The Legacy of James Moffett

The Legacy of James Moffett

His Shaping Influence on Writing Studies, English Education, and the Teaching of English

Edited by

Sheridan Blau
Teachers College, Columbia University

Jonathan M. Marine
George Mason University

Paul M. Rogers
University of California, Santa Barbara

Kathleen (Buchan) Kelly
Teachers College, Columbia University

NCTE

National Council of Teachers of English
340 N. Neil St., Suite #104, Champaign, IL 61820
www.ncte.org

Staff Editor: Cynthia Gomez
Manuscript Editor: Bonny Graham
Interior Design: Jenny Jensen Greenleaf
Cover Design: Pat Mayer
Cover Image: iStock.com/4kodiak

ISBN 978-0-8141-0201-5 (paperback)
ISBN 978-0-8141-0202-2 (ebook)
ISBN 978-0-8141-0204-6 (PDF)

Library of Congress Control Number: 2024940848

Contents

Preface

This volume is part of a larger ongoing project created to preserve, celebrate, and advance the study of the path-making work of James Moffett. The early fruits of that project include making digitally available in open access format six of Moffett's major works on the WAC Clearinghouse site, including *Teaching the Universe of Discourse, Student-Centered Language Arts, K–12, Coming on Center, Detecting Growth in Language, Harmonic Learning,* and *Storm in the Mountains.* All of these important books by Moffett can be found and downloaded as searchable PDFs free of charge at https://wac.colostate.edu/books/landmarks/moffett/. The project also involves a currently ongoing effort to digitize and make publicly available previously unpublished materials from the James Porter Moffett archive in the library of the University of California, Santa Barbara.

The first new publication emerging from this project is an edited collection of original scholarship on Moffett titled *Toward a Re-emergence of James Moffett's Mindful, Spiritual, and Student-Centered Pedagogy* (2023) edited by Jonathan Marine, Paul Rogers, Sheridan Blau, and Kathleen Kelly. Our present volume is designed to complement and extend that work, with an emphasis on Moffett's influence on the modern field of English education and its community of theorists, teacher educators, prospective teachers, and classroom practitioners who shape instruction for students in English language arts classrooms at every level.

Acknowledgments

Our team of editors would like to acknowledge our gratitude to the many friends and colleagues and organizations that contributed in important ways to the completion of this volume. First, we want to express our personal thanks and deep professional appreciation to Kurt Austin and the publications office of the National Council of Teachers of English (NCTE) for their recognition of the importance of this project to the membership of NCTE and to English teachers everywhere, and for their indispensable professional expertise in helping to make our dream of this volume into a beautiful reality. We must also add a note of special gratitude to our brilliant and tactful editor, Bonny Graham, whose keen eye and professional expertise corrected and guided us masterfully through the sensitive editing stage of this project. We also want to thank the organizations, publications, and authors who generously granted us permission to reprint key articles for this volume. We have reprinted those articles essentially as they originally appeared, but have taken the liberty of correcting some fugitive errors.

We also owe a huge debt of gratitude to colleagues and friends who were themselves close to Jim Moffett and willing to share with us their personal and professional memories of Jim and of his work. Most notable among these informants are Mary Ann Smith, Tom Gage, Sondra Perl, and Sherri Swain. We also want to acknowledge the cooperation and assistance of the special collection librarians at the University of California, Santa Barbara (UCSB), where they serve as guardians and curators of the James Porter Moffett Collection, an archive of Jim Moffett's literary and professional remains, including professional correspondence, manuscripts of published and unpublished works, lecture notes, teaching materials, and drafts of creative and professional work in progress. A supplementary and important portion of that collection is housed in the offices of the South Coast Writing Project (SCWriP) in the UCSB Gevirtz Graduate School of Education, where it is made accessible to visiting scholars through the good offices of SCWriP Director Tim Dewar and Associate Director Camille Despain, to whom we are indebted for the assistance they generously provided to authors preparing chapters for our volume.

We also want to add a note of affectionate and grateful remembrance to Jim and Jan Moffett's late daughters, Judy and Lisa Moffett. Judy was instrumental in designating the UCSB Library and SCWriP as recipients of the Moffett archive, while her older sister, Lisa, more recently granted us permission to reprint articles written by her father and to use materials from the archive in our book project. Additional thanks go to the subsequent executors of the Moffett estate. Our editorial team also wants to acknowledge the cooperation and substantive support given to this project by Teachers College, Columbia University and the English Education Program of Teachers College; by the UCSB Writing Program and the office of the UCSB Faculty Senate; as well as by the Department of English of George Mason University. We also wish to thank NCTE's convention planning committees and the Commission on the History of English Education of NCTE's English Language Arts Teacher Educators (ELATE) for opportunities we have had to share the ongoing development work of this project with colleagues across the nation.

Finally, we want to acknowledge the support and sacrifice selflessly contributed by our life partners whose weekend plans and quiet evenings were frequently forfeited to our editorial meetings and emergency phone calls or text messages. With loving appreciation, we thank Cheryl Smith, Rob Kelly, Karyn Kessler, and Heidi Marine.

INTRODUCTION

SHERIDAN BLAU
Teachers College, Columbia University

Moffett's Life and Legacy to Us

James Moffett (1929–1996), whose name and work are at least familiar to most professionally knowledgeable English teachers and specialists in college composition, is largely unknown to other teachers and researchers in the educational community. In fact, outside the field of English language arts education and composition studies, almost no one—neither intellectuals nor classroom teachers nor other educators—is likely to have heard of Moffett. Yet it is probably the case that no teacher or teacher educator in the entire history of education has had such a profound and lasting influence on the teaching of any subject taught in schools as James Moffett has had on the teaching of the English language arts from the early elementary grades through middle and secondary school and into college and beyond.

Much if not most of that profound and lasting influence derives from his publication in 1968 of two books at once, both of them finished while he was on leave from his position as an English teacher at Phillips Exeter Academy, a prestigious private secondary school in New Hampshire. The first, directed to teacher educators and scholars, as well as to veteran classroom teachers, was titled *Teaching the Universe of Discourse*, wherein Moffett elaborates a new theoretical basis, grounded on the psychological, social, and linguistic development of children and young adults, for a comprehensive instructional program across the grades in the English language arts. The second and larger volume, *A Student-Centered Language Arts Curriculum, K–13: A Handbook for*

Teachers, is essentially a methods text for preservice and inservice English teachers, emphasizing *student-centered* (a term Moffett appears to have invented) classroom practices in all the language arts that are conventionally taught across the grades and into the first year of college, along with a brief account of the supporting theory to help teachers understand why as well as what constitutes intellectually responsible and practically effective instruction.

What made these books revolutionary as well as indispensable was that they were informed by two original ideas about English as a subject for study in school. First, they offered for the first time in the history of the teaching of subject English (which began in the mid-nineteenth century) a theoretical basis for a curriculum in the arts of language that derives from an understanding of the development of the learners rather than from arguments about the importance of existing knowledge about the structure or history or cultural or economic or social value of the subject to be taught. Second, they recognized that the subject known as English, unlike academic subjects such as history or geography or biology, was not essentially a body of existing knowledge about which students were to be taught, but that, like music or mathematics, it was basically an operating system—in this case, a linguistic and intellectual and aesthetic system—to be developed through use in the arts of language, which means in speaking, listening, reading, and writing. And this meant that the role of instruction was to provide students with rich and challenging experiences in the use of language, in a manner and with the tactful kind of assistance that would promote and enhance student development in those arts. Essentially, what Moffett did was to turn education upside down for the subject of English by defining the problem and focus of schooling not on teachers and their teaching, nor on information and an established body of existing knowledge, but on learners and their learning, and their acquisition and understanding of their own growing and always provisional knowledge.

Not surprisingly, then, most of what Moffett argued for in his two revolutionary books and in the articles and conference presentations that immediately preceded and followed them, as well as through his example in his own classes and workshops, ran counter to what was at the time standard practice in schools and what continues to represent standard practice in too many schools. Hence, virtually every practice Moffett modeled and advocated was resisted and rejected and even violently opposed by advocates of traditional practices in the teaching of English and by stakeholders who were generally opposed to experimentation and innovation in the teaching of the English language arts. Most notable, however, for contemporary English teachers is the fact that virtually every innovative and unconventional practice Moffett introduced in the teaching of English, along with the theoretical and philosophical arguments he advanced for his practices, has been confirmed and empirically supported by the great body of research and theory that has emerged over the past fifty years or more in such arenas of discourse as educational psychology, situated learning theory, activity theory, rhetoric and composition, neuroscience, linguistics, language acquisition, semantics, and literary theory.

Given the modern confirmations of Moffett's theory and teaching practice, it is perhaps not surprising that many readers of Moffett's seminal books and essays (including essays printed in this volume) from the 1960s, 1970s, and 1980s find themselves feeling that Moffett's account of instruction in English classes represents a kind of prophetic vision, as if he didn't merely anticipate what was coming but saw and understood concepts and research findings that had not yet been discovered. And this prophetic quality in Moffett's writing has led many of his disciples to speak of him in almost mystical terms, as if he were some kind of modern-day prophet with more than ordinary mortal human vision and understanding.

This view of Moffett seemed supported for many of his admirers by the somewhat unconventional lifestyle of Jim and his wife, Jan Moffett, who, in the years following the publication of Moffett's most influential books (and after a year of rest and creative writing in Barbados), moved their family from New England to California, where Moffett taught from 1969 to 1970 in the English education program at the University of California, Berkeley, and began work on his Interaction project, a commercial instructional program in the English language arts, sponsored by the schools division of the Houghton Mifflin Company. It was also during this period that Moffett became more open about his deep and well-informed interest in Yoga and meditation, eventually turning their house in Berkeley into an ashram (a spiritual retreat) where Jan and Jim together taught Yoga and meditation and provided a living space to an Indian swami, who seemed to function as a spiritual advisor to the Moffett family.

The spiritual exploration and experimentation that might have seemed to casual observers an exotic eccentricity in Moffett's lifestyle represented a serious and increasingly important development in Moffett's reading life, research agenda, and personal commitments, and eventually led the Moffett family in 1978 to sell their large house in Berkeley and move to a small ranch not far from the Yosemite Valley, where they grew most of their own food and Jim taught himself how to build wind-driven and solar power systems to serve their home and the separate, large, pentagonal studio that he designed and built for himself as his writing retreat. From that rural retreat, Jim supported his family financially through continuing royalties from his earlier books, advances on forthcoming books such as new editions of *Student-Centered Language Arts*, lecture fees and income from frequent short-term summer residencies at sites of the National Writing Project, along with occasional college and university teaching appointments, including several summers, starting in 1978, at the Bread Loaf School of English.

Moffett also produced a stream of new books in the 1980s for the guidance of teachers of writing, including *Active Voice: A Writing Program Across the Curriculum* (1981) and a series of four subsequent books under the title *Active Voices*, each volume from a different level of schooling (elementary, middle school, high school, and college) collecting a range of writing assignments and sample student essays as models of various kinds of writing. His most important book of that decade, and perhaps his most important book of all for the broader field of education, was the award-winning *Storm in the Mountains: A Case Study of Censorship, Conflict, and Consciousness* (1988), a dramatic account and analysis documenting Jim's attempt to understand the violent opposition in one school district to the adoption of his huge, highly innovative, multigenre, multicultural, and multigrade-level instructional program for schools, called *Interaction: A Student-Centered Language Arts and Reading Program*, published in 1973.

While Moffett's heroic status among professionally knowledgeable English teachers and teacher educators seemed unquestionable and intellectually unchallengeable throughout the decade of the 1970s, he found himself and his expertise challenged and publicly criticized from within the profession in 1981, when he published a long-awaited collection of essays under the title *Coming on Center: English Education in Evolution*, which includes headnotes with useful biographical and contextual information available nowhere else and some of his most insightful essays about standards and testing and authorship, along with a surprising and professionally courageous major new essay titled "Writing, Inner Speech, and Meditation." In this essay, Moffett devotes considerable energy to showing writing teachers how to teach meditation and also takes on the broader task of domesticating or justifying meditation as a natural and widely practiced method of focusing attention and controlling, deepening, and suspending inner speech. He also explains how in the suspension of inner speech the mind or thought is held still and transcends all discourse as it "merges with cosmos in trance" (165). That last phrase and Moffett's insistence near the end of the essay that "[w]riting should be taught unabashedly as a spiritual discipline" (174), along with a number of mystical and esoteric references, pushed the essay beyond the cultural and intellectual tolerance of many scholars and teachers in the fields of English education and writing studies. The result was that Moffett's intellectual authority was called into question in some precincts of the profession, while in Australia, according to Bill Green and Wayne Sawyer (in this volume), "Moffett was effectively eclipsed."

In America, Moffett was attacked for his mysticism in a couple of reviews in leading journals, while his closest colleagues and friends made apologies and excuses, but few were able at the time to explicate Moffett's ideas about meditation and spirituality in a way that was entirely satisfactory to members of the community of scholars and teachers who had long thought of Moffett as the leading theorist and instructional guide for the teaching of English. In the meantime, Moffett himself, insistent on the legitimacy of his vision, published a version of the same essay (with fewer references to esoteric or mystical thinking) in NCTE's journal *College English* in 1982 and in the next year a somewhat shorter essay, "Reading and Writing as Meditation," in *Language Arts,* NCTE's journal for elementary teachers. Clearly, Moffett was ready to advocate for a broader concept of what constitutes and informs thinking and how writers arrive at their best ideas, but he hadn't yet discovered how to explain his advanced spiritual conception of that process in ways that seemed authoritatively rational to most of his readers.

Moffett's last three books, published in 1992 and 1994, complete his critique of conventional schooling and advance his more radically new and spiritually oriented conception of schooling and the role of education in human experience. That none of them sold many copies might suggest that Moffett's own intellectual and spiritual development as it came to inform his later writing was more alienating than illuminating for many English teachers who had once been his devoted readers. Fortunately, the current renewal of interest in Moffett's intellectual and pedagogical contributions and professional legacy is instigating new, renewed, and newly receptive interest in Moffett's last books and in his most advanced thinking on educational problems, and this renewal is already expanding the readership of books that many otherwise devoted readers of Moffett had deliberately and now regretfully ignored (see *Toward a Re-emergence of James Moffett's Mindful, Spiritual, and Student-Centered Pedagogy* edited by Jonathan Marine and colleagues).

Of Moffett's last three books, only the first is written for an audience of classroom English teachers and teacher educators, and that one is *Detecting Growth in Learning* (1992), in which Moffett shows teachers how to observe and track student development in the various arts of language without relying on unreliable and educationally counterproductive assessments. This short volume also includes a masterful and elegantly reasoned introduction demonstrating the utter folly of a schooling system obsessed (as American schools were and continue to be) with the testing and assessment of students in a process that merely humiliates students, discourages genuine learning, and inevitably leads to the practice of teaching only what can be reliably tested, which means removing almost everything worth learning from the school curriculum.

In that same year, Moffett published the first of his two books that explicitly build on some of his more advanced and unconventional, esoteric thinking, *Harmonic Learning: Keynoting School Reform*. In this short book, Moffett makes his case for a system of schooling that moves beyond the culturally provincial and intellectually jejune curriculum of most US schools to a curriculum that embraces a larger conception of human culture and a deeper and more spiritual understanding of human development. That book, in retrospect, seems the prelude to his more radical major volume of 1994, *The Universal Schoolhouse: Spiritual Awakening through Education*, where he abandons conventional notions of schooling altogether and argues for a new model and new purpose for educating the young, finally presenting a view of life on earth as "one big soul school [that] runs on an individualized curriculum" (338) and is designed ultimately to advance the evolution of human consciousness and the transformation of human culture, which includes the insights and wisdom of esoteric knowledge. If that idea seems difficult for most English teachers to swallow, we may find the same idea more palatable when it is expressed by Moffett more provisionally or tentatively:

> Suppose it is true, as spiritual traditions maintain, that people are here on earth to grow, not primarily to achieve or acquire except as doing so enhances inner growth. . . . Suppose we do not learn merely in order to be able to get by, get along, get around, and get ahead. These are all essential, but they fare better when education aims beyond them on the assumption that *they* are the means and *education* the end. Suppose we don't so much learn to live as live to learn. Once understood this way, knowing becomes a different matter—and a much more important one. Making a living and making a life become part of making sense of life, so that everything in it has meaning. (331–32).

Moffett's Roots and Education

Whatever readers today might think about Moffett's last books, anyone who reads Moffett's early and most widely influential articles and books will find few, if any, traces of esoteric thinking in them, although the insight exhibited in Moffett's deeply thoughtful and well-informed observations about how children and young adults best learn the arts of language, and what sorts of activities and contexts seem most likely to support such learning, might appear to represent wisdom far beyond what most readers could imagine possible for an educator in the 1960s, especially one with Moffett's limited teaching experience and lack of formal advanced study in education. For Moffett had no doctorate in English or English education. He had a bachelor's degree in English literature and a master's in French, both from Harvard. But as a senior English major at Harvard, he had won the coveted Bowdoin Prize, awarded since 1791 for undergraduate essays distinguished for their originality and great literary merit (previous winners include Ralph Waldo Emerson, Arthur Schlesinger, and John Updike), certainly a sign of Moffett's extraordinary intellectual promise.

Moffett graduated from Harvard with his bachelor's degree in English in 1952, needing five years to get his degree because he took a leave from Harvard after his sophomore year to spend a year in Paris in a self-sponsored program of study (presumably self-funded with his earnings from summer jobs) to fill in gaps in his literary knowledge and, as he told Eric Shroeder and John Boe in a revealing 1994 interview, to catch up with all "the private school kids" in his classes who were always "crowing about books I hadn't even heard of" (6).[1] In Paris he also took courses in French civilization at the Sorbonne and managed to become fairly fluent in French.

After returning to Harvard for his junior year, he surprised his friends and family by marrying his college sweetheart, Janet Lee Whaley (a Radcliff student), and completed his senior year living in an off-campus apartment with his bride. Then, with his English degree in hand, he remained at Harvard for another year to complete a master's degree, not in English but in French, and upon graduation in 1953 found himself almost immediately drafted into the Army, just as the Korean war was ending. After honorably completing his two-year tour of duty, he found himself in need of a job to support himself and his wife and their expected child. And that's when he accepted an offer to teach French at Phillips Exeter Academy, where most of the faculty were, like himself, Harvard graduates.

Nothing we know about Jim Moffett or his past would have predicted that he would become a teacher at the secondary level. Nor would his upbringing have predicted his enrollment at Harvard. Biographical notes made by Jan Moffett tell us that Jim was raised in Jackson, Mississippi, where his father, Harold ("Hal"), was a drummer (and an alcoholic) and the leader of a jazz band. Jim was born on May 23, 1929, at the height of the Jazz Age, but only five months before the Great Depression hit in October 1929, ending the Jazz Age and with it the future of Hal's band and much of his career as a musician.

The family remained intact, however, in Jackson, where Jim started school and where there were early indications that he was not an entirely typical child. Jan's notes (based largely on what she learned from Jim's mother) tell us that when Jim was in elementary school in the mid-1930s, family members used to call him "the little old man" because he was so "serious, studious, quiet, and self-contained." From other documents, we know that when Jim reached high school age, his parents seem to have been forced by their poverty to move to Toledo, Ohio, to take up residence with an aunt. It was undoubtedly the luckiest misfortune of Moffett's life. For, as a resident of Ohio, Moffett became eligible for and eventually won a Harvard scholarship that was reserved by its endowment for a graduate of an Ohio public high school. It was an unusual scholarship, as Moffett described it in his interview with Shroeder and Boe, because it provided full support for its recipient, not only for an undergraduate education but also for whatever graduate work the recipient wanted to undertake at Harvard, through the doctorate or an equivalent professional degree (6). Moffett was thereby able to use his Harvard scholarship for his bachelor's and master's degrees, though he never entered a doctoral program, perhaps because he needed a full-time income at the point where he would otherwise have done it.

Although Moffett graduated from Harvard with degrees in English and French, he wasn't certified to teach anything and had never taken any teacher preparation courses. Nor was he qualified for any decently paying position, except perhaps for a teaching job at a private secondary school, where he wouldn't need any state certification. Perhaps he thought a prep school would be a fine place to earn a living as a teacher while he tried to satisfy his smoldering ambition to be a writer—an ambition that was clearly revealed by the two short stories about his army experience that he published in 1956 and 1957, shortly after joining the Phillips Exeter faculty in 1955 as a teacher of French. It was a job at the right school, where his particular college career as an award-winning undergraduate writer with two Harvard degrees made him an ideal candidate. And though Moffett was hired initially to teach French, he soon took on some English classes, where he quickly distinguished himself as an exemplary teacher and then a teacher-researcher who was fascinated by the problems of teaching literature and composition to highly privileged and very bright adolescent boys.

Thus, Moffett gradually became a full-time member of the Phillips Exeter English department and embarked on his autodidactic career as a student and scholar in English education, eventually writing and publishing articles on the teaching of English and acquiring a reputation as a future intellectual leader for the field of English education. After his tenth year of teaching, he was awarded a Carnegie Foundation grant to conduct his own research for two years (extended to three) as a research associate in the Harvard Graduate School of Education, where he planned to complete the two books that he had already started and for which we know he had already written several chapters. Those books, described earlier, both published by Houghton Mifflin in 1968, were the more theoretical *Teaching the Universe of Discourse* and the larger volume designed to guide practice in the classroom, *A Student-Centered Language Arts Curriculum, Grades K–13: A Handbook for Teachers.*

The Contributions of This Volume

The revolutionary theory and innovative teaching practices that entered the world of language arts teaching so suddenly with those two volumes in 1968 are interrogated and explicated in many of the new and reprinted essays in this volume to help make Moffett's key ideas available for a new generation of ELA teachers and scholars. Some of these chapters were written by Moffett himself in later years to help classroom teachers better understand and enact the principles and practices he introduced in 1968. Some essays in this volume focus on Moffett's later work, including his award-winning *Storm in the Mountains*. Several essays remind us of the powerful critique of schools and schooling that reverberates through much of Moffett's writing and demonstrate how Moffett, like Freire and Dewey, saw language arts instruction as an ethical, political, and spiritual enterprise, as well as an intellectual one.

Some of the essays researched and written specifically for this volume, along with some reprints of Moffett's own essays, interpret or exemplify Moffett's turn in the 1970s to the study and disciplined practice of Yoga and meditation, showing how he found these disciplines to be resources for helping students become more disciplined thinkers and more focused and productive writers. Other essays by and about Moffett focus on his highly critical engagement with conventional assessments of student performance in the English language arts and on methods that he and younger scholars, following his lead, had developed for alternative and more intellectually meaningful methods of assessment. One new and potentially controversial essay recapitulates the history of the writer's own relationship to Moffett's thinking and traces Moffett's history of curiosity, informed opinions, and wise instincts (in the context of a half-century of reading wars) about the early steps for the teaching of reading to young children. Several of the included essays, particularly in the last sections of this volume, document efforts by currently working classroom teachers at all levels to provide intellectually richer and more engaging instruction in their English classes by adopting or adapting some of Moffett's most original, controversial, and spiritually oriented principles for teaching and learning English, thereby demonstrating the continuing relevance and classroom applicability of Moffett's thinking and practice.

A number of the essays reprinted here and some commissioned for this volume document the trajectory of Moffett's profound influence on elementary, secondary, and college language arts education in the United States and throughout the English-speaking world, largely through his writing, but also through his foundational influence on, workshops for, and deep and abiding connections to the original Bay Area Writing Project and the National Writing Project. One of these original studies documents Moffett's little known but long and consequential connection to the Bread Loaf School of English at Middlebury College and the revolutionary and long-term impact Moffett had on the teaching of writing at Bread Loaf and, subsequently, through the Bread Loaf Teacher Network, on scores of secondary schools across the nation, especially in rural schools in the South. Another original essay examines Moffett's special relevance and usefulness to teachers in rural schools everywhere. Another essay, commissioned for this volume, presents new historical findings revealing Moffett's dramatically underacknowledged influence at the widely acclaimed 1966 Anglo-American Seminar on the Teaching of English, more commonly known as the Dartmouth Conference. One new and instructionally useful chapter traces the connections between Moffett's paired publications, *Teaching the Universe of Discourse* and *Student-Centered Language Arts*, emphasizing the essential principles and teaching practices shared by both volumes.

Our volume also presents some pieces representing genres not usually found in academic books, including memoirs about Moffett and his work, eulogies written about him shortly after his untimely death in 1996, and the transcript of an interview that became a deeply felt and highly instructive conversation about memories of working with and learning from Moffett. Together, the extensive body of work collected in this volume, written by Moffett himself and by a group of authors representing three generations of scholar-teachers who have themselves learned from James Moffett in person and/or through his writing, is intended to help all current readers and future generations of ELA teachers and teacher educators to understand Moffett's legacy to our profession, especially in his distinctive vision of how the arts of language are authentically learned, and how the principles he elaborated that account for such learning must inform the crucial role that enlightened schools and thoughtful teachers can play across all grades and levels of education to foster rather than obstruct learning.

Note

1. See Eric Schroeder and John Boe's "'Individualize': An Interview with James Moffett." *Writing on the Edge*, vol. 6, no. 1, 1994, pp. 5–21.

I

James Moffett's Lasting Contributions to the Teaching of English

Chapter One

James Moffett's Legacy to English Journal

Elizabeth Spalding
University of Nevada, Las Vegas

Damian C. Koshnick
Western Oregon University

Miles Myers
National Writing Project

Spalding, Myers, and Koshnick review the extent to which the work of James Moffett influenced conversations conducted in English Journal *from the mid-1960s through the early 21st century. As an English teacher, Moffett advocated language arts education founded on oral language and developed through interaction. Moffett's views on the role of literacy in tackling sociopolitical complexities of multiculturalism are also described.*

> *I went to grade school in Jackson, Mississippi, and a big high school in Toledo, Ohio. I had a conventional education, and I accepted it all; I never questioned anything. I just did whatever they told me.*
>
> —James Moffett, 1994 Interview (Schroeder and Boe)

Who would have predicted that this compliant young man would grow up to be a leading thinker of the English profession, who questioned everything and accepted only a little? With the 1968 publication of his companion volumes—*Teaching the Universe of Discourse*, which provided the theoretical

Originally published in *English Journal*, vol. 101, no. 3, 2012, pp. 26–33. Reprinted with permission of NCTE.

underpinnings of his practice-oriented *A Student-Centered Language Arts Curriculum*—James Moffett (1929–96) became a major influence on the teaching of secondary English in the English-speaking world. We can think of no more fitting an occasion or outlet for examining his legacy to us than the 100th anniversary of *English Journal*, the NCTE journal dedicated to the work of secondary classroom teachers.

From the 1970s up until his death, James Moffett was a frequent NCTE author and a popular speaker at conventions. He was an independent scholar, a university instructor, a continuing consultant to the National Writing Project, and the author of numerous books and articles. *Interaction: A Student-Centered Language Arts and Reading Program, K–12*, one of the most revolutionary publishing projects in the history of teaching English in the United States, was his brainchild. In 1992, he received NCTE's David Russell Research Award for *Storm in the Mountains: A Case Study of Censorship, Conflict, and Consciousness*, the book he wrote over a decade after "the most tumultuous and significant schoolbook controversy ever to occur in North America" was ignited by the adoption of *Interaction* for use in Kanawha County, West Virginia, schools (*Storm* x). After his death, the National Writing Project and the NCTE Conference on English Education co-established the James Moffett Award to recognize and honor teacher research projects inspired by his scholarship.

In this article, we examine how Moffett's work has influenced conversations conducted in *English Journal* (*EJ*) over almost four decades.[1] But how does one begin to identify and interpret the legacy of a figure such as James Moffett across multiple decades? First, we relied on the general research and knowledge gleaned from years of work in the field. Second, we identified articles published by Moffett within the journal itself. Between 1970 and 1991, he published three articles and a poem in *EJ*: "Coming on Center," 1970; "Who Counts?," 1972; the poem "Bajan Bestiary: Hummingbird," 1974; and "Student-Centered Reading Activities," 1991, coauthored with Betty Jane Wagner. Third, we gathered and studied the ways in which other *EJ* authors described him when they cited his work.[2] *Teaching the Universe of Discourse* was cited 36 times in *EJ* from 1970 to 2008; *A Student-Centered Language Arts Curriculum* was cited 39 times. While studying this collection of articles, we looked for patterns of use about how and why Moffett was cited.

In tracing Moffett's legacy, we have attempted to identify ideas and concepts that Moffett introduced or promoted (and by extension those he attempted to counter), and those reported influences, or changes in practice and belief that he helped enact or inspire. We have restricted our focus here to selected examples. We begin with a brief review of his rise to prominence in the mid- to late 1960s.

Beginning with the Dartmouth Conference: What Is Happening?

In 1966, James Moffett was on leave from teaching secondary English at Phillips Exeter Academy in New Hampshire and serving as a graduate student and research associate at Harvard University. He was one of two secondary teachers selected by NCTE to represent the organization at the 1966 Anglo-American Seminar on the Teaching of English (the Dartmouth Conference). The other was Cap Lavin of Marin County, California. They were the only US high school teachers present. Over a period of weeks on the campus of Dartmouth College, leading scholars from the United States and the UK met to address the fundamental question: "What is English?"

This question seemed urgent for schools to address the sweeping social and cultural changes of the time. Just 15 months previously, the US Congress had passed the ESEA Title I Act ("Improving the Academic Achievement of the Disadvantaged"), the nation's unprecedented federal funding of K–12 curriculum changes to meet the challenge of education for all. Driven by the *Brown v. Topeka* decision (1954) that declared racially segregated schools unconstitutional and ten years later by the Civil Rights Act (1964), US teachers were struggling with how to open formerly closed schools and classrooms to all students and how to understand the variations in the way subject matter was understood and distributed among students who varied by race, ethnicity, social class, geographic location, language, culture, age, gender, and in other ways.

Against this sociopolitical backdrop, the Dartmouth participants divided into two main factions: those who viewed English as "what one learns about" and those who viewed English as "what one does" (Dixon). Moffett was one of a handful of participants who were tracing out and defending this "doing" approach to teaching English as a school subject, an approach that came to be called the "growth" or "student-centered" model.

Moffett participated in "Drama in the English Classroom," one of six Dartmouth study groups. To this group he presented the gist of his monograph *Drama: What Is Happening*, which represented years of work that Moffett had tested while teaching English at Phillips Exeter Academy (1955–1965). Herein Moffett argued, "drama and speech are central to a language curriculum, not peripheral" (*Drama* vii). He saw "drama as the matrix of all language activities, subsuming speech and engendering the varieties of reading and writing" (*Drama* vii). By drama Moffett meant not the traditional play with a script to be memorized and performed but "any raw phenomena as they are first being converted to information by some observer" (*Drama* 1). Language was learned through interaction, not, as some influential educational psychologists of the time claimed, through imitation.

Moffett offered a revised structure for teaching English focusing on students' growth based on their ability to use language to manipulate the relations among speaker (I), audience (you), and subject (it) in increasingly abstract ways. Said Moffett, "The structure of the subject [English] must be meshed with the structure of the student. A major failure of education has been to consider the logic of one almost to the exclusion of the psychologic of the other" (*Teaching* 13). The subject English was "in the learner" and the teacher's job was to follow students' various and paradoxical expressions of it: "The sequence of psychological development should be the backbone of curriculum continuity, and logical formulations of the subject should serve only as an aid in describing this natural growth" (14).

Cap Lavin, the other high school teacher at Dartmouth, went home to California with a ditto copy of *Drama: What Is Happening*. He shared the paper with a small group of California

English teachers, including Tom Gage, then a novice high school English department chair. As Gage blogged many years later, he experienced a "eureka moment" and, "At Concord [High School] . . . in those pre-Xerox days, I read the entire monograph on reel-to-reel audiotape, which I presented to members of my department to listen to and share over the summer" (Gage).

NCTE literature is rife with similar accounts, as Moffett's work was passed informally from colleague to colleague and teacher to teacher. These informal encounters helped to disseminate Moffett's vision of a language arts education founded on oral language, developed through interaction, structured on a theory of discourse aligned with student growth, and grounded in a vision of an equitable, multicultural, and multilingual society. Unlike many of his contemporaries, Moffett was, from the beginning, acutely aware of the role of literacy in addressing the social and political complexities of a multicultural age. His ideal classroom would constitute:

> the most powerful multilingual assembly that can be brought together. This means mixing levels of ability and achievement, mixing sexes, mixing races, and mixing socioeconomic classes. . . . [T]he internalization process is severely curtailed if urban and suburban children, advantaged and disadvantaged, do not talk together. Not only will they have to "speak each other's language" in the future, for social and political reasons, but the language of each needs something from each other. (*Teaching* 93–94)

Early Citations: A Guide for Curricular Revision

Moffett's work soon became a source of inspiration for teachers attempting to create "student-centered" curricula. The first *EJ* citations were by Ruth Reeves and Dorothy Knappenberger, Carol Kuykendall, and James P. Hall—all high school English administrators and teachers. In "Sequence without Stricture," Kuykendall explained how the Houston curriculum project got started: "Three years ago, Ruth Reeves, then Director of English for Houston Schools, began a grass roots campaign to free English teachers and students from overzealous content curriculums of the post-Sputnik era" (716). Reeves invited 24 senior high teachers, including Kuykendall, "to junk all existing course outlines" (716) and to help pilot a program in student-centered English. Kuykendall and her colleagues participated in a series of conversations about what English was and how best to teach it. In *Teaching the Universe of Discourse*, they found "a whole rationale for the kind of student-centered English we had intuitively sought" (716).

Hall, chair of a high school English department in Bellevue, Washington, described a similar local initiative to redefine English as a subject and create a student-centered curriculum. Hall stated, "Moffett's thinking is reflected in much of our program" (883). He went on to outline a theme-based, elective English program grounded in students' needs, characteristics, and interests. Hall emphasized the importance of providing a supportive learning environment, small classes, and opportunities for students to teach and teachers to learn.

In 1976, faculty from SUNY Buffalo collaborated with members of the English Department at Tonawanda Middle School (one of whom was Nancie Atwell) to create a writing program that reflected "both important recent research findings on the composing process and the teaching of writing and provocative current ideas on teaching writing in school classrooms" (56). Cooper, Atwell, David, Giglia, Grobe, and Locke referenced both *Teaching the Universe of Discourse* and *A Student-Centered Language Arts Curriculum, Grades K–13* in their statement of "Principles of Writing Instruction," recommending, among other things, that students write in "great quantities" in "many different modes," that students in grades 7 and 8 write primarily in dramatic and narrative modes, and that students routinely work together "in pairs, and in small group writing workshops" (58).

A young high school teacher named George E. Newell relied on Moffett as a guide for his own curricular revisions. Lacking a collaborative community, Newell described his solitary effort to rewrite a ninth-grade English curriculum from a content to a student-centered approach, resulting in "The Emerging Self" curriculum. He noted, "James Moffett's student-centered, naturalistic learning has become the vanguard of this proposed curriculum. He has restored my belief in the potentialities of the non-academic high school student" (32).

Why was *English Journal* the first NCTE journal to take up and cite Moffett's work? At a time of existential crisis in the field reflecting the turbulent social and political climate of the late 1960s and early 1970s, it should not be a surprise that some of the first people to be affected would be middle and high school teachers in "the trenches" (Hall 882). The first articles both reflected the crisis in the field and established Moffett's books as a resource for responding to that crisis. From these articles, we can infer that his work was by this time a topic of conversation among self-organized groups of teachers across the country who were sorting through what the "student-centered" classroom should look like.

Thus, the audience at Moffett's NCTE session in Washington, DC, in 1969, who likely came to glean ideas for implementing a student-centered curriculum, may have been taken aback by his first words: "Why are you here today? What do you hope to get from me? From *any* speaker on English teaching? Bright ideas? New techniques? But is it bright ideas or new techniques you need most?" ("Coming on Center" 528). Moffett went on to pose two "haunting" questions: "How differently would you teach if your students did not *have* to come to class?" (530) and "How differently would you teach if you never had to test?" (532). He then indicted the "education-industrial complex," drawing some rather unflattering parallels between students as draftees and teachers as military officers and lambasting teacher educators for their role in maintaining a corrupt system: "It's time for teachers to quit playing dumb and passive, even if that was part of their teacher training" (533). Hardly a prescription for what to do on Monday morning!

He followed up with a collection of topic sentences first presented to a discussion group at the 1971 NCTE Annual Convention and later published in *EJ* as "Who Counts?" With this contribution Moffett delivered a revolutionary message, suggesting that the whole dysfunctional educational system be replaced with "a free-choice, open market competition of learning facilities such that . . . the learner and his family could choose and support only the kind of education that seemed to them to yield their money's worth" (573).

Part of his vision for dramatic change was realized when he published *Interaction*, which he called both a "work of love" (*Storm* 4) and a "calculated risk" (*Storm* 5). He and a team of 30 coauthors contracted with Houghton Mifflin to produce a set of instructional materials of "mind-boggling complexity" (*Storm* 4), consisting of two film series, dozens of card and board games, 800 activity cards, hundreds of recordings, and other materials in addition to 172 paperback books for independent reading. In a subsequent review, Leo Ruth, a professor in the School of Education at UC-Berkeley, called *Interaction* "a powerful force in advancing 'humane literacy' wherever schools were wise enough to put it to work" (Ruth et al. 103). On the other hand, Ruth Reeves foresaw problems:

> I could think of this as a great new program of English teaching that would imbue us all with a new life. But we need more than a voice crying in the wilderness. We need more attention to the teachers than an exhortation thrown back to them over your shoulder. Mr. Moffett, will you please go on from here? (Ruth et al. 104)

Representing a classroom perspective in the same review, two teachers agreed that their students loved the activities, but that the materials were giving teachers logistical headaches. They also reported that teachers worried whether the program would hurt standardized test scores. Moffett and his coauthors, however, never had the opportunity to revise the materials based on user feedback, because Houghton Mifflin dropped *Interaction* after it ignited the most heated textbook controversy in the history of the nation in Kanawha County, West Virginia.

Assessing the Humanistic Revolution

Closing out the 1970s was Kenneth J. Kantor's article, "The Revolution a Decade Later: Confessions of an Aging Romantic." In Kantor's view, the sociopolitical ferment of the 1960s had evoked a parallel "cry for more humanistic approaches to teaching" (29). But he was disappointed that Moffett's work and associated notions of the "student-centered" approach and the "growth model" had not done more to change the teaching of English. Feeling dispirited by the "back-to-basics" movement of the mid- to late 1970s, he applauded English teachers who resisted the reactionary movements, calling them "by definition rebels" (31). Kantor nevertheless sounded a note of optimism:

> If I seem overly effusive in my praise of Moffett, it is because I have found myself returning to his work so frequently . . . either for confirmation of my present thinking or inspiration for new ideas. It may well be that in the long run this quiet revolutionary will have a greater impact on English teaching and curriculum than any other single individual. (29)

After 1979, citations of Moffett were "post-revolutionary." The initial optimism and grand visions of a dramatic sea change in teaching were replaced by the realization that not much, or at least not enough, had drastically changed.

The 1980s Post-Revolution Blues and Emerging Nostalgia

Kantor was not the only one to paint the past with a nostalgic hue. Brewbaker, for example, wrote, "Many of us, especially those with a stylish touch of gray amid the brown and blonde, cut our philosophical teeth on the theories and teaching practices of James Moffett . . . but the Moffett in us lingers on" ("Jim" 38). Looking back on her career from the vantage point of 2004, Sara Dalmas Jonsberg proclaimed, "I Want the '60s Back!":

> I have been clearing off bookshelves getting ready to retire from a lifetime of work in education. I pull down books and that stirs nostalgia for the days when we believed we could stop an unjust war, cure poverty, bring about an equitable society. I run my finger reflectively over the names of heroes on both sides of the Atlantic: Herbert Kohl, Jonathan Kozol, Janet Emig, John Holt, Neil Postman and Charles Weingartner, James Britton,

James Moffett, Harold Rosen, Nancy Martin, Douglas Barnes, Louise Rosenblatt. (15)

Generally speaking, there is little that excites humanity more than working to overturn the status quo. This may, in part, explain the nostalgia.

Prophet, Practitioner, and Sage

Throughout the 1980s, *EJ* authors often cited Moffett parenthetically to bolster their analyses and implementations of various aspects of the writing processes, such as prewriting (Powers), peer teaching (James), and teacher response to writing (Calabrese). Other authors relied on metaphors to express their debt to him. Cheryl Sanford Jenkins, for example, wrote, "Many of us, although disciples of Moffett, Macrorie, and Britton, have no formal writing program in our schools" (66). These writing teacher "disciples" were inspired to invent new curricula as individuals, but often they acted without the explicit support of the institution. As she noted, "The school board hasn't okayed" Moffett's program. Therefore, "Believing in a general philosophy, but lacking a program, we make up our writing assignments" (66). Although somewhat eclipsed by the quest for excellence launched by the publication of *A Nation at Risk* (National Commission), Moffett's vision continued to inspire teachers toward curricular innovation. In the nostalgically and incongruously titled "Jim Moffett Is Alive and Well, Stir Frying Vegetables in Mr. Chiang's Kitchen," Brewbaker described his work with teachers in Columbus, Georgia, to design a series of student-centered instructional units he referred to as the "Chinese Menu System." In this system of thematic units, students had guided choices of learning activities such as individualized personal reading, projects with other students, and research involving interviews with parents and other adults. At "the heart of the Chinese Menu System" (40) were individualization, interaction, and integration (Moffett and Wagner, *Student-Centered Language*).[3]

In 1987, Carol Pope and Karen Kutiper called Moffett "that teacher, thinker, sage who has profoundly influenced English education for at least three decades and who offers an alternative to the standard curriculum" (86). They also noted that "Moffett continues to be a force with which to be reckoned" and that his "works remain important sources of study in teaching writing courses, English education methods courses, and composition bibliographies" (86).

Meanwhile, Moffett continued to create and compile practical materials to help teachers enact his curricular vision.[4] In the 1980s, he published a guide for writing teachers, *Active Voice: A Writing Program Across the Curriculum*, the Active Voices series comprised of student writing from grades 4 through college produced in response to assignments he had originated and revised, and the nonfiction anthology *Points of Departure*, a companion to the earlier short fiction anthology *Points of View*.

The 1990s: The North Star

Several generations of English teachers had by now been educated by James Moffett and Betty Jane Wagner's *Student-Centered Language Arts*. Many of the authors who cited Moffett throughout the 1990s had first encountered his ideas in their teacher education programs. Catherine W. Kroll, for example, in a column dedicated to "New Teachers," described her experience with asking students to transform texts from story to script, an idea she attributed to Moffett. But an important term she did not attribute to him is her use of "the World" as an arena for student written and oral discourse and most likely taken up from Moffett and Wagner's text: "You need not fear you have no subject and try to manufacture one by making kids read about writing and write about reading. Words on words strengthens nothing but doubts, because they merely shadow what you're trying to teach, which is words on worlds" (23).

Other teachers first encountered Moffett's work in graduate school, after having acquired some years of classroom experience. Collin T. Wansor described reading *Teaching the Universe of Discourse* as a "seminal experience" (64). "Afterward the teaching of English became a genuinely noble experience, putting the learners (including me) at the center of a discipline that integrated all the language activities in a psychologically developmental sequence" (64). While acknowledging his debt to other composition scholars, Wansor called Moffett "the North Star and always reliable" (65). Kristie Fleckenstein was introduced to Moffett's book "after ten years of using Warriner's to teach composition" (37). She was inspired to recreate her writing curriculum as a series of spiraled writing events modeled after Moffett's I-You-It continuum.

And then the North Star was extinguished. James Moffett passed away in 1996. It was fitting that the *English Journal* memorialized Moffett in a themed issue (1997) on "Censorship" (NCTE), a practice he opposed to the end of his life. Death did not diminish his influence.

Lois Weiner attempted to "distill and focus" what new teachers could learn from Moffett and Wagner by writing a succinct explanation of how individualization, interaction, and integration should guide instructional decisions. Weiner theorized: "I think English teachers who are not acquainted with Moffett and Wagner's work but who are skilled at creating lessons . . . have internalized the 3I's [individualization, interaction, integration] and use them unknowingly" (79). Here Weiner has described the process known in the sociology of science as "obliteration by incorporation" (Merton), when an idea has become so accepted that its source is no longer cited or is forgotten.

For NCTE, the 1990s was the decade of standards (Myers 33). Among the many debates, critiques, and protests prior to their publication was Ruth Cline and Robert C. Small Jr.'s analysis of how and why US education reform has failed. Referencing Moffett's final book, *The Universal Schoolhouse: Spiritual Awakening through Education*, they rejected the assumption that measuring what children know will improve education, because "as Moffett eloquently tells us, children are not products, despite what the assembly-line mindset approach to education seems to believe" (24). And when the *Standards for English Language Arts* (NCTE and IRA) came out, Brewbaker saw Moffett's influence in a set of standards that did not break language arts down into small units by grade level (as expected by many factions) and that expanded the definition of language arts beyond the historical tripod of language, literature, and composition ("On Tuesday").

Picking up on the outdated image of the tripod, Lawrence A. Baines proposed a new metaphor of language arts as "cosmos." Baines discerned eight rather than three components of language arts in the 21st century. Seeking an organic and aesthetic symbol to represent this idea, he visualized the cosmos as a hardy, eight-petaled flower that served as "a symbol rife with innuendo" (32). He traced his expansion of the tripod back to Moffett, Britton, and the Dartmouth Conference.

The 21st Century: A Visionary

More than a decade into the 21st century, the work of James Moffett continues to inspire English teachers and teacher educators. Ben F. Nelms called him the "one visionary" 20th-century author he would recommend to "all educators and educational leaders, . . . legislators, school boards, government officials, and Congress" (47). The book he recommended is *The Universal Schoolhouse: Spiritual Awakening through Education.* Nelms used Moffett's definition of spirituality to argue that the 2011 NCTE centennial is an opportune time for a redefinition of English based on Moffett's vision: "Serving ourselves through serving our communities and redefining community in a global sense are first steps in realizing a 'cosmic consciousness'" (48). Civic literacy and responsibility are keys to the United States surviving through the 21st century and fulfilling the goals of universal public education: citizenship, employment, and personal development.

Moffett's pedagogical advice, which has been famously abbreviated as "individualization, interaction, integration," has become almost commonsensical. In fact, in 2011, it is hard to imagine how original and yet how intuitively right teachers in 1968 found such ideas as (1) students learn language by using language; (2) students need to write often and for a variety of authentic purposes and audiences in a variety of genres; and (3) students need to use language in a variety of contexts—alone, in pairs, in small groups, in large groups—to develop broad competency.

Perhaps one reason that citations of Moffett's work in *English Journal* have waned in recent years is that these ideas have been internalized by the profession. But it is also likely that the practices promoted by machine-scored testing and mandated pacing guides have encroached on the universe of discourse and teachers' ability to allow their students to explore it. Yet a Moffett-based pedagogy makes even more sense in today's diverse classrooms than it did in 1968. The need for literacy instruction that teaches students to communicate across individual and group differences and to participate in public discourse is greater than ever. Even more than native speakers, students learning English as an additional language need to talk, talk, talk. Although James Moffett did not live to see it, the universe of discourse has expanded with the advent of the digital age.

Nelms reminded us that a picture of James Moffett solely as a language or composition theorist is incomplete. Part of Moffett's genius was that he thought outside the schoolhouse and understood that schooling is a societal issue that can't be laid solely at the feet of teachers. In a 1992 forum at the NCTE Annual Convention where he described his vision for curriculum in the 21st century, he predicted, "People of the 21st century will look back on the schooling we have today with the same revulsion with which we look back on the treatment of mental patients" (Moffett and Myers). A provocative prophecy that, twelve years into the 21st century, remains unfulfilled. And strong language from a schoolboy who questioned nothing and accepted only a little.

Notes

1. Moffett also published in and/or was cited in other NCTE journals, i.e., *College English, College Composition and Communication,* and *Research in the Teaching of English.* Damian Koshnick has conducted a detailed study of citations of his work. This information is available at http:// jamesmoffettstudies.ning.com/.

2. Bibliometrics—the field focused on citation—has revealed that most published articles and most published authors are rarely, if ever, cited at all. When an author actually has a citation record to investigate, one can infer that he or she has contributed "something" to the field.

3. Individualization referred to those opportunities in a classroom when students could create their own meaning out of the material made available to them. Interaction was about creating space and opportunities for socialization between students so they could share their thinking and work. Integration was about creating lessons that enacted a broad range of the skills necessary to send and receive messages.

4. Moffett revised his original experimental program developed at Exeter Academy. He made the following major changes: (1) he put the structures of discourse into three groups that ran parallel rather than sequentially; (2) he instructed teachers to intervene and change any individual's sequence as they saw fit; (3) he added more literature to the assignments, especially poetry (Moffett, *Active*).

Works Cited

Baines, Lawrence A. "From Tripod to Cosmos: A New Metaphor for the Language Arts." *English Journal* 87.2 (1998): pp. 24–35. Print.

Brewbaker, James M. "Jim Moffet Is Alive and Well, Stir Frying Vegetables in Mr. Chiang's Kitchen." *English Journal* 71.7 (1982): pp. 38–40. Print.

———. "On Tuesday Morning: The Case for Standards for the English Language Arts." *English Journal* 86.1 (1997): pp. 76–82. Print.

Calabrese, Marylyn. "I Don't Grade Papers Anymore." *English Journal* 71.1 (1982): pp. 28–31. Print.

Cline, Ruth, and Robert C. Small Jr. "The Problem with U.S. Education: Too Much Criticism, Too Little Commitment." *English Journal 83.7* (1994): pp. 21–24. Print.

Cooper, Charles R., et al. "Tonawanda Middle School's New Writing Program." *English Journal* 65.8 (1976): pp. 56–61. Print.

Dixon, John. *Growth through English: A Report Based on the Dartmouth Seminar 1966*. London: Oxford UP, 1972. Print.

Fleckenstein, Kristie. "Criss-Crossing Perspectives: Writing Events within Writing Assignments." *English Journal* 81.8 (1992): pp. 37–41. Print.

Gage, Thomas. "Thoughts about the Dartmouth Conference." The James Moffett Consortium. Web. 16 May 2011. < http://jamesrnof femtudies.ning.com>.

Hall, James P. "A Unified View of the Subject: Some Suggestions from the Trenches." *English Journal* 61.6 (1972): pp. 882–91. Print.

James, David R. "Peer Teaching in the Writing Classroom." *English Journal* 70.7 (1981): pp. 48–50. Print.

Jenkins, Cheryl Sanford. "The Writing Assignment: An Obstacle or a Vehicle?" *English Journal* 69.9 (1980): pp. 66–69. Print.

Jonsberg, Sara Dalrnas. "Speaking My Mind: I Want the '60s Back!" *English Journal* 94.2 (2004): pp. 15–17. Print.

Kantor, Kenneth J. "The Revolution a Decade Later: Confessions of an Aging Romantic." *English Journal* 68.6 (1979): pp. 28–31. Print.

Kroll, Catherine W. "Classroom Dialogues: Connections amid Incongruities." *English Journal* 79.6 (1990): pp. 41–46. Print.

Kuykendall, Carol. "Sequence without Stricture." *English Journal* 61.5 (1972): pp. 715–22. Print.

Merton, Robert K. *Social Theory and Social Structure.* New York: Free Press, 1968. Print.

Moffett, James. *Active Voice: A Writing Program Across the Curriculum.* 1981. 2nd ed. Portsmouth: Boynton/Cook, 1992. Print.

———. "Bajan Bestiary: Hummingbird." *English Journal* 63.5 (1974): p. 55. Print.

———. "Corning on Center." *English Journal* 59.4 (1970): pp. 528–33. Print.

———. *Drama: What Is Happening*. Urbana: NCTE, 1967. Print.

———, ed. *Points of Departure: An Anthology of Nonfiction.* New American Library Mentor Series. New York: Penguin, 1985. Print.

———, senior ed./author. *Interaction: A Student-Centered Language Arts and Reading Program, K–12.* Boston: Houghton, 1973. Print.

———. *Storm in the Mountains: A Case Study of Censorship, Conflict, and Consciousness.* Carbondale: Southern Illinois UP, 1988. Print.

———. *Teaching the Universe of Discourse.* 1968. Portsmouth: Boynton/Cook, 1986. Print.

———. *The Universal Schoolhouse: Spiritual Awakening through Education.* San Francisco: Jossey-Bass, 1994. Print.

———. "Who Counts?" *English Journal* 61.4 (1972): pp. 571–74. Print.

Moffett, James, and Kenneth R. McElheny, eds. *Points of View: An Anthology of Short Stories.* New American Library Mentor Series. 1966. Rev. ed. New York: Penguin, 1995.

Moffett, James, and Miles Myers. *Curriculum for the 21st Century.* Session presented at NCTE Annual Convention, Louisville, KY, 1992. Web. 1 Mar. 2011. <http://www.ncte.org/centennial/audio>.

Moffett, James, and Betty Jane Wagner. *Student-Centered Language Arts, K–12.* 4th ed. Originally published as James Moffett, *A Student-Centered Language Arts Curriculum, Grades K–13: A Handbook for Teachers.* Boston: Houghton, 1968; reissued 1976, with Betty Jane Wagner, as *Student-Centered Language Arts and Reading, K–13.* Portsmouth: Boynton/Cook, 1991. Print.

———. "Student-Centered Reading Activities." *English Journal* 80.6 (1991): pp. 70–73. Print.

Moffett, James, et al. *Active Voices: A Writer's Reader,* I–IV 4 vols. Portsmouth: Boynton/Cook, 1987. Print.

Myers, Miles. "Buckle Up for Interesting Times." *English Journal.* 101.l (2011): pp. 33–42. Print.

National Commission on Excellence in Education. *A Nation at Risk: The Imperative for Educational Reform.* Washington: Author, 1983. Print.

NCTE. "In Memoriam." *English Journal* 86.2 (1997): p. 12. Print.

NCTE and IRA. *Standards for the English Language Arts.* Urbana: Authors, 1996. Print.

Nelms, Ben F. "Spiritualizing English: Another Dimension of Literacy." *English Journal* 97.6 (2008): pp. 47–53. Print.

Newell, George E. "The Emerging Self: A Curriculum of Self-Actualization." *English Journal* 66.8 (1977): pp. 32–34. Print.

Pope, Carol, and Karen Kutiper. "Instructional Materials: James Moffett: Prophet and Practitioner." *English Journal* 76.7 (1987): pp. 86–88. Print.

Powers, Chuck. "Structuring Creative Thinking." *English Journal* 69.5 (1980): pp. 65–68.

Reeves, Ruth, and Dorothy Knappenberger. "Preparing a Curriculum Guide." *English Journal* 59.4 (1970): pp. 520–27. Print.

Ruth, Leo, Ruth Reeves, Larry W. Dougherty, Norman M. Colb, Fred H. Sarke, and Betty Blaisdell. "Review: Teaching Materials: Interaction in Review." *English Journal* 63.5 (1974): pp. 102–5. Print.

Schroeder, Eric, and John Boe. "'Individualize': An Interview with James Moffett." *Writing on the Edge* 6.1 (1994): pp. 5–21. Print.

Wansor, Collin T. "Safe Passage through the Clashing Paradigms." *English Journal* 79.4 (1990): pp. 63–66. Print.

Weiner, Lois. "New Teachers: Designing Lesson Plans: What New Teachers Can Learn from Moffett and Wagner." *English Journal* 86.4 (1997): pp. 78–79. Print.

CHAPTER TWO

Theory for Practice: James Moffett's Seminal Contribution to Composition

SHERIDAN BLAU
Teachers College, Columbia University

In this authoritative account of Moffett's personal, intellectual, and professional life, Sheridan Blau explicates Moffett's seminal ideas, their implications for classroom practice, and their powerful influence on the National Writing Project and on the field of composition and the teaching of English more broadly.

The Genesis of a Foundational Disciplinary Figure

Like many of us who represent the previous generations of academic specialists in English education and composition, James Moffett never had a graduate course in either composition or English education and came to both fields by stumbling into a secondary school teaching job. He went to Harvard on a full scholarship in 1947 and graduated as an English major in 1952 (a year late, because he took his junior year off to study French at the Sorbonne), and then abandoned English temporarily to earn a Harvard M.A. in French in 1953, after which he was immediately drafted into the Army for two years (rising to the lowly rank of corporal). In the fall of 1955, fresh out of the Army, married, with a baby on the way, he took a job—with housing—as a

French teacher at the prestigious Phillips Exeter Academy in New Hampshire (a prep school for boys, but now coed), where he taught French for three years, before he switched to English for the next seven. Nothing in Moffett's earlier history and no document yet discovered in the Moffett archive of letters, biographical notes, manuscripts, and other literary remains suggests that he had ever thought about teaching in a secondary school or had any special interest in education before he took the needed Exeter job.[1]

Yet by the early 1960s, Moffett was deeply engaged in the teaching of English, conducting experiments in semantics, literature, and writing in his English classes at Exeter, and discovering that he could draw upon what he had learned from his research for his prize-winning undergraduate senior honors thesis at Harvard[2] to solve problems he was encountering in his teaching at Exeter. For that thesis (conducted under the supervision of his mentor, Albert Guerard Jr.), Moffett studied the relations between inner speech or interior dialogue and more externalized narrative voices in Virginia Woolf's novels. Applying what he learned from that study to his new interest as a teacher of literature in the problem of various narrative voices and the narrative perspectives they represent, he began to work out for himself and his students "a spectrum of fictional techniques scaled according to the point of view of the character" starting with inner speech and moving toward an anonymous third person perspective (1981b, 133). This schema for thinking about narrative point of view became the rationale and organizing principle for an anthology of short stories that Moffett and his Exeter colleague, Kenneth McElheny, published in 1966 under the title *Points of View*.

Then, Moffett retrospectively reports, "matters got out of hand" as he "began to see such a scale not only in narration but in all discourse." The first product of his focus on the full range of discourse types was a sequence of writing assignments that he designed for his classes and shared with his colleagues as a way of leading students from more personal and less abstract writing, up a scale of discourse types to expository and persuasive essays requiring increasingly abstract thought about a range of increasingly academic topics. (This sequence of assignments of which pirated copies were circulating widely by the late 1970s was eventually published in a revised and expanded form in

1981 under the title of *Active Voice: A Writing Program Across the Curriculum*).[3] Still obsessed by a schema that seemed to be growing in its explanatory power, he claims (1981b, 133–34) that he tried to write himself out of it (modestly minimizing the monumental theoretical task he had undertaken) by composing essays that he published individually and eventually incorporated as chapters in his 1968 book, *Teaching the Universe of Discourse*, which secured his place as a seminal theoretician for English education and composition studies.

Let us note that there is also a developmental progression in the way Moffett's obsession plays itself out: from an intellectual interest in an author's narrative style and perspective, to an interest in a range of literary strategies employed by different writers (still material for lectures or essays), to an interest in what students might do with the scales he was developing of intellectual complexity and abstraction. It is an intellectually and professionally crucial movement for a teacher to make: moving from telling about literature and writing, to helping students develop as writers themselves.

In his tenth year at Exeter, at age thirty-six, married and the father of two daughters, Moffett received a Carnegie grant to begin work in the following academic year on the development of a comprehensive curriculum and curriculum theory in the English language arts that eventually yielded the two books establishing his reputation as one of the leading spokespersons in America for the field of English education. These were the "methods" text, *A Student-Centered Language Arts Curriculum, Grades K–13: A Handbook for Teachers* (1968a), and in the same year the book he referred to as "a companion volume" designed to provide a "pedagogical theory of discourse" for the curriculum and teaching practices presented in the methods text. I am referring, of course, to the now classic book, *Teaching the Universe of Discourse* (1968b), which, despite Moffett's ostensibly modest ambition, presented a theory for the teaching of English that would be revolutionary and uniquely generative for an entire profession in the sense that it could help English language arts teachers across the grades determine what they ought to teach, and in what sequence, and through what procedures. It was a theory that would also be authoritative to the extent that it was founded on a set of nonarbitrary principles for instruction—principles that could be said to inhere in the nature of the subject of English as well as in the nature of learners and the nature of learning.

Moffett's Carnegie grant funded him for two years of study and writing, which he stretched into three and spent in residence at the Graduate School of Education at Harvard, where he held an appointment as a Research Associate from 1965 to 1968 when both of his books were published (a remarkable accomplishment, but one that will appear less miraculous when it is recognized that most of the chapters of his book on theory—or substantial portions of them—were published in earlier versions starting in 1964). During this same period, in the summer of 1966, he was also one of the fifty participants in the historic Anglo-American Seminar on the Teaching and Learning of English held for a month at Dartmouth College and known thereafter as the Dartmouth Seminar.

After 1968, Moffett never again held any long-term academic appointment, but made his living mostly as a lecturer and writer, sometimes teaching in the summer at the Bread Loaf School of English, often visiting and occasionally codirecting summer institutes at sites of the National Writing Project, and from time to time accepting short-term visiting professorships at such places as the University of California, Berkeley and San Diego State University. Up until just before he died at age sixty-seven in December of 1996, he relished travel and almost all opportunities to work with classroom teachers, and he regularly attended National Council of Teachers of English (NCTE) conferences but turned down well-paying and tenured university appointments that were—despite his lack of a doctoral degree—offered to him.

Moffett's Theory in Its Historical Context

Moffett was not, of course, the first theorist to attempt to discover some rational ground for organizing the unruly body of knowledge and constellation of practices—reading, writing, speaking, listening, language, literature, composition—that were the province of subject English. As Arthur Applebee shows us in his authoritative history of the teaching of English (1974), whenever the field of English as taught in the schools sought to find some basis for shaping its curriculum outside of the demands of college entrance exams or lists of canonical texts dictated by college English departments, theorists and theories emerged to provide what appeared to be a rational basis for identifying and sequencing what should be taught in English classes. And what emerged was almost invariably an expression of whatever broader trends in public education and in the intellectual community seem to have captured the imagination of policy makers and educational leaders. These trends included the application of science—which was translated as the principle of efficiency—to curriculum and instruction in English, and more thoughtful and promising theories deriving from the progressive movement, from reformist political agendas, from conceptions of mental health and social adjustment, from behaviorist psychology, from humanistic psychology, and the emergence of modern scientific linguistics. Not that all of these frameworks and cultural influences were intellectually impoverished (though the cult of efficiency clearly was), but they all represented a momentary fashion, a swing in the educational pendulum, that yielded a framework for the English curriculum that would necessarily pass as the pendulum oscillated in the opposite direction. What makes Moffett's theory different—among its other differentiating virtues—is that it has lasted.

Like every other modern theorist of English education, Moffett begins his discourse on theory with the observation that English is an "untidy" and "amorphous subject," whose ill-defined and undertheorized character undoubtedly explains why it is "the caboose on the train of educational renovation" (1968a, 3). He then begins to articulate the foundational principles for his theory by lamenting the widespread confusion in the field between the problem of covering content and the need to develop authentic performative capacities, which amounts to confusion about the difference between learning about something and learning how to do something. Because—as he says in his unpretentious homespun conversational style—it is easier to tell somebody about something than it is to teach somebody to do something, English is treated in schools as a subject parallel to history or geography, as if it were a body of information about literary texts and the names of language features and parts of an essay. Hence the subject of English in schools, he says, has generally been "misconstrued" and "mistaught" (1968a, 3).

What English teachers have to recognize as the first step in curricular and instructional reform, according to Moffett, is that English as a subject of study is fundamentally a symbol system, like mathematics or foreign languages, and as such it is not a discipline of information about its own content, but an instrument for working with any content. To learn a symbol system, says Moffett, is not to learn information about it, but to learn "how to operate it" (1968a, 6). Hence Moffett calls for teaching practices which place students in "realistic communication 'dramas'" (1968a, 12), where they participate as writers and readers, speakers and auditors of language in real or simulated situational contexts, "with better motivation and in a way more resembling how [they] will have to read, write, speak, and listen in the 'afterlife' [Moffett's playful term for the world beyond school]" (1968a, 12). To teach writing, Moffett calls for a set of practices that anticipate the next two generations of sociocultural research and theory about rhetorical exigencies (Bitzer 1968; Miller 1984), situated learning (Lave and Wenger 1991), activity systems (Russell 1997), and classrooms as cultures (Green and Dixon 1993), recommending that students be "trained to write for the class group, which is the nearest thing to a contemporary world-at-large," getting them accustomed to having their papers "read and discussed workshop fashion" and having them write about their own experience and discoveries. "It is amazing," Moffett concludes (1968b, 12), "how much so-called writing problems clear up when the student really cares: when he is physically put into the drama of somebody with something to say to somebody else."

Moffett and the Dartmouth Seminar

Nor was Moffett the only educator of his generation to be calling for a more thoughtfully theorized and intellectually coherent English curriculum. The decade of the 1960s was, in fact, a period of considerable foment for the field of English, and reform efforts abounded, including federally sponsored summer institutes for teachers, the curriculum study centers funded by Project English, and the Dartmouth Seminar of the summer of 1966, where, as I have mentioned, Moffett was himself an invited delegate and participant (one of only three K–12 teachers among the twenty-four American delegates). That seminar—generally regarded as a watershed moment in the history of English education—was also famously contentious for the polarized theories of English education that came to be identified (somewhat inaccurately) as a debate between the British and American positions at that historical moment not only on the aims, methods, and ends of education in the English language arts across the grades, but on how to conceive of the problem in need of solution (see Dixon 1967/1969, 1975; Muller 1967; Bryan 1974; Applebee 1974; Harris 1997). The British, represented most notably by delegates from the British Schools Council and University of London, where questions of child language and development framed an agenda for research and reform, advocated a child-centered, experiential, inquiry-oriented "growth" model of learning the arts of language, and the Americans, many of whom had been involved in the federally funded curriculum study centers of Project English, were inclined to focus on the content of the curriculum itself or the scope and sequence of the body of knowledge thought to define the subject of English that teachers were responsible for teaching.

Surprisingly, given his age and his relatively junior status, Moffett appears to have been more influential for than influenced by the mostly senior scholars who were his coparticipants at Dartmouth. James Britton (a generation older than Moffett and already a respected senior scholar by his time at Dartmouth) made explicit use of Moffett's discourse schema for the project he later undertook with his colleagues at the University of London Institute of Education to classify a vast corpus of student writing samples collected from British classrooms at every level of schooling for their now classic study, *Development of Writing Abilities (11–18)* (Britton et al. 1975). Moffett, however, makes little mention in his published writing of the Dartmouth Seminar or of his delight in meeting such like-minded colleagues as he had to have found his British colleagues to be, and whose ideas about teaching he would certainly have understood in a way that many of the American delegates apparently did not (see Muller 1967).[4] But the only mention Moffett makes in *Teaching the Universe of Discourse* (1968b) of the 1966 conference is in the head note to his chapter on "Drama: What Is Happening," where, among those he thanks for helpful criticism of his manuscript (a manuscript for the version of the chapter that appeared as an NCTE publication in 1967, the year after the conference), he includes his "fellow members of the Study Group in Drama of the Anglo-American Seminar in the Teaching of English . . . Douglas Barnes of the University of Leeds, Anthony Adams of the Crutchfield Comprehensive School, West Bromwich, England, and Benjamin DeMott of Amherst." In the same note he also thanks Arthur Eastman of the University of Michigan and Alfred Grommon of Stanford, both of whom were also Dartmouth participants, but he thanks them not in their role as colleagues in the Anglo-American Seminar, but in their separate capacity as readers for the NCTE committee on publications.

Many years later, in *Coming on Center*, in the introduction to the title essay of the book, Moffett (1981b, 1–2) again recalls the Dartmouth Seminar and the status of English education in Great Britain and the United States at that time, noting that he attended the monthlong Dartmouth Seminar in the summer of 1966, right in the middle of the two years afforded him by a Carnegie grant to be in residence at Harvard, "writing up" his "two books of theory and practice." What he found, among many of the British delegates at Dartmouth, he says, was "a gratifying corroboration" of his own approach to teaching, "which included much drama and other peer interaction." On the other hand, "many of the American participants were involved either in government-sponsored curriculum centers that were more often than not perpetuating wrong-headed tradition or in efforts to found a new English on recent linguistic triumphs."

That Moffett emerged as a major influence on the profession of English just after the widely celebrated and intensely documented Dartmouth Seminar has occasioned what seems to be a significantly distorted view of the history of English education in the post-Dartmouth years. As Joseph Harris (1997, 1–17) points out in his trenchant revisionist history of the Dartmouth Seminar, the summer of 1966 has come to represent for much of the profession of English a defining moment in the history of English education, marking a kind of Copernican shift in how the discipline of English defined itself as a teaching field. Harris attributes this "heroic" view of Dartmouth to the "highly skewed" report on the conference written by John Dixon, one of the leaders of the British delegation. The report was initially published in 1967 under the title *Growth through English* and has been reprinted several times and published in two subsequent editions, with the 1975 edition extending the title to read *Set in the Perspective of the Seventies.* Peering behind the veil of the commonly accepted history, Harris points out (2) that the Dartmouth Seminar accomplished much less than Dixon seems to have imagined; that the delegates could hardly agree on anything; that the recommendations they adopted were either so vague or innocuous that nobody could object to them; and that the few that were substantive (about tracking and testing, for example) were almost entirely ignored by the profession. More importantly, he says, the conference seems to have had little or no impact on what actually transpired in American classrooms.

Harris notes, however, that the "growth model" for English education did find an advocate after Dartmouth whose writing actually influenced the field, and that advocate was James Moffett (1997, 11). In other words, if the teaching of English in American schools underwent a transformation after the Dartmouth Seminar, the transforming event was not the Dartmouth Seminar nor the subsequent publications about the seminar, but the intellectual work that, as we have seen, began before the Seminar and eventuated immediately after Dartmouth (largely uninfluenced by that Seminar itself) in the publication of James Moffett's now classic book, *Teaching the Universe of Discourse* (1968b).

Which is not to say that Moffett's theory or book was produced without any intellectual influence from the most significant currents of thought about teaching, learning, and the English language arts in his own period. On the contrary, he references and makes explicit use of the most salient developments in the early and mid-1960s in linguistics (including Mellon's experiments in transformational sentence-combining), semantics, literary theory, sociolinguistics, and sociocultural learning theory, including Vygotsky, who was just being rediscovered and made available by Jerome Bruner, whose friend and close colleague, Roger Brown, wrote the preface to Moffett's book. Brown and Bruner were both in the psychology department at Harvard (Brown as Chair), while Moffett was a research associate in the School of Education, and Moffett apparently crossed departmental and college borders either to study with them or otherwise get to know them. Where Moffett was indifferent or hostile to contemporary currents of thought was in the arena of what was intellectually fashionable or currently celebrated as the latest approach to reform in the curriculum, in assessment, in academic rigor.

It is Moffett's intellectual integrity and scrupulously rigorous thinking rather than his insularity that has accounted for his consistent stands against the meretricious reforms and theories of teaching and learning that took over professional discourse in English in recurring waves in the decades following his influential book. If he were alive today, he would speak as clearly against "the race to the top" and the culture of common standards and assessment as he did in his anti-assessment book of a generation ago, *Detecting Growth in Language*, and as he did most famously in his 1970 speech on "Misbehavioral Subjectivities" (reprinted in *Coming on Center* [1981b, 10–17]) with which he resigned from a prestigious national commission appointed to identify behavioral objectives (an earlier incarnation of standards) for English instruction.

But as Moffett's writing and workshops also demonstrated over the nearly thirty years of his life that he was a dominant figure in English education, he was never resistant to the genuine insights offered by new and intellectually rigorous research and theory, including the virtual paradigm shifts in literary theory, literacy studies, and rhetoric and composition that he witnessed in his professional lifetime and that his own theory—with an almost mystical prescience—either engendered or seemed to encompass and anticipate. Nor am I aware of any theorized account of the subject of English as a subject for study in the schools that is as independently grounded, as Moffett's is, not on intellectual fashion or the claims of tradition or unexamined ideological principles or even on an already elaborated system of thought (like rhetoric), but on a compelling newly synthesized theory of the structure and development and operation of the mind, and of the role of language in shaping and reflecting mental development.

Because English as a subject to be taught and learned is essentially and ineluctably a discipline for the exercise of language and mind in ways that are increasingly mature and intellectually demanding, a theory of learning the discipline of English that is essentially a theory of linguistic and mental development has a kind of self-evident and compelling authority, linking as it does every stage in a student's learning to the mental and linguistic faculties that must of necessity also be under development in the student to account for growth in knowledge or skill in the discipline. Moffett's theory explicitly makes these links and in doing so also presents us with a model of mental and discourse development (or cognitive maturity or sophistication or complexity) that is elegant in its simplicity and easily translatable into a taxonomy of discourse types and writing assignments.

Moffett and the Emergence of Composition as a Discipline

And this, of course, is what accounts for its early and commanding importance to the field of composition as that field was just beginning to claim for itself the status of a legitimate field for scholarship and inquiry as well as a specialized area of teaching. In the early 1970s, as composition was just emerging as a discrete discipline, those who wanted to identify themselves professionally as part of a disciplinary community (mostly disenfranchised English instructors in year-by-year appointments and wayward teaching assistants) and who were in need of a theorist to cite whose work might legitimate their practice and authorize their claim that they were in possession of some body of specialized knowledge to distinguish them from the mass of English professors and teaching assistants (who tended to think of composition as an untheorized intellectual slum presided over by professional outcasts) could and did name Moffett as the principal theorist for the field. James Gray, the founding director of the Bay Area Writing Project and the National Writing Project, frequently asserted that the writing project, as a matter of principle, must be atheoretical, deriving its collective wisdom, as it does, not from any theory but insistently from the best practices of the teacher-participants whose own successful classroom experience gives authority to what they teach and learn from each other. Yet Gray (1997) also liked to tell of the time (it must have been in the late 1970s) when he gave a talk about the writing project to a group of visiting teacher educators from the Soviet Union and Soviet Bloc nations, and at the end one of them asked him, "Who is your theoretician?" Though it was a question he wasn't prepared for, his response was immediate and came to him, he says, without thinking: "Jim Moffett," he blurted out. For most college teachers of composition, Moffett would have been a more premeditated choice, yet perhaps also the only choice they would have known to make.

I remember a time in about 1980 when I read an evaluation report written by an English department colleague of mine, reporting on the teaching performance of one of our department's temporary composition instructors, where the evaluator noted that in a conversation following up on a classroom observation, the instructor justified most of what he did with reference "to somebody called Moffett." I also remember interviewing applicants for nontenure-track appointments in our campus composition program during the mid-1980s, when most candidates spoke of being guided by a teaching philosophy based largely on Moffett's theory of discourse (though many also mentioned Peter Elbow or Don Murray, while former UCLA teaching assistants cited Richard Lanham and former University of Chicago teaching assistants were invariably disciples of Joe Williams).

Of course, other modern theorists (putting aside classical rhetoricians) were available to have been cited by then. Kinneavy's *A Theory of Discourse* (1971) and Frank D'Angelo's *A Conceptual Theory of Rhetoric* (1975) were being read in the few serious graduate programs that were already operating by 1980, like the distinguished doctoral program in linguistics, literature, and composition, run by Ross Winterowd at the University of Southern California (who also had and deserved a large group of disciples); but neither Kinneavy nor D' Angelo offered a theory of discourse that was as translatable to practice or—dare I say—as accessible as Moffett's to thoughtful practitioners, nor as readily available for summary, paraphrase, and visual representation to writing teachers in professional development contexts. In other words, the elegant simplicity of Moffett's theoretical framework made his theory the one that emerging specialists in the teaching of writing could most easily and readily appropriate for their own use in teaching and in theoretically justifying their teaching practice.

Such a description of Moffett's theory does not suggest that his theory is simplistic as well as elegantly presented or that it is insufficiently well informed by scholarship or intellectually reductive and therefore less intellectually sophisticated or demanding than some others or that it compromises complexity and depth for the sake of accessibility; but it would appear that Moffett's work is not immune to such charges. I am not aware of any dismissive critique of Moffett's theory by any scholar in the field of rhetoric or composition or English education, but it has to trouble Moffett's disciples and all exponents of his theoretical perspective that two of the major theoretical works immediately subsequent to his—Kinneavy's monumental study of 1971 and D'Angelo's (1975) deeply learned theory of rhetoric that accounts for the relationship between thought and discourse—both ignore Moffett's earlier contributions as if their authors never heard of Moffett or, more likely, regard his work as unworthy of citation in a serious scholarly study of discourse types and discursive and rhetorical operations. It is perhaps not surprising that E. D. Hirsch's eccentric *Philosophy of Composition* (1977) also makes no reference to Moffett, but it is hard to explain why Victor Villanueva's (2003) more recent and widely used collection of classic documents in modern composition theory (*Cross-Talk in Comp Theory: A Reader*) excludes any selection or excerpt from Moffett among the forty-three selections of seminal and influential theoretical documents (D'Angelo and Kinneavy among them) that he does include.

Many of Moffett's disciples might be inclined to attribute his marginalization in some precincts of the scholarly community to his acknowledgment of nonstandard intellectual and spiritual sources (most notably the European philosopher, social critic, and esoteric Rudolph Steiner)—sources that, as Moffett himself asserted, make conventional academics uncomfortable and lack the intellectual authority that is granted to university theorists in "white lab jackets" (1981b, 62). But Moffett's spirituality was generally hidden from the academic community until 1981 and would not have been known to conventional scholars like Kinneavy or D'Angelo when they were writing their widely referenced volumes of theory. A more likely explanation of Moffett's marginalization, at least by some scholars, might be the orientation of his theory to the practical needs of classroom teachers and his evocation of an audience that specifically included elementary and secondary language arts teachers. Moffett is explicit in his forward to *Teaching the Universe of Discourse* (whose title alone surely declares its pedagogical orientation) about his audience and his purpose, where he calls the collection of essays that make up his classic book "one teacher's efforts to theorize about discourse expressly for teaching purposes" (1968b, xi). Many academics in the field of English education or in composition whose work has been reviewed by university personnel committees in tenure and promotion cases will find the problem of Moffett's status in the research community a familiar one. For among traditional researchers in most fields at most major research universities, no work of scholarship can count unequivocally as research unless it is addressed to problems that are largely theoretical and to an audience of other researchers and theorists. A book addressed to classroom teachers and that theorizes strictly in the interest of the practice of teaching, in most prestigious academic communities—including leading departments of English and, ironically, even in departments of education—will be subject to challenge and discussion as a problematic promotion case (if not preemptively deniable) if it should ever be put forward as an instance of a substantial and creditable contribution to knowledge.[5]

What may be surprising about the reception of Moffett's work in the academic community, then, is not the degree to which it has sometimes been discounted or ignored, but the degree to which—despite its pedagogical orientation and acknowledgment of an audience that would include many K–12 practitioners—it has taken a prominent place among the seminal texts in the field of composition, a field dominated by expatriates from traditional university English departments whose leading figures have been engaged in a self-conscious struggle to achieve academic respectability as members of a new and legitimate field for research and theory. Although one can cite notable instances where Moffett's theoretical work seems to have been deliberately neglected by leading scholars in the field, *Teaching the Universe of Discourse* (or key essays within that volume) has nevertheless become a canonical text for composition researchers and practitioners alike, most especially, perhaps, for those who are not ashamed of its roots in a K–12 teaching practice or in its popularity among well-informed K–12 teachers. Moffett is, for example (pulling instances from my nearby bookshelf), among the most cited sources (along with Linda Flower and James Britton) in McClelland and Donavan's 1985 Modern Language Association (MLA)-published collection of essays by major composition researchers, *Perspectives on Research and Scholarship in Composition.* Moffett's discourse typology is cited as one of the three most important postmodern classification schemas by Robert O'Connors in his widely consulted and frequently taught account of the field, *Composition-Rhetoric: Backgrounds, Theory, and Pedagogy* (1997). And in Stephen North's groundbreaking study, *The Making of Knowledge in Composition: Portrait of an Emerging Field* (1987), Moffett is given more attention than any other theorist in a chapter on "The Philosophers," where North insists that philosophical inquiry produces knowledge that is not instrumental and does not lead to action, and where he claims that Moffett's contribution is a philosophical one, despite Moffett's own insistence on his status as a teacher speaking to other teachers about an inquiry into theory conducted strictly for its value to practice.

Yet Moffett's theory, contrary to what North claims about philosophical inquiry, has remained important to the profession of composition, it seems to me, precisely because it has remained of instrumental value to practitioners, including teacher-researchers and researchers on teaching who have conducted systematic inquiries into classroom practice, including their own practice. And what has been of most value instrumentally is the central trope of his discourse theory, the idea that every act of discourse can be described in terms of its location on two axes or lines of longitude and latitude, measuring degrees of "distance" that are also measures of cognitive demand or complexity (also related to intellectual development or maturity). In fact, Moffett's schema is now so familiar to practicing teachers and has been so widely employed by textbooks, by assessment systems, by curriculum guides, and by course outlines that it may not be recognized as Moffett's distinctive contribution by many of the very teachers of writing who depend on it in their practice.

Moffett's Discourse Schema

Moffett's schema, as elaborated in Chapter 2 of *Teaching the Universe of Discourse* (1968b), in case any need reminding, posits two axes of "distance," the first of which is the longitudinal axis of distance between a speaker (or writer) and an auditor that Moffett calls the "I-you" relation, the distance between first and second person being measured by how much the auditor already knows what is in the mind of the writer and conversely how much awareness the speaker or writer needs to achieve through an act of empathy or projective identification to know what cues or information to provide to compensate for the auditor's missing knowledge. The most intimately knowledgeable auditor of one's discourse would be oneself engaged in a process of inner speech or what Moffett calls "reflection" and defines as "intrapersonal communication between two parts of one nervous system." The other distance categories Moffett identifies along the I-you continuum, beyond reflection, are "conversation" ("two people in vocal range"), "correspondence" ("interpersonal communication between remote individuals"), and "publication" ("impersonal communication to a large anonymous group, extended over space or time") (33). It takes almost no effort of imagination to translate all these forms of communication to acts of writing (with virtually no change in labels). If some readers were anticipating that I would be laying out a more finely calibrated scale of discourse distances running from self to intimate others to various kinds of more distant others, that's because we have grown accustomed to such elaborated categories, introduced not by Moffett himself, but by the adaptation of Moffett's discourse schema by Britton and his London colleagues for their now classic 1975 study of school-sponsored writing in *The Development of Writing Abilities (11–18)*.

The second, and possibly more important, axis of distance posited by Moffett's schema is the latitudinal axis measuring the distance in what Moffett calls the "I-it" relation between the speaker/writer and his subject as measured by a scale of "abstractive amplitude," moving from discourse about what is here and now experienced in the moment through one's own senses, to discourses that represent experiences, events, or ideas at a further remove in time, space, or abstractive category. On this scale, discourse about one's experience in the moment, what is happening to me as I sit at my computer writing this draft of this essay, how my body feels, how I am hungry or tired or frustrated, and so on represents the least removed up the ladder of abstraction and requires the engagement of no faculties except those of sense perception and the skills required to record perceived data. But if I begin to tell about what happened to me earlier this morning or yesterday, to look back and narrate or report rather than to record, I must use my faculty of memory and organize my discourse by the logic of time or chronology, a kind of logic that requires more abstract thinking than the check on one's senses required for recording experience in the present moment. Merely having to reframe experience or events in a chronological scheme for oneself requires an act of mind that entails more abstract thinking than is required for the mere recording of what is happening as it transpires.

At the next level of abstraction, Moffett identifies a kind of thinking more demanding than remembering and one that must organize data by a more sophisticated principle of reasoning or logic than chronology. This kind of thought—which Moffett calls *analogic* or *analogical thinking*—addresses not the question of *what is happening* or *what happened*, but *what happens*, which is to say, what generally happens or what generalizations or statements can be proposed as true over time to account for how items in a data set are classified together to yield a generalization that applies to all of them. Moffett identifies this kind of thinking with the discourse of exposition, which characteristically employs the intellectual processes of generalization and classification and calls upon the faculty of mind that Moffett identifies as analogical reasoning.

At the next and "highest" level in Moffett's schema is the discourse that Moffett labels in his "happening" sequence as *what should* or *might happen*. This kind of discourse requires thinking at a level of abstraction that subsumes the generalizations and classifications of exposition and uses them as evidence in the interest of larger arguments or as the data undergirding some larger theory. When I note my experience of this morning as immediate data, I am recording it. If I later remember that experience and organize it as a narrative, I am reporting it. If I ask my colleagues about how they spent their mornings and then classify our activities and report on what sorts of things people like us do in a typical morning, I am writing exposition. If I then use those generalizations as evidence for an argument about how hard we academics work, I am writing argumentative or persuasive discourse. But if I move from those same generalizations to a claim (that looks much like an argument) about how intellectuals are people who love to play with ideas all the time so that their free time and their work time are indistinguishable, then I am writing theory. In both argument and theory I am engaged in a mental process that Moffett calls the *tautologic of transformation*, by which he refers to the way that theory and argument both operate by taking a body of information or ideas and transforming that material into either an argument or a theory, thereby reframing but not changing the underlying data. What is *tautological* (an unfortunate word choice) about that operation is that it doesn't change the underlying data at all. The data remain intact, potentially to justify an opposing theory or argument. The term *tautologic* is unfortunate, I think, because it lends itself to more confusion than clarity, since a tautology to logicians is both an infelicitous (because redundant) way of reasoning (therefore sometimes classified as a logical error) and an indisputable but useless logical claim by virtue of defining something by its own definition, as in *arguments that are tautological are those that employ tautology*. Moffett's important point, in any event, is that both argument and theory are operations of mind that transform material lower down on the abstraction scale, but that are themselves already products of abstraction built on evidence and data that have been organized by a prior act of mind (chronological thinking), which itself operates on the concrete data of perceived experience. There is, in other words, a ladder of thought based on level of abstraction and this ladder defines different kinds of discourse as they are ordinarily practiced in writing and speech and apprehended by auditors in reading or listening.

The power and utility of this schema for teaching and research in composition over the past thirty-five years are incalculable. First of all, it generates a huge array of writing assignments, allows for the development of logically and sequentially related sequences of assignments, and provides a sound basis for classifying almost any piece of written discourse. For teachers of writing who want to think about a range of assignments, for example, the scale of abstraction alone (without considering the I-you axis) can yield a chart (Blau 1983, 301) like the one in Figure 2.1.

Perspective	Discourse Acts	Informing Faculties	Examples
What is happening	Describing, recording	Discourse organized by the senses	Field notes, love notes, diary notes
What happened (or will happen)	Reporting, narrating (or planning)	Discourse organized by memory (chronological thinking)	Memoirs, news reports, summaries of field notes, plans
What happens	Generalizing (using examples), explaining, analyzing, classifying, advising from experience	Discourse organized by analogical reasoning—the capacity to recognize a basis for excluding and including instances into classes and categories (i.e., generalizations)	History, scientific inquiry and explanation, literary analysis, prudential wisdom
What might happen, what should happen	Arguing (using reasoning), advising (from theory), speculating, theorizing, disputing	Discourse organized by the formal logic of argument or by the "tautologic" that generates new theoretical frameworks, yielding new perspectives and arguments	Professional advice and speculation, literary theory, philosophical and scientific theories and proofs, legal argumentation

FIGURE 2.1. *Scale of intellectual ascent for discourse.*

Moffett's Discourse Theory in Practice

Classroom teachers who learn Moffett's schema quickly recognize it as a guide to evaluating the difficulty or maturity level required for any writing assignment and also see how it can guide them in strategically constructing assignments so that they control at what point on the I-you axis (measuring cognitive load or difficulty in terms of audience) they would have an assignment intersect with the I-it axis (measuring the cognitive load or difficulty in terms of abstractive amplitude). They can see readily, for example, how and why it might be wise to ask students to explain the motives of characters in a novel to themselves in their journals before they explain them to a classmate or teacher, while at the same time they ask students to do a brief retelling of a story for a classmate. It has served as a framework for curriculum planning in schools and as the rationale for the sequences of writing assignments included in widely used language arts textbooks for grades 6–12 in schools (e.g., *The Writer's Craft* [Blau et al. 1993]). It also serves as the framework for many of the most widely used college textbooks in writing (e.g., Axelrod and Cooper 1990/2010).

For researchers and evaluation specialists, Moffett's schema has provided a measure of difficulty and a range of types for experiments designed to examine writing competence and processes and to measure skills. It served as the theoretical foundation for the state assessment program in writing for elementary and secondary schools in the state of California in the 1980s and for a number of state assessment programs that subsequently adopted the California model. It guided numerous evaluation studies conducted by sites of the National Writing Project, where Moffett is widely read and where his theory and the instructional models that he endorsed and developed in connection with his theory are typically demonstrated and employed in summer institutes for teachers and in other professional development programs. Moffett's accounts in his 1968 methods text (*A Student-Centered Language Arts Curriculum, Grades K–13*) and in his writing across the curriculum book of 1981 (*Active Voice: A Writing Program Across the Curriculum*) of the writing workshops that he employed to support the research and thinking that are demanded for different types of writing inspired many college and secondary teachers (especially in the National Writing Project) to develop and use writing workshops for instruction in their classrooms over a decade before Nancie Atwell introduced her writing workshops to middle school teachers and the rest of the profession.

Under the influence of Moffett's perspective in *Teaching the Universe of Discourse* (1968b) on the importance of talk and conversation as the ground from which writing and all the advanced modes of thinking and discourse develop, composition classes in colleges and universities all over the country became organized as intellectual communities where students discuss their reading in small groups, share ideas for papers, conduct research collaboratively, and read each other's writing in drafts as essays develop. If these practices have been promoted by other scholars and influential practitioners in recent years—by Peter Elbow, for example, or by the model learning communities constructed in summer institutes at sites of the National Writing Project, and by a growing body of theory about communities of practice (Lave and Wenger 1991) and more recently by genre theorists of the North American School (Miller 1984; Bazerman 1994; Freedman and Medway 1994)—Moffett nevertheless anticipated and directly or indirectly influenced the writers, theorists, writing specialists, and NWP teacher-leaders whose thinking and research and workshops in more recent decades began to be reflected in leading teacher education programs and subsequently in the classrooms of professionally well-informed teachers.

Moffett and the National Writing Project

The relationship between Moffett and the National Writing Project presents an especially telling story about the influence of Moffett's theory on practice in the field of composition and the dissemination of both theory and practice. The Bay Area Writing Project, from which the National Writing Project emerged, was founded at the University of California, Berkeley in 1974 by James Gray, who was then a supervisor of teacher education in English in the Graduate School of Education. While Gray's own vision of a professional development project built on the principle of teachers teaching teachers was the foundational principle for the project, his vision was shared by a small group of colleagues from the beginning, and the design and implementation of the project was very much a collaborative effort of a group under Gray's leadership that included other teacher educators and several highly influential teacher-leaders from Bay Area high schools and junior highs.[6] These included Albert "Cap" Lavin, Miles Myers, Mary K. Healy, Keith Caldwell, Mary Ann Smith, and Jo Fyfe, among others. All of these leaders including Gray himself were among the earliest readers and exponents of Moffett's work as that work is represented in his methods text as well as in his book on theory and (by 1973) his *Interaction* language arts and reading program (from Houghton Mifflin) for K–12 classrooms.

Lavin was probably the first of that group to know Moffett personally, because he had spent a month with Moffett at Dartmouth in the summer of 1966 as the only currently working secondary teacher invited to the historic Anglo-American Seminar (the mere token representation of K–12 classroom teachers at the Dartmouth conference is today shocking evidence of the top-down structure of the profession of English in the decades before the National Writing Project overturned that pattern for the entire profession). Miles Myers (1997–1998) reports that at the urging of Tom Gage (who was later to become one of Moffett's closest friends and most knowledgeable interpreters), he read Moffett's 1967 NCTE monograph, *Drama: What Is Happening: The Use of Dramatic Activities in the Teaching of English* (eventually incorporated into *Teaching the Universe of Discourse*) and as a result changed the way he taught composition, even before he read the rest of Moffett's work, which he did as soon as it was published in the two early volumes of 1968. Myers then came to know Moffett personally when, in the course of working on the *Interaction* program, Moffett came to Oakland High School to watch Miles teach. Miles was subsequently one of the first teachers invited to field-test the *Interaction* program in his English classes, as were Mary Ann Smith and Jo Fyfe. Moffett, in one of his own autobiographical notes in *Coming on Center* (1981b, 81), mentions that beginning in the mid-1960s, even before he moved to California, he maintained a working relationship with a group of "devoted veteran educators" who were later instrumental in founding the Bay Area Writing Project, mentioning by name Jim Gray, Cap Lavin, Miles Myers, Mary K. Healy, and Keith Caldwell.

My point in recounting these incidental connections is that they all took place before the founding of the Bay Area Writing Project, and that, added together, they demonstrate that most of the key figures in the founding of the writing project actually knew Moffett himself, and virtually all of them were familiar with his theoretical and methodological writing by the time they were involved (along with some twenty other outstanding secondary and college teachers) in the process of dialogue and experimentation that constructed the historic first writing project summer institute, where Moffett was not present in person, but was surely present in the ideas and spirit of open inquiry and critical discussion and experimentation in writing that marked that institute and shaped the prototype for all subsequent writing project summer institutes. Nor was Moffett present merely in the spirit of that first institute. His theory and the practices informed by that theory were explicitly invoked and demonstrated in at least one presentation conducted by a team of innovative teachers who were later to become two of the most respected and influential teacher-leaders of the National Writing Project. As Jim Gray (2000) tells the story in his memoir of that memorable first summer:

> Mary Ann Smith and Joe Fyfe, who were team teaching at Loma Vista Intermediate Junior High School . . . had been using the James Moffett *Interaction* series, which drew on booklets and activity cards, readings and prompts, and which introduced students to many forms of creative and real-world writing. . . . Mary Ann and Jo were committed to Moffett's key pedagogical idea: students need to experiment with genres, finding topics that interest them and working at their own pace. They explained Moffett's ideas and showed us examples of student work and a video of their own classroom in action. (54–55)

All of this, of course, helps to explain how it happened that most of the characteristic features of the writing project summer institute, as it initially took shape in Berkeley and eventually took on the status of the model for all National Writing Project sites to adopt, are entirely consistent with Moffett's own model of how writing should be taught and learned in schools in the context of a community of writers. Some of the notable features of the Berkeley model include writing response groups where writers share work in progress; frequent opportunities for writing with only selected pieces taken further in the process than an early draft; rich opportunities for discussion to discover, share, and reshape ideas; and a good deal of experimentation with writing from various points of view to different audiences and in different genres. Moffett himself often spoke of the Writing Project as an ideal learning community and spent a good portion of every summer for twenty years giving presentations at National Writing Project sites around the country, sometimes remaining in residence for days or weeks at a time, and for several years serving as the co-director of summer institutes in Berkeley, Chicago, and Long Island. Through the writing groups of writing project summer institutes, he said, he found the only success he ever had in convincing teachers of the power of small groups as sites for important learning (Moffett 1981b, 82). Significantly, even at writing project sites where Moffett made no personal appearance, site leaders have almost always taken it as an intellectual and professional duty to introduce teachers in the summer institute through assigned readings and discussions to Moffett's discourse schema along with some of his published reflections on authorship, essaying, or assessment.

Moffett's Continuing Influence on Composition in the New Century

Given the degree to which Moffett's theory and models for instruction are inscribed in the discourse of the National Writing Project and in its signature practices, it is very likely that Moffett's influence on the teaching of writing will remain visible in K–12 and college writing classes, wherever the teachers of those classes have themselves been influenced by the summer institutes and extended professional development programs of sites of the National Writing Project. And the National Writing Project now sponsors roughly 200 sites (almost all of them located on college or university campuses) with at least one project site in every state in the nation and at least one site within a fifty-mile radius of virtually every public school in the continental United States and surely every college.[7]

Beyond the National Writing Project, Moffett's work and theory and pedagogical aims are most emphatically perpetuated and celebrated in NCTE's Assembly for Expanded Perspectives on Learning (AEPL), an assembly that emerged as a subgroup within the Conference on College Composition and Communication and that continues to maintain much of its initial emphasis on the teaching of writing. Moffett served during the last years of his life as the presiding guru and spiritual mentor for the founders of that assembly, and remains (along, more recently, with Peter Elbow) its most frequently cited and most revered authority. In fact, in the years immediately following Moffett's death, a number of members of NCTE/AEPL (including me) argued that the assembly should change its name to the "James Moffett Society," but the idea was rejected on the grounds that such a name would suggest a narrower focus and mission than the assembly wanted to advertise, though there was no disagreement about the significant degree to which the society recognizes itself as an organization committed to carrying on a vision of learning and of education that was articulated by Moffett in his writing and workshops for teachers, as in his turn to spirituality.

Within the past year, however, the idea of a Moffett Society reemerged in a more modern incarnation (under the technologically sophisticated leadership of my former student, Damian Koshnick), with the establishment of an online association of senior and junior Moffett disciples known as the "James Moffett Consortium," which defines itself as "a diverse consortium of teachers and researchers dedicated to dialogue on the value of James Moffett's theories and practices in English and education and our own uses of his ideas within K–16 classrooms." Interested teachers and scholars can join the consortium at its multifunctional Ning: jamesmoffettstudies.ning.com.[8] Within the past decade, moreover, subgroups of AEPL and other NCTE-affiliated teachers and scholars have organized two national conferences to share research and classroom practices inspired by or related to Moffett and his contributions to theory and pedagogy, and I anticipate that the steady growth of the Moffett consortium will lead to additional virtual and actual Moffett conferences in the future.

In the field of composition studies, I can think of only one other figure whose writing and intellectual influence have spawned a society named after him and meetings organized to celebrate, explicate, and build on his work. And that is Kenneth Burke. Moffett, it must be acknowledged, does not rank with Kenneth Burke among the leading American intellectuals of the twentieth century, revered and quoted extensively across the globe by rhetoricians, literary critics, philosophers, and other scholars in the arts and humanities. But it must also be acknowledged that Burke (himself, ironically, a college dropout) exclusively addressed an audience of university academics and highly sophisticated intellectuals, including literary critics and theorists, rhetoricians, language philosophers, and other humanists and social scientists who read the most sophisticated and prestigious intellectual and scholarly journals. Moffett, on the other hand, primarily and deliberately addressed K–12 classroom teachers of the English language arts, teacher educators, and composition instructors at every level of education—some of the least prestigious subgroups in the academic and intellectual communities. Within those subgroups and even beyond them, as we have seen, he remains, like Burke, a uniquely revered mentor and guide for two generations of his intellectual heirs and disciples who will undoubtedly carry his practices and theory and pedagogical wisdom forward to the generations that succeed them. Unlike Burke, however, Moffett is revered not only among university researchers and theorists, but by practitioners at every level of education where theory shapes curriculum, assessment, textbooks, and the experience of students. Hence Moffett's influence on the field of composition is ubiquitous, unavoidable, and probably perpetually relevant in a way that can be claimed by almost no other figure in the modern history of research and theory in composition and rhetoric.[9]

Notes

1. The biographical information I present here is drawn from my own conversations with Moffett over the course of our sixteen-year friendship, as well as from personal revelations scattered among the essays and head notes to essays he published in *Coming on Center* (1981b), along with information generously shared with me by Moffett's younger daughter, Judy, some of it based on biographical notes and other documents on Moffett collected and composed by Janet Moffett, the late Mrs. James Moffett. See also John Warnock's (2000) informative critical appreciation of Moffett, "James Moffett" in *Twentieth Century Rhetorics and Rhetoricians: Critical Studies and Sources*, which benefited from correspondence with Moffett himself and some subsequent correspondence with Janet Moffett. Researchers seeking additional biographical and bibliographical data on Moffett will want to know that in 2006 (almost a decade after the death of James Moffett in 1996 and Janet Moffett in 1997) the literary remains of James Moffett (amounting to roughly a dozen cartons containing books, published and unpublished manuscripts, audiotapes, videotapes, correspondence, teaching materials, lecture notes, biographical and autobiographical notes, and other archival materials) were donated by the Moffett family, through the good services of Judy Moffett, to the library of the University of California, Santa Barbara (UCSB), where Moffett visited every summer without fail (always accompanied by his wife Janet, who celebrated her birthday almost every year in Santa Barbara) from 1980 through the summer of 1996 (when he arrived using a walker) as a guest presenter of the South Coast Writing Project of which I was the director from 1979 until my retirement from UCSB in 2009. These materials, now archived as the "James Porter Moffett Papers, Mss 243," are available to researchers, who may make arrangements to see them by contacting the Department of Special Collections, Davidson Library at UCSB.

2. With an essay drawn from his thesis, Moffett won the prestigious undergraduate Bowdoin Essay Prize, whose prior and more recent winners have included Ralph Waldo Emerson, Jones Very, Henry Adams, Walter Jackson Bate, Delmore Schwartz, John Updike, and the current US Chief Justice of the Supreme Court, John Roberts.

3. In the introduction to *Active Voice*, where Moffett (1981a) explains its origins in his Exeter experiments, he also explains that he hadn't intended to publish his experimental sequence of assignments but felt forced to do so by the fact that photocopies of assignments made from the mimeographed version he had produced for himself and his Exeter colleagues in the 1960s were circulating ten and fifteen years later mainly throughout the National Writing Project and eventually got into the

hands of other teachers who misused his assignments and sometimes offered public criticism of what was initially produced as part of an experiment in progress and was written up only for private circulation to continue the experimentation. (It came to my own writing project site in 1979 from someone in the Bay Area Writing Project where Moffett himself must have given out one of his original mimeographed copies. We copied it for all of our teachers and many of them copied it for their colleagues.) To avoid such continuing dissemination and proliferating misuses of his outdated work, he felt obliged to produce a revised version with an explanatory apparatus and publish it for the profession at large.

4. Muller's book, *The Uses of English: Guidelines for the Teaching of English from the Anglo-American Conference at Dartmouth College* (1967), was commissioned by the conference organizers as the "report on the proceedings at the seminar designed for the general reader." Muller was at the conference to observe and write about its proceedings from his perspective as an American professor of English with no particular expertise in the teaching of English in elementary and secondary schools. John Dixon, a British scholar who was an expert on teaching English to precollege students, was commissioned to write a report addressed to "the professional community." What is frustratingly clear to any sophisticated reader of Muller's report is how much this representative American professor of English could recount ideas (advanced mainly by the British representatives, but clearly by some Americans as well, including Moffett, Wallace Douglas, James Squire, and Benjamin DeMott, among others) about a student-centered approach to learning language and literature without understanding in any deep or meaningful way what he was talking about. He possessed what Moffett liked dismissively to call "recitational knowledge." From the time I read the book in 1967, I have assumed that it typifies the way the MLA wing of the profession of English (with notable exceptions like DeMott) generally understands the discourse of the field of English education, and I have had abundant evidence in the intervening years to confirm that prejudice, though there are numerous recent signs of a more enlightened consciousness in some important precincts of the organization.

5. A notable example of how the academic community is inclined in its most prestigious precincts to ignore or dismiss important contributions to theory that are offered largely for the improvement of instruction in K–12 education is found in the reception among the professoriate in English to Louise Rosenblatt's revolutionary and now classic volume of 1938, *Literature as Exploration.* Rosenblatt's book offered a pedagogically and philosophically sophisticated theory of literary reading and its transformative applications to instruction, introducing to the field of English education a transactional, reader response pedagogy for secondary English classes that dominated English teacher education

courses in universities (if not most secondary classrooms themselves) throughout the period during which the New Criticism was virtually the only theory of criticism and teaching practice recognized by most college and university English professors (aside from the few who were professionally committed to the preparation of English teachers). Yet, Rosenblatt's work remained virtually unknown to the mainstream literary community until some years after the emergence of a reader response theory instigated by Stanley Fish (1967) and such continental theorists as Wolfgang Iser in the late 1960s and early 1970s. Hence, Jane Tompkins does not include Rosenblatt among the response theorists whose work she collects in her 1980 edited volume, *Reader-Response Criticism: From Formalism to Post-Structuralism*, but does list Rosenblatt's work in her bibliography. Then in 1983 the MLA finally acknowledged Rosenblatt's importance to the discourse of literary theory and pedagogy, when they published a new edition of her 1938 volume with a foreword by Wayne Booth.

That her groundbreaking book had been ignored for forty years by university English professors and the profession of English as represented by the MLA continued to humiliate and anger Rosenblatt until her death at the age of 100 in 2005, and she often spoke in private of the fact that she was denied the attention of the literary community by virtue of the attention she gave in her book to questions about the teaching of literature and especially teaching literature to high school students.

6. Gray tells the compelling and historically important story of the founding and early years of the Bay Area and National Writing Projects in *Teachers at the Center: A Memoir of the Early Years of the National Writing Project* (2000).

7. Since this article was written, NWP has lost federal funding. The network of writing project sites is now smaller but still active and influential.

8. The consortium and the "Ning" operated for a few years beyond 2012, when this essay was first published, but ceased operations sometime before 2019. The National Writing Project now hosts a monthly "James Moffett Reading Group" through their WriteNow app, allowing those interested in Moffett to meet to discuss his work and ideas.

9. As if to second my final point and confirm a number of the claims I make about Moffett's powerful influence on English education and composition in Great Britain as well as in the United States, there appeared, as this essay was about to go to press, a collection of articles "rereading James Moffett," written mostly by British and Australian scholars in the September 2010 issue of the international British journal *Changing English*.

Works Cited

Applebee, Arthur N. 1974. *Tradition and Reform in the Teaching of English: A History*. Urbana, IL: NCTE.

Axelrod, Rise, and Charles Cooper. 1990/2010. *The St. Martin's Guide to Writing* (now in its ninth edition). New York: Bedford/St. Martin's.

Bazerman, Charles. 1994. "Systems of Genres and the Enactment of Social Intentions." In *Genre and the New Rhetoric,* edited by A. Freedman and P. Medway, 79–101. London: Taylor and Francis.

Bitzer, Lloyd. 1968. "The Rhetorical Situation." *Philosophy and Rhetoric* 1 (January): 1–14.

Blau, Sheridan. 1983. "Invisible Writing: Investigating Cognitive Processes in Composition." *College Composition and Communication* 34(3) (Oct.): 297–312.

Blau, Sheridan, et al. 1993. *The Writer's Craft (Grades 6–12)*. Evanston, IL: McDougal Littell.

Britton, James, Tony Burgess, Nancy Martin, Alex McLeod, and Harold Rosen. 1975. *The Development of Writing Abilities (11–18)*. London: Macmillan Education.

Bryan, Jonathan R. 1974. "A Lively and a Rigorous English: Reflections on Teaching English in Great Britain." *College Composition and Communication* 25(2) (May): 160–65.

D'Angelo, Frank. 1975. *A Conceptual Theory of Rhetoric*. Cambridge, MA: Winthrop.

Dixon, John. 1967/1969. *Growth through English*. London: Oxford University Press.

———. 1975. *Growth through English: Set in the Perspective of the Seventies*. London: Oxford University Press.

Fish, Stanley. 1967. *Surprised by Sin: The Reader in Paradise Lost*. Cambridge, MA: Harvard University Press.

Foehr, Regina, et al. 1997-1998. "A Tribute to James Moffett." *Journal of the Assembly for Expanded Perspectives on Learning* 3: 1–12.

Freedman, Aviva, and Peter Medway. 1994. *Genre and the New Rhetoric*. New York: Taylor and Francis.

Gray, James. 1997. "James Moffett, 1929–1996: An Appreciation." *The Quarterly* 19(1): 33–34.

———. 2000. *Teachers at the Center: A Memoir of the Early Years of the National Writing Project.* Berkeley, CA: National Writing Project.

Gray, James, and Betty Jane Wagner. 1997. "Reflective Tributes to James Moffett's Influence on English Education." *English Education* 29(2) (May): 147–50.

Green, Judith, and Carol Dixon. 1993. "Talking Knowledge into Being: Discursive and Social Practices in Classrooms." *Linguistics in Education* 5: 231–39.

Harris, Joseph. 1997. *A Teaching Subject: Composition Since 1966.* Upper Saddle River, NJ: Prentice Hall.

Hirsch, E. D. 1977. *The Philosophy of Composition.* Chicago: University of Chicago Press.

Kinneavy, James. 1971. *A Theory of Discourse: The Aims of Discourse.* New York: Norton.

Lave, Jean, and Etienne Wenger. 1991. *Situated Learning: Legitimate Peripheral Participation.* Cambridge, MA: Cambridge University Press.

McClelland, Ben, and Timothy Donovan. 1985. *Perspectives on Research and Scholarship in Composition.* New York: MLA.

Miller, Carolyn. 1984. "Genre as Social Action." *Quarterly Journal of Speech* 70: 151–67.

Moffett, James. 1967. *Drama: What Is Happening.* NCTE Monograph. Urbana, IL: NCTE.

———. 1968a. *A Student-Centered Language Arts Curriculum, Grades K–13: A Handbook for Teachers.* Boston: Houghton Mifflin. (Reissued by Boynton/CookHeinemann in 1992.)

———. 1968b. *Teaching the Universe of Discourse.* Boston: Houghton Mifflin. (Reissued by Boynton/Cook-Heinemann in 1983.)

———. 1973. *Interaction.* Boston: Houghton/Mifflin.

———. 1981a. *Active Voice: A Writing Program Across the Curriculum.* Portsmouth, NH: Boynton/Cook-Heinemann.

———. 1981b. *Coming on Center: English Education in Evolution.* Portsmouth, NH: Boynton/Cook-Heinemann.

Moffett, James, and Kenneth McElheny. 1966. *Points of View: An Anthology of Short Stories*. New York: Mentor.

Muller, Herbert. 1967. *The Uses of English: Guidelines for the Teaching of English from the Anglo-American Conference at Dartmouth College*. New York: Holt, Rinehart, Winston.

Myers, Miles. 1997–1998. "Remembering Jim." In "A Tribute to James Moffett." *Journal of the Assembly for Expanded Perspectives on Learning* 3: 1–12.

North, Stephen. 1987. *The Making of Knowledge in Composition: Portrait of an Emerging Field*. Portsmouth, NH: Boynton/Cook-Heinemann.

O'Connors, Robert. 1997. *Composition-Rhetoric: Backgrounds, Theory, and Pedagogy*. Pittsburgh, PA: University of Pittsburgh Press.

Rosenblatt, Louise. 1938. *Literature as Exploration*. New York: Appleton-Century (5th ed. published by MLA in 1995).

Russell, David. 1997. "Rethinking Genre in School and Society: An Activity Theory Analysis." *Written Communication* 14: 504–54.

Tompkins, Jane, ed. 1980. *Reader-Response Criticism: From Formalism to PostStructuralism*. Baltimore: Johns Hopkins University Press.

Villanueva, Victor. 2003. *Cross-Talk in Comp Theory: A Reader*. 2d ed. Urbana, IL: NCTE.

Warnock, John. 2000. "James Moffett." In *Twentieth Century Rhetorics and Rhetoricians: Critical Studies and Sources*, edited by Michael Moran and Michelle Ballif. Westport, CT: Greenwood Press.

CHAPTER THREE

Moffett, Dartmouth, and the Reform of the Teaching of English: Revising a History

SHANNON POTTS
Teachers College, Columbia University

> *Dartmouth was not so much a collective as an individual experience. . . . I may generalize that each of the participants came with one set of ideas and left with another.*
>
> —JAMES MILLER, Seminar Participant (5)

A Heroic Story

In the 1970s the teaching of English in the United States underwent what Joseph Harris, in his expansive history of composition, *A Teaching Subject,* has termed a "Copernican shift," moving the focus of the field from what a student "learns about" in school into something that a student "does," thus giving greater attention to the role of student speech and writing in constructing knowledge.

The story goes that the Anglo-American Dartmouth Seminar, held in the summer of 1966, was responsible for that shift. That summer a group of mostly male, and exclusively white, educators from Great Britain and the United States (and one of their Canadian colleagues) gathered at Dartmouth College in Hanover, New Hampshire, to define the subject of English and to identify the ways it might be taught. The Carnegie Foundation sponsored their effort, which was organized by the National Council of Teachers of English (NCTE), the Modern Language Association (MLA), and the National Association for the Teaching of English (NATE).

In the most common version of the story, or the heroic one, as Harris terms it, the British delegation and their leading thinkers

John Dixon and James Britton introduced the substantive "growth model" for learning that centers the experience and needs of students in the English classroom. In his expansive history of the field, Arthur Applebee succinctly articulates the dominant story, explaining: "What the British offered the Americans was a model for English instruction which focused not on the demands of the discipline but on the personal and linguistic growth of the child" (231). The introduction of this "growth model" at the Dartmouth conference is often considered to be the foundation for a conceptual and seismic shift in the curricular and pedagogical frameworks of English Education in America in the decade that followed (Applebee; Berlin; Harris, "After Dartmouth" and *Teaching Subject*; Squire and Britton; Russell).

The trouble with this version of Dartmouth is, first, that the history of the teaching of English in the late twentieth century hardly supports this view, and, second, that to the extent that there were at least some signs or portents of a potential shift toward a new model of English instruction in the United States, it was not the result of the influence of the Dartmouth conference, but of the influence of James Moffett, who was himself probably the youngest and educationally the least experienced participant in that conference.

So here, I would like to tell a story about a shift in thinking about the teaching of English after the Dartmouth conference, about the work that James Moffett was doing in the United States before Dartmouth, and about his participation in the Dartmouth Seminar and how it impacted the seminar and the teaching of English more broadly. My story is based on a newly accessed body of rich archival evidence that illuminates the influence of James Moffett's publications and his direct personal influence on the conversations at the Dartmouth Seminar and on teacher-leaders and teacher educators in English education across the United States starting in the 1970s (also see Blau).

Nothing Startling

According to virtually all published reports on the conference (e.g., Dixon; Muller), there was much collegial conversation and even more passionate debate throughout the seminar, focused partly on the content of English as an academic subject and, even more controversially perhaps, on the role or function of teaching and teachers in the English language arts classroom. But for all the goodwill of the participants and their shared desire to learn from one another, the main achievements of the seminar seem to have been, first, a set of unobjectionable (and largely forgotten) recommendations that most participants could have agreed upon without any conference and, second, a wider recognition of the disagreements that defined two very different and possibly irreconcilable conceptions of English as an academic subject in grades K–12. These two concepts were oversimplified to represent the "American" focus on skills in reading and writing along with the transmission of cultural heritage through literature, and the "British" emphasis on students learning through their own talk as much as through their writing and reading (Dixon).

Yet before the conference came to a close on the final day, the delegates managed to arrive at eleven recommendations or "points of agreement" (Dixon). These points are often referenced in documents and histories of the conference, though they do not seem to have been widely published, perhaps because the initial conference reports and the participants who published their own reflections on the seminar do not seem to have embraced all these points of agreement as a summary of what the seminar accomplished or should have accomplished (Marckwardt; Miller; O'Neil and Dixon; Shugrue). In his own very brief account of the conference, Albert Marckwardt (professor of English and linguistics at Princeton, incoming president of NCTE, and one of the conference organizers) characterizes the eleven points of agreement as "nothing startling." Similarly, James Miller, professor of English at the University of Chicago, refers to the points of agreement as a "closing manifesto," but laments that they are "silent on some of the major issues debated at the seminar" (19). The findings are hard to argue with, Miller contends, because they "leap to a level of generality and ambiguity high and intense enough to soar beyond debate" (19). All the same, they remain sound, even if they are not particularly exciting. They center student experience on reading, writing, and drama; they urge a reform in teacher education; and they ask for the abolition of grouping students by ability and examinations—the final two points, noted by Miller, having been relatively minor points of agreement between the factions (19).

The agreements, according to Marckwardt's account (104–5), are as follows:

1. The centrality of the pupil's exploring, extending, and shaping experiences in the English classroom
2. The urgency of developing classroom approaches stressing the vital, creative, dramatic involvement of children and young people in language experiences
3. The importance of directing more attention to speaking and listening experiences for all pupils at all levels, particularly those experiences which involve vigorous interaction among children
4. The wisdom of providing young people at all levels with significant opportunities for the creative uses of language: creative dramatics, imaginative writing, improvisation, role-playing, and similar activities
5. The significance of rich literary experiences in the educative process and the importance of teachers of English restudying particular selections to determine their appropriateness for reading at different levels
6. The need to overcome the restrictiveness of rigid patterns of "grouping"; or "streaming"; which limit the linguistic environment in which boys and girls learn English and which tend to inhibit language development
7. The need to negate the limiting, often stultifying, impact of examination patterns which direct attention of both teachers and pupils to aspects of English which are at best superficial and often misleading
8. The compelling urgency of improving the conditions under which English is taught in the schools: the need for more books and libraries, for better equipment, for reasonable class size, for a classroom environment which will make good teaching possible
9. The importance of teachers of English at all levels informing themselves about the results of pertinent scholarship and research so that their classroom approaches may be guided accordingly

10. The need for radical reform in programs of teacher education, both preservice and in-service
11. The importance of educating the public on what is meant by good English and what is meant by good English teaching

Fortunately for the conference's reputation, these recommendations would not become its recognized legacy. Rather, John Dixon's *Growth through English,* with its focus on "growth" that would come to be known as the "British viewpoint," would control the narrative. The only problem: Dixon's account centered James Britton and the rest of the British delegation as the architects of the growth model, viewing Moffett's contributions as supportive of the growth model but never acknowledging him as one of the leading architects of the concept, which he in fact was, as I demonstrate here with the help of a new body of documentary evidence I have recently managed to unearth.

The Single Story Emerges

Even before the conference began, its organizers, anticipating disagreements or at least different perspectives between the delegations from the United Kingdom and the United States, and wanting to avoid a biased historical account of the conference proceedings, commissioned two reports on the conference, one to be written by a British educator and the other by an American. For the British point of view, they appointed John Dixon, a specialist in English education and a member of the British delegation to the conference; for the American perspective, they appointed Herbert Muller, a professor of English who attended the conference as a guest observer.

Muller's book, *The Uses of English*, was written, as he says in his introduction, for "the general reader" (vi). As Muller did not have a background in K–12 education, his discussion of the conference proceedings presents a record of events organized by topic with a relatively superficial treatment of the ideas presented and debated (Sublette 348). Dixon's book, however, titled *Growth through English*, having been printed in three editions (1967, 1969, and 1975), has become something of a classic resource that has clearly shaped how most educators in the field of English in the English-speaking world understand what happened at Dartmouth. In the foreword to the 1975 edition, James Squire and James Britton (respectively representing the leadership of the American and British delegations at Dartmouth) do not merely suggest that Dixon's book is an authoritative account of the conference, but that "it is unlikely that any other book in the past decade has had more influence on English work in classrooms on both sides of the Atlantic" (vii).

Dixon was already an influential figure in British education before Dartmouth. He was one of the founders of the British National Association for the Teaching of English and he also served as chair of the British Schools Council English Committee. He was therefore intimately conversant with the theory and pedagogical practices representing the British model of education in English language arts as it was presented by the British delegates at Dartmouth. In presenting the "British" position thoroughly and with an eloquence shaped by his own deep understanding of the issues, Dixon wrote persuasively about attending to genuine learning, deep engagement, and personally meaningful reading and writing that was desired and documented in the British approach to the teaching of English, in contrast to the more traditionally academic, canonical, and information- or skill-oriented practices that seemed to be advocated by many of the delegates from the United States.

Dixon made no effort to hide the fact that he was telling one version of the seminar discussions and debates at Dartmouth, writing in the preface, "[I]nasmuch as the discussions ranged all over a large subject and produced dozens of papers on different topics, my account is highly selective" (iv). Yet the general effect of his persuasive and lively account is to give the impression that the distinctively British growth model of English was the prevailing view, if not the achieved consensus of the seminar. Given that Dixon's account is the one that was widely circulated, his story that the intellectual products of Dartmouth were a result of British theory has prevailed, and has been repeated as fact in most of the historical accounts of our field (Allen; Applebee; Bryan; Harris, "After Dartmouth" and *Teaching Subject*; Parker; Russell; Squire and Britton).

The (Forgotten) Exceptional American

John Lofty tells of a British delegate to the Dartmouth conference, who later served anonymously as a reviewer of a 2009 essay Lofty wrote, who confirmed in his review much of Dixon's account, with a note of one monumental erasure. This participant recalled: "[T]he Brits had overwhelmed the Americans. (Moffett, for us, was the exceptional American)" (Lofty 33). Yet, as a result of the dominance of Dixon's account in the field's memory of Dartmouth, Moffett's exceptional contribution to the deliberations and structure of the conference that this anonymous reviewer recalled has been largely forgotten. Of course, Moffett's presence at the Dartmouth Seminar is well-known and widely cited, but the character of his participation in and influence on the discourse at the conference has hardly been properly acknowledged.

By the summer of 1966, Moffett had concluded his ten-year stint at Phillips Exeter Academy, where he had been teaching English and French. At that point in his professional life, he was also in the middle of a two-year appointment funded by the Carnegie Foundation as a research associate in the Harvard Graduate School of Education. From anecdotes and footnotes in Moffett's *A Student-Centered Language Arts Curriculum, Grades K–13: A Handbook for Teachers*, we can see that in the year leading up to the seminar, Moffett was visiting public school classrooms that were making use of the "experimental curriculum" he had created for his handbook while still at Phillips Exeter—the research that would inform his forthcoming curricular publication (ix). At this point in his career, he had already published, with Kenneth McElheny, his anthology *Points of View*, two short stories in *New World Writing* ("Suicides," "Man"), and four essays ("Second Person," "Telling Stories," "I," "Structural Curriculum") that would later be included, or serve as drafts for chapters, in his classic and most influential volume, *Teaching the Universe of Discourse*, which served as the theoretical foundation and a companion volume for his handbook for K–13 classroom teachers. Both volumes were published by Houghton Mifflin in 1968.

We don't know (though we can conjecture) how Moffett was selected to participate in the Dartmouth Seminar. Unlike virtually all of the other American delegates, he was at the time of the conference neither a recognized leader in NCTE nor a well-known literary scholar, nor was he a legendary classroom teacher. He was, in fact, a decade younger and much less experienced in teaching than any of the other delegates at the conference. But he was already known to the Carnegie Foundation, which was the funding source for the conference and for his two-year appointment as a research associate at Harvard, and that connection may have helped him get selected. However, it is also likely that the conference organizers from NCTE were familiar with Moffett's early published essay that had appeared in the NCTE journal *College Composition and Communication* (CCC), "I, You, and It," and that they recognized the potential value of his thinking to the international dialogue that would take place at the conference.

What is clear is that Moffett was not widely known or widely regarded as a leader in the field of English education much before the Dartmouth Seminar. His name does not appear on the "Tentative List of Participants" and alternates included in the proposal written by NCTE Executive Director James Squire in November 1965. Those who were included as participants, according to the language of the proposal, were those "carefully chosen" for their "unique qualifications" with respect to the various fields of English, "the major scholarly developments in English," and "the questions to be examined by the seminar." And Moffett in November of 1965 apparently did not yet seem to meet any of those criteria.

After Dartmouth, however, Moffett's stature in the field of English education seems to have shifted dramatically. In a letter dated September 23, 1966, to Peter Caws of the Carnegie Foundation, James Squire writes about the potential for international cooperation that has been generated from Dartmouth, noting that Moffett "turned out to be one of the most interesting and influential participants at Dartmouth." Significantly, the purpose of that letter was to urge the Carnegie Foundation to fund Moffett for a year in London to work directly with Britton. Quite aside from the other archival evidence that Moffett was a powerful influence on the conference, Squire's assertion must stand as most authoritative since Squire himself was the prime mover in proposing and obtaining funding, organizing, and recruiting the participants for the Dartmouth conference, and he was intimately involved in the daily events of the conference. He was also widely recognized as an intellectual and political "powerhouse," which makes his recommendation of Moffett as reliable and well-informed as any to be obtained in the profession of English at that time (Squire).

Moffett had two main areas of focus in his scholarship and writing at the time of the Dartmouth conference: a pedagogical focus on the creation of a student-centered approach to the English language arts, and a theoretical focus on thinking and discourse (based on a ladder of abstraction) that informed an English language arts curriculum. Moffett's participation at the conference was not only singularly valuable for his substantive contributions in these areas, but also for the degree to which he was noticeably able to engage conference participants from both the United States and Great Britain in his thinking, a feat that apparently set him apart from his other progressive-thinking colleagues. Paul Olson, a conference delegate who was widely respected as a literary scholar and as director of the National Defense Education Act–funded Project English Curriculum Center at the University of Nebraska, was especially impressed by Moffett's capacity for dialogue across the usual philosophical borders. In a recent retrospective interview about the Dartmouth conference, Olson remembers that "[w]hat was really crucial was that there were people [who could] talk across the factions. . . . James Moffett was one" (Vee and McIntyre). In that same interview, Olson goes on to offer a personal anecdote of how Moffett engaged him, although they had initially disagreed: "Jim Moffett was excellent. He didn't like the stuff I had done. And he influenced me a lot. And he was very thoughtful in discourse at the conference. And in developing compositional sequences that were centered on what the child knew, in the culture of the child. I came to admire him a good bit."

Finally, if there is any lingering doubt about the uniquely powerful intellectual influence of Moffett on both the British and the American delegates to the Dartmouth conference, a recent search through unpublished archives of the conference collected by the US Department of Health, Education, and Welfare and retrieved from ERIC have turned up a document listing a set of thirteen readings that were distributed "in advance to all seminar participants" to prepare them for their four weeks of dialogue about the teaching of English on both sides of the Atlantic ("Anglo-American Seminar"). Among those readings were a number of reports on the state of English teaching in the United States and Great Britain as well as three essays by James Moffett. To my knowledge, these readings are not mentioned in any of the published accounts of Dartmouth. Here is the complete list of thirteen distributed readings (with Moffett's essays bolded):

- "The Basic Issues in the Teaching of English"; supplement to *Elementary English*, October 1959, and *English Journal*, September 1959.
- *The Disappearing Dais*, Frank Whitehead. Chatto & Windus, 1966.
- *Ends and Issues: 1965-1966*, Alexander Frazier, Editor. NCTE, 1966.
- *English in the Primary School*, NATE, July 1964.
- *Freedom and Discipline in English*, Commission on English. CEEB, 1965.
- *Half Our Future*, Central Advisory Committee for Education (England). Her Majesty's Stationery Office, 1963.
- **"I, You, and It," James Moffett; reprinted from *College Composition and Communication*, December 1965.**
- "Literature, Threat and Conquest," Walter J. Ong, S.J.; reprinted from *College English*, May 1966.
- *National Study of High School English Programs: "A Record of English Teaching Today"* and *"A School for All Seasons,"* Roger K. Applebee and James R. Squire; reprinted from the *English Journal*, March 1966.
- "New Materials for the Teaching of English: The English Program of the USOE," Michael F. Shugrue; *PMLA*, September 1966.
- **"A Structural Curriculum in English," James Moffett; reprinted from *Harvard Educational Review*, Winter 1966.**
- **"Telling Stories: Methods of Abstraction in Fiction," James**

Moffett; reprinted from *ETC: A Review of General Semantics,* December 1964.

- "Who is to Speak for English" and "Elementary Teaching and Elemental Scholarship," Francis Keppel and Northrop Frye; *PMLA*, May 1964.

Three of the fourteen publications offered to conference participants as advance readings were written by James Moffett. Looking closely at the selected Moffett pieces, we can see that they are drafts in progress and whole chapters of what became *Teaching the Universe of Discourse.* The essay "A Structural Curriculum in English" became the first chapter of *Teaching*—with "slight alterations" (Moffett, *Teaching* 1). Similarly, "I, You, and It" was published in *CCC* in 1965 and then extended to become the second chapter of *Teaching the Universe of Discourse,* with the title "Kinds and Orders of Discourse." The third essay, "Telling Stories: Methods of Abstraction in Fiction," was slightly altered before being published as Chapter 4 of *Teaching,* becoming "Narrative: What Happened." In other words, Moffett's pedagogical theory of discourse had not only already been developed by the time he attended the conference at Dartmouth, but its essential elements were distributed to seminar participants in the form of three separate papers as preparatory reading for the conference itself.

This is an especially important and somewhat paradoxical observation because there persists a common and misguided narrative that Moffett's *Teaching the Universe of Discourse* was a product of the intellectual work that transpired at Dartmouth (Cianciolo; Donahue; Trimbur). Trimbur offers the following description that is emblematic of this mistaken narrative: "As conventionally represented, Dartmouth is where James Britton and John Dixon brought new and progressive insights about teaching and learning English to James Moffett and Project English people from the United States, laying conceptual ground for the process movement that was about to emerge" (142). However, we now know that *Teaching the Universe of Discourse* could not possibly be regarded and should not be cited as a product of the Dartmouth Seminar since virtually all of it had already been written before the seminar and much of it shared with participants in advance and then used in working groups during the conference itself.

Moffett appears to have been grateful to have found like-minded thinkers in the British delegation at Dartmouth, but he also makes clear that he did not develop his theory of practice from their contributions. In the preface to *Coming on Center*, written fifteen years after the seminar, Moffett recalls, "From many of the British at Dartmouth I received a gratifying corroboration of my approach, which included much drama and other peer interaction, and which resembled the open classroom, though I had known nothing of what the British were doing" (1). He acknowledges that the ideas in *A Student-Centered Language Arts Curriculum, Grades K–13* "benefited considerably . . . from reactions by . . . my fellow participants at the Anglo-American Conference on the Teaching of English" (3). He also thanks Douglas Barnes and Anthony Adams, both British participants at the conference, in his chapter titled "Acting Out" for "discussion that helped sharpen some ideas in this and later chapters on Drama" (35).

Colleague to Colleague, Teacher to Teacher

The decade that followed Dartmouth was a boon for progressive, child-centered teaching in the United States. In 1968 two of Moffett's most influential texts, sections of which had appeared in early drafts at Dartmouth, *Teaching the Universe of Discourse* and *A Student-Centered Language Arts Curriculum, Grades K–13*, were finally published, and they began to be read by teachers and teacher educators and used in teacher preparation programs across the country. Shortly thereafter, Moffett and his family moved to California so he could accept a visiting appointment as a lecturer in the School of Education at the University of California, Berkeley for the winter and spring terms of 1970.[1] From his new home on Spruce Street in Berkeley, Moffett began to consult in schools and school districts across California and would often visit the Bay Area Writing Project.

Of course, Moffett's innovative ideas as represented in his articles and books of the late 1960s could not have been so widely disseminated and embraced by the field if they were not being taken up by classroom practitioners themselves. In their memoriam of James Moffett (Chapter 1 of this volume), Spalding, Koshnick, and Myers tell the story of how after the Dartmouth Seminar, "Cap Lavin, the other high school teacher at Dartmouth, went home to California with a ditto copy of *Drama: What Is Happening*"—which Moffett had shared in his working group. Lavin passed it on to friends, including Miles Myers. A few years later, Lavin and Miles Myers became Jim Gray's closest colleagues and collaborators in the founding of the Bay Area Writing Project (BAWP), and Moffett's ideas about writing in a community of writers were infused into the original model for a BAWP Summer Institute for teachers. Moreover, as Blau mentions in his essay "Theory for Practice," the very first Summer Institute of the Bay Area Writing Project featured a major presentation on Moffett's discourse theory and practices for the teaching of writing.

It was through BAWP and the California and National Writing Projects that Moffett's work was communicated rapidly to teacher-leaders across the country. Spalding et al. remind us that "Moffett's early work was passed informally from colleague to colleague and teacher to teacher" (27–28). Moffett's words, shared and sharpened at Dartmouth, thus made their way into teachers' hands through other teachers even before and after Moffett's influential book was published. As the wildfire spread, Moffett's ideas became central to the evolution of English teaching in the United States in the 1970s.

Moffett, Britton, and Their Influence in the UK

The connection between James Britton and James Moffett after Dartmouth is also worth spending a moment considering for it adds more color to our understanding of how Moffett's thinking at the seminar went on to shape the field. After Dartmouth, Britton, who was one of the most influential thinkers in the field of English education in Great Britain during the 1960s and 1970s and until his death in 1994, and who was also one of the leaders of the British delegation at Dartmouth, began citing Moffett conspicuously in his most celebrated and influential work. His 1970 publication, *Language and Learning*, quotes directly from

Moffett twice, both times from Moffett's chapter selections from *Drama: What Is Happening*, which evidently had moved Britton as it had Lavin and so many other of their Dartmouth colleagues. Britton also recommends in his conclusion, "a theoretical study of the English curriculum, by an American writer, Moffett" as a part of his list of "good recent books about the teaching of English" (275). Even more notably and conspicuously, Britton et al.'s monumental 1975 publication, *The Development of Writing Abilities (11–18),* cites Moffett eleven times, making crucial use of Moffett's scales of abstraction and discourse typology as the basis for the study, with revisions and additions to Moffett's framework made for practical purposes.

Moffett's influence on James Britton and British theory and practice in the teaching of English is nicely summated in a special issue dedicated to Moffett's work of the international journal *Changing English*. In one retrospective article, Bill Green argues that Moffett was particularly influential in the British world as his ideas were "taken up in the writing models developed by James Britton and his associates at the London Institute of Education . . . and driving 'Growth Model' English curriculum development." Green goes on to describe Moffett as a "key architect of what has come to be known as the New English: that version of English teaching most commonly associated with and referenced back to the Dartmouth Seminar."

It is important to clarify that I am not attempting to argue that Moffett was responsible for Britton's theory of language development. Rather, I am offering additional evidence from the writing of leading British and Australian scholars as support for my argument that one of the most powerful legacies from the Dartmouth conference were the ideas—both theoretical and pedagogical—of James Moffett, ideas that seminar participants brought home and shared, thereby reshaping the field on both sides of the Atlantic and beyond.

Note

1. It is worth noting that after publishing *Teaching the Universe of Discourse* and *A Student-Centered Language Arts Curriculum, Grades*

K–13, Moffett took a sabbatical in Barbados to "clear his head" before heading to Berkeley (*Coming on Center* 63).

Works Cited

Allen, David. *English Teaching since 1965: How Much Growth?*. Heinemann Educational Books, 1980.

"Anglo-American Seminar on the Teaching and Learning of English Agenda (Dartmouth College, Hanover, New Hampshire, Aug. 20–Sept. 16, 1966); and Miscellaneous Papers: Freshman English, English in English Departments of English Universities, Some Technical Terms; and the Breadth and Depth of English in the United States." National Association for the Teaching of English, National Council of Teachers of English, Modern Language Association of America. September 1966. ED082200. *ERIC*, https://eric.ed.gov/?q=Dartmouth+Seminar&pg=3&id=ED082200.

Applebee, Arthur N. *Tradition and Reform in the Teaching of English: A History*. National Council of Teachers of English, 1974.

Berlin, James A. *Rhetoric and Reality: Writing Instruction in American Colleges, 1900–1985*. Southern Illinois UP, 1987.

Blau, Sheridan. "Theory for Practice: James Moffett's Seminal Contribution to Composition." *Composition's Roots in English Education*, edited by Patricia Lambert Stock, Heinemann, 2012, pp. 81–104.

Britton, James. *Language and Learning*. Allen Lane, 1970.

———, et al. *The Development of Writing Abilities (11–18)*. Macmillan, 1975.

Bryan, Jonathan R. "A Lively and a Rigorous English: Reflections on Teaching English in Great Britain." *College Composition and Communication*, vol. 25, no. 2, 1974, pp. 160–65.

Cianciolo, Patricia J. *Critical Thinking in the Study of Children's Literature in the Elementary Grades*. Center for the Learning and Teaching of Elementary Subjects, Institute for Research on Teaching, Michigan State University, 1988.

Dixon, John. *Growth through English: A Report Based on the Dartmouth Seminar, 1966*. 2nd ed., National Association for the Teaching of English, 1969.

Donahue, Christiane. "The 1966 Seminar." *50th Anniversary Dartmouth Institute and Conference*, Aug. 2015, https://dartmouthwritinginstitute.wordpress.com/1966-seminar/.

Green, Bill. "Re-reading James Moffett: Discourse, Rhetoric, Subjectivity." *Changing English*, vol. 17, no. 3, 2010.

Harris, Joseph. "After Dartmouth: Growth and Conflict in English." *College English*, vol. 53, no. 6, 1991, pp. 631–46.

———. *A Teaching Subject: Composition since 1966*. New ed., Utah State UP, 2012.

Hook, J. N. *A Long Way Together: A Personal View of NCTE's First Sixty-Seven Years*. National Council of Teachers of English, 1979.

Lofty, John S. "'There Is One Story Worth Telling': An Essay for James Britton and Nancy Martin." *English Education*, vol. 42, no. 1, 2009, pp. 29–60.

Marckwardt, Albert H. "The Dartmouth Seminar." *The Bulletin of the National Association of Secondary School Principals*, vol. 51, no. 318, 1967, pp. 101–6.

Miller, James E., Jr. "What Happened at Dartmouth? (A Query by One Who Was There)." Address at the Illinois Association of Teachers of English Meeting, Urbana, 17 Oct. 1969. *ERIC*, https://eric.ed.gov/?id=ED039249.

Moffett, James. *Coming on Center: English Education in Evolution*. Boynton/Cook, 1981.

———. *Drama, What Is Happening: The Use of Dramatic Activities in the Teaching of English*. National Council of Teachers of English, 1967.

———. "I, You, and It." *College Composition and Communication*, vol. 16, no. 5, 1965, pp. 243–48.

———. "The Man Behind." *New World Writing, 11*, edited by William De Witt Snodgrass and Donald Rodney Justice, New American Library, 1957, pp. 256–63.

———. "The Second Person." *IMPULSE*, 1962, pp. 32–35.

———. "A Structural Curriculum in English." *Harvard Educational Review*, vol. 36, no. 1, 1966, pp. 17–28.

———. *A Student-Centered Language Arts Curriculum, Grades K–13: A Handbook for Teachers*. Houghton Mifflin, 1968.

———. "The Suicides of Private Greaves." *New World Writing, 10.* New American Library, 1956, pp. 7–28.

———. *Teaching the Universe of Discourse.* Houghton Mifflin, 1968.

———. "Telling Stories: Methods of Abstraction in Fiction." *ETC: A Review of General Semantics,* vol. 21, no. 4, 1964, pp. 425–50.

Moffett, James, and Kenneth R. McElheny, editors. *Points of View: An Anthology of Short Stories.* New American Library, 1966.

Muller, Herbert J. *The Uses of English: Guidelines for the Teaching of English from the Anglo-American Conference at Dartmouth College.* Holt, Rinehart and Winston, 1967.O'Neil, Wayne A., and John Dixon "Conference Report: The Dartmouth Seminar." *Harvard Educational Review,* vol. 39, no. 2, 1969, pp. 357–72.

Parker, Robert P., Jr. "From Sputnik to Dartmouth: Trends in the Teaching of Composition." *English Journal,* vol. 68. no. 6, 1979, pp. 32–37.

Russell, David R. "American Origins of the Writing-across-the-Curriculum Movement." *English Publications,* vol. 219, 1991.

Shugrue, Michael F. "Resolutions of the Anglo-American Conference on the Teaching and Learning of English." *English Journal,* vol. 57, no. 4, 1968, pp. 549–50.

Spalding, Elizabeth, et al. "James Moffett's Legacy to *English Journal.*" *English Journal,* vol. 101, no. 3, 2012, pp. 26–33.

Squire, James, and James Britton. Foreword. *Growth through English,* 3rd ed., edited by John Dixon, National Association for the Teaching of English, 1975, pp. vii–xvii.

Squire, Peter. Letter to Caws. 23 Sept. 1966. *Carnegie Corporation of New York records,* circa 1872–2015. Box III.A 606 Folder 3. Rare Book and Manuscript Library, Columbia University, New York.

Sublette, Jack R. "The Dartmouth Conference: Its Reports and Results." *College English,* vol. 35, no. 3, 1973, pp. 348–57.

Trimbur, John. "The Dartmouth Conference and the Geohistory of the Native Speaker." *College English,* vol. 71, no. 2, 2008, pp. 142–69.

Vee, Annette, curator, and Megan McIntyre, contributor. *Dartmouth '66 Seminar Exhibit.* WAC Clearinghouse, 2021, https://doi .org/10.37514/TWR-J.2021.1.1.01.

Chapter Four

James Moffett in Australia: Writing Pedagogy and Post-Dartmouth English Teaching

Bill Green
Charles Sturt University

Wayne Sawyer
Western Sydney University

Introduction

The Third International Conference on the Teaching of English was held in Sydney in 1980. It was an auspicious moment in English curriculum history, not only for Australia but also more widely, right across the ex-imperial Anglophone world. It was the first time that such a conference had been held in the Southern Hemisphere, following earlier such events in the United States (at Dartmouth, 1966) and in the United Kingdom (at York, 1971). There were 800 delegates participating in the Sydney conference, with around 200 coming from overseas, "representing Canada, Great Britain, [the] United States, New Zealand, India, [and] Singapore" (Eagleson, Introduction x). Convened by the Australian Association for the Teaching of English (AATE) under the auspices of what would subsequently become the International Federation for the Teaching of English (IFTE),[1] the Sydney conference brought together an impressive range of keynote speakers, drawn from among the field's most influential figures at that time. Notable among them was James Moffett. His presence on the podium was a clear marker of his particular significance for English teaching in Australia in the immediate post-Dartmouth period. His influence was considerable and widely acknowledged. Yet this influence has since then all but disappeared, and the reasons why are worth exploring. This chapter focuses on James Moffett in Australia—in particular, the role and significance of his work on writing pedagogy. Within the context of English curriculum inquiry, it reexamines the place of "writing" in Moffett's work, with specific reference to English teaching and public schooling in Australia. The question we ask here is: What happened to James Moffett?

This is especially intriguing given Moffett's earlier widespread influence in Australia, as noted, and as signaled by his leading role at the 1980 conference, taking into account that perhaps his major works in writing pedagogy, *Active Voice* and *Coming on Center*, were published soon after. Much changed in the subsequent decade following the Sydney conference, with what was called the "process/genre" debate (Reid) emerging (perhaps somewhat misleadingly) as a central focus, followed by new perspectives associated with poststructuralism and critical literacy, and also the emergence of information and communication technology (ICT). Reference to Moffett fell away, dramatically—something that has always seemed to us curious and unfortunate, especially now, when school writing has once again been foregrounded in education policy. The "fate" of Moffett's work is therefore symptomatic in many ways of curriculum change and educational amnesia. It is well worth asking: What was possible then, what has been forgotten, and why?

Sydney 1980: A Writing "Revolution"?

The 1980 Sydney conference, as a highly significant moment in English curriculum history in Australia, marked what can be appropriately called a "revolution" in writing pedagogy and in much ensuing professional debate. As already indicated, Moffett was one of several keynote speakers from overseas, with others including, perhaps most notably, James Britton (UK) and Donald Graves (US).[2] All three were published in the edited books arising from the conference (Eagleson, *English*; Arnold). That period might be seen now as the heyday of this particular perspective in writing pedagogy and English teaching. Moffett's contributions were titled "On Language Learning" and "Excerpts from an Educator's Notebook." Both were rather idiosyncratic pieces although entirely characteristic: fragmented in form, informally voiced, somewhat aphoristic, sometimes homely, a combination of speculation and commentary, addressed to both theory and practice. Two "bits" are worth highlighting here. The first is "the Wordless World" (Moffett, "Excerpts" 116–22) and the second is "Chords and Melodies—Brain Research" (Moffett, "On Language" 101). These pieces—delivered in 1980—contain material that would be subsequently developed in *Coming on Center* while also tacitly referencing his earlier work.

The Sydney texts point in different ways to what is perhaps Moffett's most significant single statement on writing pedagogy—the extended essay "Writing, Inner Speech, and Meditation." That essay presaged a radical shift in Moffett's work, toward a more spiritual, transcendentalist, "countercultural" engagement within an increasingly hyperrationalized social world. In that context, Moffett's references in these texts to notions of "inner speech" as "the internal carrier of acculturation" (Moffett, "Excerpts" 121) and the interplay of "chords" and "melodies" as analogous to the way the twin hemispheres of the brain work together to manage the complexity of human life and being-in-the-world (Moffett, "On Language" 101) are resonant with the possibility of new and different ways of understanding education and society—and jarringly dissonant with how things have turned out, for all of us.

The essay "Integrity in the Teaching of Writing," perhaps equally important, defined writing as "revision of inner speech" and made an ultimate argument for the importance of "authentic expression of an individual's own ideas" (89–90). Yet in "The Wordless World" (and then in "Writing, Inner Speech, and Meditation"), Moffett positions language—and inner speech—as "a verbal conceptual cage" (121) and both "a curse and a blessing" from which education itself needs to escape. This is the "Grand Paradox" (Moffett, "Writing" 166): the teaching of writing must allow inner speech to be developed "as fully as possible" (170), but eventually educators must seek to "avail themselves of discourse and still transcend it" (170–71)—a challenge, indeed, and more than just pedagogically. How did the profession respond? What happened next? One thing that is clear is that Moffett was effectively eclipsed.[3] Nonetheless, the "Writing, Inner Speech, and Meditation" and "Integrity in the Teaching of Writing" essays remain powerful and evocative statements on writing pedagogy and well worth revisiting today.

Moffett's Influence in Australia

Moffett had long been a central figure in English curriculum thinking in Australia, as it happens. His formal influence is most clearly evident in the 1971 junior secondary English syllabus in New South Wales, described by one commentator as "[t]he first 'personal growth' model syllabus anywhere in the English speaking world" (Brock 30), an endorsement no doubt facilitated by Australia's federal system of states-based government as distinct jurisdictions.[4] It is worth noting that this was just five years after Dartmouth and three years on from the publication of *Teaching the Universe of Discourse*. The syllabus presented a highly unified vision of subject English, with explicit reference to then emergent "growth model" English curriculum theorizing. Sawyer ("Structuring," "Writing") has indicated elsewhere how this curriculum innovation played out, with a key local figure here being Graham Little, an inspector in the NSW Department of Education. As chair of the Syllabus Committee, Little was essentially the architect of the new syllabus. He was able to articulate this body of theory within the characteristic liberal-bureaucratic character of Australian schooling, understanding that theory worked best when local circumstances and conditions were taken into account.

Importantly, Moffett as represented in *Teaching the Universe of Discourse* was a key and explicit reference point. Little was reported as saying that "the single most important influence" on him prior to his appointment as chair of the Syllabus Committee in June 1969 was his "reading of Moffett's book" (Nay-Brock 212). The focus in the syllabus was on "language in use in context," with subject English aimed at "develop[ing] in pupils the utmost personal competence in using the language" (NSW Secondary Schools Board 4). Language was seen in the syllabus as *activity*, first and foremost, which meant in turn a view of "*English* as activity," a view entirely consistent with Moffett's emphasis on usage and practice.

Equally significant was Moffett's insistence on the notion that "wholes" teach "parts," and on "context" as crucial to meaning and effect: "Only in the largest context—the whole composition—can meaning, style, logic, or rhetoric be usefully contemplated" (*Teaching* 5). This, alongside the crucial concept of *abstraction*, constituted Moffett's distinctive contribution, as registered very clearly in the syllabus. His influence was particularly noticeable in the central statement of what English *was* in this syllabus, viz., "WHO says WHAT to WHOM? WHY? HOW with WHAT EFFECTS" (NSW Secondary Schools Board 5, punctuation as per original; see Sawyer, "Structuring"). This draws explicitly from Moffett's "superstructure of discourse," his classic formulation of "the set of relations among speaker, listener, and subject—first, second, and third persons" (*Teaching* 18): *I-You/I-It*. This was resumed in *Active Voice* in the concluding essay, "I, You, and It." This is Moffett's notion of discourse, then, and it is central to his view of writing.

On Writing

Moffett provides a rich and comprehensive view of writing that comprises a number of "levels," each representing a distinct view or "definition" in itself. Writing is presented historically, as it developed over eons, as well as contemporaneously and individually. The levels range from "drawing and handwriting" through "transcribing and copying," "paraphrasing, summarizing, plagiarizing," and "crafting conventional or given subject matter" to "revising inner speech" ("Integrity" 90). The question is: What counts as writing, and to whom? (Although from another angle, it might be more appropriate to ask what counts as *school* writing) Importantly:

> Writing consists of not just one of these activities but of all of them at once. [. . .] When people write, they are simultaneously *drawing* letters, *transcribing* their inner voice, *plagiarizing* concepts and frameworks from their culture, *crafting* their thoughts into language forms, and *revising* the inchoate thought of their inner speech. ("Integrity" 90)

For Moffett, while the highest form of writing is what he calls "revising inner speech," this does not mean leaving the other forms behind. Rather, writing best conceived includes and comprises all of them, working simultaneously and bridging the visible and the invisible. As noted above, Moffett calls for writing to be understood as "full-fledged authoring"—"authentic expression of an individual's own ideas, original in the sense that he or she has synthesized them for himself or herself" ("Integrity" 89). This is writing that is fully *intentional*, in something like the phenomenological sense. In that spirit, and notwithstanding his humanism, Moffett points to "the personal nature of all good writing *even when content goes well beyond the individual*" ("On Essaying" 125, emphasis added). "Good" writing here is writing that works, then, that achieves its aim, is effective and meaningful, and is acknowledged as such. Such writing, in Moffett's terms, *is* "authoring."

The question arises: How feasible is this, in schooling or society? In such a light, it may become clearer why Moffett's influence dropped away as his work moved into radical territory. Can writing-as-authoring be accommodated in school in the twenty-first century? How much "real authoring" can be tolerated? As Moffett himself observed, "Small wonder we're tempted to lop off the top!" Further:

> All of us, in and out of school, have tacitly conspired to lobotomize writing, precisely because, if undertaken seriously, it threatens to be dangerous, unmanageable, and untestable by current cheap instruments. Everyone senses, quite rightly, that real authoring would require radical changes in student role, classroom management and methods, parents' and administrators' heads, evaluation, and the whole atmosphere of schooling. ("Integrity" 91)

In this light, we might reassess what unfolded over the decade following the Sydney conference and beyond. As Beavis has written: "By the 1990s [. . .], as a figure of influence, Moffett was becoming increasingly less visible, as other theoretical frames and interest areas began to rise" (304). Is what happened here a further and perhaps culminating move in suppressing the countercultural possibility of the 1960s across the Western world? Certainly things changed in the final years of the twentieth century and subsequently, as neoliberalism came into its own, casting its long shadow over education in Australia, as elsewhere. Even without taking into account Moffett's subsequent explicit engagement with spirituality and transcendence, his ideas represented a real and present danger, a truly radical alternative—and one which, it must be said, may not have been at all realistic at scale, especially given the already "positivistic" orientations of Australian education. Nonetheless, there was some continuing work with Moffett's ideas, both pedagogically and conceptually.

Teaching (with) James Moffett

From 1987 to 1993, Wayne taught in two high school English departments that worked through the whole of Moffett's *Active Voice* program in writing development, spreading the program over the four years of junior high school: years (i.e., grades) 7–10. As is well known, in *Active Voice* Moffett brought together a series of written assignments corresponding to the movement in *Teaching the Universe of Discourse* along levels of abstraction and along increasing distance from audiences. There are thirty-two assignments in all across the three groups, Revising Inner Speech, Dialogues and Monologues, and Narrative into Essay. Over four years, an average of one assignment could be contained in an average overall five-week "unit of work" in a faculty's program. The assignments were embedded inside a broader unit focus that did also contain other pieces of writing, though here we are only concerned with the *Active Voice* assignments.

The context for Wayne's programming in both schools was a twofold move to address mixed-ability classes in English and, most directly, do away with marks or grades and replace these with "work-required" assessment, based on the work of Brian Johnston. In a system with no grades, English staff argued that one way of monitoring student growth was to evaluate students' ability to successfully complete writing tasks that were both increasingly abstract and addressed to increasingly distant audiences. Increasingly challenging tasks within such a framework of language growth could conceivably provide staging points or markers of writing development.

In year 8, the particular assignments to be covered from Moffett's Narrative into Essay group, for example, were, in order:

- Correspondence
- Diary
- Diary Summary
- Autobiography: Incident
- Autobiography: Phase
- Eyewitness Memoir: Human Subject
- Eyewitness Memoir: Nature[5]

To take just four of these:

- *Diary* records the here-and-now for an audience of oneself over a period of about five weeks.
- *Diary Summary* writes up material from the *Diary* that summarises the previous work reorganised into a "continuous whole piece" (Moffett, *Active Voice* 83).
- *Autobiography: Incident* is not based on a body of existing writing, as *Diary* is, and is a piece further back in time and memory, based on one incident.
- *Autobiography: Phase* is also further back in time and memory but now covering a time period of some months, with distillation and generalising more prominent.

The issue of gradual distancing in terms of both audience and abstraction is clear, as is that of their careful sequencing. Moreover, in having students reflect on each piece, the concepts and problems and the thinking that set them up for the next piece are often paramount. For example, take the movement from *Diary* to *Diary Summary*. Workshop issues following students' writing of their *Diary* included consideration of "What things would someone else not understand? What would you have to do to make them understandable? Are there threads that run through the diary? What do you notice as a reader *now* that you hadn't noticed as a writer *then*?" (Moffett, *Active Voice* 80–81). The thinking about the issues, problems, concepts, and ideas that went into the *Diary* itself would depend entirely on the context in which any individual teacher treated it, including—most importantly—any readings that were part of those discussions. A big part of using the *Active Voice* assignments was resourcing them with appropriate reading and/or viewing that would feed into discussion and thinking. Moffett himself spends a lot of time discussing the use of relevant pieces of literature for each of these assignments.

In terms of movement from one assignment to the next, then, key conceptual thinking has already begun when a student comes to *Diary Summary*. What are the decisions a writer must make in this assignment? One is around form:

- a first-person narrative from the separate diary entries,
- a more generalised character sketch of oneself based on those entries,
- a reflective essay illustrated by specific episodes from the diary?

What about mode of abstraction for such a summary:

- chronology,
- logical classification,
- the weaving together of interrelated teams?

Students can talk about what changes were made to the Diary piece in order to summarise:

- how dialogue was treated,
- how selections were made,
- whether thoughts and reactions on events were in the original or added later.

How was the summary organised:

- as a series of snapshots,
- generalisations from recurring events,

- one topic singled out and traced through to conclusion,
- several topics covered in a sequence, or
- development of a theme removed from chronology? (Moffett, *Active Voice* 83–85).

Moffett also advised assigning readings around this assignment in which narrators could be unreliable and/or generally "seen through"—the issue being one of narrative perspective (86). Well before "critical literacy" became a prominent issue in English curricula, Moffett had English teachers consider readings that "seem calculated to get the reader to see things a certain way" (86), and, significantly, these readings were students' own creations. The richness of areas of discourse thrown into consideration here could hardly form a stronger contrast to approaches to writing that focus on structure only, around formulas such as "orientation-complication-resolution" for narrative writing or (the particularly unhelpful) "introduction-body-conclusion" for persuasive writing (ACARA) developed out of Australian genre theory (Reid).

Wayne's classes confronted, then, a range of discursive issues in addressing these assignments. One of his year 8 students at the time, Carroll (a pseudonym) began the paragraphs of her *Diary Summary* with these extracts:

> This is a story of Carroll's diary.
> Carroll is a 13-year old girl with a family of four. . . .
> By reading her diary I found out that she likes writing about . . .
> Most of her entries start with . . .
> The topic of her family only enters her diary when . . .
> Her diary is filled with things she hates, such as . . .
> She says [in] her diary that her life is boring, but if she read it again, I'm sure she'd change her mind. . . .
> Every entry covers . . .
> She complains about tests, but . . .
> She talks about her friends once or twice but she is more interested in . . .
> By reading Carroll's diary we can tell she isn't a great student because . . .
> It isn't hard to tell she dislikes . . .
> The way she writes things is a dead giveaway. . . .

Consider Carroll's decisions around the discourse here: There is a first-person narrative voice ("I'm sure she'd change her mind") that nevertheless analyses and describes the diary—and Carroll herself—using a third-person perspective ("She likes writing about . . . ," "Her diary is filled with . . ."). The piece is a character sketch in which events are not really a paramount concern. Post-genre theory, we might even be tempted to reject the voice's characterisation of this as a narrative ("This is the story of . . ."), except that the narrative named is not that of Carroll but of the diary itself. Thus, this character sketch of Carroll's is also the story of the diary, so there are things to be said here about story and discourse (Chatman). Themes are interwoven, especially themes about the disjunction between Carroll's overt concerns (especially hates, dislikes, complaints) and what is "really" being revealed about her. The unreliability of the narrative voice in one piece is raised by the narrator of the succeeding piece. Finally, and most obviously, the ongoing present tense of the *Diary Summary* is testament to the truth of Moffett's belief that (and we'll confine ourselves to "native speakers" here) students will produce the grammar that is required by the discursive context:

> [S]hifting, say, from narrative discourse to that of explicit generalization necessarily entails shifts in language and rhetoric and thus tends to bring successively to the fore different language structures. . . . Tense [. . .] is one thing that changes. . . . *What will further the normal growth of sentence elaboration is practice in language tasks that are at bottom intellectual.* (*Teaching* 53, emphasis added)

As Moffett further notes: "[A] specially devised program of isolating these structures and issues for the student is unnecessary and misguided" (53). The contemporary mantra of "explicitness" is thrown into stark relief here.

Looking back, we believe that, over four years of working through these writing assignments, along with their associated thinking, reading and discussion, Wayne's students were learning to work through and along levels of discourse in ways that did indeed advance their writing skills, language development, and literacy learning. It was in *Active Voice*, further, that Moffett attempted to address the kinds of classroom pedagogy that might be put in place to help students advance along dimensions of growth—in this case, those advanced in the more theoretical work of *Teaching the Universe of Discourse*. Here, Moffett seemed to avoid any simplistic, overly linear "developmentalism" that his program might suggest. As he argued in his explanation of the *Active Voice* program, "specific sequencing—day-to-day and even month-to-month—should occur on an individual basis" (5). He wanted to stress the "evolution of one kind of discourse into another" (5). Moffett was adamant that a program along these lines had to both avoid short time spans, such as "a year or even two" (9), and remain alive to student interests, needs, and "individual differences in growth rate and growth order" (9). A challenge indeed.

Thinking/Writing Differently?

Notwithstanding its effective eclipse in Australia post-1980s, there was continuing (minority) interest in Moffett's work and various experiments in this regard. While it cannot be claimed that these reached a large audience, it is worth reviewing them here to catch a sense of the curriculum possibilities still attached to Moffett in the early twenty-first century. It is important at the outset, however, to acknowledge that his thinking clearly exhibits all the signs of both modernism and structuralism, and perhaps even an unreconstructed humanism. And yet, because Moffett was a genuinely original thinker, his work can also be read outside such frames of reference, or as conceivably exceeding them in various significant ways (Green, "Re-reading"). Rereading Moffett's work, or reading him differently, involves brushing it against the grain.

With reference specifically to writing pedagogy, Bill previously drew explicitly on poststructuralist theory to propose a way of thinking differently about writing (Green, "English Teaching"), linking this directly to Moffett's work. The idea was to work *within* the "Integrity" essay, rereading it and tackling head-on the model of writing it presents, in particular its developmental hierarchy, which exists in tension with Moffett's emphasis otherwise on simultaneity. As was noted: "Although the 'model' is not intended as a hierarchy, then, nonetheless in effect it is. Moffett's stated concern is with simultaneity, and yet the effect is one of linearity and hierarchy," itself seen as possibly "a consequence of the print context" ("English Teaching" 262). What if this was presented differently? "Rather than expressed in a manner which cannot help but imply linearity and hierarchy, it can be depicted as circular, recursive, simultaneous, and cross-referencing [. . .]. In this fashion, the model is effectively re-cycled, and de-centered" (263). The spirit here is deconstructionist, and postmodern. It is speculative—in effect, a thought experiment.

That postmodern proposal was put forward in the context of "how to re-read Moffett in the age of media culture and information technology" (Green, "English Teaching" 260). Among other things, consideration was given to digitalising the *Active Voice* program, with all the opportunity this would provide to work with it differently, especially when the writing workshops, their processes *and* outcomes, could also be made available digitally. A central feature of the proposal was the concept metaphor of "compos(IT)ing"—in the simplest sense, composing with the (networked) computer (257–59). Turning back again to the "Integrity" essay and what might now be called its "meta-model" of writing pedagogy, each of what Moffett presents as "levels" was seen as becoming available as focus and resource, interlinked, a rich data bank of curriculum possibilities. Copying, for instance, is reconceptualised through a postmodern(ist) lens and presented as an opportunity for compositional work in a new and different key, perhaps linked up with notions of art and design (sampling, "image work"). Other "levels" or "views" might be similarly reactivated or reworked imaginatively and creatively. In this way, digital writing conceived as compos(IT)ing might provide a rich resource for the future, and even now, in the technocultural present (McKnight).

There is more to consider, though. Central to Moffett's modernism is his investment in a particular notion of subjectivity and agency (Green, "Re-reading"). Hence, he presents a movement out from the first-person ("I")—i.e., inside to outside. There is a strong emphasis accordingly on what might be called the *self-subject* as a particular (realist/humanist) understanding of the human subject à la the Cartesian legacy. This is consistent with his unified, structuralist system, overall.[6] But what if it were possible to "de-centre" his model—and productively so? To do that would be to work within a poststructuralist frame of reference and to bring to bear a different notion of subjectivity, as constituted in and through discursive practice. What would such a (mis)reading yield?

Here it becomes possible to (re)engage the other key essay in Moffett's work on writing pedagogy, "Writing, Inner Speech, and Meditation," which itself makes controversial moves that quite likely factor into his declining influence in mainstream English teaching. The insight this essay provides into the significance of "inner speech" is powerful, however, and presages the increasing focus in the field on figures such as Vygotsky and Bakhtin (Blau). Writing as "the revision of inner speech": it is worth asking what this notion of "revision" entails. How is information—inner *and* outer—processed and realised as text? How is it, first, transformed into and as inner speech, and what happens then as it manifests as written communication? Both writer and writing (and also the written text) are thereby brought together in a single writing event or over time. It is in this sense that writing, notwithstanding its materiality and its worldliness, links with consciousness. For Moffett ("Writing"), meditation offered a way of thinking such matters through, recognising as he did that working on conceptualising and verbalising was crucial, organised and impelled by a focused intentionality.[7] He understood inner speech, moreover, as the "voice" in one's head—the *social* voice, or rather the voice of the social order, a stream of consciousness.[8] But this is always a matter of multiplicity and contradiction, cacophony and chaos. Learning to write and writing itself involves working on and with (and sometimes against) this inner voice. Therefore, he suggests that linking writing with meditation offers three ways of handling inner speech: *observing* it, *controlling* it, and *suspending* it (148). While the first two might (rather uncomfortably) fit within current forms and conditions of schooling, the third is much less likely to. This is because to suspend inner speech might also be seen as *transcending* it, or at least as a move in that direction.

What might this mean? From a poststructuralist perspective, it connects with the view that subjectivity is socially and discursively produced, rendered durable and relatively stable over time, and that this is always a construction, an artifice, a fiction-with-effects. It is worth recalling that Moffett was intrigued and influenced to some extent by George Herbert Mead, who might be seen as an American precursor of certain aspects of poststructuralist theory and philosophy, including its view of subjectivity. If writing is indeed associated with subjectivity and subject formation—a technology of the self, in the Foucaultian sense—then working on writing entails working on the self, and the self-subject becomes instrumental and oriented as "author." This is to take a different view of writing and writing pedagogy. All the body work associated with writing, the training and discipline, individually and collectively, the need to focus on and develop mind *and* body, emergent literacies and interim textualities, becomes intelligible as social practice, involving reproduction and repetition *and* renewal. The links between social order and writing pedagogy are thus made very clear as a matter for both critique and reconstruction.

All this might seem rather distant and removed from the practical business of teaching writing, and indeed from Moffett's own writing program, at least as commonly understood. But it is consistent, we believe, with his overall *project*. He increasingly attended to issues and challenges of spirituality and transcendence, and to the ways in which modern Western society was becoming, as he saw it, increasingly alienated and alienating, hyperrationalised. Moffett was a visionary, operating on the edges of conventional meaning and decorum, pushing the boundaries. Then again, consistent with what he was doing all throughout his career, he was always situated "on the edge." What remains is an invitation, a sense of possibility, a challenge: a way of thinking and writing differently. That there has been little formal take-up in this regard, in Australia or indeed elsewhere, might be due to a lack of imagination as much as anything to do with the undoubtedly constrained possibilities of current educational reality.

Conclusion

In closing, there are two qualities we want to highlight in Moffett's work: first, its conceptual power, and second, its use-value in teaching and classrooms. This can be seen as bridging the professional "divide" often claimed between "scholars" and "practitioners," a somewhat questionable distinction featuring in various commentaries in the field, from Dartmouth on.[9] Moffett clearly embraced and exhibited both a distinctive scholarship *and* a practitioner sensibility, and in the early 1980s this was as clear in the pairing of his books on writing, *Active Voice* and *Coming on Center*, as it was at the beginning of his career in the 1960s, with *Teaching the Universe of Discourse* and *A Student-Centered Language Arts Curriculum, Grades K–13*. As Blau writes, Moffett's work "has remained of instrumental value to practitioners, including teacher-researchers and researchers on teaching who have conducted systematic inquiries into classroom practice, including their own practice" (91). Nonetheless, this work remains conceptually rich and, as such, an ongoing provocation as much as a resource for thinking differently and anew.

In our 2010 editorial introduction to a special issue on Moffett's work for the UK-based journal *Changing English*, we described him as "surely one of the most interesting and innovative figures, historically, in the field of English teaching" (Green et al. 240). We remain convinced that this is the case, even though his work seems little known or appreciated today. This is evident especially in a recent policy focus on the teaching of writing in Australia that seems almost willfully blind to such a rich legacy. Yet James Moffett's work remains powerful and provocative, we believe, and still insightful. The theory is crucial in this regard, supplemented necessarily by ongoing engagements with practice. This can be seen very clearly in his work on writing and writing pedagogy. It is why Moffett's work remains a significant reference point for the field even now—and further reason, surely, to revalue the field's curriculum history.

Notes

1. Officially established in 1983 but effectively operating from Dartmouth on (Goodwyn et al.).

2. Others in these postconference publications included Nancy Martin (UK), Bruce Bennett (Australia), Douglas and Dorothy Barnes (UK), Betty Jane Wagner (US), and John Dixon and Leslie Stratta (UK), all explicitly addressing writing pedagogy from a "post-Dartmouth" perspective. In addition, the Primary English Teaching Association in Australia brought out an extensive series of widely read books on writing pedagogy in primary classrooms after Donald Graves's appearance in Sydney (e.g., Walshe).

3. This was notwithstanding favourable reviews by leading Australian figures such as Garth Boomer and Bernard Newsome and, in some quarters at least, ongoing endorsement of Moffett's significance, perhaps more particularly regarding *Active Voice*.

4. See Beavis for an account of Moffett's influence on English teaching in Victoria, where Moffett's work played a major role in various important initiatives and innovations in English teacher education. Moffett was also influential in other Australian states to varying degrees.

5. Assignments from Moffett's other two groupings were also included in year 8.

6. Described elsewhere, indeed, as "a typically structuralist, 'totalizing' theory" (Sawyer, "Structuring" 286).

7. Something that is *learnt*—learning to write and engaging in writing involves learning to concentrate, to focus, and this takes time and effort, as well as repeated opportunity, practice, and discipline. Not addressed here but needing to be noted all the same is the issue of the unconscious and its significance for writing pedagogy. In this context, it is worth recalling Moffett's description of writing as akin to "hauling in a long line from the depths to find out what things are strung on it" ("Writing" 148).

8. The importance of Moffett's literary background, and in particular his early work on Virginia Woolf and literary modernism, should not be underestimated (Green, "Re-reading"; Blau). Note also Moffett's own observation that "[a]rtful simulation of inner speech occurs much more in literature than merely as a rare technique of modern fiction" ("Writing" 145).

9. On this matter, see Blau on the prejudice in the American academy regarding practitioners and practice-oriented work; see also Durst regarding James Britton. A similar binary can be observed in the Anglo-Australian scene.

Works Cited

Arnold, Roslyn, editor. *Timely Voices: English Teaching in the 1980s.* Oxford UP, 1983.

Australian Curriculum Assessment and Reporting Authority [ACARA]. "What's in the Tests: Writing." *NAPLAN*, https://www.nap.edu.au/naplan/writing. Accessed: p. 6 June 2021.

Beavis, Catherine. "'A Chart for Further Exploration and a Kind of Rallying Call': James Moffett and English Curriculum History in Victoria." *Changing English*, vol. 17, no. 3, 2010, pp. 297–307.

Blau, Sheridan. "Theory for Practice: James Moffett's Seminal Contribution to Composition." *Composition's Roots in English Education*, edited by Patricia Lambert Stock, Boynton/Cook/Heinemann, 2012, pp. 81–104.

Boomer, Garth. "Rolling up the English Teaching Sleeves." *English in Australia*, no. 22–25, 1982.

Brock, Paul. "Some Reflections on Teacher Education Programs for the Prospective Teacher of English in Australian Secondary Schools: A Personal View." *English in Australia,* no. 106, 1993, pp. 24–40.

Chatman, Seymour. *Story and Discourse: Narrative Structure in Fiction and Film.* 3rd ed., Cornell UP, 1986.

Durst, Russel K. "British Invasion: James Britton, Composition Studies, and Anti-Disciplinarity." *College Composition and Communication*, vol. 66, no. 3, 2015, pp. 384–401.

Eagleson, Robert D., editor. *English in the Eighties.* Australian Association for the Teaching of English, 1982.

———. "Introduction." *English in the Eighties*, edited by Robert D. Eagleson, Australian Association for the Teaching of English, 1982, pp. ix–x.

Goodwyn, Andrew, et al. *The Future of English Teaching Worldwide: Celebrating 50 Years from the Dartmouth Conference.* Routledge, 2019.

Green, Bill. "English Teaching, 'Literacy' and the Post-Age: On Compos(IT)ing and Other New Times Metaphors." *P(ICT)ures of English: Teachers, Learners and Technology,* edited by Cal Durrant and Catherine Beavis, Australian Association for the Teaching of English, 2001, pp. 249–71. *Academia*, www.academia.

edu/10288968/English_Teaching_Literacy_and_the_Post_Age_On_Compos_IT_ing_and_Other_New_Times_Metaphors.

———. "Re-reading James Moffett: Discourse, Rhetoric, Subjectivity." *Changing English*, vol. 17, no. 3, 2010, pp. 315–29.

———, et al. "Editorial: Re-reading James Moffett." *Changing English*, vol. 17, no. 3, 2010, pp. 237–40.

Johnston, Brian. *Assessing English: Helping Students to Reflect on Their Work*. Rev. ed., Open UP, 1987.

McKnight, Lucinda. "Electric Sheep? Humans, Robots, Artificial Intelligence, and the Future of Writing." *Changing English*, vol. 28, no. 4, 2021, pp. 442–55. *Taylor & Francis Online*, doi:10.1080/1358684X.2021.1941768.

Moffett, James. *Active Voice: A Writing Program Across the Curriculum.* Boynton/Cook, 1981.

———. *Coming on Center: English Education in Evolution.* Boynton/Cook, 1981.

———. "Excerpts from an Educator's Notebook." *Timely Voices: English Teaching in the 1980s,* edited by Roslyn Arnold, Oxford UP, 1983, pp. 111–22.

———. "Integrity in the Teaching of Writing." *Coming on Center: English Education in Evolution*, Boynton/Cook, 1981, pp. 81–93.

———. "I, You, and It."*Active Voice: A Writing Program Across the Curriculum*, Boynton/Cook, 1981, pp. 140–48.

———. "On Essaying." *Coming on Center: English Education in Evolution*, Boynton/Cook, 1981, pp.125–32.

———. "On Language Learning." *English in the Eighties*, edited by Robert D. Eagleson, Australian Association for the Teaching of English, 1982, pp. 91–102.

———. *A Student-Centered Language Arts Curriculum, Grades K–13: A Handbook for Teachers.* Houghton Mifflin, 1968.

———. *Teaching the Universe of Discourse.* Houghton Mifflin, 1968.

———. "Writing, Inner Speech, and Meditation." *Coming on Center: English Education in Evolution*, Boynton/Cook, 1981, pp. 133–81.

Nay-Brock, Paul. *A History of the Development of English Syllabuses in N.S.W. Secondary Education, 1953–1976: A "Continuum" or a "Series of New Beginnings"?* Unpublished PhD thesis, University of New England, Australia, 1984.

Newsome, Bernard. "Making Use of Ideas by Not Reinventing the Wheel." *English in Australia*, no. 67, 1984, pp. 56–59.

NSW Secondary Schools Board. *Syllabus in English for Forms I–IV.* NSW Department of Education, 1971.

Reid, Ian, editor. *The Place of Genre in Learning: Current Debates.* Centre for Studies in Literary Education, Deakin University, Australia, 1987.

Sawyer, Wayne. "Structuring the New English in Australia: James Moffett and English Teaching in New South Wales." *Changing English*, vol. 17, no. 3, 2010, pp. 285–96.

———. "Writing (in) the Nation." *English in Australia*, vol. 45, no. 2, 2010, pp. 7–20.

Walshe, R. D., editor. *Donald Graves in Australia: "Children Want to Write . . ."* Primary English Teaching Association / Heinemann Educational Books, 1981.

CHAPTER FIVE

Writing on the Mountain: James Moffett at the Bread Loaf School of English

ASHLYNN WITTCHOW
Louisiana State University

For the past century, one of the oldest professional development institutions of its kind, the Bread Loaf School of English at Middlebury College has invited English teachers to spend six weeks each summer studying at its mountain campus. Students attending the school, many of whom are classroom teachers, earn their graduate degrees in English literature over the course of several summers while simultaneously continuing to teach their own students during the school year. This model for professional development was innovative for its time, and it remains innovative today, in part because of the transitory nature of both the students and the faculty. Since the earliest days of the institution, the summer faculty have been selected almost entirely from institutions other than Middlebury. Although many faculty members maintain long-term professional relationships with the institution, the very nature of Bread Loaf creates moments of encounter between key figures in the fields of literature, writing, and education. James Moffett is one such figure. However, his many contributions to the institution have remained largely unexamined.

Moffett first joined the faculty in the late 1970s at a key inflection point in the history of the institution. Through his involvement with the Program in Writing, Moffett contributed to widespread curricular changes on the mountain. Before the introduction of the Program in Writing, the curricular offerings in writing and the teaching of writing remained sparse at Bread

Loaf, generally averaging no more than two each summer. Literature courses took precedence. Yet in the decade following the program's inaugural summer, the school offered an average of ten writing classes each summer (Low 56). These curricular trends continue today with robust course offerings in writing, pedagogy, and literacy. Although Dixie Goswami would eventually take the helm as director of the program—and as a trailblazer in the field of classroom research—James Moffett was there at the very start. Indeed, during the opening remarks of the Bread Loaf in the Schools Conference in 1985, Paul Cubeta would acknowledge Moffett's early influence on the Program in Writing at Bread Loaf: "That first summer of 1978, Jim Moffett *was* our Writing Program. And what a way to begin!" (Low 58). Although Moffett taught as full-time faculty for only four summers—1978, 1984, 1985, and 1988—he maintained a decade-long relationship with Bread Loaf, spending summers on the mountain as writing consultant and guest speaker. Furthermore, his personal correspondences with institutional leadership reveals his influence even in his absence. Therefore, this brief chapter first examines how Moffett joined the faculty during the inaugural summer of the Program in Writing and then outlines the broad strokes of his role in shaping the program in the 1980s.

The History of the Program in Writing

Beginning in the summer of 1978, the writing curriculum at Bread Loaf underwent a radical transformation as a result of the inaugural summer of the Program in Writing. Paul Cubeta, then director of the graduate program, envisioned the creation of the Program in Writing as a way to recruit and support teachers working in rural communities. In collaboration with Walker Gibson, professor of English at the University of Massachusetts Amherst, Cubeta invited key stakeholders to an initial planning session in the barn during the preceding summer session.[1]

Alongside this invitation, Cubeta included a draft grant proposal, seeking $110,750 in funding from the Rockefeller Foundation to pay for financial aid for seventy-five rural teachers over the course of three summers. The funding would also cover the appointment of two faculty members for the writing program. In the draft grant proposal, Cubeta outlined the rationale for the program, which included many of the perceived challenges facing rural teachers:

> The men and women who teach in America's rural schools usually do so without the educational and cultural resources of the more populated sections of this country. . . . Their own isolation from these cultural supports—and more importantly, from each other—creates an additional burden for these teachers. Unlike most secondary school teachers who live in or near urban areas, the rural school teacher has little opportunity to participate in supportive continuing education programs that speak to the particular educational needs of their students. Moreover, they have little occasion, through summer seminars, university courses or even local workshops, to plan with their colleagues regarding goals and strategies appropriate to the needs of their students. (Cubeta 2)

The grant proposal goes on to outline how the unique positioning of the Bread Loaf School of English makes it ideally situated to address these challenges. The mountain campus is located in the heart of rural Vermont, nestled in the protected wilderness of the Green Mountains. The dense broadleaf forests surrounding the mountain campus are a far cry from the cosmopolitan centers along the Eastern Seaboard. Yet the mountain campus routinely attracts distinguished faculty from prestigious universities across the United States and England.

The Program in Writing would sit at the boundary of these two worlds. Over the course of a two-year program of study, rural teachers would benefit from the opportunity to learn from leaders in the field of composition studies. In return, Bread Loaf faculty would benefit from an increased familiarity with "the problems of rural education" (Cubeta 2). The program as proposed would consist of two core courses, on the teaching of writing and the teaching of literature, each designed to help teachers identify the literacy needs of rural students. These seminars would be supplemented by additional programming featuring guest writing consultants and lecturers. Through these support structures, the program aspired to foster authentic writing opportunities for rural students, thereby addressing concerns pertaining to illiteracy in rural America.

The grant application proved successful. Bread Loaf soon received large grants, from both the Rockefeller Foundation and the General Mills Foundation, that funded the program. In his opening remarks at the 1985 Bread Loaf in the Schools Conference, Cubeta would reflect on the process of building the faculty for the Program in Writing (Low 57–60). He quickly identified Mina P. Shaughnessy, a pioneer in the field of composition studies from City University of New York, to helm the program. However, when it became clear that her declining health would prevent her from working with the program, Shaughnessy supplied Cubeta with three names: James Moffett, Shirley Brice Heath, and Janet Emig (Low 58). Dixie Goswami, one of Janet Emig's graduate students, would join the writing faculty during the second year of the program. Under her leadership, the Program in Writing flourished, eventually evolving into the Rural Bread Loaf Teachers Network in the early 1990s. But that first summer, James Moffett laid the groundwork for the program. In the words of Paul Cubeta, Moffett "assured the success of [the] writing program from its start" (Low 59).

James Moffett at Bread Loaf

College records indicate that the Program in Writing enrolled thirty students during the inaugural summer in 1978, including teachers hailing from ten states, largely in the Northeast. In addition to the required coursework, students benefited from the support of writing consultants, including Donald M. Murray, Mina P. Shaughnessy, Walker Gibson, and Mary I. Lanigan. Moffett taught two sections of the required pedagogical course: Principles, Problems, and Practices of Teaching English. His course, as one might expect, reflected the revolutionary student-centered and growth-oriented model of the English curriculum that informed the influential two books he had published nearly a decade earlier, *Teaching the Universe of Discourse* (1968) and *A Student-Centered Language Arts Curriculum, Grades K–13* (1968).

His course description explains that the seminar would "focus on the development of the student as writer and teacher rather than on various schools of thought in English education" (James Porter Moffett Papers, Mss. 243). This description reflects his suspicion of and impatience with academic fashions and educational parlance. In his class, teachers would learn how to teach writing by writing. Of course, they would do some reading too and respond to it in their writing, and also read the writing of their classmates and respond to it as well in writing, growing as readers and writers through such an interactive process, and also developing the sensitivities and "capacities that make good teachers" (Mss. 243). These writing-centered pedagogies perhaps best exemplify the early influence Moffett had on the Program in Writing.

Although it could be argued that course descriptions do not always accurately reflect the pedagogy of the course instructor, there is ample evidence that Moffett had a significant impact his first summer at Bread Loaf. His influence on the campus writing culture beyond the walls of his classroom would set the stage for future developments in the Program in Writing. One area of the archives where his influence is readily apparent is in campus programming. Issues of *The Crumb,* the daily student newsletter, make frequent mention of Moffett. For example, Moffett regularly screened films on writing for the larger Bread Loaf community during the summer of 1978. On July 6, Moffett screened two short films on writing pedagogy before leading a discussion of the films. Then again on July 19, Moffett screened a documentary about *Foxfire* magazine. Following the screening, he hosted Moira Tingle to discuss her involvement in the project. Indeed, similar events were so frequent that on July 26, the editor of *The Crumb* declared: "The CRUMB mentions Jim Moffett at least once a week!" These weekly notices illustrate how Moffett's influence extended beyond the rural students enrolled in his coursework and into the larger community during the first summer of the program.

In subsequent summers of the program, Moffett made additional appearances to teach courses on writing pedagogy. No longer restricted to the "back to basics" sensibilities of the inaugural summer, his coursework frequently reflected his ongoing intellectual concerns. In 1984, for instance, Moffett taught two courses: Writing from Meditation and Writing from Reading. For the former, his handwritten personal notes planning for this course illustrate how the course gave Moffett the opportunity to put pedagogical principles outlined in two key articles—"Writing, Inner Speech, and Meditation" and "Reading and Writing as Meditation"—into practice. Similarly, Moffett taught Ways to Writing, Ways of Writing in 1988. Students enrolled in this course worked with Moffett's *Points of Departure: An Anthology of Nonfiction* and *Active Voices IV* as models for their own writing. Mirroring the principles of the National Writing Project, students learned about the teaching of writing by working within writing workshops as they produced their *own* works of nonfiction, which were subsequently published for the wider Bread Loaf community in lieu of an end-of-term examination. Similar practices continue today with student-written publications produced each summer on the mountain campus.

The Legacy of Moffett at Bread Loaf

Although Moffett certainly was not the only leader in composition studies to influence the curriculum at Bread Loaf—part of the beauty of the campus hinges on the ongoing interchange of scholarship each summer—his contributions to the early curriculum are frequently understated both in Moffett scholarship and in the history of the Bread Loaf School of English. Beyond the summers when Moffett directly taught courses, he remained involved in planning for the future of the program throughout the 1980s. The James Porter Moffett Papers, housed at the University of California, Santa Barbara, contain a thin folder of letters between Moffett and Cubeta. These letters reveal his support in planning the 1985 Bread Loaf in the Schools Conference. At the conference itself, when Cubeta introduced Moffett to the conference participants, his admiration for Moffett was clear as he declared that "[Moffett] represents the embodiment of the only idea I've ever had at Bread Loaf: get the best and leave the rest to them" (Low 59). Following the conference, when the institution managed to secure additional funding to expand the school's outreach into rural schools, Moffett received a letter from both

Cubeta and Goswami seeking his experience and advice on how to best use the funds to support the creation of vibrant writing communities in partnership with K–12 schools. These small gestures illustrate how Moffett established his legacy at the Bread Loaf School of English, a legacy that would continue long after his death in 1996.

Note

1. Bread Loaf is somewhat atypical in that all classes are located in a large, repurposed barn on campus. One half of the building contains three floors of classrooms; the other half is a large space where students frequently gather to study between classes.

Works Cited

Bread Loaf School of English. Bread Loaf School of English Catalog [Course catalog], 1978. Records of the Bread Loaf School of English, F7, Middlebury College Special Collections & Archives.

———. Bread Loaf School of English Catalog [Course catalog], 1984. Records of the Bread Loaf School of English, F7, Middlebury College Special Collections & Archives.

———. Bread Loaf School of English Catalog [Course catalog], 1988. Records of the Bread Loaf School of English, F7, Middlebury College Special Collections & Archives.

———. *The Crumb*, vol. 59 [Student newsletter], 1978, F7. Middlebury College Special Collections & Archives.

———. General Statistics [Enrollment records], 1978, F7. Middlebury College Special Collections & Archives.

Cubeta, Paul. Grant [Proposal] from the Rockefeller Foundation for Bread Loaf. Records of the Bread Loaf School of English, 1977, F7. Middlebury College Special Collections & Archives.

James Porter Moffett Papers. Mss. 243, Department of Special Collections, Davidson Library, University of California, Santa Barbara.

Low, Patricia Jeanine. *Literate Learners: The Evolution of Teacher Research at the Bread Loaf School of English.* Unpublished dissertation, Stanford University, 1993. *ProQuest*, http://gateway.proquest.com/openurl?url_ver=Z39.88-2004&rft_val_fmt=info:ofi/fmt:kev:mtx:dissertation&res_dat=xri:pqm&rft_dat=xri:pqdiss:9326514.

Moffett, James. *Points of Departure: An Anthology of Nonfiction.* Signet, 1985.

———. "Reading and Writing as Meditation." *Language Arts,* vol. 60, no. 3, 1983, pp. 315–32.

———. "Writing, Inner Speech, and Meditation." *College English,* vol. 44, no. 3, 1982, pp. 231–46.

———, with Miriam Baker and Charles Cooper. *Active Voices IV.* Boynton/Cook, 1986.

II

Moffett's Groundbreaking Theory and Progressive Practice

Chapter Six

The Stormy Times of James Moffett

Russel K. Durst
University of Cincinnati

This article discusses the published work and career of James Moffett (1929–96), focusing in particular on Kanawha County, West Virginia, in the 1970s, when Moffett's innovative textbook series, Interaction, *after adoption by the county, was opposed by local and national conservative activists. The series was ultimately dropped by the district following a highly publicized, protracted, and at times violent conflict, after which other districts around the country followed suit, shutting down the series. The article examines Moffett's response to the censorship battle, explores his later interest in spirituality and literacy, and considers the implications of his work and his career trajectory for the teaching of English today.*

Introduction

James Moffett's 1988 *Storm in the Mountains: A Case Study of Censorship, Conflict, and Consciousness* tells the story of a successful and highly publicized attack on several popular textbook series, including Moffett's own, in the early 1970s. A leading literacy theorist and practitioner, Moffett wrote groundbreaking, student-centered literacy texts (in fact, he was among the first to use the term *student-centered* in the title of a 1968 book). His work "had a profound and significant effect" on English teaching, according to John Warnock's 2000 essay in *Twentieth-Century Rhetorics and Rhetoricians* (264). The standard pattern for literacy educators has been to focus on the college, secondary, or elementary level, with few exceptions, but

Originally published in *English Education,* vol. 47, no.2, 2015, pp. 111–30. Reprinted with permission of NCTE.

Moffett, who died of cancer in 1996 at the age of 67, ranged confidently and expansively throughout the entire spectrum with a grand theory of literacy teaching and learning. He had a distinguished career, but it was also in many ways an unusual career, and not without controversy. Moreover, his life and work both reflected and were influenced by cultural changes in the United States from the 1960s until his untimely death. In this article, I examine Moffett's early career, the censorship battle he faced, and the path he chose afterwards, placing his work in the context of the times in which he lived. I also consider his work and his intellectual, professional, and spiritual journey in relation to the teaching of English today.

As Sheridan Blau relates in a 2011 essay, James Moffett was born in Cleveland, Ohio, in 1929 but raised in Jackson, Mississippi, somewhat before the beginnings of the modern civil rights era. His family migrated back to the Midwest in the 1940s, when he was a teenager, and he spent his high school years in Toledo, Ohio. A bright and successful student from his earliest days, he went to Harvard for undergraduate and graduate degrees in literature, completing a master's degree, though not a doctorate, because he did not wish to become an academic and a literary scholar. After being drafted and serving for two years in the military, he took a position at the elite boarding school Phillips Exeter Academy, where he taught for 10 years until the mid-1960s. At this time, he was beginning to publish work on English teaching and decided to leave the prep school classroom, taking a faculty position at Harvard University's Graduate School of Education, spending three years there, and becoming increasingly visible as an English teaching specialist with powerful ideas and applications. At Harvard, he garnered grants from the Carnegie Corporation and other funding agencies to work on curriculum, met with teachers all over the country to spread his approach, and published widely used textbooks and studies of writing.

By the late 1960s, according to Blau (2011), Moffett had become a major national figure in literacy education, known for his innovative K–12 English language arts materials. But in the mid-1970s, after a coalition of Christian conservatives in West Virginia actively opposed his and other curricula, state after state backed away from the controversial materials rather than risk high-profile opposition. Following this battle, Moffett moved in quite a different direction both pedagogically and personally, a transition he discusses in an essay published not long before his death (Moffett, 1994b). His later work drew upon New Age philosophies, self-actualization movements, and Eastern religious practices. Soon after the textbook controversy, he relocated to Northern California, home to much of the alternative spirituality movement he had become active in, and he became an independent author of English textbooks and books for teachers, but with a smaller and more specialized following than before, for the last two decades of his life.

Culture Clash in West Virginia

My own experiences in some ways dovetail with those of Moffett. In the late 1970s just after finishing college, I spent a year living in rural West Virginia, where I taught and counseled juvenile offenders at a public institution sponsored by two adjoining counties. The institution was located in the northern part of the state, in a poor white community of 2,000 people similar in some ways to the town Shirley Brice Heath (1983) called Roadville in her classic ethnography of literacy, *Ways with Words*: close-knit, with lots of churches, and a mainly blue-collar, rural population. This was a difficult but fascinating time for me. It was difficult because I was working long, intense shifts, while living around the clock in a facility with troubled youth who had been sentenced to the institution by the courts for various offenses, some fairly serious, and whom I had to teach, counsel, and supervise. But it was also fascinating, both because the kids were interesting and because the job put me, an urban, middle-class Jew, into a world I had never known before. I remember my surprise and wonderment, early in my time there, at seeing a flyer at the local grocery store announcing the upcoming church appearance of Sister Lucy, a touring revivalist advertised as having the stigmata. Reading about this event, and viewing the evangelist's radiant smile in the flyer photo, made me feel like a visitor from another planet, a feeling I would experience many times that year.

Young people had little to do in this area, particularly of a constructive nature. Teenagers would sometimes gather by the side of the main road on the outskirts of town on Saturday nights when the nearby racetrack let out, to hurl stones at cars carrying African Americans. A private drinking spot in the next town was called the Cozy Corner Club and rumored to be affiliated with the Ku Klux Klan. When I asked a fellow counselor from the southern part of the state, who had recently graduated from a nearby liberal arts college, if there were African Americans living where he came from, his shocking reply was, "Sure, they live in Colored Holler." On one occasion, a juvenile court judge contacted us about admitting an African American teenager from downstate. The placement never happened, for a variety of reasons. However, while the possibility was under discussion the director of our facility expressed concern to me because our residents attended local schools and participated in town activities, and he was worried that an African American teen would be at serious risk of harm living in this community.

One beautiful spring morning, the director showed up at the group home with some literature that a young local preacher was distributing outside of his church a few blocks away. It was neo-Nazi propaganda discussing national and international Jewish conspiracies, the Protocols of the Learned Elders of Zion, and assorted dangers to the white race. Jimmy Carter was president at the time, and one memorable flyer talked about "Karter's Kosher Kabinet." The flyer listed every Jewish or possibly Jewish person on the president's staff, an impressively large number as I recall, and declared they were involved in certain nefarious, even satanic plots as well as alliances with the Soviet Union. I do not wish to present a caricature of West Virginia or the town I lived in. There were many progressive, community-spirited folks in the area, most people I met were friendly and reasonable, and I later learned that the offending minister had to give up his job and leave town. But this was my initial exposure to religious fundamentalism, the KKK mentality, and extreme political conservatism, qualities that also figured prominently in the censorship battle in which Moffett became embroiled. I left my job after that year to go on to graduate school in literacy, relieved to stop riding herd on recalcitrant teenagers and dealing with their sometimes startlingly dysfunctional families. But since then I have maintained ties to people and places from my time in West Virginia. As a result, Moffett's West Virginia book has a special resonance for me. My experience in this small town gave me some insight into what James Moffett went through when his textbook series was banned and effectively put out of business, after a public battle that was an early manifestation of what has become an ongoing and growing censorship conflict in our nation's schools.

The censorship battle took place in southern West Virginia, in Kanawha County, which includes the capital city of Charleston, a mix of urban, suburban, small-town, and rural areas, with a diverse demographic but a strong fundamentalist influence. At the time, it comprised one of the larger and more disparate school districts in the country. Opposition to the textbooks, which Moffett discusses in *Storm in the Mountains*, and which George Hillocks also examines in a 1978 article, took the form of a protracted protest and boycott, including wildcat strikes, bombings, shootings, and other violent incidents, attracting national and even international attention. Opposing the textbooks were mostly local figures, some of the most prominent with almost stereotypical Appalachian names—Reverends Avis Hill and Ezra Graley, businessman and John Birch Society member Elmer Fike, school board opponent and preacher's wife "Sweet Alice" Moore, and others. But in the background of this controversy was a fledgling network of conservative activists from around the country, many of whom cut their teeth during this textbook battle—Texas book-banning advocates Mel and Norma Gabler; Republican direct mailing innovator Richard Viguerie; television preacher Pat Robertson, founder of the Christian Broadcasting Network; and various members of the Heritage Foundation. For some of these people and groups, this conflict was the early success story that helped propel them to national prominence.

The Textbook Materials

But what exactly were the opponents of the textbooks protesting against? In addition to Moffett's work, textbook opponents also sought to remove language arts series by D. C. Heath; McDougal,

Littell; and Scott, Foresman, but my discussion will focus primarily on Moffett's materials. In the early 1970s he created a series for elementary and high school students titled *Interaction*, an ambitious, diverse, multimedia array of English teaching resources published by Houghton Mifflin, a leading publisher of English and language arts textbooks. It was, according to the publisher, the largest set of school materials ever put together up to that point for any school subject, comprising literally hundreds of different materials (Moffett, 1988, 4), and it was quite innovative in its design. Moffett was general editor and conceptualizer of the project, but he worked closely with a handpicked team of 30 teachers and writers from around the country to produce the series. They broke all the rules; in fact, it is a tribute to Moffett's stature, persuasiveness, and creativity that a major publisher would even consider the project. Obviously, and sadly, in the educational and political climate of recent decades, none would publish it; so responsive have publishers become to the criticisms of conservative groups and to the increasing demands of large-scale educational testing (Agee, 1999).

These materials were the opposite of teacher-proof, highly directive, and dumbed down. An accompanying volume for teachers and curriculum developers explained the rationale behind the series and its many parts. However, the books, tapes, movies, pamphlets, puzzles, songbooks, joke books, lists of proverbs or insults, even card and board games contained virtually no apparatus, such as generally appear in school textbooks. This approach was taken quite deliberately because Moffett and his collaborators wanted teachers and students to use the materials for their own purposes and according to their own interests as much as possible—not to follow set guidelines, but rather to approximate organic, self-sponsored uses of reading, writing, and speaking as closely as work emanating from a school curriculum could do. The series was also designed so that the whole class would not be doing the same thing at the same time. Rather, individuals and/or small groups were encouraged to pick and choose and to work at their own pace on the materials that particularly interested them, "to ensure that any learner of any background, level of development, temperament, or interest could find plenty of ways to engage with and develop language"

(Moffett, 1988, 5). *Interaction* was extremely multigenre and multimedia, with songs, fables, ballads, proverbs, myths, films, and film strips. There were also tapes of people telling stories in a number of dialects, both regional and ethnic, so that middle-class speakers of Standard English could be exposed to a greater diversity of language use, while nonstandard dialect speakers could see their own language forms legitimately employed in a school context. The series contained about as many different kinds of texts as one could put together in a language arts collection. It was supposed to be diverse, comprehensive, and a bit zany, to look as little as possible like a textbook series and as much as possible like a disparate set of books one might find in a public library or in one's own home. Even the shapes, sizes, and colors of the books were varied to emphasize their diversity (4–6).

The materials comprised works by vast numbers of contemporary writers of all types, including a great deal of what we today call cultural diversity, though that label really hadn't been invented yet. Moffett states with pride that he was particularly effective at convincing the publishers to let him include significant amounts of contemporary writing in the collection. He points out that living writers are much more expensive to publish, with *Interaction* accruing a debt of nearly a quarter of a million dollars in permission expenses, quite a sum in the early 1970s (Moffett, 1988, 131). This is in part why so-called classic authors are pervasive in textbooks—they're long dead, are in many cases out of copyright (hence free of charge to reprint), and even if not, their estates usually don't charge so much to include in a book. The collection included books of crosswords and other types of puzzles, photos without text (so that students could supply their own), plays, mysteries, fiction and nonfiction diaries, and much more, spanning the age groups. In all, the project was not only politically and pedagogically progressive, it also had an extremely large budget and was anticipated by Houghton Mifflin, Moffett, and his collaborative team to be widely adopted throughout the country, because 1960s idealism still lived in early 1970s education, making possible some experimentation. Early indications were that the series would make a major splash. A number of states put *Interaction* on their lists of possible texts for districts to include, and Moffett crossed the country talking to administrators and school boards, the people who mainly made textbook decisions, and working with groups of teachers who would be using the materials (Moffett, 1988, 32).

One should keep in mind that James Moffett, though just over 40 years of age in the early 1970s, was at the height of his career, with some highly respected textbook publications as well as his groundbreaking theoretical work, *Teaching the Universe of Discourse* (1968a). This book had made an important contribution to the fledgling field of literacy studies. Drawing upon George Miller's pioneering work in cognitive psychology, Jean Piaget's research on child development, and Noam Chomsky's theories of language, Moffett's book provided a new and interesting way of talking about children's intellectual growth and its relationship to curriculum in English, though applicable to other subjects as well. His universe of discourse breaks down into two interrelated but distinguishable dimensions, the social and the cognitive, each placing different intellectual demands upon the writer or speaker. For the social dimension, Moffett looked at the relative distance, in time or space or both, between writer and audience, with the greater distance generally but not necessarily indicating increased complexity. Because his categories are tied into curriculum, not purely theoretical, the system is fairly tight. His primary categories, moving gradually away from the self toward ever more distant audiences, include

1. Reflection—Intrapersonal communication, thinking to oneself
2. Conversation—Interpersonal communication between two or more people in vocal range
3. Correspondence—Interpersonal communication between remote individuals or small groups with some personal knowledge of one another
4. Publication—Impersonal communication to a large and mainly anonymous group extended over space and/or time

As Moffett states, "this communication system expands throughout the progression. Each kind of discourse is more selective, composed, and public than those before. Feedback becomes increasingly slower until it tends to disappear, which is to say that two way transaction is yielding to one way transmission" (33). Assignment sequences in Moffett's pedagogical discussions were pegged to his developmental scheme.

His more internal, cognitive dimension posits an abstractive scale moving toward increasingly complex and abstruse forms of discourse, from reporting (what is happening, chronologically), to recording (also narrative but slightly more detached), to explaining (finding patterns/forming generalizations), to theorizing and speculating. All of these categories correspond to important types of writing in an English curriculum and, Moffett argued, have a kind of psychological reality and developmental progression in students' minds. Thus, as with audience, assignment sequences in Moffett's work also moved up an abstractive scale. Moffett modeled these various social and cognitive dimensions of writing in his own published work, always staying close to questions of practice, of how to put a curriculum together. *Teaching the Universe of Discourse* thus had a major impact over several decades, influencing a range of people in composition and English education (see, for example, Applebee, 1981; Britton, Burgess, Martin, McLeod, & Rosen, 1975; North, 1987). Through this book, Moffett both led and captured the tendency for other literacy specialists to move frequently and comfortably between theory and practice, exploring their interrelationships.

The same year that the aforementioned theoretical work appeared, Moffett also published an important work on English curriculum, *A Student-Centered Language Arts Curriculum, Grades K–13: A Handbook for Teachers* (1968b), also with Houghton Mifflin. This curriculum text, more than 500 pages long, was a parallel and more practical version of the accompanying book, which laid out his theoretical framework. In the *Handbook*, Moffett proposed a curriculum with four chronological levels—kindergarten and early elementary, late elementary, junior high, and secondary. Assignments and activities at each age group were pegged to the developmental scales for audience awareness and level of abstraction discussed in *Teaching the Universe of Discourse*. So, for example, the youngest students were to focus on verbal and nonverbal play, often with concrete materials, learning how to discuss in groups, and the writing of stories, songs, and sensory recording. Similar activities were to take place at increasingly higher levels of sophistication up through the high school years, including drama, Socratic dialogue, and reading and writing of haiku and other poetic forms, while the most senior secondary students would branch out into autobiography, full-scale research, reflection essays, and, finally, generalization and theory. The curriculum at each level was intended to be comprehensive, including discussion of basic reading and writing instruction for remedial students, ways of individualizing teaching and learning (always a major emphasis for Moffett), and plenty of age-appropriate games and play throughout the grade levels.

This curriculum text was an immediate success, used in large numbers in English education courses and seminars at colleges of education and purchased for inservice instruction by school districts throughout the country. In their 1993 article, "Where Did Composition Studies Come From? An Intellectual History," authors Martin Nystrand, Stuart Greene, and Jeffrey Wiemelt state that these two 1968 books "did much at this time to promote writing as a cognitive process" (279). By the early 1970s, Moffett was an accomplished figure approaching the height of his success. And yet, despite his growing prestige, he wanted to move beyond the privileged New England prep school students he had taught at Exeter and the elite northeastern school districts that had been using his materials, to make a difference in the lives of students from all socioeconomic classes and in all parts of the country. As he later wrote, he developed *Interaction* with a wide and diverse audience in mind, "very much because I couldn't bear that such a small portion of American youth should get educational opportunities that all ought to have" (1994b, p. 20). This point is key; Moffett was an idealist as well as a firm believer in the value of his approach to teaching. He was unwilling to limit his influence to the wealthy environs of a fancy boarding school or comfortable suburb. *Interaction* was to be the project that would help him accomplish this goal.

Battle over the Books

The state of West Virginia was among the first to adopt the *Interaction* series, and the Kanawha County School District comprising the state capital, Charleston, and the surrounding area was one of the first districts to attempt to use the series. But the success for which he hoped turned into a bitter defeat and a harbinger of things to come, with implications for all of us working in literacy today. Instead of seeing his materials used by large numbers of students and teachers, the result was an intense, protracted struggle in West Virginia pitting supporters of the textbooks—mainly educated, middle-class, urban liberals—against opponents of the series—mainly conservative, rural and suburban Christian fundamentalists (Hillocks, 1978, 634). This censorship conflict drew attention in the national and even international media, and in the end, the conservatives won, with the help of a national network of activists just then beginning to make its influence felt. Of the textbook opponents, Moffett (1988) writes, with anguish but also with empathy,

> My heart is with them. They are right about many things or at least right in a sense. They should not have had my books crammed down their throats. But I think the objectors are dreadfully wrong in some ways that endanger far more than outsiders the very family, country, and religion they think they are upholding. (103–04)

Interaction and other textbook series were successfully eliminated from school curricula in West Virginia after a nasty, at times violent protest and boycott by arch-conservatives and fundamentalists. The "book-banners" labeled Moffett's series "Cover to cover, trash" (Moffett, 1988, 135), zeroing in on particular points of contention as examples of specific materials and the negative comments they elicited from opponents will show in the following pages. A disparate collection of conservative groups voiced their objections to what they viewed as the anti-patriotic, anti–free enterprise, anti-Christian, pro-diversity slant of *Interaction* and other series. Fundamentalist preachers and their followers from the hills and hollers of rural Kanawha County, as well as some of their more educated conservative allies from the city and surrounding suburbs of Charleston, rose up in full rebellion against the perceived disrespect of their educational system's leaders. Thousands of people were actively involved in all sides of the dispute at its peak, with business as usual in the county seriously disrupted, and major attention focused on southern West Virginia for the first time in decades. By 1975, *Interaction* had been removed from the Kanawha County curriculum, along with other sets of work that were also deemed pornographic, politically subversive, or otherwise inappropriate for young people. Even more important, however, other states and other school districts took their cue from Kanawha County. Rather than risk having a major fight on their hands, school officials stayed away from the books under attack or removed them from the approved lists, and publishers' representatives stopped promoting them. In point of fact, *Interaction* made money, just not enough of it to reach the publishing company's fiscal projections, and that, along with the political controversy surrounding the series, is why it was ultimately dropped (Moffett, 1988, 32).

But what exactly did opponents of the series object to? Moffett relates this information in detail in Part Three of *Storm in the Mountains* (1988). Extensive written critiques were developed by a sub-group of the Textbook Review Committee appointed by the local school board after criticisms of the series, and these critiques were presented in a 450-page report that was separate from the committee's main report. Each of the six school board members selected three people for the committee for a total of 18, of whom seven chose to work together against *Interaction* apart from the rest of the committee. The group as a whole, pro, con, and otherwise, consisted of some teachers, some politicians, several ministers, a few blue-collar workers, and housewives, all of whom had been active in community affairs in one way or another and were thus known by the board members. The subgroup comprised the more conservative, fundamentalist members of the larger group. The long document the subgroup produced offered a detailed critique of the entire series, their criticisms shedding considerable light on conservative positions hostile to *Interaction*. This sub-group quickly split off from the committee as a whole, then consulted with a nationwide network of activists (including Mel and Norma Gabler of Texas, who wrote some of the critical evaluations, advising on strategy throughout). Most criticisms were directed to individual reading and writing assignments in the nearly 200 vastly differing books of the series, and with so many materials in the collection, critics found a great deal of objectionable subject matter. In general, objections from the sub-group could be categorized as political, cultural, and religious in nature, with some obvious overlap between the categories.

Where politics is concerned, critics objected to what they viewed as an anti-American bias or a questioning of US history and tradition. For example, the subcommittee critiqued a reading for advanced secondary students from an *Interaction* book called *Transcripts* that contains interviews with five Vietnam veterans who had taken part in the My Lai massacres. The objector simply wrote, "Not necessary for education." In another book with the same name, but for less advanced secondary students, were interviews with the Italian immigrant anarchists Sacco and Vanzetti (executed for a 1920 bank robbery that they may not have committed); Lieutenant William Calley, the officer in charge at the My Lai massacre during the Vietnam War; and other such controversial figures. The objector wrote, "I question why this type of literature is important for students unless it is to make them feel guilt and shame." The critics also objected to a page in a book for secondary students called (and consisting only of) *Advertisements*. The page in question contained an ad for advice on how to be a conscientious objector, surrounded by ads for, among other things, guns, padlocks, and Charles Atlas muscle-building instruction. The objection termed the ad "a springboard for the advocacy of radical ideology concerning hatred for the military and justification for rationalizing cowardice" (Moffett, 1988, 157–59).

Moffett and his coauthors wanted students to learn how to think critically and question authority, and their liberal views were surely evident in their choices of texts and genre types. However, series critics preferred to inculcate in students respect for tradition and patriotism, even if it meant ignoring questionable aspects of US history. The critics saw no reason why, even in just a small percentage of readings, school textbooks should portray the United States in a negative light, which they associated with liberal antiwar and civil rights protesters. In reflecting upon such criticisms, Moffett (1988) expressed concern for the attitude in which "war becomes an equivalent of patriotism and loyalty, to the point that pacifism means the opposite, dislike of one's country and disloyalty. Thus for the dissenters it was self-explanatory to object to a selection as pacifist, because this was their synonym for traitors and cowards" (160).

Culturally oriented criticisms tended to focus on standards and types of language and on modes of behavior depicted in the series that objectors found inappropriate for classroom use or, in a number of cases, immoral. Many such objections centered on the occasional use of profanity in some of the readings for older students. In a book of play scripts, subcommittee critics pointed to the inclusion of such terms as *tits*, *Goddamnit*, *sons-bitches*, and *Hell, no*. But the plays' subject matter also raised much ire. The drama in which the above terms appear, *Blue Denim*, concerns the issue of teenage pregnancy, and its inclusion was intended by Moffett (1988) to help students "consider such matters more maturely" (110). Protesters complained, however, that this play was pornographic and that it was entirely inappropriate for students even to be dealing with such matters in a school classroom. Similarly, a piece about beat poet and activist Allen Ginsberg in a book for advanced older students titled *Biography* quotes the poet discussing in vivid language a pot-smoking prostitute he had known while an undergraduate at Columbia University. Excerpts from this piece figure prominently not only in the subcommittee's report but in public protests against the series, in which quotes were sometimes displayed on large placards as evidence of pornographic content.

A related and equally harsh set of criticisms applied to parts of the series in which nonstandard dialects such as African American English were employed, mainly in narratives, folk tales, and fables. Linked as well in most cases with criticisms of the culture and attitudes portrayed in these texts, the objectors argued strenuously that it was wrong to expose students to nonstandard language forms; that such forms were not acceptable to educated speakers; and that the culture, attitudes, and behaviors that often went along with such dialects were hostile to and resentful of mainstream American values. An essay by the African American writer James Baldwin, written as a letter to his teenaged nephew, in which the writer denounced white racism but called upon all people to deal compassionately with others, drew the following response: "This man's letters and articles appear throughout this series of books, he obviously is a mentally scarred individual who believes in no one or nothing but himself. He appears to be anti-everything and reading this letter seems to prove the point. Enough of this type of thinking could bring about racial uprisings everywhere" (Moffett, 1988, p. 142). One pro-*Interaction* Kanawha County teacher quoted extensively by Moffett argues that racist feelings on the part of protest leaders, mainly against African Americans, motivated much of the criticism of the series, particularly the dismissal of these dialect materials as unfit for classroom use. Moffett (1988) concluded that "[t]he dissenters wanted all language study to drill on correctness and to pretend that English has an absolute form. The fear arises over and over again in various ways: if youngsters know of alternatives, standards will crumble, whether in morals or language" (126–27).

Many of the most vociferous complaints centered on questions of religion, specifically, the depiction or non-depiction of Christianity as well as the discussion of other religious traditions alongside of Christianity in series materials. Any readings that touched upon theories of evolution came under attack. One representative example, a section in a book for secondary students called (and containing) *Charts and Graphs,* described four stages of humans ranging over nearly a million years, from lower to upper Paleolithic. The critical sub-committee wrote: "This presentation presupposes in a matter-of-fact way that the theory of evolution is a proven fact. This is scientifically inaccurate. It is contrary to the religious beliefs of many persons, and consequently, is not admissible material for inclusion in a public school curricula when implied as fact" (Moffett, 1988, 150). As well, materials that appeared to present Christianity as simply one religion or belief system among many came in for serious criticism. Thus, a book for high school students titled *Legends* included the story of Samson, while another at the same level, *Parables*, contained one of Christ's parables. In both books, stories from other religious traditions were also included. A representative criticism argued: "The story of Samson as recorded in the book of Judges . . . is historical fact. To include this historical account in a book of 'Legends' is to cast doubt in the minds of young people upon the veracity of the Holy Scriptures. Moreover, this is at variance with and is calculated to undermine the religious beliefs of young people whose families have taught them to believe in the divine inspiration of the Bible" (Moffett, 1988, 149).

Moffett (1988) believed strongly in the potential of the *Interaction* series "to reform language instruction" by making curriculum more individualized, more intellectually demanding, and at the same time more fun (4). However, even among educators, not all agree with this assessment. One secondary school teacher who went on to become a literacy scholar remembers the series from his days as a high school faculty member. He describes *Interaction* as a "magnificent failure, so ambitious, so diffuse, so uncentered" and adds,

> My understanding at the time, based on conversations among my high school colleagues, was that it failed to catch on not because of conservative opposition in West Virginia but because of its own internal problems and the difficulty of marketing such a complex series to school faculties across the country, even those who were predisposed to embrace a more diverse and contemporary curriculum. (Smagorinsky, 2013, personal communication)

From a conservative Christian standpoint, Karl C. Priest, a former Kanawha County teacher who was involved in the protest and the author of the 2010 book, *Protester Voices: The 1974 Textbook Tea Party*, complains that primarily liberal media and educators have put forth "a biased view of the historically significant textbook protest" (xii) and that the protesters had good reason to oppose the books for their language, sexual content, anti-Christian perspective, and negative depiction of US society and institutions. He argues that "Moffett's bias is apparent" in his book on the censorship conflict and suggests that, instead of *Storm in the Mountains: A Case Study of Censorship, Conflict, and Consciousness,* a more appropriate title might be *Sulking in Liberal Land: An Example of Hypocrisy, Haughtiness, and Hatred* (46).

But however one wishes to explain the opposition in Kanawha County in 1974, after months of protest, the public outcry and general disruption surrounding the response to *Interaction* and other textbook series were too much. The superintendent and series supporters on the school board were in hiding or under constant police protection due to threats on their lives, boycotts and fear were reducing school attendance, and strikes of bus and other services plagued the county (Hillocks, 1988, 632). The board ultimately had little choice but to remove these books from the list of approved textbooks for English language arts instruction. Consequently, for Moffett and his team, this set of materials that they had spent years preparing, that they hoped might revolutionize English teaching in this country, and that represented a major financial risk for the publisher because of its unconventional approach and expensive budget, ended up having almost no impact at all on American education, except, from the perspective of an English educator, as a sad story of what might have been and as a foreshadowing of the conservative backlash that has been taking place all over the country ever since. I believe this experience effectively changed the nature of Moffett's career in crucial ways.

After the Storm

I have heard it said that the true test of a person is how he or she handles the bad times. Applying this notion to Moffett's life is instructive, as he experienced a censorship conflict of the rawest, angriest, and most divisive kind, the outcome of which caused him personal pain, a financial setback, and professional loss of standing; it also made him deeply worried about the future of education in this country. And yet, rather than this disastrous experience leaving him embittered and angry, the episode in many ways brought out the best in James Moffett: his generosity, his tolerance of dissenting views, his self-reflectiveness, and the will to understand, learn, and grow that characterizes his entire body of work. However, he did eventually move outside the mainstream of literacy education in the United States to advocate pedagogies that many considered and still consider unconventional.

But Moffett's immediate response was to research and write *Storm in the Mountains*. In the book, Moffett attempts to understand for himself, and explain to others, just what happened in Kanawha County and why. The book is kind of a giant "I Search" paper representing the type of personally motivated investigative writing that Moffett always advocated. He researched the book not just by reading all the available literature, but also by going back to the area and talking with participants on all sides of the dispute, including the people who urged the banning of the series, all of them he could find. To me, this point is particularly impressive: Moffett returned to Kanawha County and sat down with a tape recorder in the living rooms of people like Reverend Ezra Graley and John Birch Society member Elmer Fike. These people had advocated banning or even burning his books, had defended and possibly even participated in violent protests against his work, had closed down a school system out of fear and anger that their children might have to read the series he called "a work of love" (Moffett, 1988, 4). And as I have mentioned, there was actual violence in the protest. Two people were shot, wildcat strikes were initiated, even shutting down the city buses of Charleston for a time. Thousands of students boycotted school or stayed home out of fear, schools and buses were firebombed at night and shot at by snipers during the day. Several people went to prison for conspiracy to commit murder, including one of the young ministers leading the protest, Avis Hill, who, after release from prison, quietly relocated to a different town without a forwarding address, before Moffett could interview him. Most dramatically, the district superintendent and several school board members were physically assaulted and injured during a live, televised school board meeting that turned into a riot. This violent attack was even celebrated in a folk ballad written and recorded by one of the main figures in the controversy, who happens to be one of the people Moffett later interviewed for *Storm in the Mountains*. The school superintendent and several district personnel associated with the book series eventually had to go into hiding and then finally to leave town for a period, so incendiary was the atmosphere surrounding this conflict (17–25).

Clearly, this was not just a case of dueling lawyers, deal-making politicians, or grandstanding demagogues; it was a truly frightening situation, both in the violence of its immediate events and in the educational consequences of its outcome. In creating *Storm in the Mountains*, Moffett revealed an admirable desire to figure out what was going on in the minds of his opponents, to understand and find common ground with the protestors, not just to vilify them. He tried hard not to demonize, ridicule, or patronize them, though I do think his bitterness comes through at times in the book. Still, Moffett showed courage in going back to the scene of this conflict, and the resulting book helped him come to grips with what had happened at the same time that he put together one of the most perceptive analyses to date of contemporary censorship issues. In the best Moffett tradition, the book traverses a wide range of the universe of discourse, comprising story, conversation, theory, literature review, even folk ballad. He also invented a concept, which he termed *agnosis,* to describe an unwillingness to comprehend or to consider ideas that challenge one's own views (Moffett, 1988, 184).

Moffett's career underwent a major shift in the early 1980s, a move away from the mainstream in the teaching of English. Whereas his early work is primarily social and cognitive in nature, focusing on audience awareness and intellectual development, though always concerned with students' growth as human beings, his later work centers more around an increasing fascination with mysticism, yoga, meditation, and spirituality. Many teachers and scholars are interested in spirituality in one form or another. What sets Moffett's work apart from that of most other composition and English education people with an interest in spirituality is that he came to advocate regular and systematic *classroom* use of meditative techniques. Others, such as the authors of a set of articles titled "Spiritual Sites of Composing" in *College Composition and Communication* in 1994 (e.g., Berthoff et al.), are careful to stay away from saying anything that could be construed as advocating religion, spirituality, or indoctrination in the classroom. But not Moffett. He also began to write at this point about his traumatic early life, his alcoholic father and the damage he did to the family, and how Moffett's own writing and teaching were in large part attempts to deal with and overcome these early traumas (1994b).

As the field of English teaching, particularly in composition, became more and more focused on social, cultural, and political aspects of literacy in the 1990s, Moffett talked increasingly about using writing to heal personal pain and to grow spiritually. There is a definite utopian strain evident in this later work, as in his essay "Coming Out Right," where he says, "Any successful writing program has to allow, and allow for, therapy" (1994b, 28), or in his book *The Universal Schoolhouse* (1994a), where he talks approvingly about how schools in the future will come to focus more and more on these notions of inner growth and spiritual development. There is also a quixotic element in Moffett's predicting and championing such idyllic educational futures, when these futures contrasted so sharply with the narrow-minded, grammar-obsessed, conventional, bureaucratized, intellectually timid, politically conservative reality of schooling that Moffett saw was becoming increasingly powerful in our society. On some level, he must have known these utopian ideas were doomed to failure, but he believed in them and so he advocated them anyway. I would place James Moffett in the tradition of educational reformers whose best ideas are not adopted on a large scale because they are simply too different, too visionary to be accepted by the mainstream. Such reformers sometimes respond not, as might be expected, by shifting to more pragmatic, less objectionable views, but by advocating ideas that are even *more* radical and have even less chance of succeeding than the original notions. Catholic priest and educator Ivan Illich (1971), who came to advocate the total de-schooling of society, is an example of one such person.

The educator John Holt, author of *How Children Learn* (1967) and *How Children Fail* (1964), is another. Like Moffett, Holt was, in his prime, a highly respected author, Harvard professor, powerful commission member, and federal grant holder. Holt was even the subject of major articles in magazines such as *Time* and *Newsweek*. However, his plan for restructuring schools around student-centered methods did not catch on, as the idealism of the late 1960s turned to disillusionment and Nixon-era conservatism. His methods largely abandoned, Holt came to see little of value in America's massive system of public education. And so, in his later years, he began to advocate closing all schools and doing away with the entire institution of public schooling (Holt, 1976). In the place of formal education, he suggested that certain adults be designated as official "knowers" and given a badge to wear as they went about their daily business. If a school-aged person, or anyone else, was walking down the street and happened to have a question or wanted to learn about a subject of interest, they could simply look for one of these knowers and talk to that person, so that teaching and learning would be folded into the contours of everyday life rather than separated off into what Holt viewed as a monolithic, unresponsive, self-protecting bureaucratic system. Many wondered at the time if Holt had lost his bearings. James Moffett's ideas about spirituality in education were not as utopian as those of John Holt, but they did go against the grain in English teaching and in American education as a whole. However, as an independent educator—"self-unemployed," as he described it (1994b, 24)—Moffett could write what he chose to. And in the final analysis, one can say about James Moffett that he had the integrity to follow his own vision.

In these days of increasing conservative power in education and other spheres of American life, with the accompanying emphasis on fixed standards, proficiency testing at every turn, and packaged curricula, it is tempting to look back wistfully at Moffett's creative, rigorous, and intellectually challenging classroom approaches and wonder what might have been. But it is also worth considering how his ideas have fared in English education up to the present day. Clearly, Moffett would be critical of assessment-driven national programs, such as Race to the Top and Common Core, for their homogenizing effects on textbooks, curriculum, and student evaluation. As far back as 1970, he inveighed against the "education industrial complex" (p. 530) and complained that "standardized testing is no more easily dropped than cigarette manufacturing, however injurious to your health. It is packaged into materials and nested down in the souls of administrators. It evaluates curriculum and therefore dictates curriculum. Teachers teach toward the tests, and it's amazing how fast their good intentions dissolve about teaching anything else" (533). Yet in the years since he wrote these words, the forces of standardization have gotten stronger, the tests more frequent, the consequences greater, with even less scope now for teachers and textbook writers to work against the grain.

Moffett's experience in West Virginia also raises important concerns about the ongoing issue of local control in the teaching of English. He was blindsided by the unexpected opposition of conservatives and religious activists, but today, teachers, textbook authors, and curriculum developers at least know they might well encounter such opposition and can prepare for it. When faced with criticism of particular books, assignments, and curricula, they can marshal arguments to justify their choices and propose alternatives when necessary. English educator and former high school teacher Suzanne Kauer taught public school for a number of years in Utah, a very conservative state. She has experience with parents and other community members opposing her classroom choices and now studies censorship, parental concerns, and possible school responses while also preparing new generations of secondary teachers. In a 2008 *English Journal* article, she bemoans but ultimately accepts the reality that, in many instances, people in communities across the country "do not agree with what English teachers ask their children to read" and will take action to prevent their children from exposure to certain texts or classroom approaches (56). Now, she states, "I ask my student teachers to spend more time thinking about and articulating the merits of the literature they teach so they can make better-informed decisions about what to teach and how to defend their choices" (60).

There remain a number of literacy educators around the country working to broaden literacy curricula to include an affective dimension of the sort that Moffett advocated, to the extent possible within the constraints of district and state guidelines. These include, to give just a few examples, Elizabeth Dutro, who helps inner-city teachers work with students on using writing to understand and cope with personal trauma (2011); Anne Whitney, who studies and works toward "transformation through writing and sharing" among participants in the National Writing Project (2008); and Robert Yagelski, who helps secondary teachers devise activities that allow students "to experience writing as a way of making sense of themselves and the world around them" (2012, 189). And recently, a group of literacy educators established the "James Moffett Consortium," under the aegis of Damian Koshnick, whose activities and discussions can be found (and joined) at jamesmoffettstudies.ning.com. Their stated purpose is "to dialogue on the value of James Moffett's theories and practices in English and education and our own uses of his ideas within K–16 classrooms." In addition, as Sheridan Blau (2011) points out, one of the National Council of Teachers of English special interest groups is the Assembly for Expanded Perspectives on Learning, which Moffett helped to found, and which is "committed to carrying on a vision of learning and of education that was articulated by Moffett in his writing and workshops for teachers" (99). Throughout his career, James Moffett fought against the mindset he termed *agnosis*, the desire not to know, the inclination to reject ideas that seem threatening or strange. Perhaps the best way to honor his legacy is by striving to encourage a critical yet open consideration of ideas and views, in our students but also in ourselves.

References

Agee, J. (1999). There it was, that one sex scene: English teachers and censorship. *English Journal, 89*(2), 61–69.

Applebee, A. N. (1981). *Writing in the secondary school: English and the content areas.* Urbana, IL: NCTE.

Berthoff, A., Daniell, B., Campbell, J. Swearingen, C. J., & Moffett, J. (1994). Interchanges: Spiritual sites of composing. *College Composition and Communication, 45*(2), 237–263.

Blau, S. (2011). Theory for practice: James Moffett's seminal contribution to composition. In P. Lambert Stock (Ed.), *Composition's roots in English education* (pp. 81–104). Portsmouth, NH: Boynton/Cook.

Britton, J., Burgess, T., Martin, N., McLeod, A., & Rosen, H. (1975). *The Development of Writing Abilities (11–18).* London: Macmillan.

Dutro, E. (2011). Writing wounded: Trauma, testimony, and critical witness in literacy classrooms. *English Education, 43*(2), 193–211.

Heath, S. B. (1983). *Ways with words: Language, life, and work in communities and classrooms.* New York: Cambridge University Press.

Hillocks, G. (1978). Books and bombs: Ideological conflict and the schools—a case study of the Kanawha County book protest. *The School Review, 86*(4), 632–654.

Holt, J.C. (1964). *How children fail.* New York: Dell Publishing.

Holt, J. C. (1967). *How children learn.* New York: Dell Publishing.

Holt, J. C. (1976). *Instead of education: Ways to help people do things better.* New York: Dutton Publishing.

Illich, I. (1971). *Deschooling society.* New York: Harper & Row.

Kauer, S. M. (2008). A battle reconsidered: Second thoughts on book censorship and conservative parents. *English Journal, 97*(3), 56–60.

Moffett, J. (1968a). *Teaching the universe of discourse.* Boston: Houghton Mifflin.

Moffett, J. (1968b). *A student-centered language arts curriculum, grades K–13: A handbook for teachers.* Boston: Houghton Mifflin.

Moffett, J. (1970). Coming on center. *English Journal, 59*(4), 528–533.

Moffett, J. (1974). *Interaction.* Boston: Houghton Mifflin.

Moffett, J. (1988). *Storm in the mountains: A case study of censorship, conflict, and consciousness.* Carbondale, IL: Southern Illinois University Press.

Moffett, J. (1994a). *The universal schoolhouse: Spiritual awakening through education.* San Francisco: Jossey-Bass.

Moffett, J. (1994b). Coming out right. In L. Tobin & T. Newkirk (Eds.), *Taking stock: The writing process movement in the '90s* (pp. 17–30). Portsmouth, NH: Boynton/ Cook.

North, S. (1987). *The making of knowledge in composition: Portrait of an emerging field.* Upper Montclair, NJ: Boynton/Cook.

Nystrand, M., Greene, S., & Wiemelt, J. (1993). Where did composition studies come from? An intellectual history. *Written Communication, 10*(3), 267–333.

Priest, K. C. (2010). *Protester voices: The 1974 textbook tea party.* Poca, WV: Praying Mantis Publishing.

Warnock, J. (2000). James Moffett. In M. G. Moran & M. Ballif (Eds.), *Twentieth-century rhetorics and rhetoricians: Critical studies and sources.* Westport, CT: Greenwood Press.

Whitney, Anne. (2008). Teacher transformation in the national writing project. *Research in the Teaching of English, 43*(2), 144–187.

Yagelski, R. P. (2012). Writing as praxis. *English Education, 44*(2), 188–204.

CHAPTER SEVEN

I, You, and It

JAMES MOFFETT

In this short treatise, Moffett unravels the complexity of his theory of discourse by sketching it on two interanimating axes; first, across increasing distance between sender and subject (from face-to-face-vocalization through publication), and second, through increasingly abstract modes of thought from what is happening to what may, will, or could happen.

Consider, if you will, those primary moments of experience that are necessarily the raw stuff of all discourse. Let us suppose, for example, that I am sitting in a public cafeteria eating lunch. People are arriving and departing, passing through the line, choosing tables, socializing. I am bombarded with smells of food, the sounds of chatter and clatter, the sights of the counter, the tables, the clothing, the faces, the gesticulations and bending of elbows. But I am not just an observer; I am eating and perhaps socializing as well. A lot is going on within me—the tasting and ingesting of the food, reactions to what I observe, emotions about other people. I am registering all these inner and outer stimuli. My perceptual apparatus is recording these moments of raw experience, not in words but in some code of its own that leads to words. This apparatus is somewhat unique to me in the way it selects and ignores stimuli and in the way it immediately connects them with old stimuli and previously formed conceptions. It is difficult to separate this sensory recording from the constant stream of thoughts that is going on simultaneously and parallel to the sensory record but may often depart from it. This verbal

Originally published in *College Composition and Communication,* vol. 16, no. 5, 1965, pp. 243–48. Reprinted by permission of NCTE.

stream is the first level of discourse to be considered. The subject is *what is happening now*, and the audience is oneself.

Suppose next that I tell the cafeteria experience to a friend sometime later in conversation. For what reason am I telling him? Would I tell it differently to someone else? Would I tell it differently to the same person at another time and in different circumstances? These are not rhetorical questions but questions about rhetoric. The fact that my account is an unrehearsed, face-to-face vocalization, uttered to *this* person for *this* reason at *this* time and place and in *these* circumstances determines to an enormous degree not only the overall way in which I abstract certain features of the ongoing panorama of the cafeteria scene but also much of the way I choose words, construct sentences, and organize parts. Compare this discourse with the third stage, when my audience is no longer face to face with me, but is farther removed in time and space so that I have to write a letter or memo to him. Informal writing is usually still rather spontaneous, directed at an audience known to the writer, and reflects the transient mood and circumstances in which the writing occurs. Feedback and audience influence, however, are delayed and weakened. Written discourse must replace or compensate for the loss of vocal characteristics and all physical expressiveness of gesture, tone, and manner. Compare in turn now the changes that must occur all down the line when I write about this cafeteria experience in a discourse destined for publication and distribution to a mass, anonymous audience of present and perhaps unborn people. I cannot allude to things and ideas that only my friends know about. I must use a vocabulary, style, logic, and rhetoric that anybody in that mass audience can understand and respond to. I must name and organize what happened during those moments in the cafeteria that day in such a way that this mythical average reader can relate what I say to some primary moments of experience of his own. In other words, whether this published discourse based on the cafeteria luncheon comes out as a fragment of autobiography, a short story, a humorous descriptive essay, or a serious theoretical essay about people's behavior in public places, certain necessities frame the discourse and determine a lot of its qualities before the writer begins to exercise his personal options.

These four stages of discourse—inner verbalization, outer vocalization, correspondence, and formal writing—are of course only the major markers of a continuum that could be much more finely calibrated. This continuum is formed simply by increasing the distance, in all senses, between speaker and audience. The audience is, first, the speaker himself, then another person standing before him, then someone in another time and place but having some personal relation to the speaker, then, lastly, an unknown mass extended over time and space. The activity necessarily changes from thinking to speaking to writing to publishing. (Thinking as inner speech is at least as old as Bergson and William James and as new as Piaget and Vygotsky.) For me no discussion of language, rhetoric, and composition is meaningful except in this context, for there is no speech without a speaker in some relation to a spoken-to and a spoken-about.

Starting with our cafeteria scene again, I would like to trace it as a subject that may be abstracted to any level I would wish. Please understand that by "subject" I mean some primary moments of experience regardless of how dimly they may appear in the discourse. There are four stages in the processing of raw phenomena by the human symbolic apparatus, although, again, one may recognize many gradations in between. This continuum can best be represented by verb tenses, which indicate when events occurred in relation to when the speaker is speaking of them. Suppose I represent the cafeteria scene first as *what is happening*, which would be the lowest level of verbal abstraction of reality: the order and organization of events would correspond most closely to phenomenal reality, and my verbalization of them would be the most immediate and unpondered that is possible. That is, my symbolic representation in this case would entail the least processing of matter by mind. If next I treat the events at the cafeteria as *what happened*, the subject will necessarily partake a little more of my mind and a little less of the original matter. Although the order of events will still be chronological, it is now my memory and not my perceptual apparatus that is doing the selecting. Some things will stick in my mind and some will not, and some things I will choose to retain or reject, depending on which features of this scene and action I wish to bring out.

Of the details selected, some I will dwell upon and some I will subordinate considerably. Ideas are mixed with material from the very beginning, but the recollection of a drama—a narrative, that is—inevitably entails more introduction of ideas because this is inherent in the very process of selecting, summarizing, and emphasizing, even if the speaker refrains from commenting directly on the events.

Suppose next that I speak of my cafeteria experience as *what happens*. Obviously, if we consider it for a moment, the difference between *what happened* and *what happens* is not truly a time difference, or at least we must realize that what we are calling a time difference is actually a difference in the level to which I choose to abstract some primary moments of experience. I am now treating my once-upon-a-time interlude at the cafeteria as something that recurs. I have jumped suddenly, it seems, from narrative to generalization. Actually, as we have said, ideas creep in long before this but are hidden in the processing. Now they must be more explicit, for only by renaming the experience and comparing it with other experiences can I present it as what happens. No primary moments of experience recur. What we mean is that we as observers see similarities in different experiences. Only the human mind, capable of sorting and classifying reality, can do this. What I do, for example, is make an analogy between something in the cafeteria experience and something I singled out of a number of other experiences. I summarize a lot of little formless dramas into pointed narratives and then I put these narratives into some classes, which I and others before me have created. In this third stage of processing, then, the cafeteria scene will become a mere example, among several others, of some general statement such as "The food you get in restaurants is not as good as what you get at home," or "People don't like me," or "Americans do not socialize as readily with strangers in public places as Italians do," or "The arrivals and departures within a continuous group create changes in excitation level comparable to the raising and lowering of electric potential in variously stimulated sensory receptors." It is apparent that these sample generalizations could all have contained the cafeteria experience as an example but vary a great deal in their abstractness, their range of applicability, their objectivity or universal truth value, and their originality.

The transition from a chronological to an analogical discourse is of enormous importance in teaching. The student must forsake the given order of time and replace it with an order of ideas. To do this he must summarize drastically the original primary moments of experience, find classes of inclusion and exclusion, and rename the moments so that it becomes clear how they are alike or different. Most students fail to create original and interesting classes because they are unwittingly encouraged to borrow their generalizations from old slogans, wise saws, reference books, and teachers' essay questions, instead of having to forge them from their own experience. Many students leave out the illustrations completely and offer only their apparently sourceless opinions. Others, reluctant to leave the haven of narrative, tell several anecdotes and never show how they are related. But these are failures of teachers, not of students. Proper writing assignments can lead the students to good generalizations.

In what I will call the last stage of symbolizing a subject, you may wonder why I still refer to the cafeteria, since none of that experience appears any longer in the discourse, which is now a highly theoretical essay. That is deceptive; it is behind the discourse, buried in the processing and so combined with other experiences, and so renamed, that we do not recognize it anymore. The "subject" seems to be a theory, some combining and developing of generalizations. This stage is telling *what will, may,* or *could happen.* Some general assertions previously arrived at by analogical thinking are now plugged into each other in various ways according to the rules of formal logic. Suppose we take some generalizations about the behavior of Americans and the behavior of Italians and the behavior of South Sea islanders and we transform and combine these statements in such a way as to come out with an anthropological conclusion that was not evident in any of the original moments of experience nor even in the generalizations about them. It took manipulations of logic to show the implication of the earlier statements. To go beyond this stage is to enter the realm of mathematical equations. What will, may, or could happen is a high-level inference entailing tautology, verbal equations. My own essay is an example of stage-four abstraction. I am setting up a series of equations among "levels of abstraction," "distance between speaker, listener, and subject," verb tenses, human faculties, and kinds of logic. I will then conclude a theory about composition curriculum by combining generalizations about what happens in discourse with what happens in the learning process of people. What enables me to do this is that something fundamental to the operation of our nervous system underlies all these man-made conceptions.

I have traced separately, and grossly, two abstractive progressions—one in which the speaker's audience becomes more remote and diffused over time and space, and another in which the speaker's subject becomes less and less matter and more and more idea. Each relation—and of course the two must be taken together—entails certain necessities, and shifts in these relations entail changes all down the line, from the organization of the whole discourse to individual word choice. As we move through the progressions, perception gives way to memory and memory to ratiocination; chronology gives way to analogy and analogy to tautology. But each faculty and kind of logic depends on the one before. In view of what we know now about abstractive processes and the cognitive and verbal growth of children, this order seems pedagogically sound to me. In other words, the necessities inherent in devising a rhetoric for an increasingly remote audience and in abstracting moments of experience to higher and higher symbolic levels are precisely the limitations which should shape our writing assignments.

According to Piaget, and Vygotsky agrees with him, the early egocentric speech of children becomes gradually "socialized" and adapts itself to other people. At the same time his mental outlook decenters; that is, he gradually yields up his initial, emotionally preferred vantage point, and expands his perspective so as to include many other points of view. Of course, both these kinds of growth never really stop. The movement is from self to world, from a point to an area, from a private world of egocentric chatter to a public universe of discourse. Cognitively, the young person passes through, according to Jerome Bruner, three phases—the enactive, the iconic, and the symbolic. First he knows things by manipulating them with his hands, then he begins to classify and interpret the world by means of image summaries, and finally he can carry out logical operations in his head modeled on his earlier physical manipulations. Most teachers have always known that in some way the child should move from the concrete to the abstract, but the whole notion of an abstraction ladder has never been clear and still requires more study. I have found the communication engineers' definition of coding to be very helpful in all this: Coding is the substitution of one set of events for another. What I call the processing of matter by mind is in fact the substitution of inner events for outer events. These inner events are neural, and we don't yet know very much about them. We can be sure, however, that as the child's nervous system develops, these neural operations become more complicated. A series of writing assignments is a series of thinking assignments and therefore a sequence of internal operations. All stages of a developmental sequence are crucial and none can be left out. Teachers have got to become more sophisticated about this sequence and more aware of the effects in the student of his trying to do what we ask.

As a model for a composition course, imagine the trinity of discourse—first, second, and third persons—to be a single circle that separates into three overlapping circles which move out until they merely touch. The discourse unity of somebody talking to somebody else about something is what we must never lose, but we can create phases, not by decomposing composition into analytical elements but by gradually pushing the persons apart. Language and rhetoric are variable factors of each other and of shifting relations among persons. We abstract not only from something but for someone. Rhetoric, on the other hand, is to some extent dictated by the abstraction level we have chosen; in drama and narrative one appeals mainly by concrete recognitions, and in exposition and argumentation mainly by one's classes and logical justice. So the rationale of our composition course lies in some crossing of the two progressions I have sketched. This is not only possible but will spiral the curriculum. For example, we ask the student to tell what happened in four different rhetorics—to himself as he spontaneously recalls a memory, to a friend face to face, to someone he knows in a letter, and to the world at large in formal writing. Generalizations and theories can be dealt with first in interior monologues, then in dialogues, in letters and diaries, and only at the end in essays. The student is never assigned a subject, only a form, and the forms are ordered according to the preceding ideas. Thus, the assignments are structural and sequential.

Specifically, I would have the student write in this order: all kinds of real and invented interior monologues, dramatic monologues, dialogues, plays, letters, diaries, fragments of autobiography, eye-witness accounts, reporters-at-large (modeled on those in the *New Yorker*), case studies, first- and third-person fiction, essays of generalization and essays of logical argumentation. Many teachers may feel that such a program slights exposition in favor of so-called personal or creative writing. In the first place, one doesn't learn exposition just by writing it all the time. An enormous amount of other learning must take place before one can write worthwhile essays of ideas; that is in the nature of the whole abstraction process. All writing teaches exposition. Furthermore, I cannot conceive a kind of discourse which does not contain ideas; even in concrete description, contrasts, similarities, and notions of causality and progression are strongly implicit. Monologues, dialogues, letters, diaries, and narratives may either contain explicit ideas or be shaped by ideas. What do we mean by a *pointed* narrative? What are Socratic dialogues about? And why do we have students digging for meaning in literary works of imagination if they are not full of ideas? The issue is not idea writing versus other kinds of writing but rather which form the ideas are presented in. All modes must be taught. The panic to teach exposition is partly responsible for its being taught so badly. Teachers do not feel they can take the time to let a student abstract from the ground up. But if they do not, he will never learn to write exposition.

There are several corollaries of the program I am proposing. Since it attempts to exercise the student in all possible relations that might obtain between him and an audience and a subject, one corollary is that he not be allowed to get stuck with one audience or at one range of the abstractive spectrum. It is essential that he address someone besides the English teacher and get some kind of feedback other than red marks. As one solution, I suggest that he be accustomed to write to the whole class as being the nearest thing to a contemporary world at large. Compositions should be read in class, and out of class, reacted to and discussed. One must know the effects of one's rhetoric on someone who does not give grades and does not stand as an authority figure. I suggest also the performance and publication of student works as frequently as possible. Monologues, dialogues, letters, and diaries give the student the opportunity both to address a real or invented person outside the classroom and to adopt a voice not his own.

What most frequently freezes the student at one end of the abstractive spectrum is too much writing about reading. Perhaps because of the great influence of college essay exams and of literary exegesis, composition courses often boil down to "how to write about books." This is a narrow notion of exposition. Abstracting about someone else's already high abstraction, whether it be a book or a teacher's essay question, means that certain essential issues of choice about selecting and treating material and creating classes are never permitted to come up for the student. When I assign a topic such as "loyalty" or "irony in A. E. Housman," all I am asking the student to do is to find illustrations for my classifications. By doing half of his work for him, I am impoverishing his education. Rather than assign literary exegesis, I would have him write in the forms he reads. As practitioner he will naturally be a better literary critic than a student who only analyzes. Rather than assign book reports and essays on books, I would encourage the student to incorporate into his essays of generalization illustrations and ideas drawn from his reading and to mix these with his own experiences and observations; in other words, get *him* to create the classes into which he can fit people and actions drawn from both books and life. There is a real place for reading in a composition course, not as subject matter to write about but as a source of experience and as a repertory of discourse. After all, reading provides some excellent primary moments of experience.

From the perceptual level on up the student should be forced in effect to confront all the right issues of choice. Only in this way will he develop the faculties necessary to produce the ideas of exposition. On the same grounds, I am leary of asking the student to read about writing. I have spent a lot of time unteaching the dicta of composition texts and manuals of advice. Trial and error best develops judgment and taste, if this trial and error process is keyed in with the student's learning schedule. Explanations and definitions of good style, technique, and rhetoric create more problems than they solve. The issue here is not only one of cognitive development but of psychological independence. We must give students an emotional mandate to play the symbolic scale, to find subjects and shape them, to invent ways to act upon others, and to discover their own voice.

Phillips Exeter Academy
Exeter, NH

CHAPTER EIGHT

Discourse and Social Action: Moffett and the New Rhetoric

ANTHONY PARÉ
McGill University

This article makes the case that while James Moffett is typically celebrated for his efforts at reforming the language arts curriculum, his interest in discourse and rhetoric led him beyond curricular reform to a radically reconceived model of education, one in which disciplinary knowledge is subordinate to the processes of symbolic representation that creates that knowledge. This article explicates Moffett's conception of the learning process and draws links between Moffett's ideas and the focus on language-as-social-action that came to dominate North American writing studies in the 1980s.

Rhetoric is concerned with the state of Babel after the Fall.
—BURKE (1969, 23)

In 1979, James Moffett wrote an article for a Special Issue of the *McGill Journal of Education* dedicated to English Studies. In an introduction to that article, the journal editor, John Harley, wrote that *Teaching the Universe of Discourse* (1968a) had "lifted the teaching of English fifty years forward." Certainly, for many Canadians working in English education and/or composition and rhetoric in the 1970s, that book was an extraordinary inspiration. It freed the school subject "English" from the death grasp of grammar instruction, *belle lettres*, and the five-paragraph essay, offered a radical vision of language and learning, and contributed to the reinvention of rhetoric as a dynamic and pragmatic

Originally published in *Changing English*, vol. 17, no.3, 2010, pp. 241–50. Reprinted with permission.

approach to the study and teaching of writing. It was nothing short of revolutionary.

I first read Moffett in undergraduate and graduate seminars in the late 1970s with Patrick Dias, professor at McGill University in Montreal and an early supporter of Moffett's work in Canada. Patrick was involved in secondary English education as a teacher educator and researcher, and was also founding director of the university's writing centre, which developed and taught writing courses across the campus. Because of Patrick's position between the two levels of schooling, he and his students were able to field-test Moffett's ideas about language education in BEd seminars, secondary-school English classrooms, and university writing courses. Along with classmates who worked as tutors and instructors in the fledgling writing centre, I would run from Pat's graduate seminar to try Moffett's ideas in my undergraduate writing classes. With Murray (e.g., 1978), Elbow (1973), Britton et al. (1975), and others, as well as the then emerging cognitivists (e.g., Flower 1979; Flower and Hayes 1977, 1981), Moffett supplied us with inspiration, an accessible theory of discourse, and plenty of ideas for day-to-day practice. We weren't alone. James Gray, founder of the US National Writing Project, called him "a national resource for American education" (Gray 1997, 34). In histories of North American writing studies, Moffett is acknowledged as a "pioneer" (Russell 2006, 265), and, along with the work of D'Angelo (1975), Kinneavy (1971), and Britton et al. (1975), his ideas about discourse are considered foundational (McCleary 1998).

In this article I would like to re-read Moffett through a retrospective lens, not to gauge or celebrate his influence, but rather to look again at what he was saying, to reconsider his vision, and to reflect on its currency. Others writing in this volume are far better qualified than I to comment on Moffett's ideas about English education; for my part, I would like to read Moffett again in the light of theoretical and pedagogical developments in North American writing studies, or what is sometimes called composition and rhetoric, or, simply, composition.

A strong first impression on reencountering Moffett after four decades is his extraordinary prescience. To what degree he was responsible for the changes he anticipated, and to what extent he was simply tapped into the *zeitgeist* is a decision for historians, but what is unquestionable is his grasp of what could and would and should happen in education. In particular, his ideas about the nature of writing suggest a sophisticated perspective that leapfrogs the so-called "process approach" to writing and finds resonance in more recent, sociocultural theories of writing, such as rhetorical genre theory (e.g., Freedman and Medway 1994; Coe, Lingard, and Teslenko 2002). His view that "[u]sing language is essentially a social action" (Moffett 1968b, 12) places him beyond the early process concern with voice and its focus on rhetorical invention, and well past the cognitive process models that featured inputs and outputs but precious little social context. Although Moffett is sometimes identified as contributing primarily to a cognitive theory of discourse (Berlin 1987; Faigley 1992), he repeatedly insists that language, including writing, is only developed in "the ultimate context of somebody-talking-to-somebody-else-about-something" (Moffett 1968a, 5)—a decidedly social perspective on discourse.

Moffett's comment that "there should be a total program in discourse running laterally across subject fields as well as longitudinally over the years" (Moffett 1968b, 6) anticipates what became known as the Writing Across the Curriculum (WAC) movement, an approach to the teaching of writing that borrowed from British trends. No doubt Moffett was influenced here by James Britton, Douglas Barnes, and others from the UK, whom he met at the Anglo-Canadian-American seminar at Dartmouth in 1966, but his stand on this comes almost a decade before Martin et al.'s groundbreaking text, *Writing and Learning Across the Curriculum, 11–16* (1976). Moffett doesn't soft-pedal his position:

> [T]he division of learning into English, Mathematics, and Social Studies is a huge mistake. The reason I have insisted on the term "discourse" is to show that what we usually call "English" cannot be successfully conceived as merely a separate subject in an array of other subjects. (Moffett 1968a, 212)

Moffett's theory and curriculum anticipate, as well, many of the best practices in writing instruction that became common in subsequent years: moving from the "expressive" to "the transactional," engaging students in authentic discourse, assigning topics with relevance in the students' lives, working in small groups, using language rather than merely analysing it, assessing writing development in multiple ways over time by using portfolios, and so on. His suggestion that classes be divided "into five or six smaller groups for the purposes of dramatizing, discussing, reading aloud, and commenting on each other's writing" (Moffett 1968b, 7) appears well before in-class writing workshops and peer tutoring became standard practice in university writing courses.

However, as I re-read Moffett, what seems most striking to me is something captured in the excerpt above, something that I think I missed the first time around—in part because I probably couldn't appreciate it, and in part because Moffett himself may have been too modest or cautious or perhaps uncertain in his claim. What seems clear to me now is that Moffett wasn't after a mere reform in language education. He wasn't just looking to shake up the teaching of English, or to extend attention to discourse beyond the language classroom. His goal was far more profound: he was attempting to reconceive *education* itself as the "universe of discourse." His purpose was not simply to redefine discourse *in* education, but to relocate education *in* discourse. For Moffett, the latter term took primacy. The proposal seems as radical now as in 1968, and just as urgent and innovative.

The more ambitious reform project is disguised by frequent references to the narrower goal: on its cover, *Teaching the Universe of Discourse* (Moffett 1968a) is subtitled "a rationale for English teaching," and the first chapter is titled "A Structural Curriculum for English." The book touches on topics traditionally associated with the English classroom—grammar, writing, drama, literature. The companion text is titled *A Student-Centered Language Arts Curriculum, Grades K–13* (Moffett 1968b). Revising the language arts curriculum might have been his original intention, but Moffett's larger hope is expressed clearly in the concluding chapter of *Teaching the Universe of Discourse*, where he acknowledges that "I have not been talking in this book just about 'English teaching' but, inevitably, about a whole curriculum" (Moffett 1968a, 212). He continues:

> So I would like to end with the proposal that educators work toward a future reorganization of the total curriculum that would eliminate conventional subject divisions and would base learning on the central process of human symbolization. (Moffett 1968a, 212)

This is not about making language pedagogy more relevant or effective. It isn't even about WAC's goal of spreading attention to writing across the full curriculum, which frequently results in superficial add-ons like technical writing classes for engineers or public-speaking workshops for business students. Moffett's vision is more radical: "there is really only one subject . . . and that subject is discourse itself, of which science and social studies are subclasses" (Moffett 1968a, 212). For him, science and social studies "are not subjects separate from and coordinate with the native language, but specialized examples of the functioning of that language" (Moffett 1968a, 212). Before the work of Foucault, Derrida, Bakhtin, and others had pushed the notion of *discourse* to the centre of writing theory, Moffett was arguing for its importance.

The theory of discourse that Moffett develops to support his reform is not terribly consistent or elaborate. His accounts of language, cognition, rhetoric, disciplinarity, and other key phenomena are sketchy, underdeveloped, even contradictory. Noticeably absent from Moffett's perspective, in the light of current discourse theory, is any reference to power. He cites Piaget for a cognitive model that matches his notions of growth in language, but his insistence that language develops only in the context of authentic social exchange smacks more of Vygotsky, who is only mentioned in passing. Other sources are not easy to determine. In both his 1968 books, references are rare: some appear in footnotes, other names are dropped without citation, and some influences are only hinted at. He says, for example, "[w]ithin the relation of the speaker to his listener lie all the issues by which we have recently enlarged the meaning of 'rhetoric'" (Moffett 1968a, 10), but doesn't indicate who "we" are, nor elaborate on this expanded meaning. He refers to Francis Christensen (1968a, 174),[1] but sounds more like Kenneth Burke.[2] Many of Moffett's ideas seem sparked by his experience at the 1966 conference at Dartmouth, and in both books he refers to Douglas Barnes and Anthony Adams—co-participants at Dartmouth; in his curriculum book (Moffett 1968b, 5), he cites Dixon's report on that conference, *Growth through English* (1967). He mentions teaching colleagues and fellow members of the School Language Group at Harvard. Finally, however, his theory of discourse is patchy and partial, and although it is often cited as seminal, it is also considered incomplete or insubstantial (e.g., North 1987; Crusius 1989; McCleary 1998).

The sense I get re-reading Moffett is that he was searching for a conceptual framework that would help explain what he felt was "the central process of human symbolization" (Moffett 1968a, 212). He says, "Some ultimate context or super-structure is exactly what English as a school subject has always lacked" (Moffett 1968a, 3), and *Teaching the Universe of Discourse* feels like an essay, in the original French sense of that word: an *essai* or attempt to articulate that super-structure. But Moffett was primarily interested in practice. He called his work a "pedagogical theory of discourse" (Moffett 1968a, xi) and produced a rich handbook for teachers (Moffett, 1968b).[3] Moffett addressed teachers directly, without condescension, as essential partners in realizing his vision of the new classroom. Most refreshingly, perhaps, he invited experimentation and resisted orthodoxy. He even says about Chapter Two in *Teaching the Universe of Discourse* that "[t]he theory of discourse that makes up most of this chapter is meant to be utilized, not believed" (Moffett 1968a, 15). And, in the same chapter, he says, "[t]his whole theory of discourse is essentially an hallucination" (Moffett 1968a, 54). No zealot, he. Less concerned with coherence in theory than coherence in practice, he encourages teachers to see his work as tentative: "[W]hat I am presenting is not a definitive, thoroughly tried-and-proven course of learning; it is, rather, a chart for further exploration and a kind of rallying call" (Moffett 1968b, 1). His purpose, then, was not to develop a watertight theory that would withstand close critical attention, but rather to sketch out a plan of action: "I am after a strategic gain in concept" (Moffett 1968a, 15).

That concept, I believe, was a social theory of rhetoric. Moffett suggests that human activities—such as science or social studies—are specialized variations of symbolic representation, or *discourses*, and that those discursive resources are deployed to produce particular outcomes or effects. Science and social studies "are not subjects separate from and coordinate with the native language, but specialized examples of the functioning of that language" (Moffett 1968a, 212). This perspective matches what is often called *new rhetoric*, insofar as it shifts attention from the formal features of text and occasion to the actions or consequences (material, psychological, attitudinal) that discourse inspires. For Moffett, language is essentially dialogic and consequential: "Dialogue, internal or external, will establish language as *behavior*—spontaneous, ongoing, expressive, manipulative—an attempt to *do* something to or for or against or with another 'party.' This is the genesis of rhetoric" (Moffett 1968a, 41, emphasis in original). The prepositions in that sentence are telling: language exists between and among people as social interaction. Moffett's insistence on the centrality of dialogue anticipates Bakhtin (e.g., 1986), a key influence on new rhetorical theory, and predates by some years the interest in Bakhtin's notion of *addressivity*, which refers to the fact that every utterance is directed to another, or is a response in a chain of communication. As Moffett (1968a, 191) puts it, "even in our unuttered thoughts, we speak as though to another because we have long since incorporated the otherness of the social world to which language is irrevocably tied." This view of language (and thought) as essentially social was not fully understood or exploited by the expressivist or cognitivist schools of writing theory and practice that flourished in North America in the 1970s and 1980s, and finds greater resonance with sociocultural theories of discourse and rhetoric that became dominant 15–20 years after Moffett first articulated his theory.

Admittedly, Moffett did not fully elaborate his theories of discourse or rhetoric, and, as a result, filling out that partial theory requires speculation. Nonetheless, I believe that the general shape and direction of his thinking can be discerned from the work he published in 1968. His insistence on language as action or behaviour anticipated the move from cognitive to social theories of writing, and his exploration of the ways in which different discursive practices create particular ways of knowing and distinct knowledges foreshadowed notions of genre that only became central in rhetorical theory in the mid-1980s.

In fact, Moffett's emphasis on language as symbolic action echoes Kenneth Burke's definition of rhetoric: "The use of language as a symbolic means of inducing cooperation in beings that by nature respond to symbols" (Burke 1969, 43). Burke is considered a seminal influence in new rhetorical theory. In retrospect, it seems to me that what Moffett was after when he placed symbol-making at the centre of his theory was a total overhaul of education itself, not just the language classroom, and the return of rhetoric to the heart of the curriculum:

> English, French, and mathematics are *symbol systems*, into which the phenomenal data of empirical subjects are cast and by means of which we think about them. Symbol systems are not primarily about themselves; they are about other subjects. When a student "learns" one of these systems, he *learns how to* operate it. The main point is to think and talk about other things by means of this system. (Moffett 1968a, 6, emphasis in the original)

What is common across the curriculum is the use of symbol systems, and the purpose of schooling is to help people deploy those systems in all of the specialized ways that humans have developed to get their work done. As he says, "[t]he function of the school is to extend the rhetorical repertory" (Moffett 1968a, 116). And what is common to all of that symbolic action is that *someone* is talking about *something* to *someone else*. To capture that, Moffett developed a simple but ingenious, articulated relationship between two key features of any discourse event, what he called the *I–it relation* and the *I–you relation*: "The first is the referential relation; the second is the rhetorical relation. Although the informative and communicative aspects of discourse cannot in reality be separated, for conceptual purposes they may be" (Moffett 1968a, 18). However, as he develops this idea, it seems clear that both the *I–you* and *I–it* relations are rhetorical—that is, both involve symbolization in the service of social action:

> The referential relation of *I–it* must be crossed with the rhetorical relation of *I–you*, in order to produce a whole,

> authentic discourse. Rhetoric, or the art of acting on someone through words, is an abstractive art. That is, one performs the same activities in pitching a subject to an audience as one does in extracting that subject from raw phenomena: one selects and reorganizes traits of things, digests, codes preferentially. (Moffett 1968a, 31)

Moffett's articulated relationship between topic and audience creates a conceptual device that describes what he calls the "spectrum of discourse," from interior monologue or reflection—"Intrapersonal communication between two parts of one nervous system" (Moffett 1968a, 33)—to publication—"Impersonal communication to a large anonymous group extended over space and/or time" (Moffett 1968a, 33), and from what is happening right this moment (recording) to what might happen (theorizing). Within that spectrum lie all possible rhetorical situations, all combinations of rhetor, audience, exigence, text, and occasion. This is a new rhetorical theory encapsulated in an elegant conceptual heuristic.

To demonstrate its flexibility, Moffett develops an extended example of himself sitting in a cafeteria (Moffett 1968a, 36–39) and observing the passing scene. He then imagines himself doing everything from reflecting on the actual scene to writing about it as an example of human activity. The movement in discourse goes "from addressing the small known audience like oneself to addressing a distant, unknown, and different audience" (Moffett 1968a, 57). He freezes that movement at one point in this expanding universe of discourse to consider the situation in which he tells a friend about his cafeteria experience:

> For what reason am I telling him? Would I tell it differently to the same person at another time and in different circumstances? These are not rhetorical questions but questions about rhetoric. The fact that my account is an unrehearsed, face-to-face vocalization, uttered to *this* person for *this* reason at *this* time and place and in *these* circumstances determines to an enormous degree not only the overall way in which I abstract certain features of the ongoing panorama of the cafeteria scene but also much of the way I choose words, construct sentences, and organize parts. (Moffett 1968a, 37, emphasis in original)

Here Moffett has summarized many of the central notions of the new rhetoric: any utterance is a response to a particular rhetorical situation and aims to achieve some outcome, to affect change, to persuade. All discourse is situated rhetorical action. Whereas classical rhetorical studies had calcified or morphed into the form-focussed writing pedagogy often called the "product approach," new rhetorical theory saw all human discourse as strategic and utilitarian: as deliberate language shaped in response to particular needs or exigencies. As noted above, the elements and actions captured in Moffett's formulation anticipate such sociocultural accounts of discourse as rhetorical genre theory, which shifts theoretical and pedagogical attention off texts and on to consequences, relationships, contingency. Genres are human efforts to regularize the *I–it* and *I–you* relations so that outcomes—both textual and contextual—are predictable, repeatable, and productive of the ends at which they are aimed. In Miller's tight summary of this new genre theory: "a rhetorically sound definition of genre must be centered not on the substance or form of discourse but on the action it is used to accomplish" (Miller 1984, 151). It is possible to analyse any rhetorical situation by considering how adjustments in the situation's *I–you* and *I–it* relations shape the action accomplished by discourse. Moffett, too, shifted attention from "the substance or form of discourse" to "the action it is used to accomplished": variations in the *I–you* and *I–it* relations, he argued, produce reflecting, reporting, generalizing, theorizing, speculating—in other words, actions. According to Miller (1984, 165), "for the student, genres serve as keys to understanding how to participate in the actions of the community"; according to Moffett, "[w]hen a student 'learns' one of these [specialised symbol] systems, he *learns how to* operate it" (Moffett 1968a, 6, emphasis in the original).

For Moffett, participation in rhetorical action is a defining characteristic of being human: "For me *rhetoric* refers to the ways one person attempts to act on another . . . we learn at the outset of life the tremendously important art of manipulating other people. This is the genesis of rhetoric—and it begins before we learn to speak" (Moffett 1968a, 115). We are rhetorical even before we are grammatical. Moffett's 1968 vision was sweeping and radical. It relocated rhetoric at the heart of the curriculum—in fact, at the heart of human interaction—and it made symbolic action the single focus of school, with specialized discourses merely subsets of that main concern. This was *not* a modest proposal; it was not a mere revision of English education. Rather, it reconceived schooling as a process of immersion in the discourse practices that shape human activity; it engaged students as participants in knowledge-making for both personal and public ends; it dissolved disciplinary boundaries and replaced them with an infinite variety of situations and exigencies requiring collective symbolic action. Well before the rise of sociocultural perspectives on writing, Moffett was making a pitch for the centrality of rhetoric in human affairs.

Anything seemed possible in the Great Society of the late 1960s, and Moffett's proposed curriculum, developed in his 1968 companion volumes, counted on "the gradually rising quality of teachers and the increasing local experimentation within school systems" (Moffett 1968b, 4). The curriculum, he believed, depended "on a fair measure of knowledge and self-assurance on the part of the teacher and good collaboration and support within a school system bent on forging its own curriculum" (Moffett 1968b, 5). But in his 1979 *McGill Journal of Education* article, while the rest of us were still energized by his work, and attempting to exploit its full implications, Moffett seemed otherwise occupied, and considerably less hopeful.

He felt that education, "[a]long with the rest of North American culture . . . is going through a spell of depression and repression" (Moffett 1979, 102). Nixon had succeeded Lyndon Johnson, and the accountability fetish, which continues to haunt education today, had taken hold, "fetched up from Detroit and the Pentagon" (Moffett 1979, 102). Standardized testing, teacher-proof curricula, behaviourist psychology, and ability-streaming were making schools "factories turning out products from inert materials (students)" (Moffett 1979, 103). Moffett was not as upbeat as he had been, and his 1979 vision of the future included an isomorphic alphabet, alternative realities, clairvoyance, psychokinesis, yoga, and other topics that placed him beyond the pale for many, and may have reduced his earlier influence.

As I noted at the start of this article, others in this issue are better able to comment on Moffett's effect on and ongoing relevance to English education, but in 1979 he himself seemed less than rosy about the prospects for radical change. His despondence in the article is understandable, given how much his remarkable vision of a fully reconceived school had been shattered by subsequent events. He imagined an educational experience that engaged students in an infinite universe of discourse, and in 1979 he looked out on a landscape of shrinking possibility, with control and fragmentation replacing the experimentation and creativity he envisioned.

Moffett, of course, was reflecting chiefly on developments in primary and secondary education—his major concern all along. But what about developments in composition and rhetoric at the postsecondary level, and the influence of the new rhetorical theory to which Moffett had contributed? In 1979, and even today, Moffett might have had cause for greater optimism if he had shifted his gaze from schools to colleges and universities in North America. The galvanizing effects of the reinvented rhetoric led to widespread adoption of postsecondary programmes in writing across the curriculum and writing in the disciplines and to the creation of courses of study in rhetoric. There was a growth industry in rhetorical theory and research through the 1970s, 1980s, and 1990s.

But here, too, Moffett's hope for the unifying force of rhetoric appears unrealized. Berlin's (2003) proposal for a revamped English studies suggested that the field was in crisis, without a coherent mission. He called for the discipline to see its work as part of a larger project and to turn its attention "from canonical texts and their authoritative interpretations to signifying practices broadly conceived" (2003, 188)—an expanded focus reminiscent of Moffett's appeal for a curriculum concerned with the "process of human symbolization." In search of such a broader mandate, some rhetoric scholars have split off from US English departments to form their own departments (Little and Rose 1994). But creating academic units devoted to the study and teaching of rhetoric—although offering the perk of disciplinary status—actually isolates rhetoric rather than relocating it at the centre of the curriculum, and it fails to establish rhetoric as the meta-discipline that Moffett proposed. Andrea Lunsford, a central figure in North American writing studies, offers this judgement on units devoted to writing and rhetoric:

> These new departments do not yet have a firm core: some focus on professional discourse, some on literacy and language, some on media, some on history, some on technology and writing, and some try for an omnibus approach that would bring all these strands together. . . . But I have some doubts, not about departments of rhetoric and writing per se, but about departments in general: it seems clear that disciplinary boundaries are crumbling, that the old framework of departments, based on the 19th century German system, is no longer adequate for the work scholars need to do, and that some other structure needs to arise. . . . So a "new" department of rhetoric and writing may find itself "old" fairly shortly. (Lunsford 2007, 6–7)

Lunsford's concern echoes Moffett's call 40 years earlier for an "ultimate context or super-structure" for English (Moffett 1968a, 3) and a "reorganization of the total curriculum that would eliminate conventional subject divisions" (Moffett 1968a, 212). Moffett's solution was a curriculum that would "base learning on the central process of human symbolization" (Moffett 1968a, 212). He argued that "there is really only one subject . . . and that subject is discourse itself" (Moffett 1968a, 212), and although his insistence on the notion of discourse now seems prophetic, his proposal for a coherent curriculum with discourse and rhetoric at its core has failed to materialize. The effort to secure disciplinary status for rhetoric has had modest success, and writing across the curriculum programmes suggest some recognition of the centrality of writing in knowledge-making across the disciplines, but an approach to education that subordinates disciplinary knowledge to rhetoric seems as visionary and unlikely now as it did in 1968.

Notes

1. Of Christensen, Moffett says this: "His analysis is indeed rhetorically oriented, since he emphasizes how syntactic differences make a stylistic difference, but students doing his exercises are not placed in a rhetorical situation. Unfortunately, the yoking of *generative* and *rhetoric* [in

Christensen's title] suggests a utility for composition that is not borne out" (Moffett 1968a, 174–75).

2. Moffett and Burke shared a fascination with drama. Moffett (1968a, 116) writes that "[d]rama is the perfect place to begin the study of rhetoric."

3. In the UK, Doughty, Pearce, and Thornton (1971, 1972) also created companion volumes that offered a detailed, theory-based practice; and like Moffett's work, their theory and curriculum seems remarkably fresh and innovative today.

References

Bakhtin, M. M. 1986. *Speech genres and other late essays.* Trans. Vern W. McGee. Austin: University of Texas Press.

Berlin, J. 1987. *Rhetoric and reality: Writing instruction in American colleges, 1900–1985.* Carbondale: Southern Illinois University Press.

Berlin, J. 2003. *Rhetorics, poetics, and cultures: Refiguring college English studies.* West Lafayette, IN: Parlor Press.

Britton, J., T. Burgess, N. Martin, A. McLeod, and H. Rosen. 1975. *The Development of Writing Abilities (11–18).* London: Macmillan.

Burke, K. 1969. *A rhetoric of motives.* Berkeley: University of California Press.

Coe, R., L. Lingard, and T. Teslenko, eds. 2002. *The rhetoric and ideology of genre.* Cresskill, NJ: Hampton Press.

Crusius, T. W. 1989. *Discourse: A critique and synthesis of major theories.* New York: Modern Language Association.

D'Angelo, F. 1975. *A conceptual theory of rhetoric.* Cambridge, MA: Winthrop.

Dixon, J. 1967. *Growth through English.* Oxford: Oxford University Press.

Doughty, P., J. Pearce, and G. Thornton. 1971. *Language in use.* London: Edward Arnold.

Doughty, P., J. Pearce, and G. Thornton. 1972. *Exploring language.* London: Edward Arnold.

Elbow, P. 1973. *Writing without teachers.* New York: Oxford University Press.

Faigley, L. 1992. *Fragments of rationality: Postmodernity and the subject of composition.* Pittsburgh, PA: University of Pittsburgh Press.

Flower, L. S. 1979. Writer-based prose: A cognitive basis for problems in writing. *College English* 41: 19–37.

Flower, L. S., and J. R. Hayes. 1977. Problem-solving strategies and the writing process. *College English* 39: 449–61.

Flower, L. S., and J. R. Hayes. 1981. A cognitive process theory of writing. *College Composition and Communication* 32: 365–87.

Freedman, A., and P. Medway, eds. 1994. *Genre and the new rhetoric.* London: Taylor & Francis.

Gray, J. 1997. Jim Moffett: 1929–1996: An appreciation. *The Quarterly* 19, no. 1: 33–34.

Kinneavy, J. 1971. *A theory of discourse.* Englewood Cliffs, NJ: Prentice-Hall.

Little, S. B., and S. Rose. 1994. A home of our own: Establishing a department of rhetoric and writing studies at San Diego State University. *WPA: Writing Program Administration* 18, nos. 1–2: 16–28.

Lunsford, A. A. 2007. Key questions for a new rhetoric. In *What is the New Rhetoric?,* ed. S. E. Thomas, 4–14. Newcastle, UK: Cambridge Scholars Publishing.

Martin, N., P. D'Arcy, B. Newton, and R. Parker. 1976. *Writing and learning across the curriculum, 11–16.* London: Ward Lock.

McCleary, W. J. 1998. Discourse theory. In *Theorizing composition: A critical sourcebook of theory and scholarship in contemporary composition studies,* ed. M. L. Kennedy, 91–100. Westport, CT: Greenwood Press.

Miller, C. 1984. Genre as social action. *Quarterly Journal of Speech* 70, 151–67.

Moffett, J. 1968a. *Teaching the universe of discourse.* Boston: Houghton-Mifflin.

Moffett, J. 1968b. *A student-centered language arts curriculum, grades K–13: A handbook for teachers.* Boston: Houghton-Mifflin.

Moffett, J. 1979. Language learning in the eighties. *McGill Journal of Education* 14, no. 1: 102–14.

Murray, D. M. 1978. Write before writing. *College Composition and Communication* 29: 375–82.

North, S. 1987. *The making of knowledge in composition: Portrait of an emerging field.* Upper Montclair, NJ: Boynton/Cook.

Russell, D. 2006. Historical studies of composition. In *Research on composition: Multiple perspectives on two decades of change,* ed. P. Smagorinsky, 243–75. New York: Teachers College Press.

Chapter Nine

Mapping Moffett: Tracing Theory and Practice between Teaching the Universe of Discourse *and* A Student-Centered Language Arts Curriculum

Patrick Sitzer
Teachers College, Columbia University

Even though five decades have passed since the twin publication of *A Student-Centered Language Arts Curriculum, Grades K–13* and *Teaching the Universe of Discourse*, James Moffett's ideas continue to startle his readers' conception of language arts education in exciting ways. *Student-Centered* provides the reader with engaging activities for students to enact across a wide age spectrum in their English classroom, while *Universe* elaborates the theoretical foundations of the sequences of activities. Although the two were published as companion pieces in the same year, they have seldom been examined in tandem as an exploration of Moffett's continued dialogue between theory and practice.

While the instructional "handbook" that is *Student-Centered* would go on to a total of four editions across four separate decades (1968, 1976, 1983, 1992), the theoretical *Universe* would be printed only once more (1983), and this second edition would lack any substantial revisions beyond the addition of a brief foreword from the author affirming that his theories still stood the test of time. With such an incredible scope of years across volumes, which activities did Moffett choose to update with the times, and which theoretical concepts kept his thinking grounded over these decades?

This chapter explores the material, pedagogical, and theoretical dialogue between the original twin volumes of *Student-Centered* and *Universe* and the theory-based updates across editions of *Student-Centered.* I hope that teachers and researchers alike might look to Moffett's example of creating authentic opportunities for students to engage in discourse as a method of balancing our own practice and theory. His decision to publish these two volumes—one explicitly dedicated to practice, the other to theory—provides a material reminder of the exciting work of engaging, transformative language arts teaching.

Charting a Course

I begin this chapter by first outlining the major pedagogical and theoretical features shared between *Universe* and *Student-Centered*, from their initial publication in 1968 across the decades into the early 1990s. Next, I outline a few of the major philosophical underpinnings in *Universe*, included here particularly as an introduction to readers who have not yet had the chance to read Moffett on their own. Then I highlight key evolutions between printings of *Student-Centered* with the addition of coauthor Betty Jane Wagner, including noteworthy material changes.

In this chapter's second section, I identify and expand five theoretical concepts that Moffett employs across editions of each book that inform the dialogue *between* the first editions of *Universe* and *Student-Centered* and *across* the four editions of the latter text: *selective attention*, *embryology*, *particles and structures*, *audiences and feedback*, and *abstraction*. I highlight specific activities Moffett includes as enactments of these ideas as well. My hope is to bring ideas to light that have been insufficiently attended to in previous Moffett scholarship, and in that way contribute to the growing appreciation of Moffett's revolutionary importance to the teaching of English, from the kindergarten classroom to the college seminar. My decision to focus on *Student-Centered* is also motivated by the likelihood that many scholars have studied *Universe* but have not attended to its pedagogical companion with the same dedication. At the very least, I hope that the observations posited here will encourage readers to return to Moffett's two foundational texts themselves as a paired set.

With one final note, I remind the reader that my own efforts in paying "selective attention" to these texts represents just a single reader's view of two incredible works. George Saunders writes that the best teaching is like the Buddhist principle of a finger pointing toward the glow of the moon in the night sky: the moon's beauty and glow should be the object of our attention, not the finger doing the pointing. My ideas in this chapter are designed to be that finger pointing teachers and scholars toward the glow of James Moffett's pair of texts so that they might explore his theory and practice in their own teaching.

Publishing the Universe of Discourse: 1968 to 1992

English education scholar Janet Emig reviewed *Universe* in a 1970 edition of the journal *The School Review*, noting that the material differences between *Universe* and *Student-Centered* could be considered a metaphor for the role that the theoretical and the practical played out in English classrooms: with *Universe* published as a tiny paperback and *Student-Centered* released as a handsomely large hardcover, someone at Houghton Mifflin understood that many English teachers would place higher value on the practical over the theoretical. "For when in crisis, which may be every day in today's classrooms," Emig writes, "why-to-do will yield swiftly to how-to-do" (416). Her words, like Moffett's, ring eerily true all these years later when we examine the ideas at play between these twin volumes: our English classrooms are often places too focused on practice without theoretical grounding, while our research and theory can be too distant from the day-to-day experiences of teachers, especially when they are in crisis.

The formatting, materiality, and contents of the subsequent volumes of *Student-Centered* show the vibrant dialogue between Moffett's theoretical underpinnings that he crystalized in *Universe* in 1968 and the evolving practices and accepted modes of thinking in English classrooms into the early 1990s.

Companion Volumes

Despite these immediately distinguishable material differences that Emig notes in her review and their metaphorical implications for the ways English educators value theory and practice, Moffett is explicit in the introductory pages of both *Universe* and *Student-Centered* that the two are meant to be read as companions to each other. He introduces his intentions for the twin volumes in the foreword to *Universe*:

> This book is addressed to teachers, other educators, and researchers in the many disciplines related to language learning. It comprises essays written while I was preparing *A Student-Centered Language Arts Curriculum Grades, K–13: A Handbook for Teachers*, to which it is meant to be a companion volume. (xi)

The reader encounters a similar passage at the beginning of Chapter 2 in the first edition of *Student-Centered*, titled "Principles and Purposes":

> A fuller argument of rationale [for student-centered language arts teaching] can be found in *Teaching the Universe of Discourse*, which is a theoretical companion to this book and may answer many questions unanswered here about the thinking that underlies the curriculum. (11)

Moffett's theories in *Universe* are presented across seven chapters and introduce his theoretical underpinning for the activities present across all editions of *Student-Centered*. Emig is astute in noting that the seven chapters can be read as "thematically related essays" (415), as some were published previously in varying forms.

The Bridge Between the Books: Drama

The earliest pages of *Universe* emphasize the need to break down walls between academic subjects taught across elementary and college classrooms to focus instead on teaching students how to operate the methods of abstraction. The goal, he writes, is to ultimately arrive at a curriculum that distinguishes between symbol systems (e.g., language, logic, etc.) and empirical subjects (e.g., biology, history, etc.):

> I am attempting to break up the bland surface of our traditional curriculum, whereby the Carthaginian Wars, the theorems of Euclid, irregular German Verbs, the behaviors of amoebas, and the subordination of clauses all come dead-level across the board as if they were the same kind of knowledge. The failure to distinguish between kinds and orders of knowledge amounts to a crippling epistemological error built into the very heart of the overall curriculum. The classification by "subject matters" into English, history, math, science, French, etc., implies that they are all merely contents that differ only in what they are about. (6–7)

Vygotsky and Piaget earn references as Moffett discusses hierarchies, selection, and memory, noting that the goal of education is not so much to reach a particular level of abstraction, but to "practice abstracting all along the way" (25). Students should be able to categorize a pop fly on the baseball field as a kind of parabola by better understanding the relationships between hierarchies and subclasses. The "concreteness" of a pop fly, Moffett writes, should not be read as an "antonym for abstractness," but instead as a subclass of this abstraction and an "extension of the referent in time and space" (19–20).

Moffett is also keen to specify issues of abstraction in human discourse by drawing connections between concepts of time, distance, speaker, and audience. The simplest and least abstract discourse is that of a person dialoguing with themselves in the moment, which Moffett calls "interior dialogue" or "egocentric speech" (*Universe* 40). Here is the least distance between *time* of communication—this is happening in the moment—and least *distance* between speaker and audience, both occupying the same mind. Abstraction increases proportionally when any of these distances grows. A person discoursing with a distant audience by publishing ideas in a philosophical journal to be read many years down the road is carrying on a more abstract order of communication. The third chapter of *Universe,* "Drama: What Is Happening," most clearly bridges to the activities expanded on in *Student-Centered.* Notably, an earlier version of this chapter ("Drama," 1966) was provided to one of the study groups and apparently generated great interest among the distinguished delegates at the influential Dartmouth Seminar (see Dixon) and would be the chapter that first drew future coauthor Betty Jane Wagner to Moffett's work while teaching in 1968 (Wagner and Gray 147–48).

Moffett explains that drama is "the matrix of all language activities" (*Universe* 60) and the most exciting and accessible starting point to venture into the universe of discourse. In its simplest form, Moffett's philosophy breaks down into a "ladder of abstraction" (29) that students learn to climb up and down. It connects the worlds of *what is happening*, *what happened*, and *what happens*, or drama, narrative, and a union of exposition and argumentation, respectively (48). Rather than viewing these as isolated activities, Moffett explains that the goal of a student-centered language arts classroom is to teach students to make decisions of abstraction in their own communication. Rather than being limited to simply retelling what happened in a simple narrative or telling only about "implicit, embodied ideas," the student can grow toward sharing an "explicitly formulated idea" to a wider audience (57). Similarly, they can elaborate "things past and potential" (57) beyond the here-and-now.

Because an understanding of "what is happening" comes first on Moffett's ladder of abstraction, drama-based activities are the earliest activities listed in each grade-band section of the first edition of *Student-Centered.*

Student-Centered Activities

Unlike the slim paperback of *Universe* that is split into seven sequential, essay-like chapters, the first edition of *Student-Centered* is divided into five sections—a lengthy introduction and four grade-band-organized collections of teaching activities—covering thirty-one chapters that move from the kindergarten classroom to the first-year seminar in college. While the activities across grade levels certainly grow more intricate in their output, each section follows the same movement of abstraction from the dramatic toward the expository. For example, the earliest activities listed in the "Kindergarten through Third Grade" section involve "solitary play" with "toys, bits of costume, props, and sets" (37) while the later involve creating physical books reporting on observations in nature and writing telegrams, which were limited to a set word count and needed to be addressed to a faraway correspondent for varying purposes (150). The same movement from lesser to greater abstraction follows in the "Grades Ten through Thirteen" section, moving from "memory writing" (387) to invented "epistolary stories" in which students create characters with elaborate interior lives, expressed in exchanged monologues written with a specific purpose (493).

As the grade levels increase, the activities expand in detail, but Moffett is explicit in his warning to teachers of older grades not to mistake the work of their colleagues teaching earlier grades as being somehow less complex, or their own work with secondary grades to be more self-explanatory. Moffett notes at the outset of the first edition's final section that he has

> foregone further description of classroom processes in the hope that the drama workshop, the reading-group discussion, the regular small-group discussion, teacher-led class commentary on the writing, and small-group cross-commentary on the writing have been made sufficiently clear before. . . . To take this section of the book in isolation from preceding sections would create serious misconceptions. Since the purpose of the following chapters is not to present the whole program for these grades but to present the part of it that is new, the reader who is not familiar with what has been dealt with thus far may easily conclude that the grades ten to thirteen program is lopsided and riddled with omissions. (384)

To prevent the possibility of accidentally isolating these grade bands further, Moffett would opt to revise the book's organizational structure in subsequent editions.

Expanding *Student-Centered Language Arts*

The second edition of *Student-Centered* took on not only a new organizational structure but also technically a new title, dropping the indefinite article and the word *Grades* and adding *Reading* to create *Student-Centered Language Arts and Reading, K–13: A Handbook for Teachers* (see Jonathan Marine's extensive bibliographies of Moffett's works hosted on the WAC Clearinghouse for further details on title specifics across texts). Most notable to the second edition, however, is the inclusion of Betty Jane Wagner as coauthor.

Wagner, a longtime teacher, wrote to Moffett in 1968 after encountering *Student-Centered* while teaching at National-Louis University in Chicago, previously called the National College of Education. "It was as if I'd been climbing up a steep and rocky mountainside," she wrote in 1997 about her first read of the book, "and suddenly panted my way to the summit" (Wagner and Gray 147). Struck by his deft observations about the "what is happening" aspect of drama at the heart of literacy and oracy instruction, she wrote to Moffett, who was still situated at the Harvard Graduate School of Education, and to her delight and surprise, he wrote back. This exchange kicked off a decades-long correspondence that would include Wagner's input into the development of Moffett's *Interaction*, subsequent revisions of *Student-Centered* (1976, 1983, 1992), and continued partnerships for workshops across the country as well as publications in journals (see Moffett and Wagner, "Student-Centered Reading Activities" and "What Works"). Already an accomplished educator and writer at the time of their connection, Wagner would go on to wider publication and accolades on the role of drama-based instruction in the English classroom (see Wagner, *Dorothy Heathcote*, *Effects*, and *Building*).

Student-Centered's second and third editions introduced a radically new format and visual presentation compared to the first edition's measured layout. Rather than the theory-oriented and text-heavy pages of the first edition, which looked more akin to the dense pages of *Universe*, the second and third editions include elaborate visual aids, ranging from a graph highlighting

Martin Buber's *I-it* and *I-thou* principle used to build Moffett's first-, second-, and third-person levels of abstraction (1976, 7) to the inclusion of the visually striking "Unifon alphabet" as a possible avenue of phonics instruction (416).

The fourth and final edition of *Student-Centered* in 1992 returns more closely to the form of the first edition in its more muted visual layout. Most significant to the scope of *Student-Centered* are the introductory remarks the two coauthors provide in the fourth edition's opening pages:

> When the first edition of this book appeared in 1968 with its companion volume of theory, *Teaching the Universe of Discourse*, both were regarded as radical and experimental. Since then the mainstream of language teaching has shifted in their direction so that the recommendations made then and now in this book seem to partake of current trends. (2)

Sean Walmsley notes in *English Education* that the seeming trivialization the authors ascribe to these revisions are in reality an extraordinary understatement. Rather than the new edition simply "partak[ing] of current trends," Walmsley argues that entire movements within the field of English education across the decades since original publication of the first edition unknowingly owe Moffett an extraordinary debt (121). This understatement, however, does correctly enumerate the original project's prophetic power in shifting toward whole-language and whole-discourse interaction with texts, toward intentional small-group discussions, and away from the tyranny of textbooks in the English classroom (Moffett and Wagner, 1992, 3).

"In recommending that students choose and interpret texts for themselves," the authors write, "it has fostered 'reader response' and 'response to literature'" (Moffett and Wagner, 1992, 2; see also Rosenblatt, *Reader*, *Literature*). Moffett and Wagner take pride not only in their long-range vision of English education but also that the ideas they espouse so passionately were becoming more accepted in the mainstream. While no doubt visionary at the time, Moffett's call for a more engaged English classroom is still pressing in a contemporary educational climate of high-stakes standardized tests, teacher shortages, and sinking literacy rates.

Mapping the Universe of Discourse: Key Ideas across Texts

With a clearer understanding of the publishing history and editions of *Universe* and *Student-Centered*, I now begin to explore some of the key ideas enumerated in 1968 and their dialogue across editions and decades. My decision to highlight these particular ideas represents one reader's "selective attention" to detail, and my choices are by no means exhaustive. Like Saunders's aphorism about pointing to the moon, the reader will find delight in *their own* exploration of the universe of discourse across Moffett's texts.

My "map" of this universe highlights five key ideas present throughout *Universe* and each edition of *Student-Centered*. Of particular interest to Moffett scholars is the way these same ideas are introduced, expanded, or acknowledged in his other works, such as *Points of View* (with Kenneth McElheny), *Interaction*, *Active Voice*, *Coming on Center*, *Points of Departure*, and *Detecting Growth in Language*, among many additional books and articles. Of the extraordinary range of ideas covered in *Universe*, these five resonate most clearly throughout the work and find embodiment in the activities across editions of *Student-Centered*. By enumerating them here, I hope that others might bring their own curiosity and expertise to the dialogue about their presence in Moffett's wider corpus of texts.

First, Moffett highlights the need for growth in students' natural ability to observe their own inner and outer experiences, which he calls *selective attention*. Second, Moffett provides a useful metaphor of *embryology* for the type of growth he aspired to foster in English classrooms. Third, Moffett saw the need to teach students the significance of *structures and systems* instead of isolated particles. Fourth, the author wanted teachers to understand the crucial role of *feedback* in all discourse activities, beginning with dramatic interaction. Fifth, and famously, Moffett introduces the *ladder of abstraction* across relations of speakers, subjects, space, and time. I conclude, like Moffett, by outlining hopes for an increasingly student-centered approach to classroom teaching to benefit student and teacher alike.

Selective Attention

Moffett marks as first among all principles in the universe of discourse the student's faculties of observation and attention. Students should grow not only in their powers of observation and endurance in maintaining attention, but also in their own awareness of *the factors influencing their attention.* This ability to pay "selective attention" is the foundation upon which all other activities are built, allowing students the freedom to turn both inward and out into the world. Moffett appears to posit the significance of metacognition—thinking about one's thinking—years ahead of its widespread recognition as a foundation for critical thinking (Chick).

"To abstract," Moffett writes in the first edition of *Universe*, "is to select and ignore; to value is also to give priority to some things over others, to prefer" (27). Moffett expounds over the course of *Universe* that most of what teachers might flag as student deficiency in writing, comprehension, or appreciation for authorial decisions is "traceable to poor observation" (103–4). He suggests that these skills begin with recording raw sensory data to understand that "material for writing is all around [us] at any given moment" (104). Moffett emphasizes the emotional impact this practice can have on a student: not only does this practice of internal and external attention remind the student of the wealth of material about which they can write, but it also "says plainly that his individual experience is of great worth, something to turn to, not away from" (229).

Returning to these ideas in a *Phi Delta Kappan* article in 1979, interim years between the second and third editions of *Student-Centered*, Moffett elaborates that a student's inward turnings must be the basis for any worthwhile and authentic language arts experience:

> True authoring occurs naturally to the extent that the writer is composing with raw material—that is, source content not previously abstracted and formulated by others. Teaching aimed this way would emphasize subject matter lying easily at hand within and around the writer—firsthand content such as feelings, fantasies, sensations, memories, and reflections,

> and secondhand content as drawn from interviews, stored information, and the writings of others to the extent that the writer truly re-abstracts these in his own synthesis. ("Integrity" 278)

Among many other activities that begin to foster self-awareness of senses and "attention to by tuning out" is sensory recording. To see selective attention at work, I include student work from Chapter 8, "Writing," of *Student-Centered*'s third edition that Moffett and Wagner share as exemplary despite its deceiving simplicity. Consider the authenticity of voice and detail included in this elementary student's writing titled "My Back Yard":

> It sure sounds funny how the wind goes through the trees. The smell of flowers blooming. The red pail laying in the grass. Our rope swaying across the air as if it was going somewhere. The wheel barrel like a ox pulls leaves. Trees are having buds. It's a beautiful night. The fence bending back in the wind. Our shed standing still there. I can hear the rabbits eating. I can hear the toad communicait. I can see our dog. I heared a bark from the yard. Our swing is trying to keep its balance. (1976, 201)

Starting even in the early grades, becoming aware of one's own choices in attention allows students to expand this view to the texts they read and to have a go at "true" authorship. It also allows them to realize that they can hold themselves in the same high regard they give to "professional" authors. "When we behave like an author," Moffett posits in *Universe*, "we pay more attention" to decisions of style and detail. "When we act as a reader," he notes, "we need to know how such decisions are made" (146–47). In a few short lines, this student has captured some beautiful raw material from their life. Imagine the potential for continued writing and conversation that could be expanded from this short work.

Selective attention, then, becomes the bedrock for all student-centered activities in the language arts classroom invested in exploring the universe of discourse. It is a simultaneous recognition of the value of students' lived experiences and the bounty that it can yield for writing, speaking, and reading.

Students must first make decisions about what to include and what to ignore before they can begin to expand their discourse. Next, Moffett creates a central metaphor for student development grounded in his extensive reading of Piaget.

Embryology as a Model for Growth

With selective attention established as the first key concept across Moffett's texts, his explanation of *embryology* emerges as the second. The analogy of an embryo is most fully elaborated throughout *Universe,* but its message is manifested implicitly in the headnotes to each successive section throughout the first edition of *Student-Centered*, placed at the outset of the respective grade-band sections that organize the first edition of the book. Moffett explains in these notes that the activities presented in later chapters are not so much new as they are growing more specific and detailed in one direction (inward) and more unified as a whole in the other (outward). This presence throughout both texts establishes the metaphor as a central piece of Moffett's methodology. Moffett wanted teachers to understand that growth in English subsumed lower levels of learning as a student climbed higher on the ladder of abstraction. To provide a visual aid, the second edition (1976) of *Student-Centered* contains a detailed diagram of a human embryo's development in its first chapter (Moffett and Wagner 4).

Moffett begins by drawing attention to the growth of a single cell into a complex organism by continuously "differentiating itself into specialized parts at the same time that it maintains integrity by continually interrelating these parts" (*Universe* 29). In one direction, the being grows inward in differentiation and internal complexity. In the other, the being moves outward toward external relationship and continuous integration with the outside world. Moffett cites Piaget to crystallize the metaphor:

> [T]he self enlarges, assimilating the world to itself and accommodating itself to the world, as Piaget puts it. . . . In moving outward from himself, the child becomes more himself. The teacher's art is to move with this movement, a subtle act

> possible only if he shifts his gaze from the subject to the learner, for the subject is in the learner. (59)

The metaphor captures not only student growth but also the hope for a structure of teaching English. In his headnotes to section four of the first edition of *Student-Centered*, Moffett qualifies this operating belief of continuous growth by clarifying that the assignments spelled out for older grades have been explicitly developed as higher abstractions of assignments for kindergarten through grade 9 (Moffett, *Student-Centered* 384). He hopes that the teachers of older students have taken the time to understand that their students and assignments have grown in inward complexity and outward integration with the world. "The reader who is not familiar with [the elementary grade chapters]," Moffett writes, "may easily conclude that the grades ten to thirteen program is lopsided and riddled with omissions" (384). The teacher of more developed students must understand and reference the work their students completed earlier in their development to make sense of what they complete in the higher grades.

To see this metaphor at work, I include details from the final section of the first edition of *Student-Centered*, which elaborates activities for "Grades Ten through Thirteen," as a comparison to the example of elementary student sensory writing presented earlier. The exercise is the "Reporter at Large" assignment for high school students, modeled on the *New Yorker*'s blend of reportage, observational notes, and interview excerpts. This would eventually be developed by Bay Area educator and National Writing Project contributor Ruby Bernstein and become known as the "Saturation Report" (Bernstein et al.). The assignment reads as follows:

> Go visit some place of business or other enterprise, talk with people there, watch its operation, take notes, then write an account of the visit afterwards. Use your narrative to convey a lot of information about the enterprise, to catch the atmosphere of the place, and to show what the people there are like. (Moffett, *Student-Centered* 422)

Moffett adds that the combination of the student's experience of receiving "some data directly through his senses" and other data in a verbal interview forces the student to "digest all this and fuse the different modes of drama, narrative, and exposition into a whole piece of reportage" (*Student-Centered* 422–23). Note too that the *output* of telling has grown in abstraction from the first student's pleasant, poem-like account of their backyard: students must model their writing on that of a major publication to be read widely by an intelligent audience. But without practice first attending to the wind in the trees, the red pails in the grass, and the smell of flowers blooming, how can we expect to teach students to capture the spirit of a bustling business at work? Additionally important is the growing willingness to bring students out into the world beyond the classroom and have them situate themselves within it.

For Moffett the goal of student growth out into the world must first happen by teaching students to look inward into themselves. Just like the embryo grows to be more of a complex whole by growing as a more intricate collection of differentiated parts, our students' communication in the English classroom must grow in intricacy by expanding out into the world. Rather than abandon or ignore the work of earlier academic experiences, the engaging teacher must "move with the movement" and give students the chance to work with the raw material of their own lives. The third key concept to explore across *Universe* and *Student-Centered* builds on the metaphor of an embryo to caution teachers against the false assumption that movement from *small* to *large* is synonymous with *simple* to *complex*.

Particles and Structures

Like the nuanced understanding of an embryo's growth inward and outward, Moffett's third resounding theory is a caution against teaching through the "particle approach" and instead toward embedding learning within authentic structures. Smallness, he explains, does not equate with simplicity. Whether one looks at an infant or an adult, a short sentence or a paragraph, a brief exercise in class or a lengthy project, Moffett is wary of taking a small "particle" and isolating it from its necessary context or the wider picture of its "superstructure" (*Universe* 5). This precise language is employed years later in the introductory note to the fourth edition of *Student-Centered*, in which Moffett and Wagner note the growing acceptance among English pedagogies of using "whole, authentic speech acts or texts, not exercises with particles" (2). We can trace an explanation of this concept back to the earliest pages of the original editions of both texts.

First, Moffett qualifies in the first edition of *Universe* the importance of recognizing that *anything* can be considered a *system* of relations (2). A tree is a system of roots, branches, and leaves. A sentence may be small, but it is a relation of words and the ideas they represent, as well as a relation to other sentences in a paragraph, chapter, or novel. He cautions that the move from "little particle to big particle is not even an order of simple to complex" because size is not synonymous with complexity. "What does count," he writes, "is that, as context for the next smallest, each of these structures governs everything of significance in the one below" (5).

Second, Moffett clarifies this need to understand particles as parts of a wider substructure as key to recognizing the fullness and richness of the universe of discourse each child brings with them to school. A student's language, preferences, and reading comprehension "will always stand in some ratio to what an individual has done, heard, seen, and felt in his personal life" (*Universe* 19). This manifests in Moffett's work most clearly in the desire to shift writing assignments toward greater personal connection and authentic connection to life outside the classroom and away from a traditional or "corrective" model of teaching writing or texts that have been artificially manufactured for the classroom.

Nowhere is Moffett as unequivocal about moving away from particles as when writing about grammar exercises. A lengthy polemic against grammar takes up the entirety of Chapter 5 of *Universe*, and warnings about isolated grammar instruction appear in all four editions of *Student-Centered*. As one set of alternatives, Moffett and Wagner suggest that students play with the idea of transcribing actual dialogue in short verbal exchanges or when writing stage directions (see "Taking Dictation" in Moffett's first edition and "Actual and Invented Dialogue" in Moffett and Wagner's second through fourth editions). In a section titled "Grammar" in an appendix of the third edition of *Student-Centered* (1983), the authors caveat that before a teacher reads any further in the hopes of gleaning some quick resources, they should first read eight different sections of headnotes earlier in the book and try six different language-based activities that have more to do with dramatic play and recorded dialogue than they do with worksheets or corrective sentences. Moffett cautions in one of the final sections of *Universe* against

> the old saw about having to crawl before you can walk. But crawling is an authentic form of locomotion in its own right, not merely a component or sub-skill of walking. For the learner, basics are not the small-focus technical things but broad things like meaning and motivation, purpose and point, which are precisely what are missing from exercises. An exercise, by my definition, is any piece of writing practiced only in schools—that is, an assignment that stipulates arbitrary limits that leave the writer with no real relationships between him and a subject and an audience. I would not ask a student to write anything other than an authentic discourse, because the learning process proceeds from intent and content down to the contemplation of technical points, not the other way. (205)

Moffett's key concepts thus far have all been carefully related to the idea that language arts instruction must be intimately related to the lived experiences of the students. By validating students' experiences when teaching them to pay selective attention to their lives, students can begin to grow more differentiated and complex while simultaneously becoming a more unified whole of a person. Just as we should not isolate one aspect of a student's life from another if we are to truly understand them, the same must be said of the ways we teach students about language. Our priority must be on "meaning and motivation, purpose and point." The fourth key concept across Moffett's works expands on how we teach students to gather and integrate feedback into their writing.

Active Discourse, Audience, and Feedback

Moffett and Wagner's ideas come to life in the myriad activities, games, and dramas they propose across editions of *Student-Centered*. These fun—if not quirky and unorthodox, even by today's standards—activities were rooted in Moffett's deep reading in child development and what he believed was a central element to student growth: feedback. Like growth in metacognitive awareness of attention, Moffett is chiefly concerned with student growth in toggling between activities in which they are actively receiving input and generating their own output. These activities, Moffett writes—with a nod to Vygotsky—are two sides of the same coin of growth in language. The key to participating in active discourse, then, is feedback.

Nearly every writing activity across all four editions of *Student-Centered* necessarily involves sharing with peers, including in the youngest grades. Moffett cites psychologist Bruno Bettelheim when speaking of the human necessity for feedback in life, not simply in the classroom. Humans lose the willingness to communicate needs if those needs are not met with action, Bettelheim writes, from the earliest cries of hunger to a "loving gesture that goes unanswered" as an adult (Moffett, *Universe* 203, first edition). More important, a baby's cry must be met with more than sympathy: it must be met with food. Moffett centralizes Bettelheim to rally teachers to rethink the way feedback is provided not just at the end of the learning process but consistently throughout—namely, the students providing feedback for one another.

For example, when providing guidance on teaching students to enact stories as dramatic re-creations in *Student-Centered*'s third edition, Moffett and Wagner outline the student-centered decision-making process. After a teacher reads a story to the students, students make decisions about "when and where the story takes place, which character each of them is to play, [and] what they are going to be doing as the scene begins" (110). Next, students improvise the parts in small groups without needing to refer to the original text and further "change events" or "make up different endings" to their liking. Once students have settled on a version they like, they have the opportunity to perform for an audience. Not only have students been able to adapt a story in a way that interests them, but they have also blended "the printed word to the physical world of behavior and sharpen[ed] reading comprehension by translating the subject" into an entirely new format (111).

Moffett encourages teachers to shift their thinking of drama as highly staged class plays to these types of smaller moments of intimate creation and communication of a student to themself or to a small group of classmates. The associations of overly formalized plays and musicals traditionally performed in school are a "hindrance," he writes, because of the increased distance between peers and discourse participants (*Student-Centered* 35). Consider Moffett's suggested activity "Enacting without Scripts" in Chapter 11 of the first edition and the multitude of communicative tasks embedded within the short exercise:

> Dialogue enlarges considerably the range of material that can be acted out. This can include the majority of selections children read, not only folk and children's literature, but excerpts from geography and social studies. A lot of their own writing can be dramatized, and the recording of live conversations . . . will, in fact, supply actual play scripts. The procedure is the same as for pantomime and for enactment in the lower grades: the groups choose the material (separately or as a class), discuss adaptation and roughly plan the action, act out with no spectators, rotate roles, and discuss and change successive versions. (169)

Wagner's expertise in using drama in the classroom was no doubt an excellent addition to the second, third, and fourth editions of *Student-Centered,* though drama is considered a means toward growth in discourse, not an end. As later activities in "speaking out," "becoming literate," and "writing down" would highlight, Moffett was most interested in "honest student-to-student conversation." The teacher's job, then, is to help students "learn from each other" (*Universe* 95) through discourse and feedback.

While these examples of active feedback are readily illustrated in student dramas, the same spirit informs students' writing and speaking skills. Participating in the push and pull of an audience provides students with authentic chances to learn about discourse, actually "doing" discourse instead of just talking about it. As the final key concept illustrates, Moffett remains committed to ensuring that students have abundant opportunities to grow as readers, writers, actors, and speakers who are invested in dialogue with their lived experiences.

Abstraction

Teaching students to abstract follows the same pattern of embryonic growth from the earlier theories highlighted in this chapter: we cannot simply jump to teaching students to abstract, but must start with the prior and foundationally important ability to pay attention.

Moffett's efforts at teaching his ladder of abstraction are well documented in his works *Points of View* (with McElheny), *Points of Departure,* and *Drama: What Is Happening.* Like those other works, the first three editions of *Student-Centered* are filled with rich samples of student writing collected over years of managing workshops in schools. Moffett and Wagner would later remove these exemplars from the fourth edition, which is the most sparsely populated with student exemplars, including them instead in editions of Moffett's *Active Voice.* In this fourth edition, Moffett and Wagner welcomed the "opportunity to shorten a work that by its very integrative nature ran to an unusual length" by directing teachers to other complementary works (2).

Those Moffett scholars who have not ventured deep into *Student-Centered* will be delighted to hear their own students' voices in those students who traveled into Moffett's universe decades ago. In the first edition of *Student-Centered*, Moffett outlines a seemingly simple exercise called "Idea Writing" to invite increasing abstraction from students, notably *after* they have spent time in dialogue and feeding back to one another. Moffett elaborates:

> The best stimulus is probably the spin-off from discussion and reading. The results are all sorts of explicit assertion of opinions, attitudes, wishes, and ideas that are neither fictional nor factual. Whether cast in prose or in poetry, they constitute what is

> really a personal essay, though the appellation seems stuffy and certainly need not be used in class. When group concentration on a subject reaches a peak of intensity, and everyone has more to say, the teacher sends them to paper, where in a sense they continue the discussion in written monologue. (245)

Note the potential for abstraction already present: students are discussing and feeding back to each other about a relevant and engaging topic, adjusting their own understandings based on those of others. The teacher's role is simply to guide the process instead of the content. Moffett included the excerpt below from a sixth grader in Harlem who discusses living conditions and inequality in her neighborhood. Like all student writing samples across *Student-Centered,* Moffett includes the student's uncorrected spelling and usage:

> If I could change my block I would stand on Madison Ave and throw nothing but Teargas in it. I would have all the people I liked to get out of the block and then I would become very tall and have big hands and with my big hands I would take all of the narcartic people and pick them up with my hand and throw them in the nearest river and oceans. I would go to some of those old smart alic cops and throw them in the Ocians and Rivers too. I would let the people I like move into the projects so they could tell their friends that they live in a decent block. If I could do this you would never see 117th st again. (245)

The depth and breadth of this student's lived experience are immediately evident, and the layers included in a relatively short piece of writing are extraordinary: imaginative narrative ("I would become very tall and have big hands"), social commentary ("all of the narcartic people"), and acute sense of (in)justice ("those old smart alic cops"). The student is shifting between *what is happening*—her neighborhood in Harlem is equally plagued by "smart alic" police, drug addicts, and cramped housing—and an imagination toward *what happens,* or *what can happen,* if this student were given the chance to make her neighborhood better. Here we have a profound piece of writing in an inimitable student voice. What could better represent Moffett's aims for learning to play "the whole symbolic scale" (*Universe* 28) of the universe of discourse than a student working to change the world for the better? This embryonic writing, like the embryonic elementary student author, contains multitudes.

Chapter 22 in the first edition of *Student-Centered* centers on grades 7 through 9, where students have already become well-versed in moving up and down the ladder of abstraction. After students become familiar with monologue and dialogue, Moffett encourages teachers to have students begin writing their own monologues, being conscious of the distance relation of time and space between events and speakers. An eighth grader at the Brooks Academy Summer School for students composed this monologue titled "Hindsight":

> I wasn't the one that had the cigarette, Sister Marie; this is how it happened. I was out of the class room on an errand and I saw Joe standing in the doorway of the janitor's closet. I walked over to him and asked, "What are you doing?" He replied "Having a cigarette—want one?" I remembered how much trouble the eighth graders who smoked last year got into, and I wasn't ready to go to the Pastor. "No", I answered, "I don't like to smoke in the morning." I said that, Sister, so that he wouldn't think I didn't know how to smoke. He then said, "Oh, you're just a chicken and you're just teacher's pet!" I wasn't going to be called "Teacher's pet" for anything in the world, so I grabbed the matches and cigarettes out of his hands and began to light my own. That's when you came around the corner, Sister. Gee, I really am sorry. I was only trying to act, "big", I guess. (326)

I know few English teachers who would not find immense delight in the wit and complexity of this short piece. The dynamism of the relations involved—the guilty party pleading before the figure of a demanding Sister Marie, Joe the class-skipping cigarette smoker, the dripping contrition of tone—make the piece endlessly entertaining and rich for further discourse. Already the writer is moving further along the ladder of abstraction toward the world of "big" people: the piece successfully toggles between present and past action in reporting "how it happened" and the truly abstract idea that explains the student's action—"I was only trying to act big." Across editions of *Student-Centered,* Moffett and Wagner encourage teachers to think of these kinds of small writings as potential for what they call "chain-reaction assignments" in which one written assignment is adapted into another (Moffett,

Universe 200). "This amounts to a lot of rewriting," Moffett qualifies, giving students "a whole new tack under the influence of suggestions from other students (200).

These two student exemplars are particularly illustrative because of their inherent value *and* their incredible potential for further abstraction, discussion, and writing. Each stems from some lived experience of the student and could be taken in nearly limitless directions: the sixth grader in Harlem could continue with an imaginative narrative of a kindly giant working to clear the neighborhood of crooked police and squalor just as much as she could pen an impassioned letter to a city councilperson. The accused eighth grader could continue abstracting the perspective of her own voice by adding time and distance from the event, or she could expand the cast of characters involved in her plea to Sister Marie. Teachers of middle school will not find it difficult to imagine the glee of eighth graders getting the chance to dramatize this fiction for an audience of their peers.

Each student author was respected for the decisions of attention they made, and the writing is acknowledged as valuable in its own right. Like the growing embryo, each piece can continue to move inward in specificity and differentiation while growing outward to integration with the wider world. It is at once already complex and full of voices *and* can be further abstracted down the line.

Hopes for a Student-Centered Language Arts

With a better understanding of some of Moffett's important concepts elaborated across editions of *Teaching the Universe of Discourse* and *A Student-Centered Language Arts*, how are Moffett's ideas still relevant for our English classrooms today?

As in his lengthy chapter in the first edition of *Universe* dedicated to meticulously disproving the "blandly technical and humanly naïve" (157) approaches to teaching grammar, usage, and mechanics with the particle approach, Moffett was appalled by the boring and disconnected "exercises" he found in English classrooms. From the outset of the twin projects of *Universe* and *Student-Centered*, he wanted to revitalize the teaching of English for the purpose of bringing students into deeper contact with themselves so that they could be in better contact with the world around them. The spectrum of discourse, he explains, "is about both art and life" in tracking a move outward from the center of the self (*Student-Centered* 489).

Moffett's own polemics against textbooks, disconnected writing assignments, and canned sample reading would eventually engender *Interaction* and the continuation of his body of work across decades in volumes like *Active Voice* and *Coming on Center*. By the time Moffett published *The Universal Schoolhouse* in 1994, he would call for the abolition of traditional school as we know it because of its generational inability to enact the practices for which he had dedicated his career. His now decades-old hopes for an increase in more human approaches to teaching and learning in language arts classrooms remain pressing in our present day. Many of Moffett's concerns and hopes were subsequently taken up by English education scholar Arthur Applebee, whose *Tradition and Reform in the Teaching of English* elaborated a range of needs, such as broadening the types of speaking and texts we consider important in English classrooms and rethinking the ways we teach educators to teach reading and writing skills divorced from authentic peer feedback (250).

Moffett was disheartened that much of English education had become distracted by the "fingers"—textbooks, workbooks, dummy sentences, grammar drills, and inauthentic exchanges between teacher and student—meant originally to only do the pointing to the "art and life" that he wanted all students to experience. He would spend his career dedicated to the ideas originally laid out in these twin texts, establishing a dialogue of theory and practice that works toward a more authentic language arts education.

By pointing my own fingers at the companionship of *Teaching the Universe of Discourse* and *A Student-Centered Language Arts* and engaging in my own dialogue with Moffett's theory and practice, I hope my process of discovery and learning will encourage readers to do the same for themselves, entering into their own dialogue with their praxis and Moffett's thinking. My own fingers are simply pointing to moments within these twin texts that resonated with the "hubbub of voices" (Moffett,

Universe 147) within my own experience—those of the educator, the writer, and the reader. I hope that in making some of these important movements within the texts more visible, others interested in Moffett's work might make even more connections. The bright moon of Moffett's project can still provide us useful—and beautiful—guidance along the continuing path of English education for years to come. There is little doubt he would have been excited to join us along the way.

Works Cited

Applebee, Arthur N. *Tradition and Reform in the Teaching of English: A History*. National Council of Teachers of English, 1974.

Bernstein, Ruby, et al. "NWP Speaks: 30 Years of Writing Project Voices." *The Voice*, vol. 9, no. 4, 2004, pp. 8–9.

Chick, Nancy. (2013). "Metacognition." *Vanderbilt University Center for Teaching,* 2013, https://cft.vanderbilt.edu/guides-sub-pages/metacognition/.

Dixon, John. *Growth through English: A Report Based on the Dartmouth Seminar, 1966*. 2nd ed., Oxford UP, 1966.

Emig, Janet. Review of *Teaching the Universe of Discourse*. *The School Review*, vol. 78, no. 3, 1970, pp. 415–22.

Marine, Jonathan M. "A Bibliography of James Moffett." *WAC Clearinghouse*, 2023, https://wac.colostate.edu/books/landmarks/moffett/bib/.

———. "A Selective Bibliography of Influential Works on James Moffett." *WAC Clearinghouse*, https://wac.colostate.edu/books/landmarks/moffett/selective-bib/.

Moffett, James. *Active Voice: A Writing Program Across the Curriculum*. Boynton-Cook, 1981.

———. *Coming on Center: English Education in Evolution*. Boynton-Cook, 1981.

———. *Detecting Growth in Language*. Boynton/Cook, 1992.

———. "Drama in English Teaching." Dartmouth Study Group Paper No. 2, *Proceedings of the Anglo-American Conference on the Teaching and Learning of English*, 1966.

———. *Drama: What Is Happening.* National Council of Teachers of English, 1967.

———. "Integrity in the Teaching of Writing." *Phi Delta Kappan*, vol. 61, no. 4, 1979, pp. 276–79.

———, editor. *Interaction: A Student-Centered Language Arts and Reading Program, K–12.* Houghton Mifflin, 1973.

———, editor. *Points of Departure: An Anthology of Nonfiction.* Signet, 1985.

———. *A Student-Centered Language Arts Curriculum, Grades K–13: A Handbook for Teachers.* Houghton Mifflin, 1968.

———. *Teaching the Universe of Discourse.* Houghton Mifflin, 1968.

———. *Teaching the Universe of Discourse.* Rpt. ed., Houghton Mifflin, 1983.

———. *The Universal Schoolhouse: Spiritual Awakening through Education.* Jossey-Bass, 1994.

Moffett, James, and Kenneth R. McElheny, editors. *Points of View: An Anthology of Short Stories.* New American Library, 1966.

Moffett, James, and Betty Jane Wagner. *Student-Centered Language Arts and Reading, K–13: A Handbook for Teachers.* 2nd ed., Houghton Mifflin, 1976.

———. *Student-Centered Language Arts and Reading, K–13: A Handbook for Teachers.* 3rd ed., Houghton Mifflin, 1983.

———. *Student-Centered Language Arts, K–12.* 4th ed., Boynton Cook, 1992.

———. "Student-Centered Reading Activities." *English Journal*, vol. 80, no. 6, 1991, pp. 70–73.

———. "What Works Is Play." *Language Arts*, vol. 70, no. 1, 1993, pp. 32–36.

Rosenblatt, Louise M. *Literature as Exploration.* 5th ed., Modern Language Association, 1995.

———. *The Reader, the Text, the Poem.* Southern Illinois UP, 1978.

Saunders, George. *A Swim in a Pond in the Rain: In Which Four Russians Give a Master Class on Writing, Reading, and Life.* Random House, 2021.

Wagner, Betty Jane, editor. *Building Moral Communities through Educational Drama*. Ablex, 1999.

———. *Dorothy Heathcote: Drama as a Learning Medium*. National Education Association, 1976.

———. *The Effects of Role Playing on Written Persuasion: An Age and Channel Comparison of Fourth and Eighth Graders*. Unpublished doctoral dissertation, University of Illinois at Chicago, 1986.

Wagner, Betty Jane, and Jim Gray. "Reflective Tributes to James Moffett'." *English Education*, vol. 29, no. 2, 1997, pp. 147–50.

Walmsley, Sean A. "James Moffett Reconsidered: Ahead of His Time, Again?" *English Education*, vol. 25, no. 2, 1993, pp. 120–27.

Chapter Ten

Reading and Rereading Moffett on Early Reading: An Individual and Cultural History

Ruth Nathan

When I received the call for proposals (CFP) for a book that would recognize and celebrate James Moffett's legacy, my own story—one that covers half a century of transactions with Moffett's writing and with Moffett himself—came immediately to mind. The focus of the story I'm going to tell is markedly narrow—Moffett's thoughts on how young children should be enabled and encouraged to read and write words early in their lives (decode and transcribe or spell). That focus is expanded to some degree by my account of how Moffett's thoughts influenced me personally and professionally. And my narrative expands even wider as I show how his position on early reading put him in opposition to what had become the popular and standard approach in elementary education at the time and had to be seen as inconsistent with his own very advanced thinking about teaching the English language arts across the grades. Yet Moffett modestly and bravely proposed that teaching phonics, the specific ways that letters represent sounds within words, was crucial to early reading instruction, while almost all proponents of progressive education encouraged learners to use prior context and a few sound–symbol correspondences to hypothesize the word in question. However, the story that follows is not merely one of my admiration for Moffett, nor merely of my own history of reading and rereading Moffett, but of my development as a teacher of reading, aided by Moffett and sometimes troubled by Moffett, all in the context of an entire profession at war with itself throughout and beyond my own and Moffett's lifetime.

Off to School

June 1967–Spring 1968

It is June 1967. I am about to complete my degree as a teacher and begin my first job in a small Iowa town. I am scared. Student teaching had been a frightful experience, mostly helping the teacher teach the Scott Foresman spelling workbook. Flash forward to the second Monday in September, my first day as a schoolteacher. Thirty-two fourth graders are lined up outside Room 14. I'm standing in the doorway with a smile, gripping a clipboard to keep my hands from shaking. The children are quiet, well behaved, and well fed, a situation almost any teacher would deeply appreciate. As the bell rings, I open the door and they flood in. I've already put their names on their desks, which are arranged in columns and rows. I suppose the thing that sets my nerves on edge is that I don't know which seven of these thirty-two children are either nonreaders or marginal readers. I'd read about them the week before school started. My unpreparedness to support less-skilled readers has deep roots, some related to my habits as a young child: I hadn't been much of a reader. But some of my unpreparedness relates to my college education, which offered me precious little in the way of how to teach reading, let alone to struggling readers. In college the one class on reading instruction my peers and I had was devoted to learning how to use basal readers (anthologies of literature passages, one per grade level) and their accompanying teacher's manual. We read several classroom management books, which were of no help since our teaching schemata weren't highly developed, and nothing specific about teaching reading in groups, pairs, or the whole class. Just the standard three groups by skill level.

I struggled that first year over those seven children, as one can imagine, but my struggles were complex. In addition to feeling lost as a reading teacher, I had remembered the feeling of loving a book—even if I hadn't read a lot as a kid: *White Fang*, a favorite, and the whole Nancy Drew series. In my 1967 classroom, there were no books, just three anthologies arranged by skill level containing small literary excerpts, at times rewritten to control vocabulary difficulty. There was no such thing as reading a whole book in class back then, either together or in small groups. By the end of that first year, I felt a deep, ever-expanding hole in my gut.

Summer 1968

The summer of 1968 changed things; I read two crucial books that coalesced in my mind to offer educated perspectives on teaching reading, as well as how I might change my classroom environment into a more vibrant place, the one I used to imagine. The books were Jean Chall's *Learning to Read: The Great Debate* and the book whose author is the principal subject of this chapter, James Moffett's *A Student-Centered Language Arts Curriculum, Grades K–13: A Handbook for Teachers* (*SCLAC*). The Chall book gave me insight into what I probably had to do regarding my struggling readers: get a better handle on how the English cipher, good old sound–symbol correspondence, actually works and how these correspondences might be effectively taught. (Comprehension, I had realized, wasn't the major hurdle, at least at the time in my particular classroom.) Moffett's *SCLAC* also attended to this issue, but also opened my eyes to the deeper and equally important need for children to interact with one another throughout the day. Though much of this chapter focuses on Moffett's interest in and recommendations for teaching children to unlock the alphabetic code through explicit and systematic phonics, I also want to acknowledge how this icon of the profession of English, whose teaching experience was entirely at the secondary and college levels, served as a reliable and inspiring guide for me as a fledgling teacher of all the English language arts to early elementary children. So I present here a selection of passages from Moffett's 1968 edition of *SCLAC* that at the start of my teaching career helped me discover the kind of teacher I hoped to become, passages that even today show us how progressive and even radical Moffett was in 1968 and how prophetically radical he remains more than half a century later:

> Most profoundly considered, a course of language learning is a course in thinking. A writing assignment, for example, is a thinking assignment. (11)

This was radical in the sense that most writing assignments were meant to answer teacher questions and were graded. The idea that children should write to think (and not be graded on this writing) was totally new.

> What a student needs most of all is to perceive how he is using language and how he might use it. What this requires is awareness, not information. (11)

Radical? Yes, in the sense that most teachers during that time were told to inform students about proper language use and grammar and to point out syntactic errors to be corrected (with a red pencil).

> The only way, short of tutorial, to provide individual students enough language experience and feedback is to develop small-group interaction into a sensitive learning method. (12)

Again, radical because classrooms were expected to be fairly quiet, and, for the most part, it was fully assumed that learning derived from the teacher, not from students' peers.

> A good group process provides the external model for the inner processes it will foster. (12)

This point is related to the one above. Moffett felt that as children speak with one another about their writing or their interpretative response to literature, they would be "aided by practical perceptions about what [they] and others are doing when they speak and write, not generalization about what people regularly do with language or formulated advice about what they ought to do with it" (11–12). For example, when students listen to each other's work they question clarity, reasoning, development/order, and so on. These sorts of questions from others have the potential to move inward so that students might think about these things as they review their own work.

Reading these passages, pondering them, I realized I could walk a new path, and I began dreaming about how Moffett's principles and purposes might shape my approach to teaching. I might try the idea of using "thinking journals," which I had also read about recently in books on writing to learn. I might think creatively about how to teach everything from grammar and punctuation to ways to bring the mathematical constant, pi, to life. Perhaps we'd turn round tables on end, roll them, and on our own figure out the ratio of its circumference to its diameter. Writing workshops and literature circles might be the group processes that Moffett had spoken of, processes that provide the "external model for the inner processes it will foster." Could I do these things?

For a teacher who felt trapped in her own skin, the skin encouraged to develop by her college instructors, and wrapped tightly by her school administration, this was the fresh air that would set me on a path that served me well for the next fifty years, a path quite different from that of the teacher who stood in the doorway of Room 14 just a few months prior.

The Historical Context: A Century and a Half of Reading Wars

As I suggested earlier, Moffett took a great risk in advancing his highly traditional and extremely conservative thoughts on learning to read in his progressive and influential textbook for teachers, *A Student-Centered Language Arts Curriculum, Grades K–13,* a volume widely celebrated as one of the most original presentations of an English language arts curriculum to surface in the twentieth century (Emig). The history I outline in this section sets the stage for our understanding of Moffett's choice to support an early, explicit, and systematic approach to teaching children to decode words from print—a phonics approach—as opposed to other ways to begin teaching the decoding process, for example, by using memorized whole words, learning new words through analogy to words known, or using dictated sentences. I want to emphasize here that he saw the phonics approach as the best method for *beginning* instruction in reading. He took no issue with the use of more progressive strategies as soon as a child had learned to apply the alphabetical principle in decoding words. All the other approaches to teaching young children to read are fine and have been found reliable, he asserted, as long as they don't get in the way of the early, explicit, systematic teaching of phonics. In this assertion, he enlisted himself into a long and contentious (and possibly endless) history, often characterized as warfare, over the best approaches to teaching children the foundational literacy skill of reading.

Competing Traditions in the Teaching of Phonics

In colonial times, American settlers taught reading (as had been done since the Middle Ages in England) by using what was known as the "hornbook," which looked like a rectangular paddle with a handle to be held in one hand, a sheet of paper pasted to one side where the letters of the alphabet (in upper- and lowercase) were prominently printed, along with the Lord's Prayer and other pieties, as well as a syllabarium, which consisted of printed syllables for students to learn: *ma, me, mi, mo, mu, pa, pi, po, pu,* etc. (Britannica). The objective of the hornbook was to initiate children into the first phase of reading by having them learn to recognize letters and the sounds of simple combinations of letters in the form of syllables and simple words (Hofstra). Reading aloud from the hornbook was a widely employed method of formal instruction in reading in colonial days and remained in use in the new republic, though many readers also came into use, including the *New England Psalter*, the *New England Primer,* Noah Webster's *American Spelling Book*, the McGuffy Readers, and others. Yet all were based on some sort of code-oriented—alphabetic or phonic—approach to beginning reading, whereby pupils first learned the names and sounds of the letters of the alphabet and then how to pronounce small syllables and words; next they would move on to memorizing word spellings (Smith 32–34). All of these methods emphasized phonics and constituted, at a fairly primitive level, what can be called a code-emphasis approach.

However, a new and soon commanding tradition for teaching reading emerged in the mid-1800s to challenge and then replace, for most teachers, the code-emphasis approach. The new method was invented and introduced to the teaching profession by the famously eloquent and politically powerful educational leader Horace Mann. Mann, who had never been a teacher himself, was in the spotlight as secretary of education in Massachusetts and was determined to find a better way to teach reading than what he considered to be the overly strict and tedious method in common use. After observing German students learning to read using a "whole-word/look-say" approach, which emphasized meaning, he condemned the American alphabetic methods, which he derisively called "abecedarian" (Aaron et al. 59), and insisted that the German approach of skipping the boring work of analyzing letters as sounds and moving immediately to offering meaningful encounters with words and meanings, all with the aid of interestingly illustrated books, was far more stimulating for children and more consistent with his broader progressive educational agenda (Meltzer).

The response to Mann was swift and highly critical. Schoolmasters and leading educators were incredulous. Teachers couldn't accept the whole-word/look-say approach and were convinced (appropriately) that Mann "didn't understand the difference between letter names and letter sounds. Furthermore, teachers who had tried his system testified that although children could successfully learn a word in context, they were unable to recognize it later in another context" (Aaron et al. 59).

While several research-based books and scientific studies of early reading began to appear in the early twentieth century, all claiming to provide reliable data to resolve the reading debate with the authority of science, most of those studies (completed between 1908 and 1921) were poorly designed and employed methods of statistical analysis that failed to account adequately for independent variables. Which is not to say they were worthless, but that quantitative research methods and statistical procedures were still in an early stage of development and lacked even the contested authority they would later acquire (Aaron et al. 61). Nevertheless, these studies introduced a line of research and research methods that would become considerably more authoritative by the middle of the century.

In the meantime, in spite of the pushback from many reading specialists and early elementary grade teachers to the "progressive" ideas of Mann and others advocating a look-say method, the look-say approach to initial comprehension became the dominant mode of beginning reading instruction by the second quarter of the twentieth century. Words were introduced through meaning first—to be recognized holistically by sight. As Marilyn Adams describes it, "Phonics was relegated to the position of an ancillary tool; it was to be introduced gradually, invoked sparingly, and exercised only in coordination with the meaning-bearing dimensions of text" (23). Demonstration schools at The University of Chicago and Columbia University employed the same method and added significantly to its orthodox status and the number of its adherents, ignoring the more balanced methods that had been developed, even by celebrated progressive educators like Francis Wayland Parker, who in the early years of the twentieth century advocated a method of teaching reading that entailed, in addition to learning whole words, attending to pronunciation phoneme by phoneme, learning new words through analogy, and receiving explicit instruction in letter-sound relationships (DiObilda and Petrillo 122, 124, 129–30).

Thus, the "progressive" view of reading, initiated through the persuasive political authority of the largely uninformed and merely impressionable Horace Mann, continued to dominate American practice in the teaching of reading until public schools in the early 1950s came under a broad attack from a number of sources for their lack of intellectual rigor and their increasingly obvious failure to ensure the literacy of all students. The specific failure of schools to teach reading was brought most dramatically to public attention by the publication in 1955 of Rudolph Flesch's sensational and bestselling book, *Why Johnny Can't Read,* declaring a national crisis in reading and placing the blame directly on the widespread "progressive" practice in schools of teaching children the look-say method for learning to read while virtually ignoring the essential and basic reading skill of phonics. Flesch, who held a doctorate in library science and was an expert in readability and prose style but who had never taught elementary children, was a powerfully persuasive writer and impressively believable in his assertions that the look-say method doesn't work, that it was not supported by any credible research, and that the textbooks most widely used in schools merely reflected the dominance of progressive but intellectually flabby ideas about learning. Flesch's book and the newspaper articles that sensationalized his claims convinced much of the nation that the crisis in reading was real, igniting a debate during the late 1950s and early 1960s within the educational community about reading that was unmatched in its furor until the "reading wars" of the 1990s.

What appears to have brought the battles of the 1950s and 1960s not to an end but to at least a temporary truce was the publication of the 1967 landmark study titled *Learning to Read: The Great Debate* by Jeanne Chall, a professor in the Harvard Graduate School of Education. With funding from the Carnegie Foundation, Chall had spent three years analyzing all the available research, observing hundreds of classrooms where children were learning to read, and consulting with hundreds of reading specialists and experienced classroom teachers to produce what is still widely regarded as an exemplary work of scholarship and an authoritative account of the most reliable methods for teaching young children to read (Ravitch).

Based on her compelling program of research and thoughtful analysis of the data, Chall concludes with a set of mostly uncontroversial and widely appreciated recommendations, with the exception of the first, which may have seemed controversial by seeking to end the great debate by asserting unequivocally that beginning reading instruction should shift from a meaning-emphasis to a code-emphasis approach (307–10). However, Chall was also emphatic in advancing two subordinate positions that are based on her research but also seem consistent with the observations and reasoning of most teachers and parents who have witnessed the reading development of children: First, she asserted that "I cannot emphasize too strongly that the evidence *does not endorse any one code-emphasis method over another*," and second, even more important:

> Nor can I emphasize too strongly that I recommend a code emphasis only as a *beginning* reading method—a method to *start* the child on—and . . . I do *not* recommend ignoring reading-for-meaning practice. Once the pupil has learned to recognize in print the words he knows (because they are part of his speaking and listening vocabulary), any additional work on decoding is a sheer waste of time" (307).

Since Chall's findings were confirmed (and never disconfirmed) by additional authoritative studies in subsequent decades, I will not rehearse here the full history of the reading wars as they continued with more and less intensity in the 1970s and into the 1980s, partly in the context of a larger struggle between progressive and traditionalist forces in the educational community. They resumed with an unprecedented ferocity in the 1990s as the traditionalist position was taken up as a moral cause by fundamentalist religious groups that associated Dewey and all progressive or liberal educational thought with every facet of modern life that seemed to question or ignore the pieties of an imagined past (Blau).

In the twenty-first century, while the social and political divisions in America have become even more dangerously oppositional and alarmingly consequential for most educational policies and practices, the reading wars have become, somewhat surprisingly, more of a discussion given new authoritative studies (e.g., Adams; National Reading Panel) that confirm Jeanne Chall's conclusions and seem to have reanimated the spirit of her reasoned and collegially respectful discourse about reading in the language arts community and more broadly in elementary education.

And now, with this abbreviated history in mind, I take a step back in time and place to 1967 and Larson Hall of the Harvard Graduate School of Education, where Professor Chall conducted her rigorous three-year study and then wrote and published her monumental work of scholarship and professional civility.

Moffett's Response to Chall's Book

James Moffett was a research associate in Harvard's Graduate School of Education in the same years that Chall completed and published her landmark study; while we don't know how well he knew her personally, we have to assume that he had met and certainly saw her on the relatively small campus of the School of Education. We know for certain that he read and was influenced by her book. In the first edition of *A Student-Centered Language Arts Curriculum, Grades K–13: A Handbook for Teachers*, Moffett speaks explicitly of Chall's recently published volume, applauding her attempt to characterize the present state of our knowledge about reading and expressing his own reasons for appreciating her conclusions, including her insistence on the initial importance of a focus on phonic decoding, as we can see in the following passages:

> Although the findings clearly call for a reversal of the conventional emphasis [the meaning approach] . . . they do not give the nod to any one method of teaching sound-letter relations, unless one is to give weight to the indications about teaching the names and sound values of letters before introducing reading text, and about teaching the sound-letter relations explicitly rather than by inference or "discovery." (71)

Given an equal effectiveness for word recognition, synthetic phonics [the decoding approach] should be preferred over analytic phonics because it offers an extra benefit in the form of creative word building whereby the pupil may combine components into words of his own choice, according to all of the English possibilities. (78)

Rereading Moffett and Rereading My Rereading Fifty-Four Years Later

Initial Impressions: First Reading, Summer 1968, Late June and July

As I said earlier, I first read Moffett's huge volume, *A Student-Centered Language Arts Curriculum, Grades K–13: A Handbook for Teachers,* when it was first published in 1968, during the summer when I was preparing for my second year of teaching. The book seemed encyclopedic in its coverage of the teaching of the language arts and mainly left me with a profoundly troubling sense of how much I still needed to learn about teaching young children, and especially about the teaching of reading to beginning readers, though my first year of teaching had already shown me how unprepared I was to meet that challenge.

So, in the summer of 1969, between my second and third years of teaching, I returned to Moffett's huge volume to reread first what for me was the most crucial chapter, "Becoming Literate," which details Moffett's understanding of learning to read words—the need for explicit and systematic instruction in letter-sound relationships and context use. It also provides a valuable review of materials available for classroom use as well as classroom-tested practices for teachers to consider. I would have a new class to teach in just five weeks, and I yearned to do a better job than I had the year before. In the following sections, I've attempted to capture the flavor of that rereading by presenting a few of my marginal notes that eventually morphed into the interesting and productive questions that I and our profession are now in a better position to answer. I found my notes in the course of rereading Moffett to work on this essay, and I can now see that the questions I asked so long ago would ultimately parallel questions that the scientific community would seek answers to during the next several decades.

Now, fifty-four years after my first encounter with Moffett's book, I'm in a position to address my questions of 1969 from my present perspective as an experienced reading teacher and teacher educator who has completed a master's and a doctorate in reading, has published essays and books based on her own research in reading, and is intimately acquainted with the most authoritative research in the field of early reading instruction. Thus, my questions may be versions of the ones I asked in 1969, but my comments on my questions and my review of the research that has suggested answers represent my current thinking and the current state of knowledge about learning to read.

What Moffett Says, What I Wanted to Ask Him in 1969, and What I Think Now

Question 1. Reading vs. Comprehension

Moffett's "Becoming Literate" chapter in *SCLAC* opens with an account of how Moffett conceived of the relationship between learning to read and the phenomenon of reading comprehension or understanding meaningful language:

> We get meaning from the speech sounds that the letters represent. The real issue of learning to read is decoding the letters into words we already know and to which meanings are already attached. Reading comprehension is merely comprehension.

> Difficulties in comprehending are difficulties in concepts, ideas, and their relationships, not with printed words. (67)

In other words, difficulties in comprehension are essentially difficulties in understanding not words, but larger conceptual meanings. Decoding is a matter of translating phonetic symbols into syllables and words. The issue of comprehension has in some sense nothing to do with decoding or making out the words on the page, but in understanding the larger meaning represented by the words in their structures as propositions and sentences, whose difficulty would be no different if heard rather than written. That sounded reasonable and plausible to me when I read it in 1969, but my notes also reflect my capacity for critical thought as I wonder about the research that might support Moffett's perspective. And now, based on my long career as a reading specialist and researcher I can respond to that wondering by referring to research that did not exist until more than a decade after Moffett's own thoughtful account, based apparently on his observations (probably of his own children) and on his reasoning.

What the Research Says

While Moffett's account seems logically and analytically true, even for nonspecialists, it was not demonstrated by research or introduced into the research literature until 1980 in the essay "The Simple View of Reading" (Gough and Hillinger). This essay states that empirical studies have demonstrated that reading comprehension is the product of two processes: word recognition (decoding) and language comprehension. The distinction here is crucial not just for understanding the reading process; it has enormous practical importance for teaching, as, for example, when a teacher is conducting a formative assessment of student reading development and finds that the student's listening comprehension is well above their comprehension when reading silently. The teacher would then recognize that the student's capacity to understand written language, when it is read aloud, is stronger than their capacity to translate written text into heard language and would know to look more closely at the child's capacity to decode.

Question 2. On Contextual Clues and Word Recognition

How important, I wanted to know, are contextual clues and whole-word recognition in early reading? On these historically controversial issues, Moffett had this to say:

> As regards both contextual clues and whole word learning, all of the current decoding programs that I have looked at recognize, as indeed they must, that these are natural and valuable aids in reading so long as they do not prevent the child from learning to crack the code itself. Although some new programs eschew *picture* cues, they do assume that children in their later reading will always use the verbal context of a word as an aid in recognizing it. Their point being simply that children should not depend on context as the main means of word attack, for it is inadequate by itself. (76)

Interestingly, Moffett points out that one way to avoid depending on context is to give children texts they can read that include the sound–symbol correspondences they have learned:

> Reading material is of two sorts—phonetically controlled texts that the children can read by themselves on the basis of the sound-spelling and sight words presented to them so far, and uncontrolled texts that the teacher reads to them, which are limited only by what the children can understand and take pleasure in. (113)

Not surprisingly, then, Moffett particularly liked the Dr. Seuss Read by Yourself series and the Follett Beginning to Read Books for the youngest readers (113). Both series are lots of fun to read.

On this question of the importance of context clues and word recognition in early reading development, I had little to go on from my own limited experience in 1969, but I find my notes reflecting what Jeanne Chall demonstrated in her 1967 book. And Moffett on this question echoes Chall. Yet in spite of Chall's compelling research and Moffett's thoughtful agreement, the question of the relative importance of context clues and word recognition versus decoding in early reading became a major controversy in the reading wars of the 1980s and 1990s, when a large group of elementary teachers and teacher educators who identified themselves with the "whole language" movement insisted on giving equal if not greater importance to using context clues rather than phonic decoding as beginning skills in learning to read words. So I can't resist noting here a small sampling of the vast body of subsequent research that I regard as authoritative on the question of what readers see and attend to in the process of reading.

What the Research Shows

Here are three interesting findings (Adams 101–2) that help us understand why Moffett was so right in suggesting that using context to guess a word is not the most efficient way to read. Though context supports word recognition, it requires attention that then reduces attention available for understanding and reading for meaning:

1. Normal adult readers fixate most on the words of a text, regardless of its difficulty (McConkie et al.).
2. Skilled readers do spend more time on important words in a text, but this seems to be due to nonvisual processes involved in thinking about its meaning (Carpenter and Just; Just and Carpenter).
3. Regardless of semantic, syntactic, or orthographic predictability, the eye seems to process individual letters. Disruptions in adult readers' eye movement indicate that the visual system tends to catch the slightest misspelling involving a visually similar letter buried in the very middle (and thus least informative) part of a long word that is highly predictable by the preceding context (McConkie and Zola).

> In summary, the eye movement research lends little support to the notion that skilled readers use contextual constraints to reduce the visual processing involved in reading. To the contrary, when reading for comprehension, skilled readers tend to look at each individual word and to process its component letters quite thoroughly . . . [with] remarkable ease and speed with which they achieve such letter-based word recognition, requiring only a few one-hundredths of a second to recognize each additional letter (Just and Carpenter, 1987). (Adams 102)

Perhaps the journal article that most affected *teachers'* understanding of context effects, as well as the entire reading research community's understanding of the phenomenon, was Keith Stanovich's 1986 "Matthew Effects in Reading: Some Consequences of Individual Differences in the Acquisition of Literacy." One of the major findings he reviewed, supported by sixteen published studies at the time, was that all readers use context, with less-skilled readers often depending on it far more: "When skilled and less skilled readers are in materials of comparable difficulty (i.e., materials producing similar error rates), the relative reliance on contextual information relative to graphic information is just as great—in many cases greater—for the less skilled readers" (366). Again, though context supports word recognition, it requires attention, reducing attention available for understanding. In other words, the less readers have to rely on context for word recognition, the better their reading comprehension.

Question 3. Why Is Moffett So Skeptical about Research in Reading?

Question 3 relates to Moffett's highly skeptical view of the research methods used in the many studies he reviews in his volume. From my present perspective, I can agree that much of the research both he and Jeanne Chall analyzed had severe limitations, such as in "establishing controls" (Moffett 73), which is fundamental. Moffett thought that "sophisticated computering and modern methodology are still not equal to the task of controlling all the variables that are operating in a classroom situation" (73). He speaks deliberatively about the need for more adequate conceptualization in reading research:

> The power of research can be no greater than the power of the concepts by which it is designed. It is this poverty of conception, perhaps more than anything else, that accounts for the inconclusiveness, contradiction, and irrelevance of most reading research. (74)

Good research design, including an adequate conception of what constitutes "reading," is fundamental to both data collection and the drawing of conclusions from that data. This is what Moffett is getting at. For example, he questions whether researchers fully understand which variables actually need measuring. He quotes his good friend Caleb Gattegno, whom he feels has put his "finger on one telling weakness of this [reading] research":

> Reading research to date has "measured" not absolute learning, but the relative advantages of one method of teaching reading over another method. However, research in reading has not attempted to discover under what conditions a learner can acquire the skills of reading and writing as readily as he acquires the skill of speaking. (qtd. in Moffett, *Student-Centered* 74)

Chall also felt a sense of perspective was lacking, especially by people who interpreted research for the greater public. They tended, she felt, "to overgeneralize findings, especially those that fitted into prevailing educational views" (90). Too often, she felt, "the interpreters and summarizers have forgotten that no one study can stand by itself, that each must be seen in the light of other relevant research on the reading and learning process" (90). In other words, she understood what has come to be known as "my-side bias" (Stanovich, *Bias*), which occurs when people evaluate evidence in a manner biased toward their own prior opinions and attitudes.

In spite of the drawbacks, Moffett was willing to take a few generalizations about best practices in teaching reading very seriously because Chall's book didn't look only at experimental studies—many of which converged on the same conclusions—but at correlational studies, case studies, and studies of children with learning disabilities as well. While correlational studies do not give evidence of cause and effect, "when placed alongside the findings of experimental comparisons, they can help illuminate causal relations" (Chall 140).

Nevertheless, if we wish to obtain a more complete picture of Moffett's ongoing relationship to reading research, we have to read his essay "Teaching Literacy," which serves as Chapter 5 of his 1981 book *Coming on Center: English Education in*

Evolution, where he acknowledges his own lack of any formal preparation in the teaching of reading or any training at all in any area of teaching, claiming that such "innocence" amounts to an advantage because it protected him from ever becoming a partisan in the battlefield of reading instruction (39). In fact, he seems to apologize for the degree to which, at first, he took

> too seriously the research in comparing reading methods that Jeanne Chall reported in *Learning to Read: The Great Debate*, before I realized such research omitted or slighted some means to literacy, and reflected what schools do and publishers put out, not what schools might do and ought to do. (39)

He goes on to assert that "[m]ost problems children have learning literacy in school are artificial and unnecessary, but it's very difficult for teachers, caught in a frenetic world they never made, to see how much these problems are school- or teacher-induced" ("Teaching Literacy" 40). He also explains how, if he has been able to contribute to improving practice in the teaching of reading, it is based on his years of experience working with teachers and watching his own children learn to read. He then offers what seems sound and generally research-supported advice about using multiple methods of teaching reading to children, particularly endorsing for parents what he calls the "lap method," having your child sit on your lap while you read to and with the child. He also speaks of the need to put the work of improving the teaching of reading more directly into the hands of expert and successful classroom teachers by instituting a version of the National Writing Project for teachers of reading (40–41).

Contradictions, Conversation, and Conclusions

It seems appropriate also to reflect on some surprising contradictions about the teaching of early reading that appeared in later editions of *SCLAC*, starting in 1992, when Moffett took on Betty Jane Wagner as a coauthor, largely for her expertise in early reading and in drama. Wagner was a beloved professor of English language arts education at National Louis University and was widely respected as a leader in the progressive whole language movement. She was also the director of the Chicago Area Writing Project and served on the National Writing Project's Advisory Board. Her influence on later editions of *SCLAC*, particularly on the teaching of drama, is fairly obvious and widely recognized, but her influence on ways in which the later editions contradict the first edition with respect to the early teaching of reading have hardly been noticed, though they have served to represent Moffett in ways that are inconsistent with the Moffett I read in a crucial period of my own development as a teacher, as they are eventually inconsistent with the Moffett I later interrogated personally (in a friendly and collegial way, of course).

This part of my Moffett story takes us to 1993 when I am conducting a five-day professional development workshop on the teaching of reading for elementary teachers in a school district in California, not so far from where Moffett had been living since 1970. Most of the teachers attending my workshop, I am quite sure, think of themselves as whole language teachers and therefore strong advocates of a meaning approach to beginning reading. They are thrilled by the literacy activities I am modeling and the learning principles I am explaining in day one, but I know that many of them are likely to resist my plans for the three days out of our five together when I will focus on helping them learn about alphabetics (one day on phonological awareness, one on phonics and fluency development, and the third on spelling development). Actually, my audience and I would be in agreement on almost every principle and practice of the whole language movement—except on the role of phonics in early reading. They would know and appreciate me as the author of two widely read books about the teaching of writing and major articles about teaching writing and fluency in reading. However, some of them are probably already suspicious of me because they know of my professional reputation as an outspoken critic of Professor Kenneth Goodman, whose research and theory inform the beliefs and practices of the whole language movement, with its growing emphasis in early reading on the three cueing systems that my workshop will eventually consider only as a way to confirm the correctness of a pronounced word, as opposed to beginning the word recognition process by guessing what the word might be.

But nobody mentions Ken Goodman during my workshop. The theorist I hear about is Moffett. And what I hear, the day after I mention Moffett's importance to my own thinking about the teaching of literacy, are two quotations from the fourth edition of *SCLAC*, read aloud by a workshop participant:

> Phonics is the only claimant for teaching reading that is not something proficient readers also do. As only a means, in other words, not a goal of reading, phonics is the hardest of the competing methods to justify, and so the advocates of it must bear the burden of proof. (115)

> As purely a learning device, only phonics may be deemed optional. For the same reason, it incurs greater risk of such side effects as aversion, "word calling," or mental myopia. Not surprisingly, then, there is some evidence that heavy emphasis on phonics impairs reading comprehension. (115)

After that workshop, I knew I had to talk to Moffett in person, ASAP. Though we had met before at conferences and I knew he would remember me, I hesitated about calling him to challenge the quotes from his own book. But the strength of my feelings about the issue overcame my reservations and I made the call. After reminding him of some of our long-standing connections, I explained what had transpired in my workshop, and I worked up the nerve to ask him why his approach to phonics in the 1968 edition of *SCLAC* differed so dramatically from the later edition that was the source of the anti-phonics passages that had been read aloud to me. I mentioned that I knew Betty Jane Wagner had been his coauthor starting with the second edition in 1976 and then in all subsequent editions, but these passages went far beyond anything I'd ever heard her say elsewhere.

First, Moffett was glad I was involved in professional development and took alphabetics seriously. He mentioned that he had invited Wagner to work with him largely for her expertise both in elementary education (where he had no experience himself) and in the use of drama in the classroom. He also had great respect for her reputation as a teacher educator and her leadership roles in the National Writing Project, in which he himself had been deeply involved and regarded as uniquely effective in its professional development work with teachers at all levels. Second, he acknowledged that it was under Wagner's influence that they made space in the fourth edition for analytic phonics word analysis, which begins with whole words, though he himself had reservations about analytic phonics and felt that many children would not be able to make the inferences required to develop firm sound-symbol relationships with that method. He also wasn't particularly happy with the quotations I told him about that had been read to me in my workshop—as if he hadn't written them, which I suspected was the case, but he remained quiet on that question.

Certainly, Moffett was walking a tightrope. He explained that he still believed strongly that systematic phonics instruction was necessary and that even synthetic phonics—that is, the decoding approach of sounding out words or word parts (/m /a/ /t/ yielding *mat*, or /m/ /ade/ yielding *made*)—was worthwhile for many children, especially those coming from any sort of disadvantaged situation.

Third, Moffett was glad teachers were involved in the professional development work I had outlined; if teachers knew English orthography inside and out (days two and three of my training), they would do a better job of coaching children as they reviewed their students' invented spellings in their stories and journal entries. Teachers could use that information as a basis for their next instructional move, whether during reading, writing, or spelling instruction. I agreed.

Toward the end of our conversation, Moffett said he'd send me his *Sound Out* tape from Houghton Mifflin's *Interaction* program, now out of print. He had a few tapes left. I'd see how systematic phonics could be taught explicitly and with joy, he said. I told him I had read Courtney Cazden's *Whole Language Plus: Essays on Literacy in the United States and New Zealand* and had heard about the tapes, which she said were popular with her students (76–77).

During a brief subsequent call I made to Moffett after receiving *Sound Out,* we reflected on the infiltration of politics in education: the enormous funding of phonics programs, the unprofessional surveillance of teachers, and the unfortunate position of teachers in education's hierarchy of power. He encouraged me to relate our conversation about phonics and invented spelling to the next group of teachers I worked with.

As anyone reading this chapter can tell, Moffett remains a valued mentor to me. I continue to appreciate his willingness to think like a scientist, even though he distrusted most reading research given the primitive statistical tools in use at the time and the lack of a strong conceptualization that should have undergirded the experimental work reviewed by Chall. I will always honor him for taking the risk he did with phonics in 1968, tying it to his highly original and radical proposal for a developmental approach to teaching English language arts. I am still awed by his capacity to stay above the fray, to encourage open-mindedness, and to empower teachers by reminding them of what they knew and to value their own experiences and instincts. He was a great man: a detailed thinker, a clear and careful writer, and an action-oriented observer who was open-minded, considerate, and fully original.

Works Cited

Aaron, P. G., et al. *Becoming a Professional Reading Teacher: What to Teach, How to Teach, Why It Matters.* Paul Brookes, 2008.

Adams, Marilyn Jager. *Beginning to Read: Thinking and Learning about Print.* MIT P, 1990.

Blau, Sheridan. "Politics and the English Language Arts." *The Fate of Progressive Language Policies and Practices,* edited by Curt Dudley-Marling and Carole Edelsky, National Council of Teachers of English, 2001, pp. 183–220.

Britannica.com. "Syllabary." *Britannica,* https://www.britannica.com/topic/syllabary.

Carpenter, Patricia A., and Marcel Adam Just. "Cognitive Processes in Reading: Models Based on Reader's Eye Fixations." *Interactive Processes in Reading*, edited by Alan M. Lesgold and Charles A. Perfetti, Lawrence Erlbaum Associates, 1981, pp. 117–213.

Cazden, Courtney B., with Patricia Cordeiro et al. *Whole Language Plus: Essays on Literacy in the United States and New Zealand.* Teachers College P, 1992.

Chall, Jeanne A. *Learning to Read: The Great Debate.* McGraw-Hill, 1967.

DiObilda, Nicholas A., and Robert L. Petrillo. "Beginning Reading Instruction in the Nineteenth Century: The Path towards Eclecticism." *American Educational History Journal*, vol. 47, no. 2, 2020, pp. 117–41.

Emig, Janet. Review of *Teaching the Universe of Discourse: A Theory of Discourse—A Rationale for English Teaching Used in a Student-Centered Language Arts Curriculum* by James Moffett. *The School Review*, vol. 78, no. 3, 1970, pp. 415–22.

Flesch, Rudolf. *Why Johnny Can't Read: And What You Can Do about It.* Harper & Brothers, 1955.

Gattegno, Caleb. *Words in Color: Background and Principle, Teacher's Guide.* Encyclopaedia Britannica Press, 1962, p. 3.

Gough, Philip B., and Michael L. Hillinger. "Learning to Read: An Unnatural Act." *Bulletin of the Orton Society*, vol. 30, 1980, pp. 179–96.

Hofstra University Library. "The Child's First Book." *Hofstra University Library,* www.hofstra.edu/library/library_libaxn_libdepts_spcoll_syllabs.html.

Just, Marcel Adam, and Patricia A. Carpenter. *The Psychology of Reading and Language Comprehension.* Allyn and Bacon, 1987.

McConkie, George W., and David Zola. "Language Constraints and the Functional Stimulus in Reading." *Interactive Processes in Reading*, edited by Alan M. Lesgold and Charles A. Perfetti, Lawrence Erlbaum Associates, 1981, pp. 155–75.

McConkie, George W., et al. *Eye Movement Control during Reading: I, the Location of Initial Eye Fixations on Words.* Technical Report No 406, Center for the Study of Reading, University of Illinois, 1987.

Meltzer, Erica. "The Misunderstanding That Sparked the Reading Wars." *Breaking the Code: Phonics & Reading*, 7 Aug. 2020, https://www.breakingthecode.com/the-misunderstanding-that-sparked-the-reading-wars/.

Moffett, James. *Interaction: A Student-Centered Language Arts and Reading Program.* Houghton Mifflin, 1973.

———. *A Student-Centered Language Arts Curriculum, Grades K–13: A Handbook for Teachers.* Houghton Mifflin, 1968.

———. "Chapter 5: Teaching Literacy." *Coming on Center: English Education in Evolution.* Boynton/Cook, 1981.

Moffett, James, and Betty Jane Wagner. *Student-Centered Language Arts, K–12.* 4th ed., Boynton/Cook, 1992.

National Reading Panel (U.S). and National Institute of Child Health and Human Development (U.S.). *Teaching Children to Read: An Evidence-Based Assessment of the Scientific Research Literature on Reading and Its Implications for Reading Instruction: Reports of the Subgroups.* National Institutes of Health Pub. No. 00-4769. National Institutes of Health, 2000.

Ravitch, Diane. "Jeanne Chall's Historic Contribution." "A Tribute to Jeanne Chall," *American Educator*, Spring 2001, https://www.aft.org/periodical/american-educator/spring-2001/tribute-jeanne-chall.

Smith, Nila Banton. 1934. *American Reading Instruction: Its Development and Its Significance in Gaining a Perspective on Current Practices in Reading.* International Reading Association, 1965.

Stanovich, Keith E. *The Bias That Divides Us: The Science and Politics of Myside Thinking.* MIT P, 2021.

Stanovich, Keith. "Matthew Effects in Reading: Some Consequences of Individual Differences in the Acquisition of Literacy." *Reading Research Quarterly*, vol. 21, no. 4, 1986, pp. 360–40. *JSTOR*, https://www.jstor.org/stable/747612.

III

The Uptake of Moffett in the Classroom

Chapter Eleven

Bridges: From Personal Writing to the Formal Essay

James Moffett

First published in 1989 in the National Writing Project's "Occasional Paper" series, this essay is a modified version of a transcript of a talk from notes that James Moffett gave as part of the Center for the Study of Writing Seminar Series. In it, Moffett elaborates on the relationship between thought and speech and in doing so offers a metacommentary on how the "scales of abstraction" he first sketched in 1968 might be taken up by students writing in the classroom. Peppered with his homespun wit, and written in his inimical style, Moffett movingly critiques the limitations of the contemporary teaching practices of the time in order to demonstrate the enduring applicability of his theory of the universe of discourse. In classic Moffett style, the sources appear as endnotes.

They say that writing was invented about five thousand years ago. That may be so, but it was only discovered about ten years ago in American schools, thanks to the National Writing Project movement. I don't usually feel obliged as a speaker to start with a joke. I've found from experience that I usually commit enough goofs, glitches, and faux pas that it is unnecessary to schedule comic relief. But I did come by a joke, very recently, that I can rationalize. I heard a speaker who was a humorous storyteller, a kind of cracker barrel raconteur. In one of his jokes, he told of a family from the backwoods of Virginia. There was a boy who had grown up to be about ten or eleven and had never said a word. Everyone grew accustomed to this, but one night as

National Center for the Study of Writing, University of California, Occasional Paper No. 9, 189. Reprinted with permission.

they were sitting around the dinner table, the boy suddenly said, "There's too many lumps in the gravy."

They looked over at him absolutely flabbergasted and said, "If you could talk, how come you haven't said anything before?"

He replied, "Everything has been pretty good up till now."

I submit that there's a whole theory of language function secreted within this joke if you bother to extract it.

A speaker has a choice of whether to say something general and inspirational and uplifting, or to say something of some practical value. For better or for worse, I have opted for the latter. My subject is how writing teachers get students from the personal-experience theme, with its many colloquial terms, to the formal essay. This seems to be a national issue. We are under pressure to do the thing that colleges seem to value most—to teach the kind of essay that corresponds to term papers or essay questions. Colleges emphasize this because it is part of their testing program, and this pressure passes all the way down to the elementary school. I believe we are gearing up for this sort of thing far too early. At any rate, this tends to determine the bent of the writing curriculum we have. What I'm going to try to aim at here are ways of doing justice to other kinds of writing that will at the same time prepare for what colleges want.

There are two main ways I think we can bridge from the personal narrative to kinds of informal and formal essays. One is by way of intervening kinds of discourse, kinds of writing, that students might practice in between personal writing and essay writing, kinds of discourse that schools could take much more advantage of. The other way is by parlaying personal writing directly into essay. I'll try to give some examples of that later. I like the term "parlay." It comes from the French "to speak," but in Anglicized use it means to transform something into something else and that's exactly what we are trying to do here in getting from personal writing to essay writing. We will look for ways of parlaying first-person narrative into essays.

I've been involved a good while in anthologizing student writing. This work has come out in four books called *Active Voices I, II, III,* and *IV*. These are anthologies of student writing. All they have in them are brief directions and samples of student writings to illustrate the assignments. The reason the project lasted longer than I would have liked is that I had difficulty getting writing in certain categories. That's one of the things I hope to emphasize—we don't ask for a broad variety of writing from our students.

I didn't go for just the top students or top schools, and I didn't run national contests. I worked partly through National Writing Project sites here and there, and partly from other contacts I had from previous curriculum work. I asked some teachers to send student writing to me from a variety of levels and backgrounds. Some of the pieces were very accomplished, and some authors, as you will see, are not so very experienced. All the selections have vitality, and they illustrate the kind of writing that I thought other students would appreciate and want to emulate.

The idea is that you use former students' writing to work with current students. Many teachers are doing this on their own, and I think that's excellent. I would certainly encourage that. You can array for students what the various kinds of writing look like when done by their peers. I also anthologize professional writing, but the problem with professional writing is that it is so intimidating that students sometimes do not identify with those writers. But I believe in using both.

In putting together these anthologies of students' writing I worked across the boards, up and down all the grades, from elementary school into college. I wanted a repertory that would hold good for all the years. I didn't invent tricky assignments or cute stuff to write; I simply looked at what's going on outside of school. If school is a preparation for life, let's see what's going on out there. What do people outside of school who practice writing really do? These samples represent the main repertory of writing possibilities, more certainly than can be done in a single year. Although I won't go into how to use the repertory (a whole subject in itself), I do want to suggest that it can be used to individualize writing, which I think we should do much more.

Figure 11.1 is my way of breaking down the main kinds of writing, the writing repertory, into five groupings. At the bottom is a category called *Noting Down*. The reason it's at the bottom is that journals, logs, diaries, and all sorts of notes are really the base for the kinds of writings above. I think you understand what I mean by the base. You write down things, and later you can write them up. This is a way of garnering material, jotting things down. Journalists write down everything that might possibly be used later as ideas for writing. At first, they plan to use most of it, but they usually just use some of it. Many professionals take field notes and lab notes. They accumulate materials that they write up into one of the above forms on the schema.

FIGURE 11.1. Kinds of Writing

THINKING UP
(Imagination)
Fiction
Plays
Poetry

THINKING OVER/THINKING THROUGH
(Cogitation)
Column
Editorial
Review
Personal essay
Thesis essay

LOOKING BACK
(Recollection)
Autobiography
Memoir

LOOKING INTO
(Investigation)
Biography
Chronicle
Case
Profile
Factual article
Feature article

NOTING DOWN
(Notation)
Journal
Diary
Logs

At the next level I have two groupings or very important domains of discourse called *Looking Back* and *Looking Into*. The one on the left is undoubtedly a lot more familiar to teachers, for that's really where you have the personal-experience themes, the first-person narrative. I use the traditional terms "autobiography," which is focused on the author, and "memoir," which is focused on others. So those two represent a shift of focus, and we are already on our way to essay. Memoir is somewhere between personal writing and essay, precisely because of that shift of focus from author to other. The less familiar category, *Looking Into*

(Investigation)—which deserves a lot of attention it isn't getting—is reportage and research. It includes traditional third-person types like "biography" and "chronicle" as well as journalistic forms like "cases," "profiles," "factual articles" and "feature articles." Investigation is an important domain in our society, for I believe most people who read are getting their information and ideas through newspapers and magazines and certain kinds of nonfiction books. In fact, many literary writers and novelists, such as Joan Didion and Norman Mailer, sometimes shift back and forth from fiction to nonfiction. Investigation deserves a lot of attention, in part because it has the attention of some of our major writers but also because this writing has gotten very good in our day.

I think people with a literature background are apt to look disdainfully at journalism. We create this little specialty of journalism, and it goes off in a box on the shelf, available only to a few students who elect it. But it ought to be mainstreamed, and I'll try to explain why. Reportage and research represent an important bridge between personal writing and transpersonal writing. (I don't like the term "impersonal." It sounds like nobody's home: there's no face, no voice—just some sort of ghost writing—so I use the term "transpersonal.") I had the most difficulty getting writing in this category, and it is fascinating to think about why schools have neglected the main way to bridge between first-person writing and essay writing.

I think you will agree that investigative writing has been almost universally ignored in the schools. There are many reasons, some of them practical, some having to do with our backgrounds. Even very good teachers, who have a strong background in writing, often don't bother with it. What I found is that most teachers, even very good writing teachers, work with only a few kinds of writing. I am sure they will say they don't have time for more, and it may very well be true. We need to understand why even the best teachers don't require a broader range of writing from their students.

There's a lot to be said about *Looking Into* precisely because we haven't been trained to deal with it, unless you happen to have had some journalism experience. Most teachers probably haven't written in this area, so they don't feel too comfortable with it.

Nevertheless, we all have done this kind of reading, *New Yorker* reportage and the excellent kind of reportage that we often get in newspapers and magazines. We feel confident to assess this, so I think we shouldn't feel so wary about assigning student writing in that area.

What do you do when you do investigative writing? You go look, you go ask, or you go look it up—three main things that reporters and researchers do. They go on site, visit, observe, and take notes. Or they interview one or many people, and again they take notes. Or what they can't get from looking and asking they go look up and see what other people have said about this. They go to records, documents, books, and so on. This is where the library research comes in. As you notice, what happens here is that you move more and more from firsthand into secondhand information, and that's part of the movement from personal writing to essay writing. From first person you can draw an arrow, if you wish, going from the left over to the right in Figure 11.1, from *Looking Back* to *Looking Into*. One of the movements involved is in that direction, going from first person to third person, from writing about self to writing about others, and from first-hand information to second- and third-hand information. I believe this is a very natural movement.

Let's go to the top level. The reason it's above is that *Looking Back* and *Looking Into* form a concrete data base for these other two. The memory is a tremendous storehouse of materials that all professional writers use. It's not narcissistic or solipsistic or just about oneself; it's about all sorts of things. If you think of your own memories, you will recognize that they are about everything, everything you ever had a chance to observe, experience, or participate in. The memory has all sorts of potentialities for the transpersonal writing that goes into essay. The other domain, *Looking Into* (Investigation), includes many sources of materials outside oneself. These are the two main sources on which the top two categories are built.

Thinking Up (Imagination) is most familiar to English teachers, who generally have a literature background. It's what we call "creative writing," but I don't like that term and I never use it. In fact, I never use the word "creative." It sounds sentimental. Creative writing is one of those specialties I wish we didn't have. I wish we would mainstream the writing of fiction into the composition program and not regard it as a specialty like journalism. Few kids will ever take such a specialty, and as a result we remove again one of the main bridges into essay writing.

We generally think of all fiction writing—poetry, plays, short stories—as being very different from the writing of ideas. I regard *all* writing as idea writing. To me the difference is not whether the writing has ideas but how buried the ideas are, how implicit or explicit the ideas are. In literature and recollection, the ideas are more implicit. They are there, but they are embodied, incarnated in personages, incidents, and events. If this is not true of literature, why do we have students digging for meaning all the time? Why do we have them chasing symbols and doing vivisections of poems and postmortems on novels, digging, digging, digging, all the time for meaning?

Here is a great irony. We have a curriculum in which students *write exposition*; but when they read, they *read literature*. We should have them do *both* types of reading and writing. It's very important for them to have the chance to do some writing in these figurative, fictional modes, because for one thing, these modes are an implicit way of stating ideas. All stories are statements. We can use the term "conclusion" for both fiction and nonfiction. In stories, the conclusions are inherent in the "logic of the events." If that's not true, then we should quit having kids analyzing novels and plays for their meaning.

It is evident that folk literature—fables, parables, legends, and myths—exist mainly to convey ideas, but they convey them in a kind of subconscious or preconscious way. Today we have a heavy industry in analyzing myths. We have whole disciplines mining myths for their meaning—Jungian analysts and anthropologists and literary critics. Legends, fables, parables, and myths all exist as stories that make statements. The fable is right on the hinge between story and statement because the meaning is distilled out as moral at the end. It is interesting to look at folk literature because it tells you a little more clearly about what's going on in modern literature that we are more familiar with.

Let's move into a consideration of the category labeled *Thinking Over/Thinking Through*. I am all for the essay, and I think we should do as much of it as we can. However, I believe that if we move into it developmentally we will get better results. This category includes "Column," "Editorial," and "Review," the journalistic forms of essay. I imagine most people read essays of this sort, and those who are writing them are writing in these journalistic forms. Many of them do exactly what we want students to do in writing—make a generalization and then support it with examples, documentation, and illustrations.

There are many avenues to this, two of which are *Investigation* and *Imagination*. A third way is to go directly from *Recollection* up into *Cogitation*, because memory is a main source of ideas. All we have to do is extrapolate memories, which is what many essayists do. It always amuses me that George Orwell's "Shooting an Elephant" has been anthologized *ad nauseam* in all the college anthologies under Essay. If a student had written it, it would be called a personal experience theme. Most of it is narrative, first person, telling about how he was compelled to shoot an elephant against his will under pressure of the group when he was in civil service in Burma. He knew how to extract and extrapolate the transpersonal aspect of his personal experience so that in the end we think of it as an essay, although it is a piece of autobiography. But the point is that it is very hard to tell the difference because *memory is one of the main routes to get into the essay.*

What I am suggesting here is that all writing is thinking; it is simply a question of whether the thinking is explicit or implicit. What I suggest is that on the left side of Figure 11.1, the thinking is implicit and on the right side, it is explicit. Exposition, argumentation, persuasion are on the right-hand side. What we call persuasion and argumentation are not precise terms but general terms for kinds of thesis essay writing. All of the group called *Looking Into* is expository. It bridges into argumentation and persuasion because that is the natural effect of reportage, research, and journalism. After a while an investigator tends not only to gather information but to generalize it, to argue points. The reporter on the beat becomes a columnist in print media, a "commentator" in broadcast journalism. So draw another arrow from *Investigation* to *Cogitation*.

The implicit (categories on the left side) roughly corresponds to the functioning of the right hemisphere of the brain, and the explicit (categories on the right side) to the functioning of the left hemisphere. But the trouble with that is that it gets to be a little too neat. First thing you know, we'll be back to that awful division of Bloom's into affective and cognitive, which I think is one of the abominations of educational movements. It's not the case that one hemisphere of the brain is cognitive and the other affective, of having mushy emotion on one hand and dry rationality on the other. Both hemispheres—and both the implicit and explicit—are ways of cognizing. They are both cognitive. It is not that half the head is emotional and the other half rational. It is a disservice to education that we ever accepted that kind of dichotomy.

The only other general thing I would say about the schema in Figure 11.1 is that the movement, if you go upward here, is generally inductive. That is, it works from particulars to generalities, moving from the concrete particulars of personal experience and narrative ("*once* upon a time") to generality, which is not "once upon a time" but *any* time. We speak of the "present tense of generalization" in grammar, and that is exactly what essay is. So this movement from the concrete particulars to the generalities is an inductive movement in terms of logic. I believe that we have not offered in writing programs enough opportunities to students to work inductively, but that is the way they build their own knowledge structures.

There is a lot of hue and cry today about "thinking"; the buzz word is "critical thinking." If we look seriously at thinking and writing, we soon come to realize that we don't have to add thinking because it is already part and parcel of writing. If we are serious about thinking, we will allow students to work far more inductively than they have in the past, building up from sources of plenty instead of employing a strategy of working from scarcity. I will explain what I mean by that. The deductive approach is to work from the top down, from the higher-level abstractions to the lower. If you are given a topic, or if you choose a topic, or if the essay exam gives you some quotation and you are supposed to refute or support it, and your grade is on the line, then you start at a higher generalization and go downward, looking for something to support or illustrate the generalization. That is what I call a wrong strategy, working from scarcity. What we should work from is plenty, from too much material, so much that you have to waste it, throw some of it away, edit it, winnow it out—in short, compose and select, abstract. Memories and investigations represent materials both inside and outside, wealthy positions, a source of plenty and not a position of scarcity. That sort of wrong-headed strategy comes from working too deductively, starting students at high-level abstract topics, or generalities, and then asking them to go down. It puts us in the position of being professional naggers. We are nagging for details, nagging for evidence, nagging for support, illustrations, and examples, no matter what the kind of writing. This shouldn't happen. It is one of those problems to which we think up brilliant solutions, but it is a stupid problem. It comes from wanting to control the subject matter of student writing and from riding herd on essay before honoring other kinds of writing. If we really want to teach thinking and writing together and get from personal experience to essay, then we should emphasize inductive thinking, which is itself a bridge to deductive thinking.

Now I would like to turn to some selections from student writing. What I want to emphasize here is the parlaying from personal-experience writing directly into the essay, which I think is a very natural movement if we know how to work it. I try to get my students (who are all teachers, by the way, with a lot of experience) to think about what is generic in some of their personal experience. I ask them to choose a personal incident in their life, something interesting, and then to write about it. Then I ask, "Of what is this incident a metaphor?" Maybe nothing will come, but when it does, you are on the road to an essay. Of what is this personal incident a metaphor? Or an emblem or symbol? What does it represent? Of what type is it a token? As soon as you begin writing about types, through the tokens, through the particulars, you are dealing with what essay essentially consists of, which is coordinating an idea with an incident or instance.

Another way is to pluralize personal experiences. I sometimes ask, "Can you think of other incidents, other experiences, to go with this one? Here you would put together a collection, a category of incidents or experiences, which all show the same thing, which all point the same way. They go together, and in that you have your thesis idea. That is the inductive approach. You transpersonalize by including incidents and experiences not just from your personal memories but from what you've heard from other people and what you've read, thus connecting incidents in your own life with incidents in the lives of characters in fiction and drama and of other people you know about. Pluralizing is generalizing.

Now the samples. The first couple are from senior high, grades 10 to 12. The first is an Autobiographical Incident, something very specific that happened in a very small time and space, something that happened one day.

Wonder Woman Strikes Again

Vicki Bilik

It was Monday, the first day of kindergarten after Easter vacation. School had gone well that day. I arrived early that morning with a little baggie full of left-over jellybeans in my lunch. A complete repertoire of stories for my friends, ranging from what the Easter Bunny brought me to the egg hunt in my grandmother's backyard.

The day had gone well. I had convinced all my classmates that I had received the biggest Easter basket of all of them, and I even succeeded in trading a mere two jellybeans for an entire marshmallow bunny. I was shrewd and unfeeling in my business affairs. So, there I was in front of the school, waiting for my mother and contemplating the day's victories. All of a sudden, a sparkle caught my eye. I looked down and there they were, my brand new, black, patent leather shoes, the pride of Miss Bradey's kindergarten class. I had got them to wear on Easter Sunday along with my brand new dress. I was so proud of them.

As I sat there admiring my prized possessions, I felt a shadow fall upon me. I looked up, and there was Jeffrey Wilson. He thought he was so cool just because he was in first grade and I was only in kindergarten. For absolutely no reason at all he looked down and sneered.

"Those are the ugliest shoes I've ever seen!" Then if that insult to my precious shoes wasn't enough, he leaned over and spit on them.

I felt the tears rush to my eyes, but I held them back. I wasn't going to let that beast know how deeply he had hurt me.

Suddenly I became aware of something heavy in my right hand. Of course! My Wonder Woman lunch box! Wonder Woman wouldn't let me down. I reached my right arm back and then swung forward, Wonder Woman hitting Jeffrey in the face with all her might.

> "That'll show that creep!" I thought.
>
> Just as I watched Jeffrey go crying into the boys' bathroom, my mother pulled up in the station wagon. I got in the car and relaxed against the seat. Defending one's honor is very hard work, you know.[1]

Of course, you can see this is a very aware girl. She knows exactly what she is doing. The story includes a very brave picture of a not so admirable side of herself, at least back when she was in kindergarten. You can see she doesn't make many explicit statements; this is pure story. And yet it is full of so many ideas, so many potentialities, so many generalizations you could make if you wanted to. You could add other incidents that would lead to more general notions about boys and girls of that age, or their relationships, or relationships between the sexes generally, or about smugness and complacency, or about unwittingly tempting other people. You see so many potential themes.

It's always interesting to me that we use the term "theme" for any type of student writing. "Theme" means a kind of thesis or a generalization. I think essay consists mainly of bringing out some of these latent ideas.

The next piece is from a high school boy who lives in rural Oregon, east of the Cascade Mountains. It is a Memoir of Nature, as I call the assignment.

> **Cougars at Bay**
>
> Scott Stephens
>
> About three years ago I witnessed something very few city folks get to see.
>
> I was archery hunting in a remote canyon, known to most people as Fiddlers Hell. This was not irregular at all since Doug Anderson and I hunted there quite often. It's a steep canyon that most people won't dare to venture into.
>
> I didn't quite know what I was doing there. I saw many deer and elk and didn't even bother to shoot.
>
> About noon I stopped to rest on a large rock. I was sitting there enjoying the scenery, when I spotted a slight movement in the brush. I was hoping to see a big bull elk.
>
> To my surprise two full grown cougars strolled out into the meadow. They were playing happily, wrestling with each other.

The wind was blowing in my face and I was sitting above them. As long as I was still I could watch them play.

They played in the meadow for about an hour, and then as if a signal from nature beckoned to them, they raced off. I wasn't quite sure what made them run off. I attempted to follow them.

As I stepped off my rock, I caught a faint sound of braying dogs. Then I knew. Poachers! I thought for sure the cats would be shot.

I ran up on the ridge, leaving my bow lying on the ground. I spotted the dogs. I was shocked. These were no pure-bred hunting dogs used by poachers. Instead, they were a mangy crew of about seven dogs, led by a big redbone. It was the wild pack that I had heard so much about. I spotted the cougars just ahead of the pack. One cougar climbed a tree, the other prepared to fight. With a rock cliff at its back and the pack at its front, it fought.

I ran back to get my bow. When I reached the fight one cougar and five dogs lay dead. The other two dogs ran off. I went up to the cougar. It was a large male. The female was still in the tree.

I never understood why the male didn't tree, or why the female didn't help. About three months later I figured it out. In the first place if he had climbed the tree the dogs would have waited for them to starve. And the male fought the dogs to give the female a chance for her life; she was bearing young. I've often gone back to Fiddlers Hell to look for the cougars, but I've never found them.[2]

One of the things interesting to me about this piece is that the writer is always trying to figure out things. He is thinking about what he observes. The story is straightforwardly told by a boy who tuned into nature and was a good observer. He probably hunts just as an excuse to get out there in nature and observe it. He really didn't do any hunting here, but he's thinking about what he observes. I believe this is the main thing that makes an essay successful. As you can see, this writing is not really focused on the author himself. It's told in the first person, but it's focused on what he's looking at. So it is on its way to exposition because it tells you about what goes on in the world; it's information and reflection.

The next piece is from an eighth-grader. It is a poll from that domain call *Investigation*. Essentially you think of some question you want answered and then go out and find the answer. Kids think of something they want to know more about, and the teacher helps them find out how to know more about it. The author wanted to know more about what people think about nuclear energy. This piece is from Spanish Harlem, New York City, where we've collected a lot of writing from junior high.

A Poll on Nuclear Energy
Gemma DiGrazia

This poll was conducted mainly among middle-class New Yorkers. Almost all of the adults had a college education. The majority of them live on the Upper West Side. There was an equal amount of females and males. Most people who answered were over forty or under twenty. The questions asked were:

1. Do you think nuclear energy is necessary as an alternative energy source? If no: What are the alternatives?

   36% thought nuclear energy was necessary. All of them mentioned that other energy sources would run out.

   64% said it wasn't necessary. Energy alternatives they listed were: coal, solar, waterpower, and conservation of existing energy.

2. Describe what you think the effects of radioactivity on humans are. All people mentioned some physical symptoms as effects of radiation and radioactivity. These are:

symptoms	*% of people who mentioned each symptom*
death	60%
genetic damage	58%
radiation sickness	56%
general sickness	52%
cancer	36%
sterility	12%

3. Do you think the public is fully informed about nuclear hazards and safety? All said no, the public wasn't fully informed.

   25% said no because they think most people aren't educated enough to understand the problems of nuclear energy.

50% said no, because they think information is deliberately withheld in lies and coverups by the government and nuclear energy people.

5% said they think nuclear energy is too technical and complex for almost everybody to understand.

20% said the public is not told everything because there is no reason to panic them when they can't do anything about it.

4. Would you know what to do in case of a nuclear disaster (i.e., melt down) in your area?

    55% said no.

    45% said yes. Those who don't feel nuclear energy is dangerous had faith in the authorities to tell them how to avoid harm. Everyone else was afraid of dying and said they would run or hide, listen to T.V./radio but not believe everything they heard, or hold their loved ones and pets.

5. Do you think that children should be educated to the benefits and dangers of nuclear energy? Why or why not?

    2% said no, people at that age shouldn't be burdened with such things.

    98% said yes, they are our future. Future decisions depend on them. Yes, so they are more fully informed about the world we live in. Some people wrote yes, though wait until they're old enough.

6. Do you think you can do anything to educate others about nuclear energy?

    18% said no, they were not educated enough themselves to teach about it.

    12% said yes, educate people to its benefits.

    60% said yes, they would tell people the facts and were sure that these would convince them of their dangers.

7. Are you in favor of using nuclear energy?

    12% said yes only if for medical purposes or if safety is drastically improved.

    48% said yes, either now or in the future. Most of these people thought it was necessary to have nuclear energy and it was just a matter of making it safer.

> 40% said no, because of obvious dangers and lack of possible safety ever.
>
> 8. Do you think we can have safe nuclear energy?
>
> 42% said no because of either total unsafeness of any nuclear energy or because those in control will push it on us before it can be made safe.
>
> 30% said maybe. They said this because of lack of information or belief that it can be safe, but it might be safe long after it is in use.
>
> 28% said yes. These people believe either that nuclear energy is safe now or will be very soon.
>
> The people who were for nuclear energy contradicted themselves a bit on the question that asked if you think the public is fully informed on nuclear energy. All of them thought that not all the information about nuclear energy was available to the public, yet they all thought that they had enough information to feel safe and in favor.
>
> The people who were unsure felt they didn't know enough.
>
> The people against nuclear energy also felt that information was kept from them. One of the issues everyone agreed upon was the issue of the public's awareness of the information about nuclear energy. They all seem to think we need to know more.
>
> Everyone thought that a nuclear energy accident would be harmful to people, and yet some people felt nuclear energy was safe or will be soon. And these people were in favor of using nuclear energy as an energy source.
>
> Before I took the poll I had some ideas of what kinds of answers would be given back to me. I had hoped that most of the people would have been against nuclear energy, but the majority of the people were for nuclear energy. Another thing that surprised me was the amount of people who were uninformed or unsure. I had hoped that people would be surer on an issue like this.
>
> From this poll I have learned a lot. I have learned how people have such different opinions from each other and how rigid some people are. The most surprising thing is that people have such opposite opinions while using the same information to get their opinions.[3]

That's not a bad conclusion. The writer arrived at it inductively from her own information. She did the legwork to find out what people thought about something. She thought about what they said; she related responses to the questions and drew her own conclusions.

Next is a piece from elementary school. I use these domains for all grades, but it is obvious that in the lower grades you are not going to get as much of some kinds of writing. For example, you wouldn't expect a lot of thesis writing in the elementary school. I think it should be available for those who can, and in this way individualization can occur. Kids can do extraordinary things in elementary school, but you shouldn't insist that they all do the same thing at the same time. Those who can should go ahead and do it. Some groups will be writing at one level, some at other levels. There are many possibilities for expository and persuasive writing, and the essay included here, a review, goes into only some of those possibilities.

Cat Calls

Nina Billone

Suddenly the whole stage turned red, and colored lights flashed on and off. Two cats cautiously crawled out of a pipe. The trunk to a broken-down car opened with a creak, while more cats filled the stage.

My mother and I had seats in the mezzanine, which is just above the first floor of the Schubert Theater in Chicago. I was extremely excited because I was watching *Cats*.

The stage was decorated like a junkyard. There were four Rice Krispies cereal boxes about two feet high, a tennis racket, and a garbage can, but best of all there was a tire that was about four feet around.

After minutes of dancing, the cats all went back to their hiding places except one. He started singing, "I have a Gumby Cat in mind. Her name is Jenny Anny Dots. Her coat is of the tabby kind with tiger stripes and leopard spots . . ." As he sang, the trunk to the car opened. Inside was a cat with tiger stripes and leopard spots acting out every move that the cat sang about Jenny Anny Dots.

Many songs went by such as "Growl Tiger, Gus" (the theater cat), Mongojerrie and "Rumpleteazer," etc.

Then a very interesting song came on, "The Rum Turn Tugger," which started out, "The Rum Turn Tugger is a curious cat . . ." The Rum Turn Tugger was a teenage cat whose coat was black and stuck to his body. I decided he was my favorite cat. He acted a lot like our cat Benjy. The play ended.

> On the way home I sat in the back seat of the car with my mind full of scenes from the wonderful play I had just seen.
>
> I like cats a lot, and seeing Cats made me realize that other people understand cats the way I do and know that they are like people.[4]

Of course some of those "other people" include T. S. Eliot. She's in good company. This girl doesn't do everything that can be done in a review but she comes to some generalizations in the end, and elementary kids should have some opportunities for writing real reviews. The form will grow as they grow.

Finally a couple of samples of what we call personal essay, which is not a very specific category, but much of our best literary writing falls into this category, from the eighteenth century on through to modern authors.

This piece is from junior high school.

> **Funny Feelings**
>
> Jennifer Levi
>
> Lately, walking down the street has not been the most pleasant thing for me to do. I feel very self-conscious because men are always looking and saying things to me. I don't think I do or say or wear anything to get myself noticed. I think it is disgusting that men feel that they have the right to say things to women they don't even know. I don't think they know how it makes women feel; I don't even think they care. All they care about is themselves and having their fun.
>
> It makes me angry, but at the same time it makes me scared. It makes me angry that they can make me feel like I can not walk around without being watched. It makes me scared because at any given moment they might hurt me.
>
> I remember when I was just starting to develop and I was very embarrassed about it. There was only one other girl in my class that had started to develop too. I remember hearing some boys in my class talking about their bodies—they were so proud about their bodies, but I never really talked to any of my friends about it then. Now we sometimes talk about it, but not a lot. It seems like boys always talk about their bodies. Sometimes I even get embarrassed listening to them talking about their own bodies.
>
> I felt real weird because in one way I was being told to be showy about my body from movies and TV. At the same time I was being told to be quiet about my body from my own fear of

> what other people would think. For a while I was very confused until I finally decided to go with my own feelings. Now I do not show it and I do not hide it. I just wear what I want and I do what I want to do. I don't let my fear or what I see interfere with what I do or wear.
>
> I think that as you grow up you become less ashamed and more proud of your body (male or female). I know that men, well at least the men on the street, are very proud and showy of their bodies. Some women, the ones on TV and in movies, are showy, and some women just don't do anything either way, like me.
>
> I know that I can not make the men on the street stop looking and saying weird things to me; all I *can* do is not make them or anyone else feel the way they've made me feel.[5]

This could have been put in fictional form or in a poem. In fact I found that a lot of what I really felt were essays were done as poems in junior high. I included some of them under the category of essay because that's what they were, and then it occurred to me that poetry may be a natural way for junior high kids to express some of their emerging generalizations.

I'm going to end with a personal essay written by one of my students at the Breadloaf School of English in Vermont, herself an experienced teacher. What she does here is to pluralize personal experiences, tell two incidents that show the same thing. She does here exactly what Orwell does in an essay which is virtually unknown. I anthologized it in a book called *Points of Departure*, which is a collection of nonfiction arranged in the same way student writing is arranged here.[6]

As you know, Orwell was a reporter or journalist. In World War II, he went in to Europe right behind the liberation forces, with other journalists. From that experience he did a piece called "Revenge is Sour," based of course on one of our platitudes, revenge is sweet. So his thesis is his title. He tells two incidents which he witnessed that document his point. The first incident occurred somewhere in France when he was with another journalist. The American troops had rounded up some SS officers who were a miserable-looking lot. There was one in particular who had clubfeet and looked psychotic. A Jewish American officer came up and began kicking the SS officer. The American officer said he felt that this was his moment when revenge would be sweet. But Orwell says that when that moment comes it isn't sweet; you think the victory is going to be sweet when you are helpless and hapless and out of power, when you are the victim. When you're back in power, you get revenge, but it really isn't sweet. That's what Orwell is saying. Then he related that to punishment in Germany after World War II, to events such as the Nuremberg trials. He told of a second incident in which he and a Belgian journalist were entering Stuttgart just after the forces had gone in. The Belgian journalist was prepared to hate the Germans when he saw them—"the Boches," he called them, using the old World War I term. When he saw a dead German soldier on the way in, he noticed that somebody had strewn a spray of lilacs over the body, perhaps as a kind of funeral gesture. It was the first dead person the other reporter had even seen. By the time he had actually seen German prisoners, he wasn't able to savor their downfall as he thought he would. He gave them coffee instead.

This construction is very similar to what we will read next. The writer was not emulating the Orwell essay at all. Our class hadn't read it; she just came up with it spontaneously. She put together two incidents which she felt showed the same thing.

A Work of Art

Shirley Rau

I recently served on a panel on a three-day writing conference in Boise, Idaho. Eight teachers of English from grade school through college were arranged in a small semi-circle on a stage, responding to questions from conference participants. Toward the end of the afternoon, everyone was getting tired. We were all thinking about the half hour that remained between us and release from the cramped auditorium. Valorie leaned toward the small hand-held mike with a three by five card, the last question from her discussion group: "What is a teacher's responsibility when a student turns in writing that is confessional or that reflects a troubled perspective?" Her voice reverberated as I met the blank eyes of those opposite from me. Pat took the mike:

"The best thing to do is treat the piece as a work of art and comment on it as such. We are not trained to deal with counseling matters." Her businesslike finality signaled another panel member to go on to the next question. The rest of the section was a blur. My mind kept turning over and over "treat the piece as a work of art." That clinical, rubber-glove theory of dealing with writing was echoed by members of my

> own department. Literary majors all, they analyzed narrative perspective, imagery, character, plot, genre and theme. They analyzed everything in literature except its connection to reality.
>
> Last year every student in my class kept a literary response journal. Charlotte Britton's journal was filled with poetry, which reflected her fragility and sensitivity. Each week writing groups met to share sections of the journals for comments. The poem that Charlotte shared in February was stark, devoid of the romantic softness so typical in her writing. And though I heard the poem that day and have read it many times since, I can only remember torn snatches:
>
> a dove
>
> the clang of a metal door
>
> a gun
>
> the question to one who remains
>
> I don't remember exactly how the writing group responded; perhaps we didn't, perhaps the words of her poem turned over and over in our minds until the businesslike finality of some response signaled another reader to go on to the next piece. One week after writing the poem, Charlotte went into the bathroom between classes and shot herself in the chest. She lived through the suicide attempt but I've died it a thousand times.[7]

What the author has done here is put together two instances of teachers distancing themselves from student emotion, and she has put them together, exactly as Orwell did, to illustrate a thesis, which she too states in her title, "A Work of Art," though more obliquely than Orwell.

My own assignment today was to talk about how students might gradually write their way from personal narrative to transpersonal essay. I have not tried to deal with the composing process or with classroom management for writing, important as these are. I took on the assignment about bridging because I think that forcing exposition and argumentation defeats itself and forces out those other kinds of writing that not only lead naturally into essay but that should be fully honored for their own sake. Such development will not only teach thesis writing best but will open up the school writing repertory in sorely needed ways. Formal essay should not be the goal of the writing curriculum, only the outgrowth of it.

Notes

1. Moffett, J. (1987). *Active Voices III*, p. 36. Upper Portsmouth, NH: Heinemann Educational Books and Boynton/Cook.

2. Moffett, J. (1987). *Active Voices III*, pp. 75–76. Upper Portsmouth, NH: Heinemann Educational Books and Boynton/Cook.

3. Moffett, J. (1987). *Active Voices II*, pp. 110–112. Upper Portsmouth, NH: Heinemann Educational Books and Boynton/Cook.

4. Moffett, J. (1987). *Active Voices I*, pp. 257–258. Upper Portsmouth, NH: Heinemann Educational Books and Boynton/Cook.

5. Moffett, J. (1987). *Active Voices II*, p. 310. Upper Portsmouth, NH: Heinemann Educational Books and Boynton/ Cook.

6. Moffett, J. (1985). *Points of Departure: An Anthology of Nonfiction*, pp. 380–84. New York: New American Library.

7. Moffett, J. (1987). *Active Voices IV*, pp. 303–304. Upper Portsmouth, NH: Heinemann Educational Books and Boynton/Cook.

CHAPTER TWELVE

Student-Centered Reading Activities

JAMES MOFFETT

BETTY JANE WAGNER

James Moffett and his long-time coauthor, Betty Jane Wagner, argue that good reading habits for high school students can be strengthened by providing activities that extend the students' capacities. Activities are suggested to foster more mature reading practices and deeper involvement in literature.

People fit reading into diverse personal patterns and schedules of seeking fulfillment. We read various sorts of discourse for various reasons at various stages of individual development. It is futile and mischievous to try to codify all this into one program for all. Just array the kinds of reading and help individuals make their way around the repertory. This is the here-is-God's-plenty method. Watch students' patterns of choice and play to that, as knowing parents do. Freely make suggestions based on what you perceive about them, but let them decide. The power to choose what one reads makes for the best reading program you can devise.

Structuring literature around concepts of either form or content interferes with individualized reading, and individualized reading should be initiated as soon as children can read at all and preserved through the years at all costs. Nothing you or anyone else can cook up by way of units or sequence will teach reading so well as guided individual choice in an interactive setting. The real learning will occur as individuals and small groups make up their own sequences as well as thematic or formal units.

Originally published in *English Journal*, vol. 80, no. 6, 1991, pp. 70–73. Reprinted with permission of NCTE.

Your structuring best comes when you organize a classroom library, provide directions for reading activities, and confer with individuals about choices of texts. If you predigest form and content for your students, you will rob them of their education by short-circuiting their thinking.

The tradition in secondary school of organizing literature around nationalities, periods, or themes works against individualization. It would be more interesting for groups or individuals to pursue a subject of interest *across* national or ethnic literatures. Organizing literature by time and place doesn't do justice to the nature of literature, which is not mainly national or historical. Thematic organization pre-interprets. By focusing readers at the outset on preselected frames of reference, both historical and thematic approaches meddle terribly with reader response. Such approaches have made too many students dislike both reading and literature. While taking control of texts away from readers, they also misrepresent literature, which affects people personally, what they think and feel. It is a figurative, artful mode of discourse, an experience itself as well as a perception about experience, created not merely to be understood but to be undergone.

The historical and ethnic aspects of literature are indeed worthwhile in themselves and often illuminate the texts, as all other aspects of context do. The relations, in fact, between texts, authors, and their environments will naturally interest youngsters. But if background becomes foreground, it will filter the text so much as to prevent readers from knowing what their native responses would have been. It is far better education to let individuals and groups explore contexts within their own programs. One thirteen-year-old girl became so fascinated with French history after reading *The Three Musketeers* that she read an adult biography of Madame Pompadour and other works about the seventeenth and eighteenth centuries. Teachers and aides can serve as resources.

Presenting literature through concepts and terms of literary criticism poses a similar problem. For one thing, both literary history and literary criticism contain differing schools of thought, not to say, at times, vehement disagreement. Students should not be brought up in one or another camp, and surveying all the various factions takes time away from the literature itself. Even old Aristotelian concepts like plot, character, and theme risk stereotyping the way readers think of fiction and drama. The priority for students is to experience the literature itself. Parallel to choice of texts is the second issue of control—who decides interpretations.

The currents of literary theory flow around three poles—the author, the text, and the reader. Which is most authoritative for determining meaning? Factions differ over emphasis on one or the other or over the relations among them. These relations are so basic that if students are enabled to select and deal with texts in the ways recommended here, they will reinvent the schools of literary theory for themselves, which is how they should first know them. Literary history and critical theory can enhance response, but you would do best to bring these spontaneously into students' discussions, performances, or other reworkings of texts, when they can use such ideas to extend their initial responses. Terminology is unimportant.

The following are selected means to reading maturity and involvement in literature.

Partner Reading

Partner reading is taking turns sight-reading aloud to each other in a group of two to four students who have chosen to read a text together. Partners may have a copy each of the same text or may pass one book around. The activity teaches more if all have a copy to follow while others read. One purpose is to allow weak or dependent readers to read collectively while socializing and to pool their skills to read a text that any one of them alone might not have enough knowledge, courage, or motivation to get through.

Part of the point is not even to help each other but to read collectively for the sharing of responses. Asides are more than welcome. Excellent discussion, in fact, often follows from casual comments interjected into the reading. Members compare interpretations or predictions, swap observations or tales prompted by the text, and generally enrich each other's comprehension at the same time that they become more aware of their own reactions to the text. This is how students come to value personal responses to reading. This is also the genesis of literary criticism.

Dramatizing and Performing Texts

Dramatizing and performing texts entail close interpretation in order to know what to render and how to render it. Players working up a performance must think about and discuss many aspects of the text, and this experience pays off handsomely during silent reading. Students become attuned to tone and style by imitating characters and playing roles. The structural cues and patterns of texts encountered in silent reading can often be translated through drama into visual, auditory, and spatial equivalents.

Reading aloud is the base from which performing a text is a natural extension. Working up a reading with one to three partners prepares well for bigger script rehearsals. A small group can render a text by simply reading in unison or by reading aloud one at a time. The goal may or may not be presentation to an audience. As a development of partner reading, playing with the text may itself be enough of an incentive. Or the group may rehearse until students perfect a version to record.

The general procedure for rehearsed reading is to sift and discuss some reading selections, talk some about the main point and approach of the text chosen, try reading parts to get a sense of who should take certain voices and how the piece should be treated, then cast and rehearse. Typically, this process interweaves silent reading (as members study the text a bit to size it up), trial oral readings (as they sound out the text to listen for ideas about meaning and the best rendering), consulting the dictionary and other people for pronunciation and definition and other information, discussion of author's intention and characterization and so on (as they work out the content to be expressed), and textual analysis (as they dig for helpful particulars).

Acting out memorized scripts is what most teachers think of first when they envision performing texts. This often evokes images of hours of rehearsal and the frantic tension of the final production of a play—complete with costumes, stage, lights, properties, and so on. If this is what performances of texts were as a regular routine, few teachers could justify them as a staple classroom process, as we recommend. Occasional performances of memorized scripts for a large audience are enjoyable and stimulating, of course, but regular rehearsed reading, text in hand, for an audience of people at hand is by far the more valuable experience for the total language development of the student.

Any rehearsed reading or singing can be recorded on audio- or videotape and played later for an audience. As students listen and discuss changes between tapings, they become sensitized to various voicings of text. Producing a tape provides a stimulus to read. And the tapes become part of the classroom library for other students to listen to themselves or to use with the text and read along.

Listening to and Watching Performed Texts

Read large quantities of stories and poems to students, sometimes assembled as a whole class, sometimes in small groups. Before youngsters can read much themselves, this practice is, of course, a necessity if their appetite for literature is to be both nourished and satisfied. It also makes reading a common part of everyday life and shows many children of nonreading parents what books are all about and what pleasure and stimulus can be associated with them. It also puts you in a giving position. While receiving this gift, learners develop an urge to assume the teacher's power, to become able to do themselves what the teacher does. In this respect you become a model to emulate.

Continuing to read to youngsters who have themselves learned how to read serves to show what good oral reading is like—how it recreates a storyteller's voice, how it brings out moods and feelings and meanings, how it follows cues of punctuation and typography. Your interpretive readings prepare students to read to other people. Hearing a text read aloud well while following it with the eyes helps students to learn to read better both aloud and silently. From good recordings they can hear all aspects of print brought skillfully to life—letters, typography, paragraphing, punctuation marks, and line settings of poetry. Pronunciations of words rarely heard in common speech are sounded while the listeners are looking at the words, enabling them to read those words aloud when encountered and also encouraging them to use those words in conversation without fear of mispronouncing them.

Modern technical texts can become accessible also despite unfamiliar terms, heavy loading of thought and information, and difficult sentence structures. Hearing Shakespeare can almost obviate the need for textual notes, for professional actors can not only give pronunciations of old words and proper names but also make clear the meaning of words that have changed sense and unravel difficult syntax caused by older grammar and poetic compression. This is in addition to bringing out the drift of whole speeches, the characterization of speakers, and the dramatic interplay among characters. Excellent discussion is often prompted by students' surprise that the voice they hear on a recording does not sound as they imagined it when reading silently.

Transforming Texts

To transform a text is to take the essence of what it expresses and transfer it to another form of writing or to another medium altogether.

- Any tale that learners have read can be shared with others by paraphrasing.
- A prose fable can be rewritten as a poem, an anecdote as a script, a story as a series of letters, a biography as an autobiography, a diary as a memoir, or a mystery story as a film script.
- Rewriting prose or poetry as a script automatically shifts the medium from book to stage, radio, film, or television. Or texts might be recast into a nonverbal medium through music, dance, drawing, or mime.

Reading Journals

Students reading silently need a way to *register* their responses—bring them to awareness—equivalent to uttering responses in collective reading. Annotating the margins of a text would be the most direct way, but most often the text is not the student's own. Occasionally, however, students can photocopy a short text so as to leave unusually wide margins for annotating. Suggest sometimes that a group silently reading a text in common do this and bring their annotations to the ensuing discussion. Or individuals could do this for a one-to-one conference with you.

Annotations link responses directly to words, phrases, or passages that prompted them. Encourage students to underline, circle, draw arrows, or invent other graphics to single out and relate these citations to each other and to the marginal remarks. Make clear that they may jot down anything that comes to mind while reading that text—memories, images, feelings, observations, all sorts of associations. These may not have anything to do with *explaining* or *evaluating* the text, though they might, if desired at some point, be used for that. Annotations are a record of a reading experience for later reference in discussion or other follow-up. Annotation should lead easily into journals and establish the idea of registering responses immediately and relating them specifically to certain parts of the text.

Some readers find a double-entry journal useful. On one half of a journal page they note what occurs to them about a text and leave the other half for a later response to the response. They may ask the teacher or someone else to write on this blank half what occurs to them about the original entry. This can become a valued and valuable dialogue about reading experience. (See the periodical about dialogue journals of all sorts, *Dialogue*, edited by Jana Staton, Joy Kreeft Peyton, and Shelley Gutstein, Center for Applied Linguistics, 4646 40th St NW STE 200, Washington, DC, 20016.) Or the readers themselves might make the second entry at a more removed moment, perhaps after reading something else during the interim.

Readers bring their journals to conferences or group discussions and refer to them while sharing. They can also mine them for writing ideas, which are often triggered by reading.

Discussing Reading

When a group has finished reading a selection, members may come together to raise questions about things they did not grasp, things they want to know more about, or issues in the selection they want to talk about. They can jot these down and bring them to the group. They also just share opinions or feelings about what they have read and compare interpretations. This comparing is of vast importance, for it allows readers to discover that their reactions or interpretations may not be the only ones justified by the text.

Such a group is, of course, ideal for sharing entries in the reading journals. Once students are familiar and fluent with discussion based on reading journals, there is no more powerful way to enrich understanding of texts and increase the range of reader response. It will do more for the study of literature than any other activity you can sponsor.

Writing in Literary Forms

Students who have tried their hand at writing fiction, poems, and scripts have an inside track on understanding what professional authors do with those forms. Participating in writing workshops focused on them enhances considerably the appreciation of literature, because not only are learners role-playing the poet, playwright, or short story writer, they are reading drafts of similar efforts by partners. Being part of the creation of these texts as both author and audience sensitizes them to many issues of the writer's craft that increase enjoyment and perception manifold.

We believe such democratic and collaborative ways of learning to interpret will carry all students to their maximum development in literacy and literature.

Mariposa, California 95338

National-Louis University
Evanston, Illinois 60201

Chapter Thirteen

Who Counts?

James Moffett
Free-Lance Educational Consultant and Writer
Berkeley, California

In this lively series of vignettes, Moffett ties together the social, educational, and governmental, and in doing so demonstrates some of his earliest attention to educational policy and reform, and the intertwined nature of society and schooling.

Personal responsibility is to fiscal accountability as lovemaking is to a gynecological examination.

* * * * *

Whenever the learner cares less about evaluating his learning than someone else does, then the educational system is already in grave trouble, and we have a clue to why it is.

* * * * *

Each party in education should assess his own and only his own work—learner, teacher, administrator, parent—and never ask anyone else to do it for him or agree to do it for anyone else.

* * * * *

No administrator or teacher can possibly exert enough control over learning results to be held truly accountable for them and must therefore, to protect his livelihood, resort to measures that inevitably impair learning.

* * * * *

If I'm to be held accountable for my students' performance, then I must be granted powers far exceeding any ever accorded teachers

Originally published in *English Journal*, vol. 61, no. 4, 1972, pp. 571–74. Reprinted with permission of NCTE.

heretofore—to control the materials purchased, the methods permitted, learning sites, scheduling, grouping and mixing, style and atmosphere, and to abolish censorship, centralized adoption and curriculum determination, grammar teaching (though it cost the superintendent his job), and grades and testing (though it render accountability itself difficult to implement).

* * * * *

If it's true, as most educational research tends to show, that student performance correlates more with socioeconomic background than with any school factors, how can I as teacher control the learning for which I'm accountable—especially if it's language that's being learned, and if preschool or out-of-school influences are stronger than those in class?

* * * * *

Everywhere that strict fiscal and job accountability has been tried, it has led to the undermining of the institution's function in favor of CYA (the Army term for Cover Your Ass).

* * * * *

The same Federal administrations that squandered eighty billion dollars in a worse than useless war have said that education must tighten its belt because it is wasting money.

* * * * *

Minority reformers and white liberals often think that behavioral objectives, programming, planning, and budgeting systems, performance contracting, etc. will alleviate corruption and incompetence, whereas such systems are bound to fail, being unnecessary for the good people on whom they place a hampering burden, and being ineffectual for the dishonest and incompetent, who merely cheat and use the accountability system itself as a means of getting more than they give.

* * * * *

State by state—with California leading the way of course—this nation is starting to bet its children on a system of measurement, PPBS, that is itself unmeasured and unmeasurable.

* * * * *

The first rule of evaluation is that the means of measuring must never dictate, displace, or distort what is being measured, but no public school system now honors this rule.

* * * * *

The kind of full reporting system required to compare costs with benefits or one teaching program with another requires in turn the converting of school systems into vast labs and scoreboards, because such a strict accounting cannot function without ascribing learning results to teaching causes, and this futile effort to control variables must *of necessity* end in decomposing learning into units so small, fragmented, and rigidly sequenced as to make the accountability system the determiner of school activities rather than the measure of them.

* * * * *

Whenever a performance contractor cannot succeed by juggling numbers, teaching directly to the payoff tests, eliminating all learning but the payoff targets, showing temporary short-term gains, or bribing students to do their cheating for him, he has only to avail himself of all those powers especially granted to him but denied to regular personnel—to waive the usual curriculum and bureaucratic routines and to choose his own methods, materials, setting, scheduling, staffing dispositions, etc.

* * * * *

The job of schools is not to prescribe *what* should be learned but to facilitate *how* to learn *anything*, from which it follows that statements of specific objectives and of performance criteria for ringing a bell when they have been reached are pointless and can only impede reaching the main goal.

* * * * *

Since increased school costs have led to the call for tighter accountability, and since the main rise in school costs is caused by union-negotiated increases in teacher salaries, it is difficult not to see in the job accountability trend a goodly measure of management retaliation against recently organized labor.

* * * * *

If such movements as Program Planning Budgeting Systems (PPBS) and performance contracting succeed, within three to five years most students, and probably teachers too, will abandon schools in revulsion to this final turn of the screw.

* * * * *

It is no random freak that the atomized breakdown of instruction into itsy-bitsy steps that is the logical end of fiscal accountability so closely resembles the programmed materials that the education industry is trying hard to plug into schools.

* * * * *

The so-called problems of learning to read and write are not *learning* problems but *institutional* problems, the chief one of which is and always has been some form of accountability, for the institution to check and control itself.

* * * * *

Except perhaps in some very small, monolithic communities, any school board in this splintered nation that claims to have drawn up a set of specific and commonly agreed on objectives is deceiving itself or the customers, for only on a few general human universals is consensus possible.

* * * * *

Systems of fiscal accountability inevitably prefer the reactionary divisions of learning into grades 1, 2, 3, etc. and into science, social studies, reading, and language arts, because they have to have breakdowns that can be made good, reportable budget categories and that, furthermore, won't change in a year or so, whereas even the mildly revolutionary trends such as nongradedness, team teaching, elective courses, and humanistic syntheses tend to make the systems unworkable, so that any truly radical reform of schools away from breakdowns toward wholeness of learning will run into fierce resistance from a technocratic organization stretching from Washington down through the local district.

* * * * *

Since the improvement of schools depends on offsetting the negative side effects of their own institutionalism, any deep or honest effort at reform will not focus on increased accountability but on protecting learning from the already disastrous effects of the institution's obsessive self-monitoring.

* * * * *

Accountability is a red herring used to cover up real problems such as tax inequities; the exploitation of schools for jobs, markets, and votes; the strengthening of Federal centralization and Presidential control; and the diversion of public money into such powerfully lobbied private sectors as the defense industry.

* * * * *

It is the learner who should be developing performance criteria—to find out what happens when he says things this way or writes things that way—by having constant opportunities to get and give reactions about language action.

* * * * *

If we were serious about accountability, we would work it up from the people, not down to them, by replacing the present monopolistic, captive-clientele system of *compulsory* education with a free-choice, open-market competition of learning facilities such that, by some means of redistributing tax money, the learner and his family could choose and support only the kind of education that seemed to *them* to yield their money's worth, but you won't hear bureaucrats and businessmen lobbying for that sort of accountability, truly based on the people's choice—nor perhaps teachers either, for that matter.

* * * * *

Only a few basic ways of learning exist, which we already know and can easily assess—motivated trials by a learner to reach his goals, plentiful response from his environment that tells him where he may have missed, and his self-corrective response to this response—and so the best educational strategy is to give those fundamental processes everything we've got, evaluate only whether those processes are working unimpeded, and quit pretending that learning and its assessment are great mysteries that only the creation of many more technical jobs and markets will solve.

* * * * *

The most serious single cause of reading and writing failures—and it makes hash of all our shuffling and mumbling about materials and methods—is the negative set of feelings and attitudes induced in learners by the constant quizzing, testing, questioning, grading, criticizing, prodding, and, in effect, *punishing* that occurs every time they attempt to read or write but that is required to answer the question, "How am I doing?" or "How is he doing?"—or required just to force out enough performance to assure everybody that we have a going concern here about which such questions can be asked.

* * * * *

If the main goal of education is, precisely, to learn how to set and reach goals, then the more that adults do this *for* children, instead of helping them develop good judgment in making decisions, then the more the adults are robbing children of their education to solve their own problems, which, for lack of such an education themselves, they do not know how to solve any other way.

CHAPTER FOURTEEN

Speaking Truth to Power: Remembering "Who Counts" in English Education

JORY BRASS

In this 2018 English Journal *column, Jory Brass recalls Moffett's "Who Counts?" and its scathing critique of educational accountability reforms in the 1970s in order to posit that the same questions and concerns that Moffett had fifty years ago are just as relevant and timely today.*

Accountability is a red herring used to cover up real problems such as tax inequities; the exploitation of schools for jobs, markets, and votes; the strengthening of Federal centralization and Presidential control; and the diversion of public money into such powerfully lobbied private sectors as the defense industry.

—JAMES MOFFETT, "Who Counts?"

Forty-five years ago, one of the National Council of Teachers of English's (NCTE) most influential figures unleashed a scathing critique of educational accountability reforms that Richard Nixon's administration launched with the support of corporate America. Writing on behalf of NCTE's commission on "The Teacher and Accountability," James Moffett listed more than two dozen reasons why NCTE opposed policies to hold teachers "accountable" for student performance measures. *English Journal* published Moffett's provocative essay with

Originally published in *English Journal*, vol. 107, no. 4, 2018, pp. 85–88. Reprinted with permission of NCTE.

NCTE's 1971 "Resolution on Accountability" to elaborate on NCTE's opposition to the teacher accountability movement.

Moffett's commissioned article played with the double meaning of its title, "Who Counts?" On one hand, Moffett argued that English teachers did not "count" because English could not be reduced to countable or observable measures, such as learning objectives, outcomes, and competencies. On the other hand, he believed the English education profession would no longer "count"—professionally or politically—if government and corporate leaders ever gained control over their field of professional judgment. In his view, any meaningful reform of education would not *increase* accountability, but protect teaching and learning from its "already disastrous effects" (Moffett 573).

Moffett's rejection of teacher accountability drew from a series of NCTE resolutions that opposed learning objectives, standardized testing, and any curriculum or accountability structures that failed to involve students, teachers, and the public in the governance of public education. Today, however, NCTE has shifted its positions on teacher accountability and "partnered" with the federal government, venture philanthropy, and the private sector in education reform. In the interest of "speaking truth to power," this column revives Moffett's forgotten article on teacher accountability to highlight how NCTE's recent policy positions constitute radical shifts in NCTE's political agenda. In doing so, I also hope to spur debate within the broader NCTE community about "who counts" in English education.

Who Counts?

As accountability reforms emerged in the 1970s, Moffett and the NCTE discussion group declared it was fundamentally unfair to hold administrators or teachers accountable for student performance measures: "No administrator or teacher can possibly exert enough control over learning results to be held truly accountable for them" (Moffett 571). Moreover, any "statements of specific objectives and performance criteria for ringing a bell when they have been reached are pointless and can only impede" the teaching and learning of English (572).

Moffett noted that accountability measures impeded reading and writing development by forcing students to demonstrate pre-specified performance criteria. The focus on student performance measures obscured the intrinsic pleasures and social nature of reading and writing; it also led to punitive teaching and assessment practices that sabotaged learning and engagement by triggering "the negative set of feelings and attitudes induced in learners by the constant quizzing, testing, grading, criticizing, prodding, and, in effect, *punishing* that occurs every time they attempt to read or write" (Moffett 574; italics in original).

Accountability measures also narrowed English teachers' already limited control over their work. It placed a "hampering burden" on good teachers and encouraged "obsessive" surveillance and management in schools (Moffett 572). Indeed, Moffett predicted, if schools would fully implement the emerging standards and accountability agenda, it would take only three to five years "for most students, and probably teachers too, to abandon schools in revulsion to this final turn of the screw" (572–73).

In Moffett's view, teacher accountability also violated the first rule of educational assessment. Any system to hold teachers accountable for measures of student performance would, "*of necessity* . . . make the accountability system the determiner of school activities rather than the measure of them"—an obvious misuse of assessment (572; italics in original). Standardized assessments also served the commercial interests of the for-profit education industry by priming the education market for prepackaged materials aligned with standards and accountability measures: "it is no random freak that . . . the logical end of fiscal accountability so closely resembles the programmed materials that the education industry is trying hard to plug into schools" (Moffett 573).

For Moffett, the increased commercialization and outsourcing of teaching and assessment under the accountability model was part of a broader attack on teachers, teacher unions, and socially progressive approaches to teaching English. If educators paid any attention to politics, Moffett explained, "it is difficult not to see in the job accountability trend a goodly measure of management retaliation against recently organized labor" (Moffett 572). He also lamented how accountability spawned "a technocratic organization stretching from Washington[, DC] down through the local [school] district" that worked against progressive, humanistic, and radical approaches to English (573). Lastly, if academic achievement correlated with a student's socioeconomic status more than with any school factors, the logical target of reform was not schools, but social and economic inequalities (571). However, Nixon-era Republicans and corporate leaders mobilized the language of "accountability" to rationalize policies that cut educational funding, shifted public resources to the private sector, and scapegoated teachers for the nation's social, economic, and political problems—the "red herring" that masked how government policies and corporate practices contributed to social and economic inequalities (Moffett). Thus, English teachers had compelling reasons to resist reforms that held them accountable for student performance measures and that shifted educational authority to the federal government and corporate America.

NCTE's Present Agenda

Many of Moffett's fears concerning educational measurement, the private sector, and federal policy have been realized through standards and accountability reforms supported by the Bush and Obama administrations. At the same time, NCTE's political agenda has shifted from the oppositional positions it drafted in the 1970s and held into the 2000s. The organization's shifting positions on "who counts" in English education become obvious when juxtaposing its recent positions on teacher evaluation, the Common Core, and federal-corporate partnerships in English education with its 1970s opposition to teacher accountability.

First, the NCTE Executive Committee's 2012 position on teacher evaluation has combined two forms of accountability that Moffett considered oppositional in the 1970s: test-based accountability and professional development-based accountability. Echoing several NCTE positions of the 1970s, Moffett identified the former as a threat to the latter, as teacher accountability reduced English to behavioral measures and positioned non-educators to steer educators' work through high-stakes standardized assessments (Moffett). In contrast, NCTE's present position on teacher evaluation "acknowledge[s] the *dual* purposes of evaluation of teachers—professional development *and* accountability"—as they now aim "to align quality assurance purposes with professional growth" and recognize performance measures that "assist school leaders in making major personnel decisions such as retention, tenure, and dismissal" (NCTE Executive Committee; italics in original).

NCTE's 2012 position explicitly rejects "an overemphasis on accountability rooted in testing" and notes that teacher evaluation systems should consider "a wide range of evidence, including classroom observations, teacher-developed materials, student products and performances, and student feedback." At the same time, however, NCTE's "characteristics of a fair and effective teacher evaluation system" now validate statistical and behavioral measures that Moffett rejected as reductive and inappropriate assessments: "test-based accountability," "clearly defined standards of teacher performance," "effective teaching behaviors," and "quantitative measures of student achievement" (NCTE Executive Committee). Ironically, accountability measures that Moffett dismissed as "unnecessary, ineffectual, distorted, and bound to fail" (572) now constitute what the NCTE Executive Committee identifies as necessary measures of "a fair and effective teacher evaluation system."

NCTE's "neutral" stance on the Common Core State Standards (CCSS) marks another shift from its 1970s opposition to standards and accountability. Official NCTE publications claim the organization neither endorses nor opposes the Common Core. At the same time, NCTE and its affiliated National Writing Project (NWP) have mobilized their teacher networks to support and accelerate the implementation of the CCSS—standards that philanthropic foundations, testing companies, and edu-businesses developed through a process that deliberately excluded students, teachers, and professional organizations (Williamson). NCTE has joined with the NWP and private sector partners to produce online resources, a book series, professional development, and commercial materials to help English teachers understand and integrate key instructional shifts determined by the standards movement that excluded them (www.ncte.org/standards/common-core). This move to align English teaching with standards and accountability measures set outside of the education profession constitutes a radical shift from NCTE's political agenda in the 1970s—when Moffett found it hard *not* to see standards and accountability as an attack on the teaching profession and a corporate agenda to commercialize and outsource education to the private sector.

In 2009, however, former NCTE executive director Kent Williamson announced NCTE's commitment to "putting into practice" educational initiatives funded by federal grants, philanthropic foundations, and private sector investors. For example, NCTE strategically (and successfully) positioned itself for a share of the $110 billion that the US Department of Education made available to education providers who would support the implementation of the CCSS, CCSS assessments, and data systems designed to hold teachers and teacher educators accountable for student progress on standardized tests (Williamson). Williamson conceded that these ventures posed "something of a quandary" for professional organizations, but NCTE would align itself with educational initiatives funded by the federal government, philanthropy, and private sector partners: "While we are wise to look critically at the emerging plans, it is hard to argue about the gigantic sums they are making available . . ." (Williamson).

Since 2010, NCTE and NWP press releases have promoted more than $66 million in funding from federal grant schemes, the Bill and Melinda Gates Foundation, and private-sector matching grants to develop curricula aligned with the CCSS (NWP), support implementation of the CCSS (NCTE), accelerate CCSS implementation by scaling awareness of the CCSS's instructional shifts across their networks (NWP), and align professional development and teacher leadership with the CCSS (NWP). Moffett feared the demise of the English teaching professions if "bureaucrats and businessmen" ever steered English teachers' work through externally defined standards and accountability measures. Today, the US Department of Education and the Bill and Melinda Gates Foundation recognize the NCTE and NWP as official "partners" in K–12 education as they fund the organizations to align English education with a standards and accountability regime developed by entrepreneurs, testing companies, venture philanthropists, and edu-businesses.

Democratic Accountability

James Moffett could take for granted that the NCTE community opposed these teacher accountability reforms. NCTE's 1971 position laid out in the "Resolution on Accountability" did not hold English teachers accountable to externally defined performance measures, standards developed by entrepreneurs and testing companies, federal SEED and Investing in Innovation grants, or the Gates Foundation. Instead, NCTE's 1970s leadership chose to defend a social democratic position on educational accountability:

> English teachers recognize their accountability to various groups—to students, to colleagues both within and without the discipline of English, to parents, to the local community which supports the schools, and to the wider communities beyond it. However, they reject the view that their goals and objectives can be stated only in quantifiably measurable terms, describing the behavior their students will display at the completion of instruction. (NCTE)

NCTE's 1971 position also asserted that accountability applied to students, parents, communities, and government—each of whom needed to provide financial, cultural, and social support to teachers, public schools, and the public good.

Today, however, NCTE's political agenda has radically reconfigured "who counts" in English education. NCTE has muted its former critiques of behavioral measurement in English, aligned "accountability" and "quality assurance" measures with its externally funded "professional development" initiatives, and now partners with the federal government, philanthropy, and the private sector to align English teachers' practice with curriculum and accountability frameworks developed outside of the education professions.

Moffett's 1972 essay is timely today as it helps educators to remember and imagine a very different NCTE. At the onset of teacher accountability reforms, NCTE commissioned a prominent teacher-scholar to elaborate more than two dozen reasons to oppose the federal and corporate movement to hold English teachers "accountable" for student performance measures. With NCTE increasingly aligning itself with a political agenda that resembles and extends the accountability agendas it opposed from the 1970s into the 2000s, the broader NCTE community might engage NCTE's past positions to evaluate how its present positions on teacher evaluation, the Common Core, Gates Foundation, and federal reforms may or may not impede the teaching and learning of English, diminish the teaching profession, extend surveillance and management in schools, elevate private sector and market interests above those of the public sector, accelerate the commercialization and privatization of education, and legitimize a "red herring" that erodes democratic accountability, the public interest, and broader struggles for social and economic justice (Moffett).

At the very least, English teachers, academics, and NCTE leaders might remember James Moffett's timely question as they work out their positions, practices, and partners in English education: Who counts?

Works Cited

Moffett, James. 1972. "Who Counts?" *English Journal*, vol. 61, no. 4, 1972, pp. 571–74.

NCTE. "Resolution on Accountability." National Council of Teachers of English, 1971, www.ncte.org /positions/statements/accountability.

NCTE Executive Committee. "NCTE Position Statement on Teacher Evaluation." National Council of Teachers of English, 2012, www .ncte .org/positions/statements/teacher evaluation.

Williamson, Kent. "Policy into Practice: CEE and NCTE." CEE Conference. Chicago, IL: NCTE, 2009.

CHAPTER FIFTEEN

Assessment as Storytelling: Inviting Preservice Teachers to (Mis)Behave When Writing about Students' Learning

JESSICA RIVERA-MUELLER

Assessment theorists in English studies argue that assessment is a process that can help educators create better teaching and learning experiences (Huot; Adler-Kassner and O'Neill; Gallagher and Turley). Local teaching conditions, however, support assessment as "an instructional tool, not a policy tool," to varying degrees (Gallagher). As a teacher educator, I know my students—future middle and high school English teachers—will need to create their own assessment practices within the conditions of their local teaching context. While I want teachers to enact assessment practices that value language resources from all students and support students' ongoing learning, I recognize that teachers must make these decisions within their school's established structures. For this reason, I am invested in helping my students develop conceptual frameworks in my courses that can support their decision making when they become teachers. As they make decisions about how to design their own assessments and how to engage with assessments designed by others, I want them to be mindful of what is measured in the assessments and how they discuss those assessments with a range of stakeholders, particularly when assessments narrow what counts as learning.

Narrowing what counts as learning is especially problematic for literacy learning. Reading, writing, speaking, and listening—the four areas of literacy instruction in secondary English classrooms—are practices created in and mediated through social contexts and intertwined in the development of literacy. What counts as "good" or "successful" uses of literacy are socially constructed and contextual, and the connection between language and power shapes how the language resources students bring to the classroom are or are not valued. April Baker-Bell offers an example of the relationship between language and power when she argues:

> [T]he ubiquity of whiteness in schools erroneously positions White Mainstream English-speaking students as academically prepared to achieve because their cultural ways of being, their language, their literacies, their histories, their values, and their knowledges are privileged in classrooms. From this assumption, linguistically marginalized students of color are falsely positioned as linguistically inadequate because their language practices do not reflect White Mainstream English. (20)

Learning outcomes that seek measurable and observable progress toward narrow conceptions of literacy constrain teachers who want to value and support language resources from all students.

The challenge to center students' language resources and learning experiences is not a new challenge, a point richly elaborated in the scholarship of James Moffett. Throughout his career, Moffett argued for learning activities that create meaningful learning experiences rather than simply producing documentable student performances. In his masterwork on assessment, *Detecting Growth in Language*, Moffett argued that *observing* students' in situ processes and products can greatly inform teachers' understandings of student learning; however, the activities and products should be connected to "the goals themselves of speaking, reading, writing, and thinking—of communicating, collaborating, decision-making, problem-solving, creating, and interpreting texts—not some exercises that are means only, alleged to eventuate sometime in these goals" (4). Moffett believed that "testing activity . . . betrays the learning goals to the extent that it differs from them" (2). In making these claims, Moffett challenged educators to keep learners and their learning experiences at the center of instructional decision making.

Because the problem of narrowing what counts as learning persists, preservice teachers need frameworks for navigating assessment structures that require them to produce evidence of students' progress toward predetermined learning outcomes. Storytelling, as a practice of crafting stories about literacy learning, is one way for teachers to navigate the relationship between literacy learning and assessment activities without narrowing what counts as learning (Adler-Kassner; Fleischer and Garcia). When preservice teachers reflect in writing on their teaching as part of their clinical requirements, or when inservice teachers tell stories that are crafted for a variety of audiences (including students, parents/guardians, administrators, and community members), they contextualize the information that assessments communicate, creating and shaping broader cultural narratives about literacy learning.

Storytelling for the purpose of reflecting on learning and teaching also remains critical because "[t]oo often these days, the kind of thoughtful, research-based instruction that is at the core of pedagogical content knowledge appears at odds with calls for mandated curricula, standardized approaches to pedagogy, and standardized assessments" (Fleischer and Garcia 4). For this reason, scholars have called on teacher educators to help preservice teachers develop storytelling skills that enable them to engage in "everyday advocacy." For example, Fleischer and Garcia argue that "[s]uccessful educators in this new era need to go beyond the *what* and *how* of teaching literacy; they need also to be confident in their knowledge of *why* they teach in certain ways and, most importantly, *how* they might help others understand their reasons" (5, emphasis in original). Through storytelling, teachers can create a fuller picture of literacy learning, which can help them work within and against assessment structures. While working steadily to help my preservice English teachers conceptualize assessment as storytelling, I found a concrete approach for this activity when I returned to Moffett's scholarship. In this chapter, I share how I repurpose elements of Moffett's scholarship to encourage and invite preservice teachers to approach their necessary engagement with assessment as storytellers.

Repurposing Moffett's Argument

At the time of composing this chapter, my university requires all preservice teachers to complete the Praxis Performance Assessment for Teachers (PPAT) during their student teaching experience. The exam was created by Educational Testing Services to "effectively [measure] how teacher candidates apply content knowledge and teaching skills in the classroom," and passing the exam is required to obtain a professional teaching license in the state of Utah ("ETS Performance Assessments"). In the exam, preservice teachers must write detailed accounts of their own teaching performance and their students' learning to demonstrate their ability to be a reflective teacher. To craft these stories of learning and teaching, preservice teachers need to identify and evaluate the way learning is framed in the PPAT exam in order to decide how they want to utilize and/or disrupt that frame of learning in writing up their own responses. By combining Moffett's ideas about learning with the notion of assessment as storytelling, I aim to help preservice teachers understand how their words and actions create stories about student learning and how crafting stories that center on language resources for all students is an aspect of becoming an "equity-oriented teacher" (Bieler).

These conversations occur in my "Teaching Literacy in Diverse Classrooms" course, one that is paired with a thirty-hour clinical teaching experience in a secondary classroom. Together, the coursework and the clinical experience create a process-oriented learning environment in which preservice teachers examine definitions of and perspectives on literacy learning. Because my students practice teaching in this course, I have designed an assignment that requires them to practice writing responses for one of the four tasks included in the PPAT exam. Most of my students will complete the PPAT exam the following semester, so they appreciate the opportunity to learn about and prepare for the high-stakes exam in my course. Our work with the exam, however, is critical. Rather than simply studying how to perform well on it, we study how the exam is a context for studying and practicing how they construct stories about student learning and their own performances as teachers. As a teacher educator, I believe this high-stakes and compulsory exam is a context (like future ones they will encounter) where they can practice navigating competing conceptions of literacy learning and move (uncomfortably) between resistance and compliance, freedom and constraint.

My teaching approach is an activity of repurposing, creating "something new out of existing conditions," because I use Moffett's scholarship, especially "Misbehavioral Subjectives" (*Coming on Center*), to help preservice teachers critically engage with the writing they compose (about their students' learning) for the exam (Stenberg 11). "Misbehavioral Subjectives" is a powerful teaching tool because it historicizes the field's relationship with assessment practices and offers specific language for analyzing the behaviorist underpinnings of many contemporary assessment practices. Because the text supports both pedagogical goals, I introduce it in the first half of the semester to build a shared vocabulary for class discussions throughout the course. With this approach, Moffett's voice circulates with contemporary literacy scholars, which enables us to recursively examine our definitions of literacy learning. In this way preservice teachers' intellectual growth is like "a circle that becomes filled with more and more detailed and interfused figures" (Moffett, *Detecting Growth* 8).

Put simply, I use Moffett's scholarship to transform a test preparation experience into a learning experience that focuses on understanding the concept of assessment as storytelling. In particular, I use Moffett's critique of behaviorist assumptions—ones that often shape the kinds of stories that are told about literacy learning—to help preservice teachers interrogate the specific narrative choices that operate in their own and others' stories about literacy learning. In the final section of this chapter, I elaborate on the elements of Moffett's ideas that I share with my students and provide examples of student writing to show the ways in which they take up Moffett's critiques of behavioral objectives in their own development as teachers. In doing so, I do not make an argument about the PPAT exam, nor do I make an argument about whether I agree with my students' perspectives. Instead, I aim to share how Moffett's scholarship has been an important teaching tool for developing my students' critical awareness of assessment practices.

"Misbehavioral Subjectives"

The primary work of Moffett's that I use with my students comes from Chapter 2 of *Coming on Center*. In the essay, he argues that an uncritical use of behavioral objectives distorts and corrupts learning processes: "No one has ever tried to measure the incalculable negative effects of keeping children perpetually under this kind of spotlight and of regarding them as score-sources while they are trying to grow up" (*Coming on Center* 11). Reducing learning to what is *only* linear, measurable, and observable limits students' opportunities to learn, carries broad implications for teachers (preservice and inservice), and raises important ethical questions about the consequences of using *only* these types of standardized and quantifiable assessments—which we no longer call "behavioral objectives" but that nevertheless remain focused on observable performance or behaviors. When a teacher or evaluation process frames student learning in terms of behaviors, that process ignores the complexity inherent in the process of learning and limits the kinds of learning activities that educators imagine and create.

More than fifty years later, Moffett's harsh condemnation remains relevant both as a prescient warning to educators today and for the way it illuminates the context of the era from which it emerged. "Misbehavioral Subjectives" includes two parts: a statement that served as Moffett's resignation from his role as a consultant in the "Tri-University Project on Behavioral Objectives" and a reflection on the conditions surrounding his decision to write this statement. The statement—which Moffett composed in 1969—was first published as "Misbehaviorist English: A Position Paper" in *On Writing Behavioral Objectives for English*, a collection edited by John Maxwell and Anthony Tovatt in 1970. In this collection, Moffett challenges educators to critically examine their use of behavioral objectives as the standard for describing learning; in doing so, he was a critical voice in a period when "behavioral objectives" were the prevailing fashion for describing the aims and outcomes of instruction in schools. Moffett's "Misbehavioral Subjectives" offers readers an account of an important moment in the field's history, which creates a context for discussing how and why we have arrived at our current milieu of contemporary assessment beliefs and practices. For preservice teachers, it is a sobering educational experience to notice how relevant Moffett's arguments feel today.

In the headnote to the chapter, Moffett explains that the "Tri-University Project on Behavioral Objectives" was created through a two-year grant from the US Office of Education to produce "'A Catalog of Representative Behavioral Objectives in English, Grades 9–12'" (*Coming on Center* 10). Moffett shares the following explanation of the project and his role in a 1969 meeting of well-paid consultants to the project:

> During its first year, a couple dozen "consultants," including me, were to convene for a total of five days to write objectives for this catalog. Consultants comprised some leaders in English education and administrators representing schools where the objectives were to be field-tested during the second year in a "controlled" comparison between schools not using the objectives and those blessed with them. . . . The Tri-University directors were to revise and edit our objectives and, after field-testing and garnering reactions from outside readers, publish the Catalog for professional use. (*Coming On Center* 10)

Moffett explains the logic of the project by citing from the project's abstract: "'Behavioral scientists may provide some assistance [in defining the subject of English]. They focus upon the learner—the learner as a doer, as a reactor, as a person whose behavior can be influenced in measurable and desirable ways by the classroom and by his reading, viewing, listening, speaking, reading, and reasoning'" (*Coming on Center* 10).

Moffett contends that these policy positions that "pos[e] as child-centered while actually generating a very destructive 'constant focus upon the child' . . . [are] exactly parallel to the fraudulent doublespeak claims of programmed instruction to be 'individualized'" (*Coming on Center* 11). Moffett describes his increasing discomfort with the project throughout the three days that he convened with fellow consultants to write these objectives. He tells readers the following:

> For two days I was a good boy and went along; then at a cocktail party the evening before the third day I told the directors that I couldn't stomach it any longer. They understood, they said, and we agreed that I would spend the last day writing a paper on my position. (*Coming on Center* 11)

Together, Moffett's statement and reflection provide preservice teachers with a powerful model of inquiry, reflection, and professionalism, one that invites them to reflexively examine and critique current assessment practices. While preservice teachers may know that they don't want to teach to a test or let test results function as the only story of students' literacy learning, it can be difficult for them to identify and articulate problems with standardized approaches to assessment. The specific critiques of behavioral objectives that Moffett offers in "Misbehavioral Subjectives" help preservice teachers identify and examine how concepts—a teacher's role, assessment results, and learning goals—are framed, which is important for their ability to discover the specific frames they want to utilize and/or disrupt in their own practice.

When I introduce "Misbehavioral Subjectives," I begin by explaining that behavioral objectives are observable and measurable, and contemporary forms of behavioral objectives often include the following sentence stems: "At the end of this lesson, students will be able to do x" or "I can do x," a statement written from the student's perspective. Then, through a lecture, I narrate the story of Moffett's decision to write his statement, as I just articulated. Following the lecture, my students study three specific arguments that Moffett offers as critiques of behavioral objectives:

- They deny the importance of the interpretive work that occurs when teachers explain the meaning of student learning.
- They fail to acknowledge the complexity inherent in the process of learning.
- They limit the kinds of learning activities that teachers imagine and create.

Discussing these notions in small groups, whole-class discussions, and course projects throughout the remainder of the course, then, provides an opportunity for preservice teachers to learn from one another and refine and/or revise their beliefs about literacy learning, assessment practices, and storytelling.

To support the critical nature of the learning experience, the assignment I have designed includes two parts. The first part prompts students to practice writing responses for one of the four PPAT exam tasks. I ask students only to practice writing exam responses; I do not grade their responses. I want the process of writing responses to the exam's questions to teach them something about their beliefs and values as storytellers. In the second part of the project, I ask students to compose a "learning narrative," which shares the insights and questions that emerged through the first part of the project. In my prompt for the learning narrative, I ask students to consider the following questions:

- What narrative practices are valued in task 3?
- What stories are you encouraged to tell about student learning?
- What stories might be harder to tell within this exam? Why?
- How do your emerging notions of literacy function within these narrative practices?
- What are the ethical dimensions of representing students and their learning in these ways?
- How will this experience shape your future storytelling?

Again, I want the process of writing to help my students construct their own conception of assessment as storytelling.

I also provide an opportunity for students to discuss their narratives with one another. In this course, I have worked with most of the students in prior classes, so I trust them to use the processes of writing and dialoguing to (de)construct their beliefs about the assessment of literacy learning. Our conversations about Moffett's scholarship are an essential component of this approach because the critiques provide my students with specific ways to examine the definitions and values that operate in the PPAT exam. In the following section, I describe how I repurpose three of Moffett's claims about behavioral objectives and share moments from my students' writing that illustrate how they are navigating these concepts when they are positioned to represent student learning and their own teaching in the professional context of the PPAT exam.

Framing a Teacher's Role

The first critique I present to my students is Moffett's claim that behavioral objectives deny the importance of the interpretive work that occurs when teachers make claims about student learning. Moffett points out how the application of behaviorism to education has conflated the notion of observability with objectivity:

> [O]bserved behavior can be badly misinterpreted by a psychology that in the name of objectivity refuses to infer what is going on in the black box of our head but does not refuse to infer the meaning of observed behaviors because the latter are supposedly self-evident and entail no inferences. But any observation entails inferences. The claim to be an objective observer is really unscientific. The mere fact of being overt does not make a behavior objective. (*Coming on Center* 13)

Moffett adds to this critique that behaviorism's lack of "respect for inner processes" means that observers "can misinterpret certain confusions in the thought and speech of students as task failures when actually these confusions indicate arrival at a more complex stage of growth where more errors *can* be made" (14, emphasis in original). In making this claim, Moffett explains that a student's engagement with an assessment may be shaped by thinking or personal experience that is unknown to the observer. Moffett's claim challenges all educators to acknowledge the role our own inferences play in interpreting student learning, and to examine critically the kinds of sources we use to create our understandings of students' learning.

This critique also has the power, then, to help educators (re)frame a teacher's role in the assessment process—moving from a neutral observer of behaviors or correct answers to an invested stakeholder in students' lives, someone who actively shapes learning experiences. As I listen to my students grappling with the role of a teacher in the assessment processes—through their participation in the PPAT exam—I notice students' appreciation for what the exam signals about the duties of a teacher. Students notice how the exam questions "push the student teachers to look at how the nuts and bolts of the lesson connect to the bigger picture of standards and learning goals," thereby showing "how much thought should be occurring in the back of our minds at each moment." Students begin to grasp how purposefully designing instruction supports student learning. One student offered the following explanation:

> What was super important to me was that teachers need to know all the factors that go into helping students and differentiating instruction. . . . Teachers are not just going to school to teach kids some material out of a book. We need to be able to relate to their lives, use resources around us to help kids interact with their community and make a difference in it.

From these responses and others like them, I hear students framing the role of a teacher as someone who plans purposefully, continually questions their work, and learns about their students and community to create a meaningful context for learning. Their comments highlight how interpretation in examining student work includes more than an interpretation of the students' expressed thinking; it includes inferences about the learning context and students' literacy histories.

Students also note the additional roles that the exam doesn't seem to include. Students assert that the exam "pushes the student teacher to tell about student learning only in the form of their performance on learning activities"; therefore, the exam "looks at students at times as simply a product of what they can do based on our teaching." One student noted that she "was extremely frustrated by the small scope we see of the students. To add to the narrow view, it's from OUR narrow view." In these moments, I hear my students framing a teacher's role as a person able to tell a story about student learning but understanding that the story is not a full or definitive story.

I also hear students grappling with the kinds of tensions they anticipate encountering as they purposely consider the role of the teacher in the work of storytelling. One area is the relationship between planning and what my students name as "teacher intuition." One student explained this tension in the following way:

> Another thing that I struggled with is that while there are lots of things you can record and write out and plan for a lesson, so much of teaching is also intuitive and in the moment, particularly differentiation. I think it is always important to have a plan, but adjustments have to constantly be made on your feet as a teacher, and the task does not provide space to evaluate or demonstrate this well.

This issue emerged in another way as students reflected on the ways their interactions might shape their relationships with students. One student wrote, "We need to observe students to see how they react to our teaching methods; it's an important part of reflecting on your praxis. My concern is accurately describing these things without turning students into objects of study rather than people I am observing." This same student noted that she kept her own personal journal of her clinical experience, and she found that "narrative writing like this [was] much more productive" than her expository answers on the exam because it captured more of the classroom "activity."

Listening across these reflections, I hear my students applying an ecological perspective to the role of a teacher; they are striving to craft meaningful learning experiences and recognizing that literacy learning is sponsored in multiple contexts for multiple purposes. Within this framework, teachers must acknowledge their role in constructing interpretations and seek multiple opportunities and contexts for gathering the information that is used to create interpretations of student learning. In this way, my students echo Moffett's belief that "[t]o judge language growth, [teachers] have to sample a learner's speech on many different occasions and make a composite judgement" (*Detecting Growth* 6).

Framing Results from Assessments

The second critique I present is Moffett's claim that behavioral objectives fail to acknowledge the complexity inherent in the process of learning: "Some goals in English imply overt behavior and some do not. In insisting that desirable behaviors be *observable*, the behavioral approach rules out a great deal of learning" (*Coming on Center* 13, emphasis in original). Narrowing the curriculum to observable behaviors, then, narrows our conception of literacy learning. Adding to this critique, Moffett states that the

> effects of certain reading, acting, and writing on a student's social, emotional, and cognitive growth tend of course to be long-range and inextricable. Although it helps to acknowledge that many of these effects will occur years later and often out of school, in practice these effects will either not be observed by evaluators or be falsely attributed to more recent school treatment—or, most likely, be ignored because they cannot be causally traced. The greater the time-space span, the less likely it is that effects can be ascribed to their proper causes. (*Coming on Center* 13)

Because the behaviorist paradigm inherently seeks causal relationships, Moffett warns educators that we need multiple perspectives on students' learning. Results from assessments, in other words, become more meaningful when they include multiple perspectives and are contextualized as providing partial knowledge.

> The only hope for truth through observation is to synthesize the totality of observations—from different times and vantage points—into a full picture. This certainly must include the student's statements about what he had or had not learned, how and when. The interior and external views correct and corroborate each other. Discrepancies stimulate new insights. (*Coming on Center* 14)

This claim challenges educators to examine the causal relationships that are purported by any assessment and the perspectives that are present or not in any assessment.

Using Moffett's language about including students' perspectives, I challenge the students in my class to engage in conversations with their own students about their learning, a practice that can also help educators (re)frame the meaning of results from assessments. Listening to my students' reflections, I hear them making arguments for deeper attention to student feedback. One student, for example, explained that a student demonstrated her learning verbally but did not "capture it the same" on her written assignment, the evidence used for the exam's analysis of student work. From this experience, she felt that "it's unfair to evaluate our students' development, literacy, and learning based upon a single piece of work." Another student argued for student feedback because she recognizes that she "may describe and observe [behaviors] that are extremely off base." She writes,

> Yes, students may have succeeded in the learning activities, but did they really respond well to what I did? Students may have even failed the learning activities but could have learned and responded to the rest of the lesson plan. How could I possibly know that without their feedback. . . . WE are discussing students and observing them, but never asking them what they think and what they need.

This student (like others in the class) wants to ensure that her evaluations support her students' growth in meaningful ways.

In addition to wanting student feedback, I hear my students arguing for a closer attention to context. One student wrote, "[I]n the process of looking through the nuts and bolts of my instructional strategies, learning activities, and data, I felt that some of the questions seemed to ignore other aspects of being a student." Some students pointed out that the focus on individual achievement "overlooks the social aspects of a good learning environment. . . . Appreciating individual students for who they are is impactful, but it's very important to look at the bigger picture, too." Another student points us to the impact of time on assessment results, arguing that "[w]hat a student learns, how they succeed in school is an ongoing process, and [it] doesn't begin when we decide it does and it doesn't end when we decide it does." Students also noted their feelings that the exam doesn't account for the fullness of a student as an individual and the learning relationships that are present in the classroom. One student explained, for example, "Teachers don't know what is going to happen in the classroom that day—students are humans, and humans are highly unpredictable because we don't know what is going on in their lives after school."

Because "most learning is never shed but, rather, becomes assimilated or transformed into more advanced skills and knowledge," teachers' stories about learning need to be shaped by students' own understandings of their learning and attention to contextual factors (Moffett, *Detecting Growth* 8). In arguing for student feedback and closer attention to the learning context, I hear my students planning to frame future assessment results by contextualizing what is not present in the assessment and reflecting on the relationship between individual learners and the learning environment. Both storytelling strategies enact the idea that growth is "cumulative, not linear" (Moffett, *Detecting Growth* 8).

Framing Pedagogical Goals for Literacy Learning

The third critique I present is Moffett's claim that behavioral objectives can limit the kinds of learning activities that teachers imagine and create. I believe Moffett makes this claim most powerfully when he states:

> [M]ost major drawbacks in the present curriculum stem from just this self-defeating effort at systematization. Instead of reading, talking, acting, and writing for real, students are taking comprehension tests, doing book reports, writing "critical" papers about literature, parsing sentences, filling in blanks, etc., to make their learning visible to the teacher. Thus, the main impact of behavioral formulation in English will be to perfect the error of our present way. (*Coming on Center* 15)

Moffett explains that when learning objectives are specified through the behaviorist approach, they "become transformed into activities, which is necessary since [the more specified level] is the one that is actually behavioral or observable" (*Coming on Center* 15). He further argues, "[A]t least half of the activities are ones I would never consider desirable, such as filling in cloze passages[1] or listing the items of evidence in a speech or an essay" (15).

Beyond being undesirable, Moffett notes, "the amount and kind of activities that would have to be run off in the classroom in order to evaluate behavioristically would drive out and distort hopelessly the learning activities themselves" (*Coming on Center* 14). In making this claim, Moffett also advises educators to include student perspectives. He asserts:

> [B]ecause objectives determine evaluation, it is absolutely essential that the learner have a hand in formulating objectives. Otherwise, some kinds of learning behavior of value to him will never be written into the curriculum because they are not destined to be assessed. (14)

Moffett's claim challenges educators to reenvision the process of assessment with students at the center.[2]

Drawing from Moffett's critique, we can (re)frame pedagogical goals for literacy learning, from uniform and teacher centered to dynamic and student centered. This shift provides a framework for preservice teachers to critically analyze their roles and goals as they seek to enter the profession. Listening to my students' reflections, I hear them calling for richer pedagogical goals. One student wrote, "For the future, I want to focus on the multifaceted dimensions of a student's learning. It is not always well-represented in the work they turn in, but that doesn't mean a student is not learning." Based on my conversation with this student and others, I know my students want to create learning projects that encourage students to utilize the range of literacy resources they possess—even if those specific skills (e.g., adding artwork to complement an essay) are not formally assessed. Underscoring this idea, another student wrote,

> My job as an educator is to help students achieve literacy, but I need to ask myself, to what end? Why do my students need to read and write? For what purpose are my students going to use their literacy skill? Task 3 of the PPAT does not seem to ask these questions at all; rather, I feel that all the literacy skills we teach are for the purpose of achieving "learning goals" and "content standards." This is a rather limited view of what students do with reading and writing because of its

> narrow context: schoolwork. . . . In other words, the task seems to limit literacy and content learning to what students do in our classroom because it limits that learning to observable schoolwork.

While it is challenging to work within and against already established goals for literacy learning, framing literacy learning as dynamic rather than teacher centered is an approach I hear from my students. One student noted, for example, that the exam

> structured the questions to fit the narrative of what we do *to* kids: "What learning activities do *you* plan to implement in this lesson?" "To what extent did the lesson, including instructional strategies, learning activities, materials, resources, and technology, help to facilitate student learning?" "How does the evidence you collected support this finding?" Only one question asks what students did: "How did the students use the content presented to demonstrate meaningful learning?" Though the task asks us to plan for students, it does not give us time to really detail and describe what they did with the lesson, nor did it ask us what the students *thought* about the learning activities.

As this excerpt illustrates, a deeper focus on what students learn prompts educators to consider how we use students' language resources and learning goals.

As preservice teachers focus on the connection between learning activities and authentic learning experiences, they may also discover opportunities to revise their understandings of language learning. In *Detecting Growth in Language*, Moffett argues, "A lot of evidence supports the idea that many changes accepted as necessary growth are cultural and that in some respects it would be better for the culture than for the child to change" (68). Attention to students' experiences, especially as we value language resources from all students, can lead us to deeper conceptions of literacy. In this way, teachers can meet the National Council of Teachers of English's call for secondary teachers to "acknowledge that we all have cultural frameworks within which we operate, and everyone—teachers and students alike—needs to consider how these frameworks can be challenged or changed to benefit all peoples" (NCTE Commission on Reading).

(Mis)Behaving

When Moffett submitted his position paper, he asserted his belief that "[l]osing this battle means losing a lot more in the future" (*Coming on Center* 17). Today, his words seem nothing short of prophetic. Because attempts to standardize education have relied on behavioristic assumptions, we find ourselves aiming to reclaim learning experiences that have been lost and advocating for more inclusive conceptions of literacy learning within those experiences. Through repurposing, however, we can still learn from and apply Moffett's critical perspective on learning outcomes. Drawing from Moffett's ideas, teacher educators can help future teachers begin to create the language and practices that lead to fuller storytelling in assessment contexts, ones that often require teachers to make and communicate data-driven decisions. Through repurposing, preservice teachers can learn about the behavioristic assumptions that shape the kinds of stories that are told about teachers' roles, the results of assessments, and goals for literacy learning. Moffett's thinking is a valuable tool for helping future teachers develop a critical perspective that is necessary when beginning their English teaching careers.

Notes

1. A cloze passage is a contextual analysis strategy that asks students to learn to predict and verify the meaning of unfamiliar words or familiar words that have new or unusual meanings by searching for clues in nearby words, sentences, and paragraphs of a text. It is used before reading a text.

2. For a contemporary example, see Inoue, Asao B. *Labor-Based Grading Contracts: Building Equity and Inclusion in the Compassionate Writing Classroom*. WAC Clearinghouse, 2019.

Works Cited

Adler-Kassner, Linda. *The Activist WPA: Changing Stories about Writing and Writers*. Utah State UP, 2008.

———, and Peggy O'Neill. *Reframing Writing Assessment to Improve Teaching and Learning*. Utah State UP, 2010.

Baker-Bell, April. *Linguistic Justice: Black Language, Literacy, Identity, and Pedagogy*. Routledge / National Council of Teachers of English, 2020.

Bieler, Deborah. *The Power of Teacher Talk: Promoting Equity and Retention through Student Interactions*. Teachers College P, 2019.

"ETS Performance Assessments." *Educational Testing Services*, https://www.ets.org/ppa/.

Fleischer, Cathy, and Antero Garcia. *Everyday Advocacy: Teachers Who Change the Literacy Narrative*. W. W. Norton, 2021.

Gallagher, Chris W. *Reclaiming Assessment: A Better Alternative to the Accountability Agenda*. Heinemann, 2007.

———, and Eric D. Turley. *Our Better Judgment: Teacher Leadership for Writing Assessment*. National Council of Teachers of English, 2012.

Huot, Brian. *(Re)Articulating Writing Assessment for Teaching and Learning*. Utah State UP, 2002.

Moffett, James. *Coming on Center: English Education in Evolution*. Boynton/Cook, 1981.

———. *Detecting Growth in Language*. Boynton/Cook, 1992.

———. "Misbehaviorist English: A Position Paper." *On Writing Behavioral Objectives for English* edited by John Maxwell and Anthony Tovatt, National Council of Teachers of English, 1970, pp. 111–16.

NCTE Commission on Reading. "A Call to Action: What We Know about Adolescent Literacy Instruction." *National Council of Teachers of English*, 17 July 2018, https://ncte.org/statement/adolescentliteracy/.

Stenberg, Shari J. *Repurposing Composition: Feminist Interventions for a Neoliberal Age*. Utah State UP, 2015.

CHAPTER SIXTEEN

Insider Knowledge: Reading and Writing with James Moffett's Points of View

KATHLEEN (BUCHAN) KELLY
Teachers College, Columbia University

"A student writing in all the same forms as the authors he reads can know literature from the inside in a way that few students ever do today" (Moffett, *Teaching the Universe* 7). Is Moffett right? What "knowing" literature entails and whether students can come to do so intimately through writing was what I aimed to find out.

Why Moffett and Why Now?

In the summer of 2020, as schools remained in remote-instruction mode as a result of the COVID-19 pandemic, and at a time when the world as I had always known it was only nominally available in data streamed through fiber-optic lines and cellular transmission towers, I began to think a lot about distance. On what does our connection to and communication with one another depend?

James Moffett had my attention. Maybe it was his claim that the farther away we are from ourselves and the stories we tell, the greater the demands on the storyteller. Moffett takes up this idea in his short story anthology, *Points of View* (Moffett and McElheny). He describes a "narrator's increasingly complicated job of compiling and assimilating materials from more and more remote sources" when writing for a distanced, more "public audience" (569). In this remote time, how would we tell our stories to one another? Consciously or not, distance and proximity came to inform my planning for the high school Narrative Fiction course I would teach in the coming fall.

As the syllabus began to take shape, I decided I'd run this elective course for eleventh and twelfth graders using a writing workshop model. Absent real human connection, I wanted to build a writing community that would help to bridge our distance, as we remained unsure how much longer we'd have to remain quarantined. I also decided that Moffett's narrative spectrum, which he puts forth in *Points of View* (Moffett and McElheny), would guide my course design. I opted to employ a read-one, write-one approach to our study of literature. Imitation pieces would follow units on varied narrative perspectives. This course design would give me a chance to "test out" Moffett's theory about how, through the imitation of selected literary works, students can come to know literature more intimately. Along the way, we would enact the kind of English curriculum that Moffett calls for in "A Structural Curriculum in English," whereby students "learn language and literature through reading, writing, and discussing whole, authentic discourses" (*Teaching the Universe* 7). I also hoped such an experiment in teaching and writing might help the students and me to forge connections despite our remoteness to one another. In what follows, I report on what happened that fall.

I first explain the theory underpinning Moffett's narrative trajectory in *Points of View*, especially as it is informed by the work of semanticist S. I. Hayakawa. Then I describe the ways I both drew from and adapted Moffett's approach in *Points of View* in my coursework that term. Next, I offer a look at the data: student writing assignments, class notes, and end-of-term portfolios, with an eye toward seeing whether students' writing and analysis of their own writing gesture toward an understanding of the shifts in narrative perspective Moffett suggests. I also look to see the extent to which, through this process, they might be said to have come to know literature "from the inside." Finally, I consider the implications of this study for ELA writing classrooms. I begin with the idea of abstraction and the ways it is integral to Moffett's theory of narrative perspective.

On Abstraction

Moffett considered an awareness of abstraction integral to the work in the English classroom. He claimed that "a very large measure of what educators mean by 'teaching students to think' is in reality making them conscious of abstracting" (*Teaching the Universe* 27). Abstraction here is based on S. I. Hayakawa, who defined the process of abstracting as a process of "leaving characteristics out" (Hayakawa and Hayakawa 86). Moffett went to San Francisco to work with and make himself a student of Hayakawa in the 1960s, so it is not surprising that Hayakawa's ideas about how language functions show up subsequently in much of Moffett's writing. Hayakawa spoke of language as a collection of symbols (or abstractions), so that "[l]earning language is not simply a matter of learning words [the symbols]; it is a matter of correctly relating our words to the things and happenings for which they stand" (86). Understanding how symbols function within a language system was central to Hayakawa's work; he considered abstraction an essential aspect of epistemology. His illustration of the ways the process of abstraction shapes how we know what we know appears in his famous Abstraction Ladder (based on Alfred Korzybski's "Structural Differential"), represented in Figure 16.1 and explained in Table 16.1. Hayakawa's work would inform Moffett's narrative trajectory and design of *Points of View.*

In the Abstraction Ladder, Hayakawa instructs the reader to start reading from the bottom up to understand the process of abstracting: to read from "concrete" up toward "abstract." We can see that at the base level, the cow is something consisting of atoms and electrons and a specific DNA pattern resulting from an almost infinite set of possible combinations of such elemental units. At this "process level," we have a direct experience with the creature before us. As we follow a concept up the ladder, the symbols (or words to refer to the concept) continue to change, allowing for more and more of the essence of the original idea to become less concrete. Eventually, the word *Bessie* is the name we give to the object of perception of level 2. This ultimately becomes, at level 8, the word *wealth*, a term that omits almost all of the

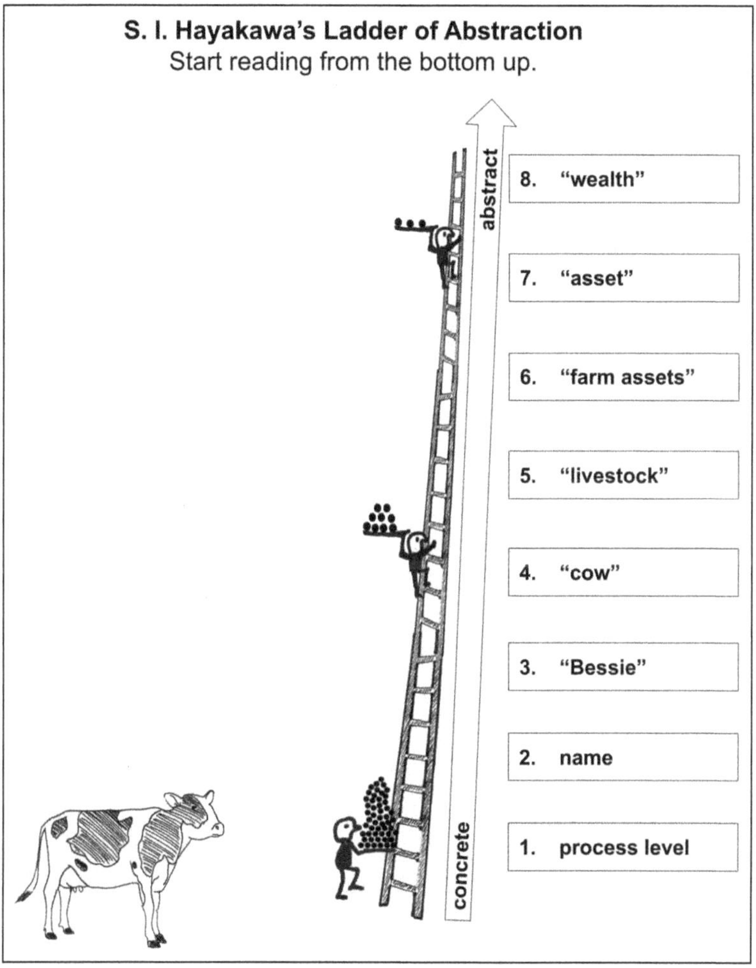

FIGURE **16.1.** *Source: Robert Kelly's* Ladder of Abstraction, *2023. Used with permission.*

characteristics of "Bessie." To correctly relate "wealth" to "the things and happenings for which it stands" requires some work on the part of the language learner. According to Hayakawa's theory, each step along the way subsumes the previous steps. Thus, statements and uses of language need to be "referable to lower levels" as we move up the Abstraction Ladder. He explains this abstraction process as follows:

TABLE **16.1.** Hayakawa's Explanation of Each Rung of the Abstraction Ladder

(Read from the bottom up.)	
8. "wealth"	The word "wealth" is at an extremely high level of abstraction, omitting *almost* all reference to the characteristics of Bessie.
7. "asset"	When Bessie is referred to as an "asset," still more of her characteristics are left out.
6. "farm assets"	When Bessie is included among "farm assets," reference is made only to what she has in common with all other salable things on the farm.
5. "livestock"	When Bessie is referred to as "livestock," only those characteristics she has in common with pigs, chickens, goats, etc., are referred to.
4. "cow"	The word "cow" stands for the characteristics we have abstracted as common to cow_1, cow_2, cow_3, . . . cow_n. Characteristics peculiar to specific cows are left out.
3. "Bessie"	The word "Bessie" (cow_1) is the *name* we give to the object of perception of level 2. The name *is not* the object; it merely *stands for* the object and omits reference to many of the characteristics of the object.
2.	The cow we perceive is not the word, but the object of experience, that which our nervous system abstracts (selects) from the totality that constitutes the process-cow. Many of the characteristics of the process-cow are left out.
1.	The cow ultimately consists of atoms, electrons, etc., according to present-day scientific inference. Characteristics (represented by circles) are infinite at this level and ever-changing. This is the *process level.*

> The test of abstractions is not whether they are "high-level abstractions" or "low-level" abstractions but whether they are referable to lower levels. If one makes a statement about the culinary arts in America, one should be able to refer to the statement down the ladder in particular American restaurants, American domestic science, American techniques of food presentation down to Mrs. Levin in her kitchen. (Hayakawa and Hayakawa 93)

Figure 16.2 is a representation of Hayakawa's concept.

Moffett's theory of narrative perspective, a schema of discourse predicated on Hayakawa's communication theory, hinges on this concept of the abstraction ladder and makes its first explicit

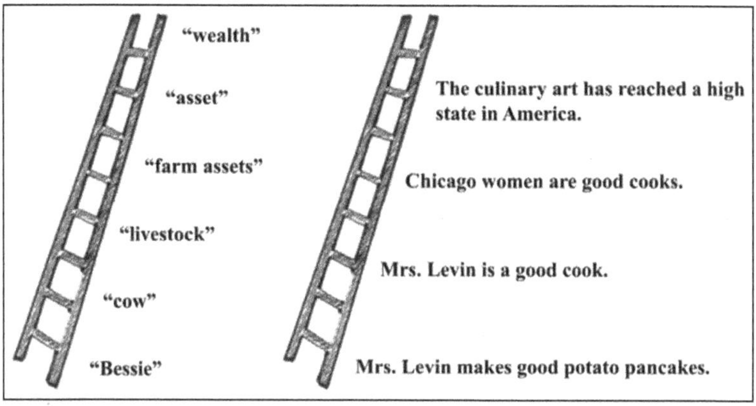

FIGURE 16.2. *Source: Robert Kelly, Ladders Side by Side, 2023. Used with permission.*

appearance in 1964 under the title "Telling Stories: Methods of Abstraction in Fiction" in *ETC.*, a journal edited by Hayakawa. It may be the case that Moffett's interest in narrative perspective stemmed from his senior thesis at Harvard, a work that focused on the consequences of different narrative perspectives in the work of Virginia Woolf. Sheridan Blau has suggested as much, indicating Moffett remained interested in what narrators in different subject positions (first person, third person, omniscient, etc.) can know and report. Blau has also indicated Moffett found in Hayakawa's Abstraction Ladder a model for thinking about the positional relationships between speakers and listeners in what they are talking about (Blau 2022). In "Telling Stories," Moffett defined and described narrative method in terms of "a certain level of abstraction, and as the communication system operating among teller, told-to, and told-about" (447–48). Further, he claimed that the narrative spectrum he proposes is "also a progression up the abstraction ladder" (447–48). The links to Hayakawa are very clear, even if they are not referenced explicitly: both communication system models require increasing distance from the concrete to reach the abstract. And, like Hayakawa, Moffett indicates that "each technique subsumes the previous ones and is built up out of them" (447–48). Moffett would later publish a revised version of the "Telling Stories" essay in 1966 in the first edition of *Points of View*, in a form almost identical to what came out in *ETC.*, although he renamed some of the original categories.

A few more specifics of Moffett's abstraction ladder in *Points of View* bear mention as they inform both the organization of his anthology, which guided my own course design, and the work Moffett suggests is incumbent upon authors who use particular narrative perspectives in fiction. These storyteller specifics also shaped the original writing students in my course did according to the read-one, write-one model. Moffett describes the increasing distance of the narrative trajectory as follows:

> [E]ach technique in this spectrum, regarded as real-life reportage, is more comprehensive and abstract, takes in more territory, than the ones before it. This comes from the narrator's increasingly complicated job of compiling and assimilating materials from more and more remote sources. . . . Throughout the spectrum, the narrator of the story becomes less confined to a particular time and place of telling and being listened to. . . . [H]e floats more freely . . . and his broadening vantage point implies greater and greater selection and organization of his original information; at the same time, his more public audience demands of him a more universal style, rhetoric and logic. (*Points* 569)

Figure 16.3 illustrates the narrative spectrum Moffett describes above.

What Moffett details here are the ways that increasing narrative distance from a subject and a known audience inform the kinds of stylistic choices a writer must make. Movement outward from a mutual understanding of events and storyline between narrator and audience—what we might encounter in, for instance, an interior monologue—will change what a writer needs to do to meet the reading needs of an increasingly distant audience. Traveling along a trajectory toward a less familiar audience changes the set of assumptions from which a writer must operate. These assertions in *Points of View* are in some ways reminiscent of "the communication system operating among teller, told-to, and told-about" (447–48) that Moffett described in "Telling Stories." Each movement outward along the narrative spectrum requires each variation in point of view to become more comprehensive

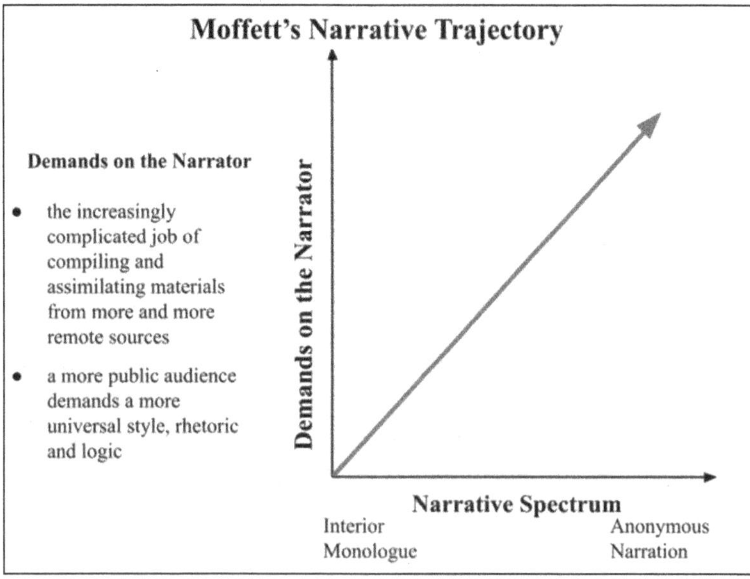

FIGURE 16.3. *Source: Author.*

and more abstract; each one needs to take in more ground. And as a reading audience becomes more public, less known, it gets more complicated for writers to meet the demands of that public.

Now that I've explored abstraction, Moffett's abstraction ladder in relation to the work of Hayakawa, and the ways Moffett's own theory of narrative spectrum informs the design of *Points of View,* one further point bears mention. In Moffett's distancing theory, which appeared in "I, You, and It" in 1965, he spells out a possible writing curriculum, suggesting that teachers have students write in a particular order "all kinds of real and invented interior monologues" outward to essays of "generalization and logical argumentation" (reprinted in *Active Voice* 201). To some extent, I followed his lead here too in my study: the assignments began with interior monologues and moved outward.

Before I move into the specifics of the classroom study, I want to recall the "Schema of Discourse" that Moffett later suggests in *Active Voice,* for if we read down in Table 16.2, we can see the outward movement speakers must engage in as they try to reach an increasingly distant audience.

TABLE 16.2. Schema of Discourse

(reading down) *Progression of Speaker-Audience Relationship*	
Thinking to oneself	Inner verbalization
Speaking to another person face to face	Outer vocalization
Writing to a known party	Informal writing
Writing to a mass, anonymous audience	Publication

Since Moffett's narrative spectrum and exemplar texts set the standard for and guided my course design, the schema he sets out in *Points of View* is noteworthy, and I include it below. The perspective in this anthology of stories moves from what Hayakawa might term "concrete" to the "abstract." The links between the schema of discourse mentioned above and the narrative sequencing to come are useful to recall. Both move from thinking and writing to oneself to writing to a mass, anonymous audience.

Reading and Writing with *Points of View*

What follows is a look at students' work with narrative perspective and narrative sequencing in my own classroom. I examine the ways students' writing and their analysis of their own writing gesture toward an understanding of the shifts in narrative perspective Moffett suggests. I explore the extent to which, through this process, the students in this course might be said to have come to know literature "from the inside" as Moffett claims they will if they write in the same forms as the authors they read.

My study took place in the fall of 2020 "at" a small independent school in Southern California in a mixed eleventh- and twelfth-grade semester elective course whose focus is narrative fiction. There were eleven students in the class: eight juniors and three seniors. The expectation for the course is that texts and excerpts by published writers, artists, filmmakers, and musicians are the springboard for exploring student lives and experiences. I taught the class exclusively over Zoom.

The day-to-day workings of the course varied, but I ran it according to a writing workshop model. I instructed the students on day one to get a journal. We would use it every class period and for homework assignments. Students wrote during every class: the day always began with a free, private writing and then, depending on the activity or text, students wrote together, sometimes independently, sometimes in concert. I broke the semester down into four units, all driven by narrative perspectives taken from and guided by Moffett's *Points of View:*

Unit One:	The "Secret" Inner Voice: Interior Monologue; Dramatic Monologue
Unit Two:	The Epistolary and the Private: Letter Narration; Diary Narration
Unit Three:	An "I" Appears and Watches: Subjective Narration; Detached Autobiography; Memoir, or Observer Narration
Unit Four:	A Voice and Voices Appear and Report: Biography or Anonymous Narration—Single Character Point of View; Anonymous Narration—Dual Character Point of View; Anonymous Narration—Multiple Character Point of View; Anonymous Narration—No Character Point of View.

The Project in Action: Course Readings and Coursework in Narrative Fiction

Though I did follow Moffett's lead as far as narrative perspective in my course design, I did not limit my course readings to those in his collection. I include his list of perspectives and exemplar texts in Table 16.3, as they informed the study I conducted and the curriculum I created for the Narrative Fiction course.

While the class did read many of the texts listed in Table 16.3, I tried to include other voices as well, more diverse, more current voices; thus, I drew from *Sudden Fiction*, *McSweeney's*, *The New Yorker*, *Harper's*, and *Best American Short Stories 2018* and *2019* to supplement *Points of View.* All of the readings I selected were short texts. I use the word *text* liberally, as these varied. What we read included film, art, podcasts, poetry, novel excerpts, television clips, etc. In our unit on the dramatic monologue, for example,

TABLE 16.3. Moffett's Narrative Trajectory in *Points of View*

Narrative Perspective	Moffett's Exemplar Text
Interior monologue	"But the One on the Right" by Dorothy Parker
Dramatic monologue	"The Lady's Maid" by Katherine Mansfield
Letter narration	"A Novel in Nine Letters" by Fyodor Dostoevsky
Diary narration	"Flowers for Algernon" by Daniel Keyes
Subjective narration	"A&P" by John Updike
Detached autobiography	"First Confession" by Frank O'Connor
Memoir or observer narration	"The Fall of the House of Usher" by Edgar Allan Poe
Biography, or Anonymous Narration—single character point of view	"The Five-Forty-Eight" by John Cheever
Anonymous Narration—dual character point of view	"Unlighted Lamps" by Sherwood Anderson
Anonymous Narration—multiple character point of view	"The Suicides of Private Greaves" by James Moffett
Anonymous Narration—no character point of view	"The Minister's Black Veil" by Nathaniel Hawthorne

we watched a film clip from *Good Will Hunting*. The narrative perspective was the focus, and the questions about the narrator's purpose in addressing a particular audience remained the same as those we might ask of a short story from this perspective: Why this story? Why this listener? My efforts to stay faithful to the design of Moffett's *Points of View* were in the choices I made in introducing students to narrative perspective of particular kinds at particular times. We studied texts in the same order that Moffett follows in *Points of View*—of increasing distance along a narrative trajectory. As far as materials used in this study, everything we read needed to be accessed online; I uploaded and shared all materials with students.

I now briefly explain how I ran the course, as I see the student narrative writing and their analysis of that writing as born out of all the work we did together. Course design is also important to the discussion portion of this study.

I ran the course using a read-one, write-one model. The three steps involved in this approach were (1) Students read a text. I followed Moffett and let the narrative perspective rule the mentor text. But we did not study short stories exclusively; film, poetry, art, etc. were all on the menu. We typically read three to four texts in each narrative mode. (2) The class engaged in a close reading. Through Harkness discussion (a student-led discussion in which the teacher functions as facilitator at the Harkness table [or Zoom room in the time of COVID]), writing-to-read, and writing-to-learn activities, we closely studied these texts, examining form and content as respective and relational entities. (3) Students wrote a story.

Students crafted their own original tales in the modes we studied; these stories were often born from the daily writing we did. And the imitation pieces followed units on varied narrative perspectives. The tales went through several drafts, workshopped in pairs, in writing group teams, and in consultation with me. A final aspect of the work students did for this read-one, write-one model was a metacognitive piece. For every assignment, students were required to analyze their work for content and form. For content, I had them identify the elements they opted to include for each assignment; each narrative perspective required different story elements. For form, I asked them to offer a rationale for the particular elements they included and provide an explanation for their stylistic choices in relation to the respective points of view. For example, when writing in imitation of the epistolary mode, the prompts were:

> ***Content:*** *Identify the letters, diary entries, other kinds of correspondence you included.*
>
> ***Form:*** *Why three letters and a newspaper editorial (for example)? Explain how you tried to make the language intimate, real, and unique to the relationships you sketch in the story.*

Here is a snapshot of the assignments I gave in relation to four narrative modes:

Interior Monologue: Exemplar Text/Inspiration: Edward Hopper's "Soir Bleu"

My Writing Assignment: Craft a stream of consciousness/ interior monologue for your assigned character in the painting.

Dramatic Monologue: Exemplar Text/Inspiration: Gus Powell's *Departures*

My Writing Assignment: Select one photo from Powell's portfolio and create a dramatic monologue.

Epistolary Form (Letter & Diary Narration): Exemplar Text/ Inspiration: Real Life

My Writing Assignment: Craft an epistolary story.

Subjective Narration: Exemplar Text/Inspiration: Ian Frazier's "Tomorrow's Bird"

My Writing Assignment: Using subjective narration, write one of the "scenes" in "Tomorrow's Bird" from the perspective of the crow.

Getting to Know Literature: Data Collection

Thus far I've covered course setup; now I describe what happened. By considering classwork, compositions, and writing portfolios from my eleven study participants, I report on the extent to which they could differentiate points of view in their own writing and the ways in which their work reflected an understanding of the writerly moves a writer needs to make as narrative perspective moves outward from interior monologue toward anonymous narration. First I describe the data.

What did classwork consist of? Though we often had conversations about what students noticed about the narrative trajectory, these comments were not always documented. In Harkness discussions, board notes are not the norm. However, sometimes *after* a discussion, I would prompt the class to see what our conversation yielded. And students would write responses to the prompts into the Google Doc for that day's class. Also, we did not engage in Harkness all the time; sometimes I would present a prompt to the group and students would write their responses beneath it. These prompts were germane to the narrative perspectives we were studying. The class notes I cite below make the student observations visible. The first of two sets of class notes is a look at students' ideas after our discussion of interior monologue. These notes offer a way to see what students can glean of this first narrative perspective and the inner workings of texts that employ that narrative perspective. The second set of class notes offers a look at how students see the shape and demands of narrative perspective within the epistolary story versus interior monologue and dramatic monologue. These notes are tantamount to those for a unit review; they provide some basis for contrastive analysis. And they may offer a sense of whether students see the writerly demands that Moffett discusses as texts move along the narrative spectrum.

The end-of-term portfolio assignment is a final, crucial part of the data. This assignment was to be a collection of student writing they chose from the entire semester's work; they had to assemble it, share it, and analyze it. The original compositions students wrote all semester long were fair game as inclusions in the portfolio. The only stipulation was that at least two be newer pieces, from the second quarter of the school year. The portfolio entailed an explanation and analysis of their choices of works to include, insights into self as a thinker and a writer, and a discussion of narrative perspective—what various modes require, challenges in crafting assignments, new understandings, etc.

Now to what happened in the study. I first report on class-wide trends in what students had to say about narration. Then I highlight three students' comments about narration as they may offer some insight into Moffett's theory of what pupils stand to gain by writing in the same way as the authors whom they study. After that I describe the analytical responses of other students in the class, especially as they bear on coming to know literature intimately via writing.

Data Analysis and Discussion

In analyzing the data, I studied the class notes, looking to see what students said they noticed about narrative demands and discernable differences in the crafting of stories as we moved away from the interior monologue. I tracked their remarks about stylistic and fictional elements. I also studied the student portfolios to see what students came to understand about narrative trajectories.

If the question is *What will or do students know about the inner workings of literature after studying different narrative perspectives and writing in the same form as the literature they read?*, the answers ought to lie in what they noticed, how they wrote, and how they analyzed what they wrote. Two sets of class notes shed light on what students had to say about what they came to know of the inner workings of literature. In each set of notes, the teacher prompts appear in bold; the student responses follow.

> 1. *Class Notes on Narrative Perspective within the Interior Monologue:* Lowell's poem, Parker's short story, and the speeches we all crafted in response to "Soir Bleu" are examples of interior monologue, also referred to as stream-of-consciousness narration.
>
> **Given our small sample set, what can we surmise about stream of consciousness narration/ interior monologue? Specifically, what can we identify as its features?**
>
> - Dialogue is present; there are also responses to that dialogue.
> - Unfiltered thought features prominently.
> - Texts offer an analysis of actions of others or self.
> - There may be a dark tone to them—but not always.
> - Characterization of narrator may be shown as an inferiority complex; self-loathing; unhappiness.
> - Dichotomy between the performed self and the true self is apparent.
> - Mention of context or setting.
>
> **What can we identify as its purpose? Why bother with this perspective?**
>
> - Others can relate to it, perhaps.
> - It enables authors to comment on a true aspect of people or of situations.
>
> **What can we identify about its crafting? Its possibilities?**
>
> - Dark; comedic; satirical; character arc is possible.

The first set of class notes suggests that students recognize an intimacy that is present in the interior monologue. In the examples our class studied, we looked at the ways dialogue with an interlocutor can highlight the internal conversation of a character in a literary work. Students picked up on that. That's not necessarily a feature in every interior monologue, so I'm not sure how truly important it is. But it is at least a craft move they recognized. Student remarks also highlighted the interiority of a character. This is evident in what they called "unfiltered thought" and the ways they saw characters somehow critically responding to their selves and their own actions. Other student remarks that bear on Moffett's claim about students "knowing literature from the inside" are their observations about a constructed self versus a real self, what they termed "performed vs. true." That there can be a dichotomy in what a character is thinking and may or may not reveal to the outside world is an important, accurate observation of this narrative perspective. Other nifty writerly moves like the use of setting or dialogue with another character or some trends like darkness or depression did not bear much on the particular narrative perspective, and may have just been identified because of the particular texts I chose and/or students' own original written work, their frames of mind in crafting their pieces, etc. Nonetheless, it seems important to acknowledge that some of the students' observations seem fairly accurate given the corpus examined yet don't seem to bear on the genre of narrative perspective more broadly. Lastly, students' comments that stream of consciousness functions as a way to "comment on a true aspect of people or a situation" was astute. They seemed aware of the way a figure might have to perform in a particular setting. This is often a reason why a writer opts for the interior monologue narrative perspective.

2. *Class Notes on Narrative Perspective within the Epistolary Story vs. Interior Monologue and Dramatic Monologue:* **By the end of this discussion, what can you say about the epistolary (letter) form as a genre?**

- important information on the header (date, to/from whom) is easiest to manipulate the reader

- timeline/progression adds drama
- The epistolary form is sincere and formal way of writing

How does it compare to or contrast with what we've already studied—the interior and dramatic monologues?

- Monologues feel more profound and complete as they reveal the mostly unfiltered thoughts of the speaker. Epistolary form reveals characterization more slowly and through certain moments, in which the character is writing themselves.
- more of a dialogue between two people instead of just one person in a monologue
- you can see the emotion of the questions more than in a monologue because you have 2 people's sides (like text message, emotions read differently)
- Both the monologue and the epistolary forms give a sort of in-depth look at the speaker's thoughts/perspectives
- I think these letters don't reveal as much character as an interior monologue, because when you are alone with your thoughts you tend to [be] much more open then when talking to someone else, where you can come across as guarded even in a letter. Therefore, it's much more like a dramatic monologue, because while you are expressing your feelings to another person they aren't truly yours and yours alone.
- seems more comparable to a dramatic monologue rather than interior because they address the "you's" that are both of them
- dramatic because they call each other out & Ivan considers Peter to be deceiving him
- The letters don't reveal as much of a person's thoughts in the moment because they have time to go over their letter and decide what they want to include and take out. The monologues feel like more of an ongoing thought in their head with no edits.

How does the distance affect reader, writer, and text?

- The distance makes the reader have to do more legwork and interpret more

- distance affects the reader because while the writer may be one place at the time of the letter, their location could change when the letter is received

This second set of class notes mentions some stylistic features that don't necessarily get at the heart of the epistolary form. Students' observations about timelines or dates and headers may simply be a by-product of the particular literature we studied. These notes also clarify that students have an awareness of the way dialogue is distinct from monologue and how dialogue will be used in an epistolary form in a manner distinct from its function in the interior and dramatic monologues. That the nature of the correspondence hinges on this back-and-forth communication is what students' observations gesture toward. Students also seem aware that there can be a communication breakdown when two interlocutors are in conversation. The example of the "text message" is a case in point. Another important observation is the idea of having to be guarded in a letter versus being more open "in your own private thoughts." They point out that that makes the interior monologue more honest. Students also note the ways a dramatic monologue or an epistolary story has stops and starts in the ways that an interior monologue need not. So there is some awareness of narrative boundaries. One keen observation students made is the role of distance as it shapes what the reader has to do—"more legwork and interpretation" as we move outward from the interior monologue. Their observation does seem to correspond to Moffett's claim of the writer presenting a more universal kind of text for an audience who is not as well known. Students also saw that having an audience requires a speaker to edit him/her/their self. That is an accurate distinction between the interior monologue and the other two narrative perspectives. Again, perhaps this is evidence in support of Moffett's claim of students having a knowledge of the inner workings of the literature they study on account of "writing in all the same forms as the authors [they] read" (*Teaching the Universe* 7).

I now report on class-wide trends about narrative perspective in student portfolios. It may be helpful to see the actual prompt:

> **Offer an analysis of the narrative perspectives in the body of work you have created. As we have moved from the interior monologue outward, what has happened to your tales? What challenges have you faced as a writer? What insights have you uncovered about the writing processes involved in crafting stories from these various stances? What else have you learned and/or what else seems worthy of mention?**

At the outset, I want to make clear that some of the students interpreted this prompt as asking about their opinion of narrative or their own stance as a reader of a narrative; therefore, not all of the data were relevant or usable. Nonetheless, I can report on some trends. Comments on narration, what I also term *narrative perspective*, all tended toward what I call evidence of "How Fiction Works" (to borrow from Wood). Their responses indicated an understanding of how fictional elements—e.g., characterization, stylistic choices, communication between interlocutors, etc.—function. Students reported they were trying on writing styles, felt encouraged to look at art, and experienced a freedom in the work we did. Moreover, they recognized that reading like a writer requires analysis and an ability to consider the views and thinking of others. Students also demonstrated an awareness that writing along the narrative trajectory outward from the interior monologue made new demands of them as writers. Not every student seemed to agree on what the demands were, nor could they always articulate those demands. Still, there was an awareness that they had to do things differently when writing an epistolary story versus a dramatic monologue versus a memoir, etc. A number of students reported that writing in the modes of the authors we read (from different points of view—narrative perspectives) required stepping into another mindset. This kind of perspective shift was prominent, and expressed as "gazing at others," "an awareness of others," "empathy for others," "requiring a new perspective of others," and "required [them] to think of the world and of others differently." I did not anticipate this real-world link. The project, based on their reports, brought about a kind of humanity for and in them in ways they themselves hadn't been able to see before. In a related but not exactly same way, students also reported that narrative writing forced a consideration of others in relation to self. And it caused them to question their perceptions of and beliefs about others. Additionally, some students claimed that imagination was required for perspective shifts. This all amounted to new understandings about the craft of writing and new ways to conceive of and write about other people. Two students reported that movement outward from self required an "out of the box" kind of thinking, a cliché I took to mean a novel approach to their thinking about craft.

Three particular students gave explicit answers to what they learned about writing in different narrative perspectives. I read these comments in relation to Moffett's claims about students coming to know literature "from the inside" by writing in the forms that they read. I also explore these responses as they bear on Moffett's narrative trajectory, specifically his abstraction ladder. Remember that according to his schema of discourse, each technique in the spectrum is more comprehensive and more abstract, takes in more territory, and gets more complicated for writers as the audience becomes more public; the style needs to be more universal. These students' responses appear in Table 16.4.

TABLE 16.4. On Narrative Perspective and Moffett's Abstraction Ladder: Three Student Reports

(All names are pseudonyms)
Lisa: "I found when reading back on my different works throughout the year that as we shifted from one side of the spectrum to the other, the stories I wrote went from private to increasingly more public."
Cathy: "By reading stories and then emulating them I was able to focus not only on the specific form, but how I as a thinker process human interaction and emotion through writing. Through the gradual transition from internal monologue to an external viewpoint, I wrote not only more honestly, but took a greater interest in what I was writing about."
Annie: "As I've moved from the interior monologue outward, my tales have become less personal and have required a more advanced 'stretch for creativity.'. . . Most writing requires us to draw upon our own experiences of the world, yet I found that as we moved from the interior monologue outward, my tales relied less upon individual experience and more upon creativity."

We begin with Lisa. Lisa recognizes that there is a narrative trajectory, as seen in her use of *spectrum*. Her adverbial *increasingly* and her use of *spectrum* both signal the sort of incremental approach toward outward narration that Moffett describes. And she suggests that she is moving along a trajectory from "private to increasingly more public" writing. This comment suggests she grasps the idea that the movement outward from the interior monologue requires a shift; her diction "private" versus "public" makes this obvious. That she sees there are "sides" to a spectrum is important. This signals an awareness that narration comes in different forms and exists along some kind of trajectory. Moreover, that she is writing in the same way, mirroring this approach, suggests she may understand what is required of narrative perspective shifts outward toward a more universal audience. Her report may suggest she is also able to make the writerly moves required of a distancing narrative perspective. She seems to have embraced the read-one, write-one approach here, and perhaps has internalized what narrative perspective shifts demand.

Cathy's remarks echo the incrementalism Lisa describes, especially evident in Cathy's description of a "gradual transition." She also seems aware of an outward movement, evinced by the claim that she had to "transition from internal monologue to an external viewpoint." Cathy's first sentence also suggests a benefit. Knowing the concept of moving from an interior monologue to a narrator-less text may be indicative of her comprehending the narrative trajectory. Moreover, her ability to focus on writing about people and emotion suggests a metacognitive awareness, seen in her statement, "I was able to focus on . . . form . . . and how I as a thinker process." Whether Cathy fully grasped what the narrative demands are as we move along the abstraction ladder is unclear. Her second sentence seems to run counter to what an interior monologue can afford a writer; the "unfiltered self" earlier mentioned in class notes is not necessarily what one would expect to find in a narrator as we move along the narrative trajectory. Possibly she just wrote more honestly and took a greater interest in writing as the assignments progressed. But if she understood the social situation entailed in each of the narrative positions, why would she think that the narration would become more rather than less "honest"? On the other hand, she might mean that as she took on more demanding tasks and thereby took an increasingly greater interest in each task, her writing became more honest in the sense that she was more genuinely engaged in the process.

Finally, Annie, like Lisa and Cathy, recognizes a movement away from self. She describes the writerly move she needs to make as grounded in a need to "become less personal" and requiring "a more advanced 'stretch for creativity.'" Here, her use of "the stretch" seems to echo Moffett's description of the narrator's increasingly complicated job as we move up the ladder of abstraction and outward from the self. This work entails reaching. Like Lisa, Annie seems to "get it." She grasps and can apply Moffett's claim of what's required of a writer as the narrative perspective moves away from the "I." The fact that she talks about having to rely on "creativity" as she moves outward seems to suggest she must imagine a self and an audience that is not her. Invention is at work here. Can she not assume that the reader of her tales will know what she does, read her signposts? Maybe. That this requires some extra effort is implicit in what she's saying.

Taken together, these three student responses seem to suggest that Moffett may have been on to something when he claimed that students who write in the same modes as the authors they read will "know literature from the inside." These students' reflections all offer some evidence that they understand that shifting narrative perspectives makes changing and increasingly complex demands on writers. Lisa points out having to meet public demands. Cathy realizes the extra work she needs to do. Annie sees that creativity is in order if she wants to write away from herself. She looks on it as a more demanding work of art.

These analyses are certainly thought-provoking and seem to suggest there is great value in both the abstracting *from* (moving up the ladder of abstraction) and the abstracting *for* (increasing distance from audience) paradigm in designing ELA curricula. These processes appear to expand the narrative experience and thus the narrative repertoire of student writers. But we need to also ask, what of the eight other students?

These students also responded to every writing prompt over the course of the semester. And they were vital, active members of our writing community. Their final portfolio analyses, though important and interesting, don't necessarily help me to gauge whether they left our course with an intimate or a more intimate knowledge of literature because of the writing they did. But there are some hints. Mostly, the following seven analytical remarks (one student skipped this question altogether) shed light on the limits of language and the trouble with interpretation. As before, all student names are pseudonyms.

In response to the prompt: **What insights have you uncovered about the writing processes involved in crafting stories from these various stances?**, the responses varied. One student offered a list of the writing assignments; three offered accounts of development as writers; two wrote descriptions of personal growth; and a final student commented on the universal nature of voice.

Sally is in the first category. In her response, she remarked, "As I looked through everything I have written in the first semester, I noticed a shift in my narration. I started out the year with the stream of consciousness piece . . . then I expanded on that skill with the dramatic monologue." Though with her verb choice of *expanded* she does suggest that some more detailed expression is required, which might make us think of the subsuming that Moffett discusses in his account of the ladder, her analysis is mostly a plot summary of the many narratives she penned.

Three students responded to this prompt by offering a historical look at how they have changed as writers. The first is Ned. His analysis consisted of a description of the personal boons of writing: "The biggest thing I've learned about myself from writing from different perspectives is how much I genuinely enjoy writing fictional stories." In effect, he details *his* change, not the ways his writing moves changed for varied audiences. The second student in this category is Pete. He also described personal growth: "Over the course of the semester, I think I have widened my thoughts and sight when approaching an assignment and this has helped me produce more interesting and better writings." Though the verb phrase "have widened" suggests some awareness of a need to stretch as a writer for new narrative demands, this is mostly a look at the quality of his work and a change in that realm. Timmy offered a similar kind of response, indicating that the course as a whole was beneficial to him: "All in all, over the course of this semester I feel that I was able to truly evolve as a writer." What has led to this "evolution" is unclear, yet personal change is suggested by his diction. There is no mention at all of narrative perspective demands in his analysis.

In response to the prompt above, two students reported on their own development as thinkers and people as a result of the work we did. Gary states that "[the coursework] has all led me to be a more open person and to me becoming someone I would actually want to get to know." Gary's remarks about growth concern the general ways writing has served him in his life, which is wonderful but not a direct response to the question. Carmen answers in a similar way. She does not report on the demands of a writer when encountering more distant narrative stances, but she recognizes that some things require shifting as new audiences are written for. This is clear in her claim that "through the gradual transition from internal monologue to an external viewpoint, I wrote not only more honestly, but took greater interest in what I was writing about." Hers is somewhat of an answer to the prompt blended with a *what happened to me and my writing approach* answer.

A final, puzzling response comes from Kenny. What he gleaned about narrative perspectives is unclear. He mostly disregarded the prompt and wrote about the elements of storytelling. One remark that seemed somewhat on topic is this: "The voice in [my] head is spontaneous and conversational, just like everyone else in the world." That he offered this in response to a question about narration suggests he knows a narrator has a voice. This is an important observation. Yet his words here tell me that he sees a universality in how things are communicated in narratives, which ignores or shows he is unaware of the kinds of writerly moves an author needs to make along a narrative trajectory from the internal monologue to the anonymous narrator. Or we might read his response as a comment on the different narrative personae or voices he adopted for the changing narrative perspectives. Perhaps his claim could be taken to mean that in each persona or voice he had to adopt to suit a new perspective, he found himself thinking spontaneously and conversationally just like anyone else, but from a different perspective to a different audience. This could suggest that Kenny managed to comfortably inhabit each new perspective, even if it required (as it had to) adjustments in abstraction and vocabulary and detail. It may be that to the degree Kenny managed to fulfill the assignment and take on increasingly demanding narrative perspectives, he did different kinds of intellectual work but didn't recognize how his language and thought had to be adjusted.

The analytical responses from the entire class do seem to suggest that classroom conversations around differentiation on points of view are possible. Students can observe what's required of writers when writing from various narrative perspectives for different audiences.

Yet given how little many students in the study had to say about the insights they discovered about how different perspectives changed their writing or thinking processes, we might conclude that some high school students can manage to make the intellectual and verbal adjustments required to adopt a variety of narrative stances for different audiences, but they don't necessarily recognize or have the background knowledge to talk about what those shifts required of them intellectually or verbally. This doesn't mean that Moffett was wrong in claiming that writing different types of narratives allows students to learn about literary genres from the inside, or from the perspective of a writer. Instead, it might suggest that adolescents who can be seen to develop intellectually, verbally, and tactically as writers over the course of a semester of exemplary instruction in writing won't be able to explain how or in what ways they or their writing developed.

Implications

The implications of this study fall into several categories. I see the work having a bearing on the role of daily writing in a classroom setting. I think this activity can create a space for reflection and the ground from whence seeds of storytelling can grow. The workshop model I used all semester can provide inroads to literature; we wrote to access texts, and these writings helped to generate discussion and future papers. A narrative awareness seems to emerge from the methodological approach we used. Some facility with naming, using, and discussing the function of particular story elements becomes apparent, maybe as a result of a read-one, write-one approach. Another outcome of our work is the possibility of creating and inhabiting real, honest writing communities even in the absence of physical proximity. The work from this term and the student portfolios also suggest that drawing from real life makes for meaningful assignments and real compositions, as revealed by student reports.

As far as Moffett's narrative trajectory, reports from Lisa, Cathy, and Annie suggest that although students saw that narrative perspective moving away from the interior monologue required something, was more demanding, they did not necessarily agree on the particulars of the demand. Still, they recognized it, which may in and of itself be a win. The other students in the class may not have witnessed these changes to the same degree, but I believe the read-one, write-one approach was still edifying for them as writers and thinkers.

Working with *Points of View* caused me to question the nature and worth of studying genres in isolation. Moffett's idea that each narrative perspective is broad enough to be studied through different media makes much more sense than isolating genres, studying them one at a time, a practice many schools still engage in. The narrative perspective approach enables a diversity of reading and may even cultivate a broader interest in the arts. Plus, it normalizes reading literature from different perspectives. Inviting students to see that there is more than one vantage point from which the world is experienced seems like an important move.

One question I have about a narrative trajectory approach, however, is whether all students can truly understand what's required, precisely because of the mixed media. Though I agree with Moffett's claim that "*what* a story is about is a question of *how* it is told; you cannot separate the tale from the telling" (Moffett and McElheny 569), I think that unless students can grasp the many structural and even stylistic elements that each angle of vision requires, it's hard work, especially if you've got to write an imitation piece. Moreover, while three students clearly made the abstraction ladder connection, not everyone did, or at least not so explicitly in this portfolio assignment. That doesn't mean they didn't learn about structural differences in storytelling along the way, but it might mean that they had difficulty understanding form's relation to content. And this naturally affected what they were able to do in their imitation pieces. And, as mentioned earlier, these high schoolers may not have the vocabulary or background knowledge to report on their own development.

Finally, this study speaks to the enduring relevance of James Moffett's work. I hope this project will invite another look at his legacy as a theorist and teacher. It turns out that in some very important ways, he was right. Students came to know literature, their thinking, and their abilities "from the inside."

Works Cited

Blau, Sheridan. Personal interview. 19 Apr. 2022.

Hayakawa, S. I., and Alan R. Hayakawa. *Language in Thought and Action*. 1939. 3rd ed., Harcourt Brace Jovanovich, 1972.

Kelly, Robert. *Ladder of Abstraction* [Digital Art]. 2023, San Diego, California.

———. *Ladders Side by Side* [Digital Art]. 2023, San Diego, California.

Moffett, James. *Active Voice: A Writing Program Across the Curriculum.* Boynton/Cook, 1981.

———. *Teaching the Universe of Discourse.* 1968. Boynton/Cook, 1987.

———. "Telling Stories: Methods of Abstraction in Fiction." *ETC.: A Review of General Semantics,* vol. 21, no. 4, 1964, pp. 425–50.

———, and Kenneth R. McElheny, editors. *Points of View: An Anthology of Short Stories.* New American Library, 1966.

Wood, James. *How Fiction Works.* Farrar, Straus and Giroux, 2008.

CHAPTER SEVENTEEN

James Moffett and the Promise of Rural Education

KIM DONEHOWER
University of North Dakota

> Suppose it is true, as spiritual traditions maintain, that people are here on earth to grow, not primarily to achieve or acquire except as doing so enhances inner growth. . . . Suppose we do not learn merely in order to be able to get by, get along, get around, and get ahead. . . . Suppose we don't so much learn to live as live to learn. . . . Making a living and making a life become part of making sense of life, so that everything in it has meaning. (Moffett, *Universal Schoolhouse* 331–32)

This vision from the concluding chapter of James Moffett's *The Universal Schoolhouse* can seem impossibly utopian if we think of all the structures in place to focus K–12 schooling on learning to "get by, get along, get around, and get ahead"—i.e., to be "college- and career-ready" (Council of Chief State School Officers). The notion of school as a stepping-stone to some kind of advancement, especially a financial one, is a well-known story. This chapter argues that if Moffett's more spiritual or metaphysical and less materialistic perspective on education could ever find a home in any existing school, it would probably have to be a rural school. The structure and culture of the rural schoolhouse is likely to be much more hospitable to the kind of education Moffett calls for in *The Universal Schoolhouse* and in much of his earlier work than any urban or suburban school we could imagine.

What's more, the possibilities for literacy instruction in rural schools are ripe for implementation of the kind of curriculum Moffett describes in *Teaching the Universe of Discourse*—a profoundly rhetorical curriculum in which students are "realistically put into the drama of somebody with something to say to somebody else" (12). In Moffett's vision, students "play" at different roles in their relations to subjects, speakers, and listeners until they have mastered "style, logic, semantics, rhetoric, and literary form continuously through practice" (13). Such a curriculum can be logistically difficult in any classroom, as students must rotate through a series of assignments that place them in a wide variety of relations to subjects, speakers, and listeners. Additionally, all of these should simulate real literacy experiences in which students are authentically positioned to say something to someone else, with any requirements for what is to be said also corresponding to the student's "own intellectual and emotional growth" (12–13).

The problems in implementing a curriculum such as this one have to do with the structure and culture of schools. A teacher who is responsible for 120 students is much less likely to be able to tailor assignments to individual students' intellectual and emotional growth, compared to a teacher with 40 students. Moreover, culturally, the grading structures that prevail in urban and suburban schools tend to penalize the kinds of play and experimentation required for students to try on different rhetorical stances and moves that Moffett perpetually advocated throughout his career (Moffett, *Teaching*; Moffett and Wagner). Additionally, the very heterogeneity of urban schools in contrast to the typically deep cultural connections among the students in rural schools means that rural schools are likely to provide students with a variety of roles they feel willing and prepared to enact.

To investigate the possibilities of the rural schoolhouse to implement the kind of writing curriculum Moffett advocates, I interviewed ten rural teachers, all of whom participated in a National Writing Project summer institute for rural teacher-leaders. Participants in this institute were not exposed directly to Moffett's ideas, nor had any of them read Moffett. I focus here on the experiences of two teachers, Lisa and Rachel, very different teachers with different teaching histories. The school at which they both ultimately taught, pseudonymously identified here as Westport, provides a case-study example of the ways in which two different teachers find a typical rural school to be well suited for Moffett's curriculum.

Rural School Structures

Rural schools are diverse by type and structure. One useful way to categorize them is by their distance from metropolitan or micropolitan centers, as the US National Center for Education Statistics does. The NCES designates rural schools as "fringe," "distant," or "remote"; "fringe" schools are within five miles of an urban or regional center; "distant" schools are within six to twenty-five miles; "remote" schools are more than twenty-five miles away (NCES, "Rural"). Research has shown that the distance from metro- and micropolitan centers in turn affects the culture of rural schools (Theobald and Nachtigal; Barter; Howley and Howley). This essay defines "rural" schools as those located in "distant" and "remote" districts; "fringe" schools tend to blend characteristics of rural and suburban schools.

Another structural difference among rural schools is whether all grades are housed in the same building. Single-campus K–12 schools may be fringe, distant, or remote. However, it is common for secondary schools in rural areas to consolidate grade levels across a wide swathe of geographic locations into one location. As a result, rural students often have to commute to school across vast distances. Rural students may also have to commute to a different high school even after their K–8 experience took place in a local building. This is all to say that the experiences of distant and remote rural students often don't match those of their nonrural counterparts both in terms of the demands they face in getting to school and in the array of grade levels and types of students housed in the buildings where their education takes place.

Across these differences, though, the hallmark of the rural school is lower enrollments and student-to-teacher ratios (US Department of Education). To handle staffing issues that arise from low enrollments, it is not uncommon for rural schools to combine grades, or to have a single teacher responsible for multiple grades. One of my informants, Lisa, began her career teaching English at Turner, a rural-remote school in which she was responsible for grades 6–12 and the elementary library; that school currently has an enrollment of forty-two students across grades K–12.

Lisa's Experience

Lisa describes her goals for high school students this way: "You want them to leave better people—regardless if they go on to college, or the workforce, or the military. Maybe they've learned to see the world in a slightly different way, or to be kind, or even when to hold their tongues." In other words, regardless of students' choices about "how to get by," they should be personally transformed, as people, by the high school experience. Elsewhere in our interview, Lisa repeatedly used the word *growth*. Here, *growth* refers to development toward emotional and intellectual maturity, a bettering of self by way of setting and achieving personal goals, thinking through and embracing challenges, and persisting in the face of obstacles. Lisa's second teaching job was at Westport, a rural-distant school that embraced a variation of standards-based grading school-wide (Vatterott). Lisa explained her love for Westport's assessment system this way: "The goal is to get students to keep growing. The focus is on the growth and the actual learning."

Lisa describes several one-on-one conferences with students in which they get to determine the amount of learning growth they want to aim for in her classes. Students track their own learning in Westport's grading system, and those who are pleased with their growth in Lisa's English classroom may choose to hold steady with what they can do or push for even more growth. At the end of each grading period, students receive the highest grade they achieved on a major assessment during the marking period. In other words, all the grades in the term are not averaged together. Instead, students receive a 1, 2, 3, or 4 based on the highest level they were able to achieve during the term. Students can therefore choose to accept a 2 or 3 on some literacy skills and push themselves to accomplish a 4 on others. By constructing the assessment in her classroom to embrace the aspects of the curriculum students feel most invested in and motivated by, Lisa is not only embracing the type of student choice that Moffett argued was so essential to education (*Teaching*) but also avoiding the types of assessments that he suggested "pos[ed] as child-centered while actually generating a very destructive constant focus on the child" (*Coming on Center* 10).

Lisa's notion of "growth" is expansive and matches Moffett's idea that a language learning curriculum should "correspond to [the student's] own intellectual and emotional growth" (*Teaching* 12–13). She explains that in her own high school student experience, she went largely unnoticed because she wasn't either a star student or a star athlete. She attributes this to attending a "class A" school. (Many teachers in rural regions in the US distinguish between metro-/micropolitan schools and rural schools using state high school athletic association designations of "class A" and "class B" schools.) Lisa explains that she is glad she began her career in class B (rural) schools this way: "It was great to start in class B because you got to really *see* all your students." Lisa attributes this increased ability to see her students to the rural school structure: smaller school size, smaller surrounding communities, and lower student-teacher ratios.

"Really seeing" students, for Lisa, means seeing beyond academic or athletic accomplishments to the whole person. Lisa asserts, "We're telling kids unless you get an A, your contributions aren't important. A lot of kids leave high school feeling like it was a waste, and it *was* a waste for them, because they weren't recognized for the things they bring to the world." Lisa's examples of these kinds of things include being kind, a deep knowledge of hunting or some other subject outside the curriculum, or simply providing a kind of "positive energy" in group interactions. My conversations with Lisa suggest another way to interpret her statement—unless students get an A, their learning experiences are not seen as particularly significant or successful. But in Moffett's curriculum, with its emphasis on repeated practice with a variety of rhetorical situations, any experience, even an "unsuccessful" one, is valuable because language learning is ultimately an experimental endeavor in which students need the space to try, and fail, and try again, having learned from the experience, and not merely seeking the "psychic security" of pleasing the teacher (*Teaching* 95). Lisa does not use the same language that Moffett does to describe the advantages of her assessment system, but it was clear in our conversations that she sees too much emphasis on grades as detrimental to students' learning.

Moffett's focus on encouraging individual goals as a path to true fulfillment is apparent in his suggestion that "[l]earning is joining a certain culture. . . . [M]ost learning is by acculturation. . . . Instead of trying to teach everybody the same things, it is far more sensible to encourage individuals to learn different things. . . . Rippling across a whole community ensures, in fact, the maximum sharing of knowledge" (*Universal Schoolhouse* 50). In the culture of Lisa's rural classroom, knowledge is defined broadly and distributed across students rather than stuffed into each individual student. For Lisa, curricular design involves choice and tailoring of teaching materials to meet the needs and interests of individual students. Lisa emphasizes choice in her classroom, using literature circles, where students talk about the different books they are reading, and self-chosen topics for writing. In this way, the student who has expertise in hunting has that expertise recognized and shared. The element of choice allows for the "maximum sharing of knowledge" among students and teachers and puts teachers in the position of being a more authentic audience for students, one to whom they actually have something to say.

In the Turner school, Lisa at one point had a single student for senior English. He was interested in farming, and Lisa describes teaching him a course in "farming through English" for the entire year. She notes that she hates standardized curricula, and she would agree that it is "far more sensible to encourage individuals to learn different things" (Moffett, *Universal Schoolhouse* 50). She doesn't have to say how much easier it is to encourage individualized learning in a rural school, where it is not so uncommon to have a classroom with a small handful of students or even only one. She adds, "English especially is such a unique subject matter; . . . any curriculum is automatically dated. You have to use current events and bring the things that the kids like, or you're missing a tremendous opportunity." With this approach, combined with standards-based grading, Lisa's students are assessed in what they can do with texts regardless of what texts those are. Additionally, they learn to make meaning—to "see the world in a slightly different way," as Lisa says—of the stuff of actual, immediate life, because students can focus on events happening in their worlds in the here-and-now. The level of choice, independence, and individual attention required by Lisa's approach is much more realistic and achievable in a rural school environment because teachers have fewer students and typically teach the same students for several years as they progress through the grades. In the case of the single student class, Lisa is in a position to help the student shape his own curriculum, to take a path he himself can design, not so much to be able to "get by, get along, get around, and get ahead," but to enable him instead to "live to learn" what best serves his inner motions and capacities.

Rural School Cultures

Rural schools generally occupy a different place culturally than do metro- and micropolitan schools. As Thomas Lyson notes,

> [S]chools in rural communities play many roles. . . . They serve as social and cultural centers. They are places for sports, theater, music, and civic activities. . . . Schools serve as symbols of community autonomy, community vitality, community integration, personal control, personal and community tradition, and personal and community identity. (131)

This is why, Lyson notes, "school consolidation has been the bane of rural communities for at least the past 50 years" (131). When a school goes, it is often felt, it will not be long before the rest of the community goes with it (Sell and Leistritz).

Compare Lyson's list of roles played by rural schools with some of the things Moffett advocates in *The Universal Schoolhouse* that schools should do. He argues that public services should be incorporated into schools (298–99), which reflects schools as community hubs. Moffett writes that schools "should not merely mirror the society but should fashion selectively a special culture that will correct and complement the society" (57), which connects to the idea of schools as key to local culture. Moffett also argues that education plays a key role in "regenerating" culture (66) by developing a higher consciousness through choice; this echoes the notion that schools are important for community vitality. Last, Moffett writes that "[s]pirituality is connectedness. The more spiritual a person, the more he or she identifies with the rest of humanity and nature" (71). This suggests the idea of schools as integral in the evolution of identities because of the unique way schools shape the values and knowledge of their attendant communities.

Because they are not subject to the same levels and complexity of bureaucracy as urban and suburban schools, rural school cultures can also "enhance inner growth," not only when students are given choices but also when teachers have it. Moffett suggests teachers will need a high degree of curricular autonomy in the education he describes (*Universal Schoolhouse* 122). And rural schools often foster a culture of autonomy. Lisa reports being told by her first principal to "teach whatever you want," though she did have to turn in weekly lesson plans with links to the state standards. Since those standards were about what the students needed to be able to do with texts, not the texts themselves, Lisa was free to choose texts that matched her students' interests and needs. While this lack of oversight could cause problems in the hands of a less conscientious teacher than Lisa, it does provide opportunities for a dedicated teacher to experiment with structural changes in the curriculum.

At Westport school, a rural-distant single-campus K–12 school located in a town with a population of 945, two teachers cover each subject area across grades 7–12. One of those two English teachers, Rachel, was free to design teaching materials within her own classroom but was also encouraged to coordinate curriculum and methods with her colleagues. Similarly, Lisa's colleagues in subjects such as science, keyboarding, nutrition, and social studies sought her out for across-the-curriculum opportunities for her students to read, write, and think about subjects other than English. Nationally, rural teachers report more job satisfaction than their urban and suburban counterparts, despite lower pay. One factor in this satisfaction is the degree of autonomy they enjoy (US Department of Education; NCES, *Job Satisfaction*).

Moffett also advocates for community integration when he writes that students should "interact in activities composed of mixed ages and backgrounds . . . [and] . . . range afield to learn from others at work and interact with the broader environment" (*Universal Schoolhouse* 49–50). In general, rural schools report higher rates of parental and community involvement than do urban and suburban schools (US Department of Education iv). The Westport school offers a strong example of a community integration project: In 2007 the school was destroyed by a tornado a few days before the start of the school year. For a year, students attended school in empty classroom spaces in another town's school nearby. When they returned to their new school building, Rachel could see that the whole community still needed help processing the experience of the tornado. Her classes began a community writing project, collecting various people's tornado stories and writing their own. The resulting book was sold as a fundraiser for the school. In the text, you can see people grappling not only with the fear and helplessness occasioned by the tornado, but also with the loss of the school, a place central to Westport's identity and of which it is justifiably proud. This incredible story illustrates Moffett's vision in action. The tornado book goes beyond mere desire and theoretical hope of what education can do for a community. It makes community identification and change real. In the last chapter of *The Universal Schoolhouse*, Moffett argues that "spiritual education centers on personal growth, which will solve more social ills and material problems than any other sort of educational orientation" (331). In the example of the tornado book, we see how a series of personal essays addresses both a social ill (the devastation of the tornado) and a material problem (the need to raise funds and awareness to rebuild the school).

The production of the tornado book also hewed remarkably close to the writing curriculum Moffett lays out in *Teaching the Universe of Discourse*. He advises starting writing instruction with the closest relations between speakers and listeners (classroom peers) and speakers/listeners and subjects (topics about which students have immediate, personal knowledge), and then moving gradually into modes that assume more interpersonal distance between speakers/listeners and more abstract, less immediate relations to subjects. The process of the Westport tornado book began as personal writing about personal experiences, sometimes for an audience of the writers themselves, what Moffett calls "reflection—intrapersonal communication between two parts of one nervous system" (*Teaching* 33). But as the students and the teacher began to conceive of the collection of their stories as a valuable document for the community, essays were workshopped and revised for a less well-known audience and finally for a more general audience. Moreover, as the revisions of the individual pieces of writing developed, the students gradually reconceived the purpose and audience for their writing in a sequence that moved their project along a continuum from known readers to less familiar readers to a wider public audience, including future audiences of readers, thereby recapitulating the movement Moffett calls for in a growth-oriented and rhetorically authentic curriculum.

This sort of progression also marks a development in the writer's role and sense of power with respect to the world that serves as an audience, offering us a glimpse of what Moffett means when he writes in *The Universal Schoolhouse* of the potential of education to shape identity:

> It is much harder to determine who you are and what you may do even in the worldliest matters when others are constantly forcing things on you and planning everything for you—that is, when you are reactive. It's essential to assert feeling and will and thought proactively enough to establish your own *patterns of action*. Then you manifest something of yourself out there for you and others to respond to so that with their help you can chart past and future. (340)

Moffett's vision of identity here is not a wholly autonomous, individualistic one. While there is the individual's assertion of feeling and will and thought, those then bump up against others' responses, "so that with their help you can chart past and future." This flexibility and freedom of choice in school promotes the kind of identity work that a project such as the Westport tornado book can make possible as individuals share their own thoughts and experiences of the tornado for others to respond to. For that process has the power to instigate and eventually lead to some kind of collective understanding of the various meanings of the tornado for the community, making the experience, the thinking, and the writing of the students for the audience of their classroom and their community a valuable community resource.

Rural Literacies and the Universe of Discourse

I have argued in this chapter that rural education is one educational setting more suitable than others for the realization of the goals and principles Moffett set forth in both *Teaching the Universe of Discourse* and *The Universal Schoolhouse*. I now want to argue that Moffett's ideas are especially relevant, adaptable, and valuable for rural education. The last decade and a half have seen a growing interest in the concept of "rural literacies"—the literacies required "to sustain life in rural communities" (Donehower et al. 4). One strand of research in this area emphasizes the importance of literacies that build and manage relationships both inside and outside rural communities. These include relationships with urban and suburban constituencies, whose consumption of rural communities' resources affect their livelihoods (Schell), as well as relationships within the community and region itself, whether with people, institutions, or landscapes (Edmondson; Donehower, "Connecting Literacy").

The latter category is integral to the survival of rural places as outmigration poses a major threat to many rural communities. In the last USDA study of rural outmigration, published in 2010, half of nonmetropolitan counties had experienced population loss due to outmigration, with a third losing 10 percent or more of their population (McGranahan et al.). Schools themselves, through the relationships they shape, can educate students to leave the community (Carr and Kefalas; Corbett). I argue elsewhere that "rural stayers and returners . . . live in their communities . . . from a conscious choice that is continually made and remade" (Donehower, "Why Not" 38). This "continual choice to stay" entails a constant renegotiation of one's relationship with a rural place and people to withstand the pressures that lead to outmigration and the negative images of rural life that are prevalent in many media. I argue that "this choice requires both emotional and intellectual work, and as such, literacy activities . . . can . . . locat[e] people within a web of relationships [and] create nuance and enjoyment in rural life" (38). Moffett's description of an English curriculum in which students "role-play . . . first and second persons in all the possible relations that might exist between the student and a subject, and between him or a speaker and listener" (*Teaching* 10) is training in using literacy—the symbol system of the English language—within specific social contexts to shape relationships with people in varying degrees of proximity to the speaker/writer/reader/listener. Moffett's inclusion of speakers' relationships to subjects opens up the potential to shape relationships with the nonhuman aspects of rural life, also an important aspect of the choice to stay (Rautio, "Children," *Writing about Everyday Beauty*). This is an optimistic portrayal, I admit, but the research on rural outmigration suggests that lack of economic opportunity, which significantly affects many rural counties, is not always the primary factor in rural outmigration (McGranahan et al.). Instead, a perceived lack of amenities, particularly natural amenities, is (McGranahan et al. 3), which suggests that reshaping rural people's relationships with their physical surroundings is key to stemming outmigration. In other words, the more extended category of relationships, those between rural and urban/suburban people, is vital to shape the management of rural resources—agricultural, natural, extractive—that benefit all three constituencies.

Imagine the effects of the rural curriculum outlined above on the Kanawha County residents Moffett describes in *Storm in the Mountains*. One of the most noteworthy features of *Storm* is the middle section of transcripts of Moffett's interviews with the rural Appalachian people who wanted to censor his high school literacy curriculum, *Interactions*. The result of Moffett's interactions with these people was a complete stalemate. Moffett characterizes the problem as the censors' *agnosis*, or willful ignorance; I would suggest instead that there is a complete failure of identification—the censors' inability to relate to Moffett and, to some extent, Moffett's inability to relate to the censors.

Identification work and identity work can go hand in hand. Lisa describes her process of choosing books for her Westport classroom as an effort to balance the need for individuals to see themselves with the need to identify with others. She refers to Rudine Sims Bishop's notion of "mirrors and windows"—that students need texts that let them see themselves reflected within the larger culture, as well as texts that give them a "window" into the lives of those different from them. Moffett's curriculum moves from mirrors to windows in another way—from "mirroring" interactions between speakers and those closest to and most like them, to "window" interactions between speakers/writers and those distant from them in space, time, and culture.

The identification and identity work described here would benefit students in any school context, rural, suburban, or urban. But the specifics of Moffett's curricular ideas in *Teaching the Universe of Discourse*, and their conceptual underpinnings in *The Universal Schoolhouse*, are a particularly good fit for rural schools. They match the traits and needs of rural schools for teacher autonomy, student choice, and exploration of identity and relationships. They also provide a road map for rural schools to take advantage of their structural and cultural particularities to produce student-centered, individually tailored education that reverberates throughout local communities. While some of Moffett's ideas may seem utopian, he notes that most of the obstacles facing his vision are practical. He writes, "[L]etting students do different things at the same time will entail radically restructuring the procedures of education. It means, for example, mixing ages, learning modalities, and subjects—in other words, abandoning standardization of both the subject matter and the learners" (*Universal Schoolhouse* 51). As Rachel's and Lisa's classrooms show, such "radical" tactics are already starting to happen, suggesting that in rural school spaces the time for Moffett's ideas has come again.

Works Cited

Barter, Barbara. "Rural Education: Learning to Be Rural Teachers." *Journal of Workplace Learning*, vol. 20, no. 7-8, 2008, pp. 468–79.

Carr, Patrick J., and Maria Kefalas. *Hollowing out the Middle: The Rural Brain Drain and What It Means for America*. Beacon Press, 2009.

Corbett, Michael. *Learning to Leave: The Irony of Schooling in a Coastal Community*. Fernwood, 2007.

Council of Chief State School Officers and National Governors Association Center for Best Practices. Common Core State Standards Initiative. *College and Career Readiness Anchor Standards*. http://

www.corestandards.org/ELA-Literacy/CCRA/R/. Accessed 12 Aug. 2021.

Donehower, Kim. "Connecting Literacy to Sustainability: Revisiting *Literacy as Involvement*." *Literacy, Economy, and Power: Writing and Research after* Literacy in American Lives, edited by John Duffy et al., Southern Illinois UP, 2013, pp. 97–110.

———. "Why Not at School? Rural Literacies and the Continual Choice to Stay." *Rethinking Rural Literacies: Transnational Perspectives*, edited by Bill Green and Michael Corbett, Palgrave Macmillan, 2013, pp. 35–52.

———, et al. *Rural Literacies*. Southern Illinois UP, 2007.

Edmondson, Jacqueline. *Prairie Town: Redefining Rural Life in the Age of Globalization*. Rowman & Littlefield, 2003.

Howley, Craig B., and Aimee Howley. "The Power of Babble: Technology and Rural Education." *ERIC*, Opinion Papers, 1995, ED382437.

Lyson, Thomas A. "What Does a School Mean to a Community? Assessing the Social and Economic Benefits of Schools to Rural Villages in New York." *Journal of Research in Rural Education*, vol. 17, no. 3, 2002, pp. 131–37.

McGranahan, David, et al. *Nonmetropolitan Outmigration Counties: Some Are Poor, Many Are Prosperous*. US Department of Agriculture, Economic Research Service, 2010.

Moffett, James. *Coming on Center: English Education in Evolution*. Boynton/Cook, 1981.

———. *Teaching the Universe of Discourse*. Houghton Mifflin, 1968.

———. *Storm in the Mountains: A Case Study of Censorship, Conflict, and Consciousness*. Southern Illinois UP, 1988.

———. *The Universal Schoolhouse: Spiritual Awakening through Education*. 1994. Calendar Islands Publishers, 1998.

Moffett, James, and Betty Jane Wagner. "What Works Is Play." *Language Arts*, vol. 70, no. 1, 1993, pp. 32–36.

National Center for Education Statistics. *Job Satisfaction among America's Teachers: Effects of Workplace Conditions, Background Characteristics, and Teacher Compensation*. Statistical Analysis Report, 1997.

———. "Rural." *Locale Definitions*, https://nces.ed.gov/surveys/ruraled/definitions.asp. Accessed 28 June 2017.

Rautio, Pauliina. "Children Who Carry Stones in Their Pockets: On Autotelic Material Practices in Everyday Life." *Children's Geographies*, vol. 11, no. 4, 2013, pp. 394–408.

———. *Writing about Everyday Beauty in a Northern Village: An Argument for Diversity of Habitable Places*. University of Oulu, 2010.

Schell, Eileen E. "The Rhetorics of the Farm Crisis: Toward Alternative Agrarian Literacies in a Globalized World." *Rural Literacies*, Southern Illinois UP, 2007, pp. 77–119.

Sell, Randall S., and F. Larry Leistritz. "Socioeconomic Impacts of School Consolidation on Host and Vacated Communities." *Journal of the Community Development Society*, vol. 28, no. 2, 1997, pp. 186–205. *Taylor & Francis Online*, doi.org/10.1080/15575339709489782.

Sims Bishop, Rudine. "Mirrors, Windows, and Sliding Glass Doors." *Perspectives: Choosing and Using Books for the Classroom*, vol. 6, no. 3, 1990, pp. ix–xi.

Theobald, Paul, and Paul Nachtigal. "Culture, Community, and the Promise of Rural Education." *ERIC*, Opinion Papers, 1995, ED388464.

US Department of Education. *Status of Education in Rural America*. National Center for Education Statistics, https://nces.ed.gov/pubs2007/ruraled/chapter3_6.asp. Accessed 12 Aug. 2021.

Vatterott, Cathy. *Rethinking Grading: Meaningful Assessment for Standards-Based Learning*. ASCD, 2015.

IV

Moffett and Mindfulness, Moffett in Memory

Chapter Eighteen

Meditative Practice and Feminist Rhetorical Resilience

Karen Tellez-Trujillo
California State Polytechnic University, Pomona

I see myself as one of the teachers James Moffett described in his 1994 article, "Women's Ways of Writing, or, Images, Self-Images, and Graven Images: Responses," as having "reasons for choosing the profession they're in, and going about it in the way they do, that concern their own efforts to heal, grow, and find themselves" (259). My teaching practice is very much informed by how I use writing as a way of caring for myself and healing as a result. The more I write, the more I listen to myself and the more I think about the writing teacher I am and want to be. In thinking about writing in this way throughout the years, I have decided that as much as I value personal writing in my classroom, students will also benefit (as Moffett insists in his controversial essay "Writing, Inner Speech, and Meditation") from meditating prior to personal writing. Although a lifetime of experience and countless hours of writing have shaped the writer and writing teacher that I am, two major discoveries in my education have led to the most significant changes in my goals for myself and, more important, the goals I have for my students.

The first major discovery in my writing practice took place during the time I spent as a Borderland Writing Project (BWP) fellow. This experience was much like what Moffett writes about in his 1979 essay "Integrity in the Teaching of Writing" where teachers "wrote, talked shop about writing, and worked up a presentation they could make as consultants for other teachers during the following school year" (278). Far more took place during that summer institute where relationships were formed between teachers of all levels, and with each interaction, new perspectives were shared and, for the most part, adopted. It was also during this seminar that I was introduced to Moffett and meditation for the first time.

The Moffett I was introduced to was the pedagogue that Jonathan Marine and Paul Rogers describe in their introduction to the recently published *Toward a Re-emergence of James Moffett's Mindful, Spiritual, and Student-Centered Pedagogy*, a teacher who believed "that students should be the center of the classroom and learn from one another ('student-centered learning') and that they should write authentic texts wrought from the plenitude of their own experiences to perpetually rediscover the limits of their own perspectives" (2). Student-centered learning was what had drawn me to become an English major; I believed my professors were more concerned with student growth than with growing their egos as scholars. As a result of courses taken in the English department and gender studies, I knew that I wanted a dialogical classroom where my students' well-being and experiential knowledge were honored and valued.

The second discovery occurred when I began researching Elizabeth A. Flynn, Patricia Sotirin, and Ann Brady's 2012 concept of feminist rhetorical resilience. During this time, I began recognizing that the belief system I'd created around resilience and responses to adversity was harmful not only to myself but also to my unrealistic expectations of others. I often thought about the types of adversity my students were coming up against inside and outside the classroom and how much of that adversity surrounded reading, writing, and their relationships with language. At the time, as now, I was learning and teaching in a Hispanic-serving institution (HSI), although then I was only forty-five miles from the United States–Mexico border. Like my students, I and many of my peers raised in this geographical location had been denied our home language of Spanish in school. Many of us had also been raised in environments where the "bootstraps" (Villanueva) mentality we uncritically accepted contributed to the idea that any resistance we felt to injustice was to be faced without complaint or outside help. This unreasonable approach to resilience applied to our negative experiences with language as English speakers from Spanish or Spanish- and English-speaking homes, as it did to other oppressive situations inside and outside the classroom.

In this chapter, I first discuss the relationship I now see between meditation and feminist rhetorical resilience and why enactments of both can and should take place where writing is occurring as a way of creating an opportunity for students to notice and control their inner speech, particularly when their inner speech gives attention to the various adversities they face daily and their responses to these adversities. I then share my vision for integrating Moffett's meditation into the writing classroom. Last, I discuss the potential limitations to my argument in support of meditation in the writing classroom but do not stay long with the limitations, as I acknowledge that Moffett's alternative approaches to teaching were met with resistance (Rogers and Marine), and still—he persisted, as should I.

Relearning Resilience and Pairing It with Meditation

Nearly ten years after being introduced to Moffett's work, I learned about feminist theorists Elizabeth A. Flynn, Patricia Sotirin, and Ann Brady and their concept of feminist rhetorical resilience, introduced in their edited collection, *Feminist Rhetorical Resilience*. For Flynn and colleagues, resilience is an attribute enacted not just by some but by all. They also assert that one does not need to have access to power or vast resources to enact resilience, but only access to personal and community resources, as well as to relationships with others. For Flynn et al., reaching the end of an adverse situation is not the goal of the person who is experiencing adversity; instead, continuous forward movement is what matters, which calls for progression through consistent, small gestures aimed toward affecting change for both the individual and the community. I was captivated by this concept and chose to write my dissertation, "Enactments of Feminist Resilience in the Composition Classroom: Re-scripting Post-Adversity Encounters through Writing," in response to my study of student essays and interviews centered on students' resilient responses to adversity. In the study, composition students from three first-year writing classes explored their definitions of resilience, the times and places they believed they witnessed resilience in action, and their beliefs about how one already is or becomes resilient.

Flynn et al. "define resilience using three tenets: agency, mêtis [from Greek mythology, intuitive intelligence], and relationality, and resist conceptions of it that assume that it is an inherent and unchanging personality trait" (Bourelle). I found this definition personally resonant because I have been ever aware of my own struggle for agency, my own consistent need to assess and adjust my social positioning to fit my surroundings, and my own reliance on relationality within my community as a support system. Like many students, I have spent a lifetime among the writers that Eli Goldblatt referred to as those "who are marginalized in such a way that their voices hardly register in the public arena" (440). I know firsthand what it means to rely on others for access and power, how important it is to shapeshift, and why relationships are necessary for survival.

I learned early in my teaching career that the first tenet of agency could be attained through writing, and that students were less hesitant or fearful of using their voice in the knowledge that oftentimes their voices were all they had. Flynn et al. assert that feminist resilience "allows us to focus on those who have neither available resources, nor taken-for-granted access" (7). I often ask students to list the tools needed to write, and although they have not listed meditation, they have listed quiet spaces, reflection, and time to think without pressure. The second tenet, mêtis, in the discourse of feminist resilience refers to "intuitive knowledge," and Debra Hawhee's case for mêtis noted by Flynn et al. describes it as "embodied intelligence" (qtd. in Flynn et al. 12). To access the embodied intelligence and knowledge required of feminist resilience, students must take the time to first listen to themselves, which few have time for or practice in doing, and pay attention to what their bodies are telling them in the moment, whether it be that they are fatigued, strong, or stressed. The third and last tenet is relationality. Writing, like meditation, can be as charged by the energy of writing in a community as it can be when done in private. Because I anticipate that meditation will be new to most students, having a group with whom they can share their challenges and triumphs with meditation will be beneficial as students accept and realize that meditation is not as difficult or otherworldly as they might have imagined.

I share these tenets in relation to meditation to set the foundation for my belief that meditation not only has a place in the writing classroom, but that it is imperative for students who are not accustomed to taking stock of the resources they possess or have access to or the relationships and skills within themselves that empower them in times of adversity. Given that meditation is an unusual practice within university classrooms, and considering the benefits that can come from integrating it with deep consideration, I have spent many hours envisioning the writing classroom where meditation is practiced.

Vision for Integrating Moffett's Meditation into the Writing Classroom

When reflecting on my ideas for meditation in the writing classroom, I have asked myself the questions I typically ask when considering activities and practices for my writing courses: (1) Will integrating time for meditation into the course schedule benefit students? (2) Will the choices speak to the objectives of the department and course curriculum? (3) Do these decisions uphold the teaching philosophy to which I adhere? With positive responses to these questions, I recall Moffett's assertion that we should "consider what therapy, spirituality, and the university's missions are essentially about: . . . getting better—getting better in the sense of healing, getting better in the sense of becoming a finer person, and getting better in the sense of becoming more competent at some activity" ("Women's Ways" 261). Being fully aware of my experience level with meditation, I believe that over time not only will I get better at teaching meditation in connection with writing, but also that my students and I will, with time, get better at controlling inner speech. Therefore, I am confident in proceeding with meditation in the classroom to the level of my ability.

Moffett also suggests that "just taking part in this world gives you enough reason to want to assess what you are up to" ("Women's Ways" 259), and I argue further that before one can take a meaningful part in this world, time must be spent caring for and giving attention to the self. Students will benefit from learning that there are varying magnitudes of adversity they will face daily, and that regardless of the gravity of that adversity they do not automatically bounce back through resilience after experiencing strain, as if they were a Rubbermaid box. Students will benefit from recognizing their capacity to respond to adversity in a manner consistent with feminist resilience, but also from the knowledge that resilience does not have an end but rather is ongoing. Through meditation before writing, students can learn to control their inner speech and write about what is present in themselves, thus avoiding superficial writing that is crafted toward what they believe others want to read. A further, lasting benefit is students accepting that they will not emerge from adversity unscathed but will continue to grow and change, which should be revealed as their writing and meditation practices mature over time.

My vision for a writing class that integrates Moffett's meditation is one where, after a meditation session, students write about, discuss, and reflect on their resilient responses to day-in-and-day-out challenges. In this vision, students spend time practicing witnessing their inner thoughts, or a version of what Moffett refers to as the "stream which has been more verbally distilled and which can hence more directly serve as the wellspring" ("Writing" 231). This is a way for students to check in with themselves while also becoming comfortable with silence and stillness, which, like meditation and writing, requires practice. Among the earliest steps in learning to control inner speech is the practice of "letting inner speech flow spontaneously, but witnessing it" (Moffett, "Writing" 231). From this beginning step, the developing meditator might begin to experiment with slowing down the flow of inner speech to focus the mind on a single thought or idea or experience. And in this slowing down and focusing practice, we find an opportunity and resource for rewitnessing and reprocessing some of the challenges we have faced and continue to face, reflecting on our responses, and identifying our moments and acts of resilience as a way of acknowledging the growth and change we have experienced from facing adversity. This is not to say that the effects of enactments of feminist resilience are always positive, but I know from experience that there is benefit in taking time in our reveries or meditations to slow down the flow of inner speech to focus on moments of discomfort and adversity and our endurance and response, taking stock of how we have reckoned with our day-to-day challenges—how we have responded to them, what we have learned from them, and how we might respond in the future.

This narrowing down and focusing of inner speech as it is witnessed allows the writing student to hold "the mind without distraction, focusing on it with special intensity, and developing it to an understanding not achievable by ordinary, relatively wayward reflection" (Moffett, "Writing" 236–37). I agree with Moffett that the teacher should not try to play the psychiatrist when students are working toward healing, but there is no reason to deny our students or ourselves the well-known therapeutic benefits of writing ("Writing" 234). Moffett's approach to meditation is not therapy, but "[p]recisely because it is not thought of as therapy and works toward another goal, writing can affect fine therapy sometimes. At any rate, self-awareness is the means in both cases, and this requires focusing attention on one's inner speech" ("Writing" 234). Further, a brief meditative retreat will provide students a new approach to writing as they feel less hurried and can focus on what they would like to write rather than in response to what they believe others want to read.

Having taken into deep consideration the benefits of meditation with writing and honoring one's vision, I need to consider logistics. Students at my university meet for only fifteen weeks during the semester in classes that last one hour. Over the course of the semester, it takes time for students to build trust and community, so meditation will need to be introduced after students have had time to get comfortable with one another, and this could take four weeks or more. Students will also need to learn about the reasons I have chosen to put meditation on the syllabus. This conversation would not take place until at least week two. During the fifteen weeks spent together, I feel confident that I would have time to "coach students on how to get themselves into a meditative state of unusual absorption in a subject that interests them and then to visualize, imagine, feel, and think everything they can about that subject without at first concerning themselves about writing something down" (Moffett, "Writing" 243). How deeply students get into the practice will be up to them, as is their option to start meditating on their own if they don't already do so.

However and whenever students take up the practice of meditation for themselves (if they ever do so), I believe meditation will be helpful in getting them to focus their attention in a way that is rarely asked of them in their earlier schooling, and that in operationalizing Moffett's theory, students will learn to focus intensively for a time on their inner speech and thereby "channel and intensify inner speech in a state of heightened consciousness and self-communication" ("Writing" 243) that enables them to summon all they are capable of saying about a subject. To help my students learn to control and focus their attention, I recommend a progression of steps I have pulled from Moffett's approach to meditation that, coupled with journaling, I have found to be a workable program for allowing students to recognize what they can do and be comfortable with their practice. It also allows them to determine for themselves at each step whether they find that meditation techniques are serving them as writers. The following list of activities, borrowed largely from Moffett's "Writing, Inner Speech, and Meditation" article, describe a progression of steps in controlling and focusing attention that can lead students (and has worked for me) into a comfortable and productive experience of meditation and a practice that can deepen and enrich their performance as writers.

Step 1. Gazing

Gazing is a contemplative practice best done in private. Moffett notes that gazing is simply "staring . . . and visualizing," exactly as we see children doing quite naturally, yet a practice that helps to develop the capacity to perceive and notice what is happening in both one's exterior and inner worlds, which is a prerequisite for thoughtful, attentive writing ("Writing" 236). Because gazing requires open eyes, it might be a challenge to practice it in a classroom setting where students could be distracted by the presence of others. Also, many students may depend on closing their eyes to focus. For these reasons, a teacher could assign gazing as homework to be done in private. Wherever the gazing is done, it should be paired with a written reflection on how the process of gazing did or did not contribute to the writing process.

Step 2. Witnessing

Moffett claims the following approach to meditation to be the "simplest and easiest" and is a method I could envision taking place in the composition classroom. The act of witnessing, with eyes open or closed, "consists of letting inner speech flow spontaneously but of witnessing it. Instead of floating along on this stream and being borne away from the center of the self, one sits on the bank, so to speak, and watches it flow by, staying separate from it, not trying to influence it, but above all not being carried away by it" ("Writing" 236–37). This meditative practice has been the easiest for me to achieve and has encouraged control over inner speech that has led to writing from thoughts I might not have accessed otherwise. The writing done following witnessing is more clearly focused than when not paired with meditation. Following meditation that precedes writing, I find myself less prone to a clenched jaw, tense hands, and a propensity to pull my shoulders up to my ears as I type. Moffett encourages, "Once able to still himself, turn inward, and witness his thoughts, the meditator may deliberately attempt to narrow down and focus his inner speech to exert some control over it." He further suggests that "[w]ill comes more into play" at this point, and notes that "even to observe is to alter, so maintaining the witness distance and not getting 'lost in thought' already asserts some influence no doubt on the direction and content of inner speech." Moffett summarizes the process as follows: "setting a subject, holding the mind to it without distraction, focusing on it with special intensity, and developing it to an understanding not achievable by ordinary, relatively wayward reflection" ("Writing" 237). I suggest that ten- to fifteen-minute witnessing sessions could occur in classes that range from fifty-five to seventy-five minutes. This practice can also happen once per unit in a fifteen-week semester separated into four units, or more often as time permits in each class. For the teacher who is more adept and practiced at meditation, a more complex approach to visualization than shared here could take place in the next, more advanced step.

Step 3. Visualization

Using visualization, "[t]he meditator closes his eyes and transfers the image inward to the middle of the forehead. Alternately gazing outward and visualizing inward teaches one to develop inner attention and imagination without forcing verbalization. Other pure visualization meditations can follow" (Moffett, "Writing" 236). If this step is done properly, with the meditator staying focused in or out, Moffett suggests that this "frees the meditator from the excitations of the environment and lets him or her feel the strength of the self, the deeper self that abides at least somewhat independently of the outside. Writing presupposes just such inner strength." I suggest this as an advanced step, as Moffett notes that "[a] writer of whatever age has to feel full of herself and have a degree of confidence, belief that she has something to say, faith in her will and control of her attention ("Writing" 236). This type of practice may need to take place in private or in a class that is nearing the end of the semester where silence and trust are valued.

Holding Attention

I am also mindful of Moffett's recommendation that "[h]olding attention on regular breathing is perfectly safe and may be an easy, fitting focus for many students, offering an alternative to visual and auditory focuses" ("Writing" 244). Holding attention and breathing is also an appropriate alternative for students who may be hesitant or feel vulnerable at any attempt to work to achieve a meditative state. Moffett writes that most students can access "a quiet location and a comfortable sitting position," essential to meditation. He also recommends "[s]itting cross-legged on the floor or sitting on a chair (preferably without touching the back of the chair)," as "one keeps the spine erect but not stiff, releases muscles, and slows and deepens breathing." This position also requires considerations of mobility and access, but it is still possible. He then reminds the practitioner, "The key to meditation is a relaxed body and an alert awareness," which is likely not easy to achieve without practice ("Writing" 244). Each of these steps is reasonable and productive for writers of all levels.

◆ ◆ ◆ ◆

Most days I benefit from seeking quiet, sitting for a few moments, paying mind to my breathing, and reaching for relaxation, expecting that I will achieve awareness, whether I have writing to do or not. I hope that my readers (presumably teachers) and their students, who have not yet experienced meditation, will follow Moffett's advice to practice such a discipline of relaxed breathing and alert attention to discover the benefits it offers to thinking and deepened consciousness, at home and in academic settings.

Limitations and Possibilities of Meditation in the Writing Classroom

It was by chance while building an understanding of Moffett's meditation that I came across Russel K. Durst's "The Stormy Times of James Moffett" (see Chapter 6 this volume) and wondered whether asking students to meditate in the classroom would be seen by some students or their parents as somehow alien or even threatening to their cultural traditions or religious beliefs. I thought that maybe it's just too early in a student's education to integrate meditation into a college first-year composition class or high school college prep writing course. In fact, I must confess that each time I plan for meditation in my classroom, I come up against the worry that my students will treat the exercise as just another arbitrary school assignment, and in their writing and discussion perform in the way they believe their peers or I want or expect of them. However, I also try to remember Moffett's belief that even such performative writing can represent a baby step or half-hearted action that comes before one learns how to free oneself to pay genuine attention to one's own thinking and begin to listen to one's own inner speech. I worry, in other words, that students will privilege writing for an audience over learning to write for themselves, at the same time that I recognize that my writing class must prepare my students to write as members of an academic community.

I also worry, of course, that my own relative lack of experience in meditation, when compared with Moffett's, disqualifies me for the task of teaching my students a discipline that takes many years to master. But I continue to promote focused attention and mindfulness, as well as the art of listening to and recording one's inner speech, because I have experienced the value of such disciplined attention to the quality of my own thinking and writing, and because I have every reason to trust the wisdom of Moffett's advice to teachers like me.

Conclusion

I conclude this chapter so grateful for the opportunity to write about and continue Moffett's legacy while encouraging other writing teachers to do the same. Consistently returning to Moffett's writing throughout my teaching career has empowered me, knowing that he was not sidetracked by what others thought about his approaches to teaching, nor was he deterred by the reluctance of others to accept spirituality in learning institutions. Durst shared that "James Moffett fought against the mindset he termed agnosis, the desire not to know, the inclination to reject ideas that seem threatening or strange" (129), and I see this as a fight that might be risky, but worth the risk. My own growth and healing through meditation, paired with what I have gained in productivity and depth as a writer, give me the confidence to continue following the advice and example of my spiritual and pedagogical mentor, James Moffett.

Works Cited

Bourelle, Tiffany. "Kairos, Resilience, and Serendipity: An Interview with Elizabeth Flynn." *Composition Forum*, vol. 35, 2017.

Durst, Russel K. "The Stormy Times of James Moffett." *English Education*, vol. 47, no. 2, 2015, pp. 111–30.

Flynn, Elizabeth A., et al., editors. *Feminist Rhetorical Resilience.* Utah State UP, 2012.

Goldblatt, Eli. "Don't Call It Expressivism: Legacies of a 'Tacit Tradition.'" *College Composition and Communication*, vol. 68, no. 3, 2017, pp. 438–65.

Marine, Jonathan, and Paul Rogers. "Moffett's Turn to the Spiritual and Meditative." *Toward a Re-emergence of James Moffett's Mindful, Spiritual, and Student-Centered Pedagogy*, edited by Jonathan Marine et al., Peter Lang Publishing, 2023, pp. 1–24.

Moffett, James. "Integrity in the Teaching of Writing." *Phi Delta Kappan*, vol. 61, no. 4, 1979, pp. 276–79.

———. "Women's Ways of Writing, or, Images, Self-Images, and Graven Images: Responses." *College Composition and Communication*, vol. 45, no. 2, 1994, pp. 258–63.

———. "Writing, Inner Speech, and Meditation." *College English*, vol. 44, no. 3, 1982, pp. 231–46.

Rogers, Paul, and Jonathan Marine. "Meditation and the Writing Process: An Interview with Don Gallehr." *Toward a Re-emergence of James Moffett's Mindful, Spiritual, and Student-Centered Pedagogy*, edited by Jonathan Marine et al., Peter Lang Publishing, 2023, pp. 95–106.

Trujillo, Karen R. *Enactments of Feminist Resilience in the Composition Classroom: Re-scripting Post-Adversity Encounters through Writing.* Unpublished dissertation, . New Mexico State University, 2020. *ProQuest*, https://www.proquest.com/openview/8835359bbdeba19e60d17d0777bc0f12/1.pdf?pq-origsite=gscholar&cbl=18750&diss=y.

Villanueva, Victor, Jr. *Bootstraps: From an American Academic of Color.* National Council of Teachers of English, 1993.

CHAPTER NINETEEN

Moffett, Yoga Philosophy, and Pedagogy: Teaching for Embodied Learning

DENISE MALTESE
Onteora Middle School, Boiceville, New York

In a state of Yoga, comprehension is different from comprehension at other times. It is closer to the true nature of the object.

—T. K. V. DESIKACHAR, *The Heart of Yoga*

I began teaching middle school English in 1992 in a progressive New Jersey school district that supported our department in terrific ways. One way was to send us all to the National Council of Teachers of English (NCTE) Convention in Orlando in 1994. I was amazed by all of the famous authors, researchers, and thinkers who attended the Convention, my mentor teacher pointing them out. I remember, going down the escalator, hearing her whisper reverently, "There's Moffett." Isn't it funny the way certain memories persist? I remember a white-haired man with a distinct, distinguished face glancing at us as he passed us going upward. There is a term in Yoga philosophy, *samskaras*, that refers to the idea that purposeful action or intent by an individual leaves an impression or imprint; it's related to memory and the way the mind stores these impressions. The mind is full of *samskaras,* both positive and negative, and they shape who we are.

James Moffett passed away in 1996, the year that I began graduate school at the University of California, Santa Barbara, so I have only known him through others who have known him and through his writing. I heard from Moffett acolytes at the Assembly for Expanded Perspectives on Learning conference in Estes Park in the early 2000s, and over discussions about Moffett at NCTE Conventions, that he was a guru, a yogi, a visionary, a *mystic* even, but I didn't understand the significance of these titles as I was trying to maintain my footing on the shaky ground that was the pattern and practice of teaching English language arts in a public school.

As an early career teacher, I began by first clinging to practices that gave me the structure and the lessons for my middle school English class. When I was introduced to Moffett's work, however, I received a philosophy for implementation: how to teach language arts in a sensible way, one that was student centered, varied audiences and purposes for using language, and considered how abstraction levels affected students' understanding and use of discourse. I found Moffett's explanations clear and easy to understand, enabling me to design an effective curriculum. I was also fortunate that experimentation was accepted in the schools where I taught, and therefore I could run a workshop model so that students could "play the scale" (Moffett, *Detecting Growth* 69).

I was so deeply influenced by Moffett that in the fourteenth year of my teaching practice, I published an essay on the impact that Moffett's work had had on my teaching practice and curricular choices, "Out of the Narrow Tunnel and into the Universe of Discourse." However, it wasn't until a few years later that I began a personal yoga practice, which, as in Moffett's own case ("Yoga" 119), led me to a yoga master, in my case, Linda Lalita Winnick, with whom I studied Yoga philosophy and Ayurveda, and I eventually received my 200-hour yoga teacher training certificate. Moreover, as my study of Yoga philosophy moved beyond a simple exercise routine, I was surprised and pleased to discover a new depth to my understanding of Moffett's writing and particularly what Moffett had to say about growth of consciousness, a concept I had seen multiple times in his writing and assumed I had understood but now apprehended and appreciated in a new and deeper way.

While I had read what Moffett wrote explicitly about Yoga philosophy in his articles "Yoga for Public School Teachers" and

"Writing, Inner Speech, and Meditation" in his collection *Coming on Center*, I was most familiar with his earliest and now classic book of 1968, *Teaching the Universe of Discourse*, where he makes little mention of his interest in Yoga or in any esoteric texts. Nor is it clear how much Moffett had read in such texts before he wrote his classic works. Those who knew Moffett personally, from the time he moved to California in the early 1970s, often spoke and eventually wrote about how his yoga practice was an important part of who he was, and we know that in the early 1970s he actually turned his home in Berkeley into an ashram, where his wife gave yoga lessons (Potts 13). One legendary story I heard from his friends was that Moffett could hold a headstand for an exceptionally long time. Yet, even if Moffett didn't study Yoga intensely until the 1970s, it now seems clear that he had intuitively and deeply come to understand the relationship between Yoga and writing earlier, and returning to his work as often as I do, I can see the threads of his understanding of Yoga permeating much of his early writing about discourse and mastering the arts of language, as it does more explicitly and with greater elaboration in his later essays. The relationship between Moffett's deep understanding (intuitive and acquired) of Yoga philosophy and its practice has barely been touched on by previous scholarship on Moffett but seems to me a necessary part of understanding Moffett's thinking about teaching and learning, and can help us better understand his amazing prescience as an educator and guide for many of today's most successful classroom teachers.

Yoga's goal is to join mind, body, and spirit, bringing one back to an egoless consciousness where there is no confusion of mind and body, akin to the newborn's response to the world. "At birth, the mind of a child is integral with the world, because it has never had to deal with the world," Moffett tells us (*Detecting Growth* 9). As a child grows and develops an independent sense of self, the ego forms, and according to Yoga philosophy, this is when the difficulties begin. Eastern philosophies like Buddhism and Hinduism recognize that suffering is inevitable. While tragic events are out of our control, how one's mind responds to everyday difficulties can be altered with practice. This is relevant for all humans, but I would like to make the case for its special relevance for adolescents, for whom much everyday suffering is unquestionable. Bodily changes, cultural pressures, peer interactions, the need to be simultaneously seen and invisible, and, perhaps, the desire to receive unconditional love are all among the inner conflicts that might distinguish adolescence as the most painful transition period in the lives of most human beings, especially in Western culture. It's probably why, when folks ask me what grade level I teach and I tell them eighth grade, they recoil a bit into themselves, recalling their own sensitive and difficult growth processes.

When teaching adolescents, a way for educators to reach students is to say that by learning to control one's mind, one's emotions, and one's focus, one can reduce suffering. And as a result, by practicing these habits of mind and by developing equanimity, students can grow to be more stable adults. Only in the past few years has social and emotional learning been on the curriculum. In New York State, where I teach, the "SEL benchmarks" adopted in 2018 were formally titled "Social Emotional Learning: Essential for Learning, Essential for Life" (New York State Education Department). Moffett understood that learning about language and how to use it impacts one's emotional and social well-being.

> To be the master, and not the dupe, of symbols . . . takes consciousness and an integrated view of the hierarchical, inner processing. I am not talking here about dry data and intellectual matters. I am trying to talk simultaneously about effective thought, emotional health, and active values. The relations among feeling, thought, and values are such that this course seems not only possible, but in the end necessary. (*Teaching the Universe* 25)

It is necessary because it gives meaning to our lives; to have empathy, to care for others, to remove the differential in communication—all lead to a deeper understanding of oneself and also of the culture and the community in which one is living. School can numb students to such qualities, but in a more mindful and more engaging classroom environment, students can live in an emotionally richer and more receptive state of consciousness. According to the SEL benchmarks, "Extensive research indicates that effective mastery of social emotional competencies is associated with greater well-being and better school performance; whereas the lack of competency in these areas can lead to a variety of personal, social, and academic difficulties" (NYSED 1–2).

The Heart of Yoga

In addition to Moffett's work, I've been especially influenced by T. K. V. Desikachar's writing in *The Heart of Yoga: Developing a Personal Practice*. This book gives practical advice as to how Yoga philosophy can influence regular folks—"householders"—those of us who have day jobs and don't live in an ashram. "There are many definitions of yoga," Desikichar wrote, and some of them are:

- yoga as the movement from one point to another, higher one
- yoga as the bringing together, the unifying of two things
- yoga as action with undivided, uninterrupted attention

These definitions have one thing in common: the idea that something changes. (79)

Over the thirty years of my career as a teacher of English language arts, I have observed an exponential growth in the popularity of yoga as a form of exercise. With yoga now part of the modern collective consciousness, teachers may feel more inclined than they have been in the past to pay attention to the core concepts or arts of living that are known as the "Eight Limbs of Yoga" ("Yoga") and to recognize how much they connect to and can illuminate our understanding of what we talk about under the headings of "learning" and "growth" (see Figure 19.1). These "limbs" include the *yamas* and the *niyamas*, the first two limbs, which together provide a set of guidelines on how to live ethically and with satisfaction in the world. The Kripalu Center for Yoga and Health explains that the *yamas* and *niyamas* are "like a map written to guide you on your life's journey. Simply put, the *yamas* are things not to do, or restraints, while the *niyamas* are things to do, or observances. Together, they form a moral code of conduct" ("Yoga's Ethical Guide").

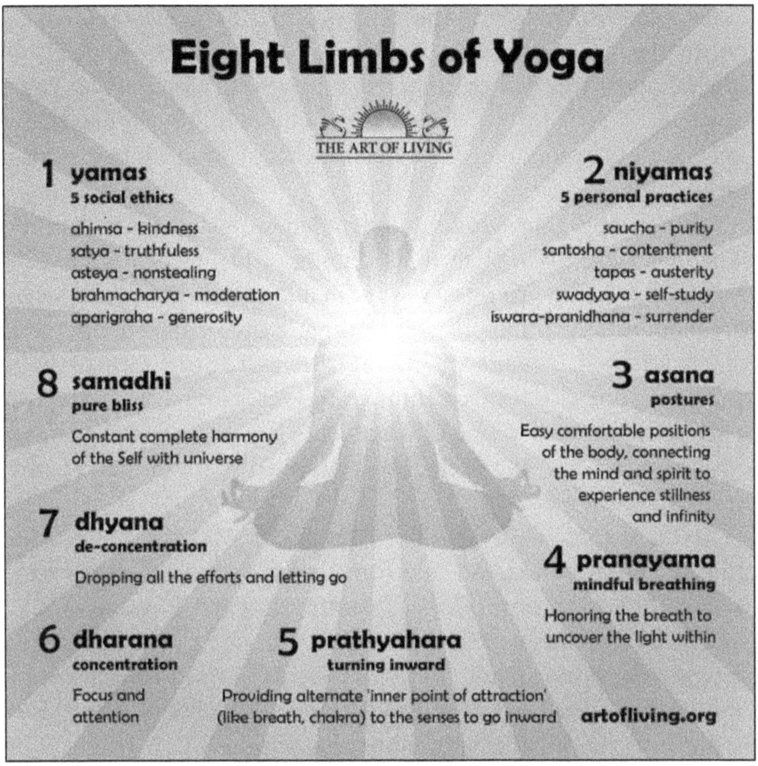

FIGURE 19.1. *The Eight Limbs of Yoga. Originally published on artofliving.com. Reprinted with permission. (Site is now defunct.)*

The third limb, *asana*, which refers to the postures or positions for yoga practice, is surely the most familiar term to casual practitioners of yoga. The fourth limb, also fairly well known to novice practitioners, is *pranayama,* breathing, which works with *asanas* to help the practitioner inhabit the body for a complete experience of the physical realm. When one is focused on a pose, or when one is practicing a particular kind of breathwork, it is the intent to create oneness, to leave behind what is known as the "monkey mind" and to inhabit the body fully, to let go of the mind's grip and allow the body to experience the sensations that the postures and breathwork bring. There is a simultaneous sense of holding and release that happens when one practices asana and pranayama. It is essential to do both, as this applies to one's experiences throughout time—life is both holding on and letting go. In classrooms outside of the yoga studio, students need not practice postures or breathing to experience the tenets of Yoga, however. The eight limbs together promote a natural process of living a deeply connected life that teachers can tap into and pass on to their students.

While applying Moffett's related theories of discourse and language development in my teaching, and being a student of Yoga, I have come to observe that in a language arts class, when a student is deeply immersed in reading, writing, and role-playing, that student is actually practicing the next four limbs of Yoga and can come close to equanimity and to "complete harmony." This state of mind is one that students can enter when they are curious and allow themselves to be moved (with an open heart) and "open-minded."

Notice that while the first four limbs of Yoga have to do with the outer world, the next four limbs are aspects of the inner world. The first, *pratyahara*, "turning inward," is a way that students begin this process. There is a blurring of the distinction between the physical and the mental self, and one's consciousness and bodily awareness together focus on the task at hand. This is the essential kind of consciousness required of a reader who has begun to master the disciplines of reading or writing that Sheridan Blau has described as "performative" or "disciplined literacy" (19). Blau describes "performative literacy in action" in ways that mirror the limbs of Yoga. For example, he notes that while this may seem obvious, competent readers need a "capacity for sustained focused attention" (19). When a student is open to such focus, there is then a merging of consciousness that occurs between the reader and the text. This is the "focus and attention" that is the basis for the next limb, *dharana*. "The mind has reached the ability to be directed [*dharana*] when direction toward a chosen object is possible in spite of many other potential objects within the reach of the individual" (Desikachar, *Heart* 109). B. K. S. Iyengar warns that "[a]t school we learn to pay attention. This is useful, but it is not in yogic terms concentration. We do not say of a deer in the forest, 'Look he's concentrating.' The deer is in total vibrant awareness in every cell in his body. . . .

True concentration is an unbroken thread of awareness" (13). I have seen students go to that place when reading or writing or playing a role; they release their defenses, their selves, and allow their minds to be carried. They are attuned to their subject; they have let go and moved into *dhyana*, described as "dropping all efforts." There is a sense of lightness, in a way, because the reader, the writer, the yoga student is not *trying* so hard anymore. There is relaxation. Everything else falls away and there is a sense of egolessness. In the life of an adolescent, this can be a welcome place, free from the worries that distract their minds. Students must be shown how to have these experiences through reading, writing, and role-playing.

"In a state of Yoga, comprehension is different from comprehension at other times. It is closer to the true nature of the object" (Desikachar, *Heart* 151). The difference is removed from the observed and the observer, and they become one. This merging is what Moffett identified as the "total fulfillment of communication's goal," which is "to remove a differential" so that "the inner and outer worlds equalize" (*Detecting Growth* 69). This fulfillment leads to *samadhi*, that blissful state, where it is impossible to separate "the dancer from the dance," as Yeats wrote in "Among School Children." In other terms, Patanjali, author of *The Yoga Sutra*, a set of yogic aphorisms, explains, "Soon the individual is so much involved in the object that nothing except its comprehension is evident. It is as if the individual has lost his own identity" (qtd. in Desikachar, *Heart* 186). In a language arts class, is it possible for students to become so absorbed in their work that they are completely integrated with the subject at hand? In my experience, these are habits that we want to encourage in our students.

Learning as Attunement

I am interested in exploring the habits of mind one must hold when learning. The eight limbs of Yoga seek to reach the highest levels of consciousness, often spiritual and ascribed to God, and the discipline it takes to achieve that is not to be minimized. However, these are lifelong skills that students can practice: looking inward, focusing attention, equalizing inner and outer worlds, and, of course, emotional equanimity. In *Harmonic Learning*, Moffett described "learning as attunement" and wrote that

> [a]ttention and concentration play paramount roles in learning of all sorts. . . . [T]here's no question about it, sustaining focus makes things happen that don't otherwise. . . . When we dwell on or dwell in something exclusively for some time, we lose ourselves and take on some nature of that object, activity, or setting. . . . [W]e start to resonate with what we are engaged with. That is attunement. (127–28)

As a yogi, Moffett would have been familiar with the Yoga Sutras and the concept of *chitta vritti nirodha. Chitta* refers to the mind, *nirodha* refers to restraint, and *vritta* is literally "waves or fluctuations"; thus, Yoga seeks to restrain the fluctuations of the mind. "That is attunement."

In "Writing, Inner Speech, and Meditation," Moffett lays the groundwork for this thinking. He explains that these three practices are naturally allied activities and that educators must draw students' attention to them so that students learn ways to communicate that help them both make sense *in* the world and make sense *of* the world. He also notes that most thought is a matter of enculturation, "hearing out the world," and that we are thereby conditioned to think of our worlds through the lens of that which is already written by society. However, through the practice of meditation, he writes, students (and their teachers) can learn to watch their thoughts (their inner speech), quiet the mind, and come to silence the mind's desire to "run to and fro" (170). Moffett says, "My own practical definition of meditation states it as some control of inner speech ranging from merely *watching* it to *focusing* it to *suspending* it all together" (151). Once one has come to this point, perhaps, "in *making sense*" one is "*making knowledge*" (148). Most important, there is a convergence of the thought, the thing studied, and the thinker himself: "Passion, memory, imagination converge with intellect and intuition like rays of different colors coming together to create white light" (153).

Moffett draws from many spiritual traditions in this essay and explicitly shows how these habits of mind can influence the way we teach and the way students can learn. Meditation, of course, is not limited to yoga and Eastern philosophies like Buddhism. Repetition of prayer, for example, is itself a meditation and a suspension of inner speech toward a focused point. While public schools must honor the separation of church and state, the lack of spirituality in many students' lives has left them with empty idols. Moffett wrote about the mindless viewing of television, but what would he make of today's endless scrolling on social media, which itself feels like a mind-emptying experience but is in fact mind-numbing? Adolescents watch so-called influencers on YouTube and TikTok for entertainment, advice, and ways to be in the world. Their viewing hours have been monetized, their minds co-opted by influencers. It is often up to the schools to give students a break from this—without their electronic devices—to spend time in quiet concentration on a task, to suspend inner speech and slip into silence momentarily so that they can "attune directly to nature instead of just human frequencies" ("Writing" 163).

Role-Playing to Release One's Ego

In Moffett's explanation of teaching discourse, he begins with drama, "the matrix of all language activities, subsuming speech and engendering the varieties of writing and reading" (*Teaching the Universe* 61). The dramatic experience is one of the first ways that students can step outside of themselves and into a role that brings them closer to the subject they're exploring. There is a shedding of one's ego during role-play. Moffett writes, "Begun at an early uninhibited age, extemporizing of this sort can head off later self-consciousness, make verbalization easy and natural, increase presence of mind, and develop inventiveness, . . . and act out and express real feelings in a situation made safe by the pretense that 'I am being someone else'" (91).

Throughout each school year, I encourage my students to try on different role-playing activities (see, for example, Wilhem's *"You Gotta"* and *Action Strategies*). One role involved a research project that asked students to pick a service organization they wanted to learn more about. After reading and researching, students designed a multigenre presentation that was displayed at a service fair to which parents, faculty, and community members were invited. Students played the role of a representative of their chosen organization, ranging from groups such as the ALS Association (chosen by a boy whose uncle was diagnosed with ALS) to the ASPCA, from The Trevor Project to March for Our Lives. The fair came at the end of "writing from plenty" (Moffett, *Active Voice* 183), when students had learned significant amounts of information about something they already cared about, like the prevention of gun violence. When students were given a real audience to which to present their knowledge, they embodied the role. This epitomizes "what is happening" (*Teaching the Universe* 60); when the student was one with the subject, the student *was* the representative for the service organization, and this is how students learn about becoming what they want to be. During this role-play, students' identities shifted as they temporarily embodied a new persona. The shift in consciousness that came from learning about service was significant, and students reported that they understood ways to make a difference in the world.

Samadhi occurs when a person is one with the subject; there is no distinguishing between the two—an actor is a role while the play is played. Role-playing opportunities give students the sense of being outside of their usual selves, their egos, and their limitations, on the yogic path toward liberation. Desikachar has said that when the mind and the object are joined in one unified space,

> *Yoga* also means acting in such a way that all of our attention is directed toward the activity in which we are currently engaged. Suppose for example that while I am writing, one part of my mind is thinking about what I want to say while another part is thinking about something entirely different. The more I am focused on my writing, the greater my attentiveness to my action in this moment. (114)

According to Desikichar, when one is in the state of *samadhi*, "the gap between the mind and the object we are focusing on is much smaller, and the understanding so immediate, that we no longer have to think" (114). When we allow students to step out of themselves and into roles they care about, they are closer to *samadhi*. Body, mind, and spirit are one, and thinking ceases to be a separate act of a mind that is distinct from the whole self of the thinker. This is the meaning of *yoga*, "to yoke," to become joined or linked, to become one as an integral human organism and one with the infinite possibilities that the universe can bring.

Another way I've had students engage in role-playing is through writing in which they take on a particular stance or voice. Recently, my students read the novel *Harbor Me* by Jacqueline Woodson. The book follows six special education students in modern-day Brooklyn who each tell stories about the challenges they face. During reading, my students wrote discussion questions and ran book clubs with the faculty and staff, who also read the book. To conclude the book study, students selected one character to whom to write a letter of advice. The resulting writing was authentic and kind, considering that students were writing to fictional characters. This type of role-play, in which a student takes on the voice of an advisor, helped students move from the self to the community and allowed them to develop empathy, which can be heard in the following letter:

> Dear Tiago,
> You and I have something very important in common. We're both bilingual! Isn't it the best feeling? Knowing that you can start a conversation with your mom in Spanish leaving others dumbfounded just adds some fun in life. It sure makes mine more interesting. Speaking two languages is like having a secret weapon or a superpower. Like in one of Amari's comics. And we can use that superpower everyday to help others who might be struggling with coming to a new country where most people don't speak their language. Unfortunately some people aren't all that fond and welcoming of our eloquence. Maybe they're jealous or maybe they're just rude, but still the side glances you get from strangers in the streets are anything but comforting. Even if they don't call out "Go back to your own country!" you can feel their eyes burning into the back of your head, judging. Perrito seemed like he was a great companion though, barking at those haters and scaring the xenophobia right out of them. He would have been your perfect superhero sidekick.
>
> I read an article the other day that was written by a bilingual woman, Natalia Sylvester, who talked about how being bilingual has affected her life and the people she has helped using that skill. She encounters people everyday who

are ignorant and dismissive of people who don't speak English. She said that she witnessed a woman trying to communicate with a cashier but the cashier, even after the hand gestures and seeing her clear need of assistance, chose not to understand. It's up to us isn't it? To help them out. It could just as easily be us. But we have the education and the opportunity to go about our day without struggling to communicate. Natalia also talked about how growing up, her parents made her speak Spanish even though she and her sister were so excited to jump right into speaking English all the time. But now she's grateful that her mother insisted on a strictly Spanish speaking household because that's a part of herself she never wants to lose. Natalia was eager to start their life in America but everyone is different and having a hard time transitioning is totally okay too. I know that sometimes when you're writing, the words don't come out in English as easily as you want them to. Though it comes with its struggles, being bilingual is really a gift. Sometimes it makes us self conscious and insecure but why should we be? Every language is beautiful and should be spoken proudly!

I really hope you learn to be comfortable speaking both English and Spanish. I definitely struggle with my Japanese but like anything with enough practice you'll be a walking talking English dictionary in no time! I know that reading books, watching movies and TV shows in the language you're trying to improve really helps, it's fun and educational. There's nothing holding you back and Amari, Ashton, Esteban, Holly, Haley, your mom, Ms. Laverne and everyone supports you all the way! Practice your English and embrace the Latino side of you while doing what you love!

Love,
Coco

Coco begins her letter by establishing the connection between herself and Tiago—"We're both bilingual!"—and then explains the challenges they both face, which were described in the book but also experienced by Coco herself. When she writes about Natalia Sylvester's article, she says, "It's up to us isn't it? To help them out. It could just as easily be us." This is where the writing blurs between lived and fictional experience, and it's powerful and transformative. She switches linguistically from "you and I" in the first paragraph to "us" in the second. This shift shows a deep identification with the character and a shift in consciousness. Coco inhabits the voice of the older sister, cousin, friend. And what is it to inhabit? To dwell in. Empathy. Attunement.

The Value of Literature

In *The Reader, the Text, and the Poem,* Louise Rosenblatt described this "live circuit set up between the reader and the text. . . . For the reader, the poem is lived-through during his intercourse with the text" (14). If yoga's end goal is to join mind, matter, and subject, then Rosenblatt's work complements that goal with its claim that the reader and the subject are both integral parts of the process of reading—again, inseparable. In the same way, Moffett wrote that "the more people at the same time make unconsciousness conscious, the more they identify with the world they are incorporating" (*Detecting Growth* 69). Coco's letter to Tiago demonstrates this identification with the world she incorporated. She wrote this letter in the spring, and it was the first time she wrote about being bilingual. Perhaps, before reading *Harbor Me*, there hadn't been space in the classroom consciousness for that information, even though it is part of Coco's identity. Once the subject was made approachable through reading the novel, her dual languaging became an important way for her to connect to the story. In this writing experience, there is no separation between fictional and lived reality; there is "us," and Coco is one with the universe of the story.

I believe, like others I've cited here, that reading literature helps students learn to attune their senses, to practice their concentration, and to let go of their attachment to their egos as they fall into the story. A former student of mine, Milo, wrote to the author about the impact that reading her book had on him. The way he describes what happened to his mind in a letter to the author aligns with both Rosenblatt and Yoga philosophy.

> Dear Joelle Charbonneau:
> I'm going to be honest when I say I absolutely hate reading. As a thirteen-year-old student I would much rather play video games or hang out with my friends. If I was that desparate I probably wouldn't eat for a day, or if it comes down to it, run 5 miles, only to not read a book. So, when I heard that we would have to choose a book to read over the course of three weeks, I bet you could tell that I wasn't thrilled. To tell you the truth, I probably haven't read a full book since maybe the 6th grade (I'm in 8th now) just because I dislike reading with

> a strong passion. So when I told my dad about the assignment I was given, he knows how much I don't like reading, and he knows I like binge watching shows, so he asked me what I liked about the shows I watch, and came to the conclusion to give me "The Testing¨ which of course when I first saw it it looked big and long and dreadful, but after reading it I think he hit the nail right on the head.
>
> I don't actually know why I like your book so much, but I've been thinking about it and might have found out why I do. I love shows that have to do with suspense and spooky bits and as though this book did not offer much of that straight out, I felt like it was there, but in a different way than what I´ve seen before. When Malencia's dad told her about the nightmares that he has had from the testing, and how now she was more scared than excited to go, it really made me nervous about what was going to happen when they got to the facility. There were also a lot of unexpected "BOOM" parts that caught my attention. For example when Malencia was walking back to her room to look for her roommate, then saw her just hanging there, it caught me by surprise. I was reading that page in class and I showed one of my best friends sitting next to me and he was pretty shocked too. Another time I jumped a bit was when Malencia and Tomas were going to get water from the spring place, then she said to wait but Tomas went anyway and it blew up. I almost jumped out of my bed cause I was spooked, and then after when she had to like patch it up after, ugh, very disgusting. Because of that scene there I don't think I would be able to watch a movie if there ever was one. . . .
>
> This has probably been one of my favorite books I have ever read, and you might be my favorite author as well, but I'm not sure, I gotta read your other books first and then decide if you are my favorite author or not. I think that sounds pretty fair. I'm not gonna lie. I think this is one of my favorite books because there are so many different aspects and genres just in that one book. It has the romance between Malencia and Tomas, has the happiness when she gets accepted into The Testing, it has the sadness of when her friend gets shot with a pencil because they messed up a challenge. And of course all the suspense.

With his father's help, Milo finally found a book that engaged him. During our reading conference and while observing Milo in class, I could tell that he was becoming deeply immersed in the story; this practice of concentration, *dharana*, and then letting go into the text, *dhyana*, and finally the blissful spot that he entered temporarily, *samadhi*, all integrated into his being. Milo described his reading process: "I love shows that have to do with suspense and spooky bits and as though this book did not offer much of that straight out, I felt like it was there, but in a different way than what I've seen before." Since the book engaged him in a "different way," it was able to hold his attention and therefore made space for the necessary concentration that *dharana* brings. Milo described a physical response to the reading in several parts, for example, "I almost jumped out of my bed." He is so moved because there is no separation of mind and text; it is one unit and therefore moves his body. He is experiencing a form of *samadhi* because he has become one with his reading experience, there with the characters that Charbonneau created, his senses completely attuned to the book, the way Iyengar described the deer in the forest. Milo is out of himself, egoless, and into the book. These activities are mechanical in that the reader must make sense of the letters on the page, but they also create changes in an individual's consciousness. As Moffett explains, "There's a correlation, for example, between absorption in reading and hypnotic sensibility; . . . people who love to read, avid readers, go into an altered state of consciousness" ("Going with Growth" 36).

Cristina Bruns describes this phenomenon in "Immersion, Transformation, and the Literature Class," asserting that "many readers have had the experience of finishing a novel or short story and feeling that they would never quite be the same after having read it" (1). Bruns draws on the work of psychiatrist D. W. Winnicott to explain the transitional space that is inhabited when one is moved by a literary work. The "inner and outer worlds" are blurred and "the reader becomes part of the text as the distinction between self and text blurs" (Bruns 2). This happened to Milo and created a physical response, "jumping," that was unexpected as he allowed himself to be moved by the book. At the conclusion of *Detecting Growth in Language*, Moffett explores this concept: "In total fulfillment of communication's goal—to remove a differential—the inner and outer worlds equalize" (69).

These two examples of student writing, along with my description of the role-playing students took on during the service fair, illustrate how the limbs of Yoga can look in education, but there are countless ways that the immersive experience can play itself out. The important thing is that we give students opportunities to make this happen. Others have theorized in the same vein. Mihaly Csikszentmihalyi, with his theory of flow, wrote that "[t]he best moments in our lives are not the passive, receptive, relaxing times. . . . The best moments usually occur if a person's body or mind is stretched to its limits in a voluntary effort to accomplish something difficult and worthwhile" (3). Sir Kenneth Robinson and Lou Aronica talk of the Element as "the meeting point between natural aptitude and personal passion" (21). Those who find themselves in the Element, Robinson and Aronica claim, "find that time passes differently and that they are more alive, more centered, more vibrant than at any other time" (21). These experiences are those that Yoga aims toward, the attunement that Moffett sought for students when learning:

> Yoga lays a base for all learning because it teaches control of mind and body. Without relaxing and concentrating, for example, no one can learn well either academic subjects or sports and artistic skills. The learner has to relax and let go of useless motion so he can conserve and channel energy. He must concentrate his attention so he can focus selectively on some activity or subject. He must center himself so he can line his will up behind the activity (be "motivated"). He must balance and integrate himself so he can summon all his resources and can experience the learning activity throughout his whole organism. So learning requires a holistic state of full access to memory and feeling, to all sensory modalities, to both halves of the brain (intellectual and intuitive) to head and heart, mind and body. (Moffett, "Yoga" 121)

Sondra Perl too in writing about the writing process, has shown how intellect and intuition, or mind and body, are indistinguishable and how we must discover the language for our ideas in our bodies through what she refers to as "felt sense."

> This process of creating new sense, of saying something fresh from all that came before and from all that lives within us, is a bodily one. In other words, knowing is embodied. But bodies—or human beings—do not exist in isolation. We are enmeshed in situations, and both situations and human beings are shot through with language. It is from within this interconnectedness

of bodies, language, and situations that a theory of embodied knowing is derived (Perl).

I don't think it is too esoteric to speak of writing this way. Recent studies of the brain have shown that impressions, impact, and trauma can create physical changes in the body. For example, a study of American soldiers' brains reported in the *New York Times* in 2016 asked, "What if PTSD is more physical than psychological?" The physical changes seen in the soldiers' brains was correlated with exposure to blasts, sometimes resulting in visible physical scarring on the body, but also visible as scarring on the brain (Worth). *Samskaras* left from battle are painful, and the "shell shock" that was written about in the past metaphorically acknowledges this. Similarly, psychiatrist, Bessel van der Kolk writes about various therapies that impact both mind and body, including yoga, to rewire the brain after trauma. But what of positive experiences that lead to growth and learning? Are those impressions the type that will move us toward a fulfilled and fulfilling life? Is it our job as educators to provide students with those opportunities? At the conclusion to Bill Moyers's *Creativity* series with Maya Angelou, she tells a group of schoolchildren, "You're at a curious time now in your age. You'll remember certain things and some things you'll forget forever, but I hope you'll remember me." Don't we want our classes to be memorable, even if the imprints, *samskaras*, are left there with a light touch?

At the least, teachers must concern themselves with growth. As Moffett says, "The primary dimension of growth seems to be a movement from the center of the self, outward. . . . In moving outward from himself, the child becomes more himself" (*Teaching the Universe* 59). At this time in my teaching, I am certain that the way to teach language arts is by transforming consciousness. Yet such an aim is entirely lost in schools and classrooms where teachers are pressured to teach skills and particular bits of subject matter content that can be learned and tested on standardized tests or large-scale assessments of the kind that Moffett identified with what he contemptuously called the "educational industrial complex" (*Active Voice* 70). Literature has the power to transform consciousness and, as Rosenblatt and others have insisted, where reading is deeply immersive and produces an aesthetic experience, it leaves impressions on the mind, *samskaras,* that change the reader's consciousness. Observing students who are immersed in reading, writing, and role-playing confirms that these impressions are integral to their growth.

> Growth means change, and educators have to concern themselves with the changeable aspects of people. . . . Even to know if or how he wants to change, the individual has to be at least partly awakened from the hypnosis of acculturation. And, education, finally, should foster human evolution. I am not interested in helping to teach young people to read well enough to follow directions or write just well enough to take dictation. (Moffett, "Writing" 139)

For years I struggled to make sense of the final sentence of Moffett's short but seminal book *Detecting Growth in Language*, my own confusion stemming from maybe a missing piece, the study of Yoga and its influence on Moffett's work. The book concludes: "Consciousness makes the difference between confusion of mind with world, and fusion of mind with world, and that difference is the most important thing a teacher needs to know about growth in language" (70). *Samadhi*—the blissful place that goes beyond time and space and where communication does not occasion misunderstanding, where one's memories and feelings are integrated into one's body, mind and spirit, where one is beyond mere language and into the intuitive realm—is a space that English language arts teachers can create for their students through everything that reading, writing, and role-playing can bring. "The final stage of growth, though, is having the best of the mystical world of unity and the practical world of plurality. . . . Pursuing differentiation and integration far enough leads out the other side, back into the nonverbal world" (*Detecting Growth* 69), the world of *samskaras* that transcends time and space, but that in fact leads us to be evolved humans and the best versions of ourselves that we can be.

Works Cited

Blau, Sheridan. "Performative Literacy: The Habits of Mind of Highly Literate Readers." *Voices from the Middle,* vol. 10, no.3, 2003, pp. 18–22.

Bruns, Cristina Vischer. "Immersion, Transformation, and the Literature Class." *Journal of the Assembly for Expanded Perspectives on Learning*, vol. 17, 2011–2012, pp. 1–6.

Charbonneau, Joelle. *The Testing*. HarperCollins, 2013.

Csikszentmihalyi, Mihaly. *Flow: The Psychology of Optimal Experience.* Harper & Row, 2009.

Desikachar, T. K. V. *The Heart of Yoga: Developing a Personal Practice.* Inner Traditions International, 1995.

Iyengar, B. K. S., with John J. Evans and Douglas Abrams. *Light on Life: The Journey to Wholeness, Inner Peace and Ultimate Freedom.* Rodale, 2005.

Maltese, Denise "Out of the Narrow Tunnel and into the Universe of Discourse." *Voices from the Middle,* vol. 14, no. 2, 2006, pp. 47–56.

Moffett, James. *Active Voice: A Writing Program Across the Curriculum.* Boynton/Cook, 1981.

———. *Detecting Growth in Language*. Boynton/Cook, 1992.

———. "Going with Growth: Fitting Schools to the Facts of Language Life" *Coming on Center: English Education in Evolution.* Boynton/Cook, 1981, pp. 61–75.

———. *Harmonic Learning: Keynoting School Reform.* Boynton/Cook, 1992.

———. *Teaching the Universe of Discourse.* 1968. Boynton/Cook, 1983.

———. "Writing, Inner Speech, and Meditation." *Coming on Center: English Education in Evolution.* Boynton/Cook, 1981, pp. 133–81.

———. "Yoga for Public School Teachers." *Coming on Center: English Education in Evolution.* Boynton/Cook, 1981, pp. 119–24.

Moyers, Bill. "A Portrait of Maya Angelou." *Creativity with Bill Moyers,* 8 Jan. 1982, https://billmoyers.com/content/maya-angelou/.

New York State Education Department (NYSED). *Social Emotional*

Learning: Essential for Learning, Essential for Life. Aug. 2018, http://www.p12.nysed.gov/sss/documents/SELEssentialforLearningandLife.pdf.

Perl, Sondra. "Part Two: Embodied Knowing." *CUNY Academic Commons: Composition & Rhetoric Community*. https://compcomm.commons.gc.cuny.edu/feltsense/part-two-embodied-knowing/.

Potts, Shannon. "Centering Moffett: A Bio-Professional Study of James Moffett's Contributions to the Teaching of English." Teachers College, Columbia University, PhD dissertation proposal, 2023.

Robinson, Ken, and Lou Aronica. *The Element: How Finding Your Passion Changes Everything*. Penguin, 2010.

Rosenblatt, Louise M. *The Reader, the Text and the Poem: The Transactional Theory of the Literary Work*. Southern Illinois UP, 1979.

van der Kolk, Bessel. *The Body Keeps the Score: Brain, Mind, and Body in the Healing of Trauma*. Viking, 2014.

Wilhelm, Jeffrey D. *Action Strategies for Deepening Comprehension*. Scholastic, 2002.

———. "*You Gotta Be the Book*": *Teaching Engaged and Reflective Reading with Adolescents*. Teachers College P, 1997.

Woodson, Jacqueline. *Harbor Me*. Nancy Paulsen Books, 2018.

Worth, Robert F. "What If PTSD Is More Physical Than Psychological?" *New York Times Magazine*, 10 June 2016.

Yeats, William Butler. *The Tower: A Facsimile Edition*. Scribner, 2004.

"Yoga's Ethical Guide to Living: The Yamas and Niyamas." *Kripalu*, https://kripalu.org/resources/yoga-s-ethical-guide-living-yamas-and-niyamas.

CHAPTER TWENTY

A Tribute to James Moffett

MILES MYERS, DONALD R. GALLEHR, RICHARD L. GRAVES, REGINA FOEHR, SHERIDAN BLAU, AND BETTY JANE WAGNER

In this memorial tribute published shortly after Moffett's passing, Miles Myers, Don Gallehr, Richard Graves, Regina Foehr, Sheridan Blau, and Betty J. Wagner all reflect on their own sense of Moffett's unique personality and character, as well as on his distinctive contributions to the teaching of the English language arts.

Introduction

A visionary and trailblazer, James Moffett recognized and wrote about trends in education long before others even considered their possibilities. With sterling scholarship he bridged learning theory and commonsense practice. He helped us to see how ancient wisdom and modern philosophy can inform each other and teaching and learning, and he articulated concepts that we knew to be true even though we were unable to articulate them. A master at seeing connections and helping others to see them, he changed our thinking about education and our professional and personal selves.

In his typical trailblazing fashion, James Moffett was AEPL's very first member. A member of the AEPL Advisory Board, he also served as featured speaker at the first AEPL conference and at other AEPL events. It is, therefore, a special honor and privilege to devote this opening section of *JAEPL* to pay tribute to James Moffett, our *original* member, colleague, and friend.

Originally published in *The Journal of the Assembly for Expanded Perspectives on Learning*, vol. 3, 1997, pp. 3–12. Reprinted with permission.

Each of the writers in this tribute to James Moffett knew Jim personally and professionally. Each was invited to contribute an informal article or personal narrative about him.

Remembering James Moffett—Miles Myers, Past NCTE Executive Director

The news was a shock. I had talked to Jim about two weeks before, and he seemed much better. Then about a week before he died, he left a phone message asking me to call. He had missed the NCTE convention again. I had heard his name for the first time many years ago when Tom Gage suggested, "You should read Jim Moffett's monograph, *Drama Is What Is Happening.*" This monograph, which later evolved into *Teaching the Universe of Discourse* and which changed my teaching of composition, was my introduction to James Moffett. I met him sometime in the 1960s after he left Phillips Exeter, when he came to Oakland High School to watch me teach. He was working on his *Interaction: A Student-Centered Language Arts and Reading Program* series, later putting one of my classrooms in a movie describing this series. The series, which was published as a collection of large activity cards, irregular sized books, games, tapes, all sorts of classroom materials organized around the principles of his Student-Centered Language Curriculum, K–13, was disliked by textbook salesmen because it was too heavy to carry around. I still remember an *Interaction* salesman huffing and puffing up and down the steps of Oakland High to deliver two sets of the Interaction series. (My principal looked at the pile of stuff and asked, "I thought you were getting an English series, Miles." "Well," I said, "Let me get back to you after we figure it out.").

When Jim and Jan moved to Berkeley, Jim was a regular at writing project institutes (we taught together one summer), a participant in our battles over behavioral objectives in PBS (Program Budget Systems, not Public Broadcasting Systems), a contributor to numerous CATE and NCTE workshops, and an off-and-on member of Berkeley groups of school reformers. In the 1970s, Jim got interested in silencing the mind as a way to enrich what one knows. It's as if he got all that talking going in schools, both internally and externally, and then decided enough is enough. He and Jan started a sort of ashram at his house on Spruce Street in Berkeley, and Celeste and I would go there every Saturday morning to do our Prana Yoga exercises, led by Jim and his co-teacher, Pingula. We were meditating, turning, breathing, stretching, sitting yoga style, standing on our heads. Jim could stand on his head for thirty minutes, I swear. (Celeste asked me, "Why can't you do that?") I was always behind in my breathing homework ("Miles, did you finish 2 repetitions of 20 breaths?" "No!" I answered.), and Jim kept pushing books in my direction ("Jim," I stated, "those yogis in those books do not seem to have to work.").

His last NCTE convention was in 1994, the last of our three public conversations at the NCTE convention, sponsored by NCTE's Commission on Composition. For my generation, Jim Moffett was our most important thinker about the teaching of writing in K–12 schools. Today, he is a very important thinker about new directions in K–12 school rethinking—harmonic learning and the relationships of body and mind, an emphasis on the individual, the internal, the space away from work and politics. He is, finally, a deeply missed friend.

Reading Jim Moffett—Donald R. Gallehr, Director, Northern Virginia Writing Project

When I first read "Writing, Inner Speech, and Meditation," I knew I needed to reread it to understand it. It is a rich essay, with one embedded sentence after another and numerous connections to composition theory and literature. The 52 footnotes alone constitute a course of studies in writing and meditation.

I was intrigued by the first sentence of the essay: "Writing and meditation are naturally allied activities." I, and a number of others, used this essay as a map to explore this alliance further. Particularly helpful to us was Jim's description of how we watch, direct, and suspend inner speech:

> Both writing and meditating watch inner speech. We see this in the gazing of children, and later in their journal writing, mapping, and free writing. In meditation, this is called witnessing.
>
> Both writing and meditating *direct* inner speech. We see this when we narrow and develop a subject. In meditation, this is bringing the mind back to a point of concentration.
>
> Both writing and meditating *suspend* inner speech. After focusing on one point, we suspend inner speech to relax the mind—to give it a rest. In meditation, this is silence.

We all know that education fiercely separates "church and state," and Jim could easily have written about meditation from a secular point of view, the way many do in such fields as sports, drama, music, business, and medicine. Instead, he acknowledged his own training in an Ashram and described the mystic traditions, both ancient and modern, that gave birth to meditation. This essay is a rock-solid theoretical foundation, and Jim helped us to build on it through his work with AEPL—through his work on the Advisory Board, as main speaker at the first AEPL Colorado Conference, and through the publications of AEPL members, including *JAEPL* and *Presence of Mind.*

I, like many others in AEPL and NCTE, came to know Jim also as a friend. In 1985 he ran a Writing and Meditation Institute at George Mason, and in 1991 an Institute on School Reform. Both times he stayed with my wife and me at my home in Warrenton, Virginia. All who met him know that, in addition to being a courageous scholar, he was a wonderful human being—just as straightforward and compassionate in person as he was in his writings.

In "Writing, Inner Speech, and Meditation" Jim wrote: "Teachers can give no greater gift to their students than to help them expand and master inner speech." He inspired many of us as individuals, and our profession as a whole, to develop our own inner speech and to make the connection between writing and meditation. We are indeed fortunate to have known him.

Jim, We Hardly Knew You—Richard L. Graves, Professor Emeritus, Auburn University

Jim, we hardly knew you.

You were taken from us before we were ready. So much more we could have learned from you. So much more you could have taught us. We listen for the sound of your voice, but all is still. Now we ask ourselves: What are those unspoken truths that remain with you? We listen and wonder.

Morning: A thin yellow finger moves across the horizon. Darkness is everywhere, but now it recedes before the coming light. Here in this sandy land, among these trees, in this silence, which is broken only by the sound of birds, the light awakens all. Light defines the landscape and warms the earth. This is a sacred moment.

When we get together it should always be like it is in Colorado. Everything is informal. Our words are honest. We listen with open hearts and open minds. You were there, Jim, and we listened to you. We heard your words, but more, we sensed a presence beyond the words. One morning you taught us how to go beyond words, how to enter another world, in the purity of sound. We remember. We remember.

The healing. The laying on of hands. The sacred oil, from a holiness church. The words. The prayers. The spirit that moves in this place, invisible, like unseen fingers. . . . Who is the healer? And who is being healed?

Did you know, Jim, that you were the first member of our assembly? When the announcement was made, you were the first to send a check, the first to enroll. Sometimes I think we ought to call ourselves the Jim Moffett Society, for you embody all that we stand for, all we believe in. You really are our Number One member. Always will be.

What is the spirit that creates a man like Jim Moffett? When he was a child, could anyone have predicted the pattern and direction of this life? Were the seeds of his spiritual depth present even then? What is this spirit that moves among us, moves within us, connecting, guiding, bringing energy and light into our lives?

Jim Moffett spoke the truth of his heart, even though in speaking he risked misunderstanding. He was a giant among us, an explorer who blazed new trails into uncharted worlds. We knew Jim Moffett as friend, teacher, and spiritual guide. We honor a man whose influence will live on long past his lifetime. We honor a wise and gentle man who willingly shared his gifts with us.

We grieve his passing, but the celebration of his life is so much larger than our grief. He would want it this way.

Thanks, Jim. You have blessed our lives. Your words and your spirit live in ours still. You will always be a part of us.

Memories of James Moffett—Regina Foehr, AEPL Chair

The week Jim Moffett died I received in the mail a manuscript he had sent of his latest book, one he had spent most of a lifetime writing. In telephone and electronic mail conversations Jim had asked me to read his manuscript and serve as agent for its publication. This book, he explained, was his metacognitive analysis in recent years from his writings of a lifetime. And, although as I write this article, I have only just begun to read the 425-page manuscript, I can see its initial title, *Writing to Heal*, he has changed to *Growing Up Sober*.

Though Jim and I had talked by telephone several times earlier in the year, our friendship began at the 1994 NCTE Convention in Orlando. Our previous telephone conversations had been initiated by an article he had submitted to *The Spiritual Side of Writing: Releasing the Learner's Whole Potential*, a collection that I coedited with Susan Schiller (1997). These conversations quite naturally always turned to other topics—to our shared Mississippi heritage where I had grown up and Jim had spent several formative childhood years, to views on spirituality, to his deep concern about the universal neglect of children in our world. But at this convention, our paths crossed rather frequently because of Jim's leadership and high visibility. And visible he was. Tall, California suntanned, and wearing a rust Indian suede leather vest over simple blue, cotton shirts, he cast a rare and curious mystique, which became more present to AEPL as the week progressed, allowing us a glimpse into the mystery and paradox of Jim.

Jim exemplified paradox; he was simultaneously simple but complex, innocent yet wise, playful and serious, shy but courageous, and reticent though bold. In one of his presentations his amusing stories of his friend and mentor, an East Indian yogi, made us laugh out loud. Then, midsentence, he'd turn our laughter and our consciousness upside down, spinning us into sudden insights with their poignant truths. He tricked us, at one level made his friend seem foolish, then showcased his genius in brilliant simplicity, raising our consciousness in the process. His friend was the classic "wise fool." So was Jim.

When I say Jim Moffett was an archetypal fool, I'm not being irreverent. I mean it as the highest compliment. I am, however, aided in this insight about Jim by Carol Pearson's discussion of archetypes in *Awakening the Heroes Within* (1991). Pearson discusses archetypes as the ego states from which we operate at different times in our lives: "warrior," "caretaker," "orphan," "fool" and so forth. Although we move in and out of these various states as circumstances and our moods call us to do, we tend to function primarily from some dominant states. When Jim attended a convention workshop I gave on archetypes, took Carol Pearson's archetypes test, and scored high in the archetypal "fool," I suspected then the potentiality for a friendship with Jim—after all, who doesn't like someone who's willing to risk looking foolish. Not surprisingly, Jim also scored high in archetypal "sage." As all of us workshop participants shared our dominant archetypes, Jim openly shared his, too, and gave me permission to do so.

The archetypal fool within is the playful part of the self, the ego state that thrives on self-expression, whose desire for self-expression outweighs the fear of "looking like a fool." The internal risk-taker, it is also the part of us that likes to have some fun. It's the court jester in ancient kingdoms who gets away with what others would be hanged for. It's a shape-shifter, seeing and presenting the world through new eyes. Jim's internal fool, it seems to me, gave him originality and the courage to publish his ideas which leaped beyond canonical boundaries of their day. His *Universal Schoolhouse* (1994) offers a reconceptualization of education as both a catalyst and an oasis for spiritual awakening and transformation within the student and society. But this concept was no more outrageous when it was released in 1994 than was his groundbreaking integration of "Writing, Inner Speech, and Meditation" in 1981 (*Coming on Center*). Jim's example evokes the internal "fool" or "clown" or "natural child" in others, giving them the courage to express their original ideas and to explore the unconventional.

In academia, we too often take ourselves too seriously and don't look at the lighter side, sometimes even fear reprisal if we explore the unconventional or write what we really believe. We favor instead the safety of tradition. When Jim and I talked about his willingness to follow his intuition beyond the safety of established boundaries—to write, for example, on unconventional topics—he always modestly downplayed any particular courage. He seemed to think he simply enjoyed a freedom of expression as an independent writer that institutional affiliation would have denied him.

Sometimes I watched Jim appearing to suppress laughter when there was no obvious reason for laughter. (The archetypal fool within is irrepressible.) As Langston Hughes reminded us, though, sometimes we laugh to keep from crying, integrating the tragic and sublime. As any wise fool would do, Jim seemed to integrate it all.

Jim's humorous side made correspondence with him and his wife, Janet, fun—not that any of us pursued lengthy correspondence, just notes and letters here and there, and then email in the last year. Jim's handwritten notes on Jan's handmade stationery showed her whimsical side, too, and always included his appreciative commentary on her art. I've heard him tell with a smile of how they had met on the steps of the Harvard School of Education. Together the two of them reminded me of two kids—in bright-eyed exhilaration eager to experience life. At least, that's my image of them the last time I saw them together in seemingly boundless energy dashing out the cabin door after our first AEPL conference in 1995. They were on their way back down the mountains to catch their flight—their early morning freedom and lightness of heart, the prize for a rigorous but successful conference that had featured Jim.

Jim was able to laugh at himself too, for example, in his story about himself as a high school English student in Ohio where his family had moved from Mississippi after the war. He chuckled as he told it, still amused these many years later at the memory of it and his behavior at the time. He told of how he used to gaze deliberately out the window seeming indifferent during class. Then when called upon, he would spin sharply around to face the teacher, giving the right answer. We both laughed at his adolescent behavior, recalling our own students' transparent games in our classes in subsequent years. Then at my query regarding his journey from simple roots to an ivy league education, he told of how as a high school senior he had been awarded one of Ohio's two Harvard scholarships from a Harvard recruitment program extended to every state.

But it was after sharing a panel on Spiritually Open Pedagogy at this conference that I came to know another side of Jim, his prophetic side. After the panel, he made a simple prophetic statement to me in the most direct but natural way, followed by the words, "But you know that." Earlier in the week, he had done and said the same thing, spoken the same words, followed by "But you know that."

Though I had heard his words but forgotten them the first time he said them, the second time he had my attention. And though I had no intellectual reason to know the truth of his words, somehow, at some deep internal place, I knew the truth of his words. Seeing Jim's way of honoring his own intuition or inner knowing and expressing it personally and in his writing has given me the courage to honor intuitions, particularly in professional matters and choices.

Jim's example has opened doors for all of us within the academy. A revered scholar on mainstream educational issues, Jim also courageously opened and led the way for further exploration through his leading-edge writing and thinking on topics far from mainstream. Jim Moffett was truly a hero on a difficult journey into uncharted territory. And even though I have shared some memories of him primarily through the mono lens of only one archetype, Jim's complexity was obvious. Fortunately for us all he has left yet another legacy, his awaiting manuscript, promising to shed more light on his many dimensions—and vicariously our own—as he made his way through the journey of *Growing Up Sober* and *Writing to Heal.*

On Jim Moffett: A Reflection and Memoir—Sheridan Blau, NCTE President-Elect

One of the most embarrassing features of professional life as an educator is that of having to endure the great changes in fashion that sweep through the educational community and dictate teaching practices and curriculum content for a few years, until one fashion is replaced by another. The changes are embarrassing not because they represent change, but because the changes they embody so clearly represent mere changes in fashion or opinion or swings in a pendulum of sentiment rather than any real progress in professional knowledge or insight into the way learning takes place. In fact, the one constant in the educational fashions to which school policy makers regularly try to submit teachers and curricula is that no version of reform or return to basics (for that seems to define the swing of the school pendulum) ever calls for any teaching practice or curriculum content that would demand anything like authentically intensive and focused thinking about substantive matters.

Jim Moffett's theory and practice, on the other hand, never changed with the fashion of the times. He never swerved from a focus on thinking, and on a curriculum that demanded increasingly sophisticated thinking on the part of students within every program of study and from grade to grade. Not that he participated in any way in the recently fashionable critical thinking movement (though people interested in critical thinking could look to Moffett for a theory of thinking) nor made the mistake ridiculed so soundly in Hirsch's most recent book, calling for a curriculum that would teach ways of thinking in place of intellectual substance. No, Jim's articles and books advocated for thirty years or more an approach to teaching the English language arts that called upon students to engage in reading and writing and speaking tasks through which they would learn the *processes* of effective composing and for which they would conduct the investigations and research—acquire the substantive knowledge—that would allow them to read, write, and speak knowledgeably.

Jim's work constitutes the best refutation I know of to Hirsch's half-baked assertion that an interest in intellectual processes entails a de-emphasis on content knowledge in a discipline. Jim's first principle in teaching writing, for example, using workshops to help students produce satisfying and rhetorically effective pieces of writing, was the principle of plenitude. Students should never be asked to write for publication or for the submission of a complete paper, until they know more about their topic than they could cover in a single writing assignment. The problem for any real author, he often reminded us, is to select and order what he knows from a body of knowledge much more vast than can be communicated in any single piece of writing. Writers write from plenitude, from an abundance of experience and knowledge, not from scarcity. Only in schools are writers expected to produce written documents from scarcity. Jim's workshop approach to teaching writing therefore emphasized the role of investigation and research or "looking it up" as the key step to be taken before "writing it down."

I was about to say that we need Jim's wisdom now more than ever, when the best ideas of progressive educators are under attack, merely for their association with progressivism. But the truth is that the ideas that Jim spent his professional life adumbrating and illuminating for language arts educators have always been the ideas we have most needed as correctives to educational trends and fashions that pose simplistic answers, slogans, and teacher-proof techniques for problems that demand no less than the most thoughtful, creative, and intellectually well-informed responses on the part of classroom practitioners. No one was a stronger advocate than Jim for the principle that writing teachers must first be writers, just as literature teachers must first be powerful and experienced readers. His attention to method in teaching was always exploratory and the outgrowth of inquiries he urged all of us to conduct on how we might classify the actual kinds of writing that are read by readers in real communities, and what sorts of investigations had to be conducted in order to produce an instance of each type of writing that a reader would value reading.

Jim was, of course, himself, encyclopedic in the range of discourses he commanded. He was thoroughly conversant with the canonical texts of the British, American, continental, and classical literary traditions and read widely in science, philosophy, linguistics, and religion. I was always surprised by how much he kept up with current literary theory and how masterful he was in appropriating, explaining, and challenging contemporary theoretical formulations. He was also exceptionally ready to read new ideas and encounter new theories, about literature, about learning, about history, linguistics, science, the arts, and religion. His books reflect the breadth and depth of his learning and offer entirely original and generative perspectives on the English language arts curriculum, on teaching writing and literature, on the nature and goals of education and the aims and obstacles to learning, on cultural conflict in education, on educational policy and the education of the soul, and so on.

Whenever he visited our Writing Project in the summer (and he did so virtually every summer for 18 years), he would do a workshop in two parts. The first part addressed the perennially refractory problem of helping students move across the gap that divides personal or expressive writing from expository or transactional writing, while the second half of his presentation was focused on whatever new book he was writing or new topic he was exploring in his own research and thinking. Our teachers found both parts of his presentation equally valuable, and I personally found every one of his presentations over the 18 years of his annual visits to be a cherished moment in my own intellectual life and in my own development as an educator. For his part, he always found something new to learn while he was with us. In the early years of his annual visits he became an expert on Chumash Indian cave paintings (of which we have excellent examples in the mountains above Santa Barbara), and then on Chumash culture and religion and California mission history and so on. He loved to hike in our mountains, and even in the last visits—even after he was weakened by illness—he managed to take hikes with me down the canyon behind my house to see the rock formations and examine the varieties of plant life native to the hills and canyons of the particular micro-environment where

I live. No companions for a hike were ever more interested or more companionable on the trails I love to hike than were Jim and Jan Moffett.

Outliving Jim Moffett—Betty Jane Wagner, Director, Chicago Area Writing Project

I never thought about outliving Jim Moffett. My most salient impression of him was as a man of great strength. He gave up smoking and drinking long before most of us in my generation gave a second thought to health, and he and Jan were vegetarians and meditated and practiced yoga for decades before it became fashionable, at least here in the Midwest. He lived as he thought and taught—with stalwart integrity.

Jim was indeed a paragon of integrity, but, in my experience, he was full of contradictions: His mind was sinewy and rugged, but his manner unassuming and almost bumbling. Wise, but offhand in his dictums. His views iconoclastic, but his response to the clichés and conventional thinking of his students, warmhearted and generous. Unmoved in his convictions, but a good listener. Unbending, but willing to negotiate. Walking away from offers for professorships that most of us would have leapt at, yet forever committed to changing the climate of intellectual life in schools at all levels. Serious of purpose, but full of wit.

The summers he came to the Midwest to conduct Chicago Area Writing Project Summer Institutes, he arrived not with an academic's but rather with a rancher's hands and tan; and his laconic, unpretentious leader's stance quickly settled the more jittery of the teachers who were our summer fellows. Jim simply amazed them with his power. Typically, by the middle of the first morning, the teachers were awe-struck with the quality of the writing they had already produced, and several of them called me to exult over the miracle that had occurred. The second summer one of them begged me to let her come back and visit the first day of the institute to see what in the world it was that Jim did. She watched closely, but she still didn't know how he got such good writing to happen. She did know that in his quiet, almost clumsy, way he communicated without question his unswerving faith in the participants' ability to produce powerful writing. And produce they did.

I first knew I was in the company of an original and groundbreaking thinker when I got my hands on the 1968 edition of a *Student-Centered Language Arts Curriculum, K–13: A Handbook for Teachers*. At the time, I was pretentiously teaching a course called "Theory and Methods of Teaching Language Arts" at National College of Education, now National-Louis University. This required preservice course for elementary teachers paradoxically defined *language arts* as everything but reading. All of the texts of the era were prescriptive with obligatory chapters on handwriting, spelling, grammar, punctuation, book reports, and sometimes speech training.

In Jim's *Student-Centered Language Arts Curriculum* I found the first comprehensive text I could use. As I read it, I recognized how oral language was the basic saddle or ground that connected all of the peaks around me—writing, reading, thinking. So I wrote this Mr. James Moffett, who was then at Harvard. And, to my amazement, he wrote back. And I wrote again. Before I knew it, I was part of the dialogue that resulted in the *Interaction* curriculum; then, before I had time to catch my breath from that overwhelming project, he asked me to help him revise *A Student-Centered Language Arts Curriculum* for the 1976, then the 1983, and finally the 1992 edition. This quarter-century dialogue with Jim has profoundly shaped and sharpened my thinking.

Jim was constantly talking about his vision for the future. He was always on a quest for a better society. Like Thomas Jefferson, the great visionary who conceived of this nation, Jim Moffett invariably had his sights on the culture we *should* create. Jim's vision of *the universal schoolhouse* reminded us of Jefferson's original vision of the University of Virginia, an academic village paid for by the public where the best minds of the age would be gathered to talk about ideas. He did not want any religion to control the curriculum, nor did he believe in matriculation or graduation or degrees. Anyone from any walk of society could simply come and freely learn.

Jim also dared to look into metaphysics that were not part of the established paradigm. As he put it, it is now *au courant* to talk about paradigm shifts, but it is still taboo to create one. Jim reminded us that "the very founders of modern science—Newton, Bacon, and Descartes—were so steeped in the esoteric doctrine that half of what they said has been passed over in embarrassment by those moderns who do not realize that physics cannot be disembedded from metaphysics" (1991, 835). There is more to be discerned from the nonmaterialist world than we have dreamed of, and Jim never wanted us to forget it.

Jim's abstract for the talk he had planned to give at the NCTE Research Assembly on February 23, 1997, in Chicago began:

> The state should no longer determine curriculum. Instead, public education should show learners how to customize each [one's] own curriculum by choosing what and how to learn from the total array of resources throughout a whole community, which becomes a universal schoolhouse for all ages and purposes and at all times.

What started 25 years ago with *Interaction* (1973) as a way to organize schools to allow for maximum student choice and ownership, became in Jim's vision a way to organize a society so maximum learning occurred. Because the whole community was the schoolhouse, learning could happen in any venue: offices, labs, farms, shops, factories. Opportunities for apprenticeship, internship, community service, job training, retraining, cross-age tutoring, and continuing adult education were automatically fostered. His vision was to decentralize teaching, so that literacy was a one-on-one, self-perpetuating culture that was not dependent on the professional, except in the role of setting up programs run by nonprofessionals. Like Jefferson, Jim wanted pedagogy to be thoroughly populist. Only *that* was consistent with a thorough-going democracy.

Jefferson wrote in one of his hundreds of letters to his colleague and antagonist John Adams, "I believe in the dream of the future more than the history of the past." Jim had the same belief. Like Jefferson, Moffett was a visionary and a prophet. Both turned their backs on institutions and power and returned to the land. Without the trail that Jim hacked out, I doubt we would have had by now the robust movement within the NCTE that's reflected in the *Journal of the Assembly for Expanded Perspectives on Learning (JAEPL).*

Jim's greatest contribution to our profession was his intuitive perception of the wider context in which any discussion must be couched. He illuminated: 1. the concept of writing as a revision of inner speech; 2. reading comprehension in the context of a broader connection with the world; 3. the rise of the Christian right as a manifestation of the nation's spiritual hunger; 4. the world of school in the broader vision of a society where school as a separate locale for learning does not exist; and 5. the universe of discourse in language in the context of the direct knowing that transcends words. Working with Jim was like following a dance partner whose right foot firmly kept the beat of the rhythm of teachers everywhere while his left was kicking wildly into outer space!

Whenever, in our profession, developments emerge that have integrity and cause learning to happen, you will find that Jim was there first. All during the dark days in the '70s when behavioral objectives dominated the curriculum, we were always heartened by the knowledge that somewhere in the world Jim Moffett was tirelessly urging us to resist this trivialization of learning. What he told us resonated deeply with our own experience as teachers and with our dreams for our students. He fearlessly forged ahead and also graciously watched our profession struggle to catch up with the sheer sanity of his vision.

It is hard to imagine wandering into the darkness of the future without his light to guide us. His death is an immense loss to our profession. I know I shall miss him very much. If there is a dimension in the cosmos where spirit transcends body and language, I'm sure Jim's consciousness is there communing with all of us teachers on this side of the dark veil that separates us.

Chapter Twenty-One

Remembering and Reconsidering Moffett: An Interview and Conversation about Moffett with Sondra Perl

Sheridan Blau
Teachers College, Columbia University

Introduction to Sondra Perl

Sondra Perl is professor emerita of English at the Graduate Center of the City University of New York (CUNY), where she directed the PhD specialization in composition and rhetoric. She is also a founder (with Richard Sterling and John Brereton) and former director of the New York City Writing Project, a site of the National Writing Project, at Lehman College, CUNY. In 2006 she founded the Holocaust Educators Network, which was modeled on the National Writing Project. In 2015 that project was renamed The Olga Lengyel Institute for Holocaust Studies and Human Rights (www.toli.us), where she now serves as the senior director for national programs in the United States.

As one of the most influential scholars of the first generation of modern composition researchers, Perl produced a series of research studies in the early 1980s that helped to uncover and describe the mental and embodied experiences of student and adult writers as they engage in the writing process. She also conducted foundational research on classroom teachers in their teaching of writing and published that research in 1986 (in collaboration with Nancy Wilson) in their powerfully influential book, *Through Teachers' Eyes: Portraits of Writing Teachers at*

Work (reprinted in 1998), a volume that served as a model for a generation of researchers who sought to provide ethnographic accounts of classroom teachers in their daily work of teaching.

In her teaching and her composition research, Sondra Perl has emphasized the importance of a writer's "felt sense" as the preverbal source for the ideas that activate a process of discovery and articulation in language. Her 2004 book, *Felt Sense: Writing with the Body*, remains an authoritative and widely consulted guide for helping writers discover and make available to themselves their own most creative and potentially influential ideas. (For a digital copy of the book and a short video of Perl discussing its history, go to https://compcomm.commons.gc.cuny.edu/feltsense/.)

Perl's attention to the nonverbal sources for a writer's ideas was of particular interest to Jim Moffett, who often spoke about it to colleagues, although in the interview transcript that follows Perl does not recall speaking with Moffett about that work when she first met and collaborated with him. In the interview here, Perl tells the story of how she and Moffett spent a week working together in the summer of 1979, providing a professional development seminar on the teaching of writing for teachers in the Shoreham-Wading River school district on Long Island, New York. During this Summer Institute, Sondra participated in workshops led by Moffett, and in this interview, she describes in great detail a few of the methods he employed. Moffett's practices were so engaging and successful, in fact, that Perl adopted them for use in her own classrooms when teaching writing to undergraduates and graduate students at CUNY, in her workshops with teachers in the New York City Writing Project, and with other educators across the US and in the EU. Teachers reading these descriptions of Moffett's teaching are likely to find in them models they too will be inspired to adapt for use in their own writing classrooms, wherever they teach.

The Interview (conducted on Zoom)

SHERIDAN BLAU: Let's talk about Jim.

SONDRA PERL: Let's do it. This is a great project honoring a great man.

SHERIDAN: Can you tell me about how you knew Jim personally and professionally and in what context and during what period of time?

SONDRA: You know, ever since you've asked me to do this interview, I've been thinking about my history with Jim. And it begins not so much with Jim himself as with my living at home in New Jersey on leave from college for a semester in the late sixties. I didn't think I was going to be a teacher, but I decided I would enroll at a local college and take a course in teaching. The professor assigned the first edition of Jim's book from 1968. [Shows *A Student-Centered Language Arts Curriculum, Grades K–13*, 1st edition (*SCLA*)]

SHERIDAN: I have that book, the same edition!

SONDRA: If you had told me then, as an undergraduate, that I would have a role to play in the field of composition and rhetoric, and that I would come to know Jim Moffett, I would not have believed you!

SHERIDAN: What college did you come home from?

SONDRA: I went to Simmons College in Boston. I came home for a semester because my sister was ill, and since I had always taken a lot of credits, I could afford some time off. I'm not even sure what led me to take this course; it was at Montclair State with a young professor, who said, "This guy [Moffett} is going to go places; this is someone you should all read."

SHERIDAN: Do you remember who the professor was?

SONDRA: Nope. But I kept the book. I've looked at what I underlined back then and, not surprisingly, found ideas that still resonate today. But after that course and as my sister was getting well, I put it aside. When, a few years later, I enrolled at NYU to pursue a doctorate in English education, Moffett's work eventually became a part of my background reading. During graduate school, I also began teaching writing at the City University of New York. That is when I understood that the standard textbooks being assigned for basic writing and freshman composition tended to be formulaic and that Moffett's *SCLA* was so much richer.

SHERIDAN: In the meantime, at NYU were your professors confirming your earlier sense of the importance of Moffett?

SONDRA: They must have been.

SHERIDAN: Who were you working with?

SONDRA: Gordon Pradl and John Mayher.

SHERIDAN: And you don't remember them emphasizing the contributions of Moffett?

SONDRA: We're talking 1970, 1971, 1972. . . . They were very influenced by Louise Rosenblatt, by transactional ideas of reading, and the London Schools Council with Jimmy Britton and Nancy Martin. Gordon had been an undergraduate at Amherst and was also influenced by Theodore Baird, who founded the Amherst school of writing. Although Moffett's work, including *Teaching the Universe of Discourse*, must have been on our reading lists, I don't know that Moffett himself was visibly on the scene yet.

SHERIDAN: Well, he was, and was already widely influential in California, but not so much, I suppose, in New York. And was Louise [Rosenblatt] still at NYU when you were there?

SONDRA: Yes, she interviewed me, but I think I was in the last cohort that she accepted before she retired.

SHERIDAN: So you never had a course with her?

SONDRA: I never had a course with her, but I did with Mitchell Leaska, who was very close to her.

SHERIDAN: Leaska himself was an important literary scholar who, by the way, wrote about Virginia Woolf, as did Moffett. You know, Moffett wrote his prize-winning senior thesis essay at Harvard on Woolf, specifically on her narrative point of view, which led directly to his interest (which he called his "obsession") with perspective and the thinking of writers in relation to audiences.

SONDRA: Fascinating! But strangely, I don't recall anyone talking about Moffett in my early days at NYU. But then I got involved in writing research, and I did a dissertation focused on the composing process. So I must have read more Moffett in that period. But to talk about when I really got to know him, we have to jump to the National Writing Project. You know, Richard Sterling, John Brereton, and I started the New York City Writing Project in 1978. In 1979 and '80, Richard and I were contracted to bring the writing project model to the Shoreham-Wading River School District, which employed some forward-thinking administrators. They decided to devote a portion of their summer budget to a three-week Writing Project Summer Institute designed exclusively for teachers in their district. They asked if there was anyone we wanted to invite to work with us that first summer, the summer of '79, and we came up with the idea of inviting Jim for a week.

SHERIDAN: That's terrific.

SONDRA: It was fabulous. We had three weeks, and reserved one of those weeks for working with Jim. It also happened that the superintendent of schools for the district was traveling during the week that Jim would be doing the instruction, and he offered us his house so that we could avoid a long commute from Manhattan. So Jim and I shared the superintendent's house and made the short drive together back and forth to the seminar every single day. At the seminar, Jim demonstrated everything he believed in. He didn't talk to us about good teaching; he embodied the spirit and the work of a good teacher. The teachers and Richard and I sat with him and read and wrote and laughed and shared and did group work, really engaging in all of the amazingly rich and complex activities that Jim understood to be the most powerful and generative way to teach writing.

SHERIDAN: How terrific.

SONDRA: That's how I got to know him well. I also learned that he only used the name "Jim" in public and professional settings, but at home he preferred to be called "Prana."

SHERIDAN: I didn't know that.

SONDRA: You didn't know that?

SHERIDAN: No, I got to know Jim and his wife well in his late years, but I don't think he ever told me that, though now that you say it, I am starting to remember something they may have told me about it.

SONDRA: He always referred to himself as "Prana" and Jan, his wife, called herself "Yamuna." I have been thinking about his chosen name because the meaning of "*Prana*" is "breath." Jim was a practitioner of yoga and meditation, practices which are grounded in breathing. It occurred to me recently that the name he chose for himself is so fitting because in so many ways Jim breathed new life into the field of English studies. In fact, in the fifties and sixties, if writing was taught at all, it was, as Janet Emig often said, both a "limited and limiting" affair, based on a linear model with strict steps leading to the creation of the five-paragraph essay. In other words, for decades the teaching of writing was focused on products, not processes, and Prana was one of the scholars in the field who worked to enlarge our understanding of writing and literacy, really breathing new life into the curriculum for so many teachers and for their students.

SHERIDAN: I love that observation about Jim's name! You know, I am now remembering that I did know about Jan's name, because they used to come to Santa Barbara every summer so Jim could do a presentation at my writing project site, and they always chose to come when they could stay over for her birthday weekend, and I'd spend time with them during the weekend, and he would refer to Jan as Yamuna. And now I remember that they told me Jim's name too, but they didn't use it around me. I would expect that he used his Hindu name more in the early years when they were running the ashram in their house in Berkeley. But by the time you worked with him, were they already living in Mariposa?

SONDRA: That's right. I went to Mariposa at one point, and he also stayed with us in Manhattan at one point. But it was working with him, day in and day out in Long Island, and watching the way he worked with teachers that showed me the richness of what he had to offer. The [National] Writing Project, as you well know, has changed the practices of thousands of teachers across the country as it changed my practice, but it was Jim who got me to understand how the methods he developed work in a classroom. I can say more about that, but . . .

SHERIDAN: By all means, say more!

SONDRA: Well, you mentioned that you would be asking me about what ideas or practices I used that came from Jim and which texts or ideas were most influential for me. And the answer is definitely material in the first edition of *Student-Centered Language Arts, K–13*. Just the idea of adding the "13" shows that he understood that really powerful generative teaching, while it may need to be adjusted for level and cognitive ability, can be based on the same ideas and principles from kindergarten through university. Good practice is good practice.

SHERIDAN: He was the first to try to cover so many grades with his theory and practice, and maybe the only one who actually did it in a book. I can tell you from experience that publishers don't want to do books that go across too many grade levels.

SONDRA: I think that's right. So what I would really say about Jim, or Prana, is that he was ahead of his time. He understood so well that composing is a meaning-making activity, and it happens when we read and when we write and when we listen and when we sing and when we dance and when we share the sense we make of the sensate world.

There are so many ways in which he was far ahead of his time. What he invited us to do that summer in Long Island—which was such a simple, simple thing—was freewriting, which he called "spontaneous flow of thoughts." He told us to just go and write. "Don't worry about punctuation," he said. "Don't worry about spelling." We all know the practice from Peter Elbow's work, but Moffett was writing about this in his K–13 methods book even before Elbow's *Writing without Teachers* was published. Moffett invited us to move around the school and record the spontaneous flow of our experience and impressions of everything we encountered—everything we were seeing and hearing and smelling and feeling. And then he suggested that we do this on different days and at different places, or even return to the same place at a different time to see what's different. Moffett then asked us to stop and to label the record of our stream of consciousness according to what was immediate and sensory—like smells and sights and sounds—and what we were thinking about in memory—images and feelings and thoughts from the past.

SHERIDAN: I didn't know he did that. That's just brilliant! And he was playing with having people write what he called their "spontaneous flow of thought" before Peter Elbow introduced freewriting? When did Peter do that? 1973, I think. But Peter says that Macrorie really invented freewriting. That must have been 1970 or '71.

SONDRA: That's right. I almost forgot. I always credited Ken Macrorie as one of the folks who introduced freewriting to get us away from what he called "Engfish." I was introduced to his work at NYU and I loved *Uptaught* (1970). But Moffett describes essentially the same process in his original 1968 methods book for teachers. So Moffett needs to be acknowledged as the inventor of freewriting as a teaching practice. That 1968 volume is filled with amazing classroom practices and ideas and suggestions, many of them, as I said before, ahead of their time. And what I just described to you was only step one. Then there are many other things you can do. You can look at your spontaneous writing for tense to see if you are recording a present experience or a memory, or for whether you're merely recording what's happening, or possibly generalizing, or reflecting, noticing when and why you might have moved into a more or less abstract level of thinking.

What Moffett also introduced to us in Shoreham-Wading River, which I have continued to use in almost every writing class I have ever taught, is something he called a "memory chain." I remember being astonished by the writing it generated. If I were planning a sequence for a fifteen-week writing course, memory chain would usually come somewhere in the third or fourth week. It works like this: You're in a classroom and you look at an object in the room and ask yourself, what does that object remind me of. It will be simpler to grasp if I demonstrate it right now for you. So I'm going to look at the artwork that is behind me, which consists of several different kinds of flowers. I'm going to ask myself: what does the artwork remind me of? And that might take me on a memory chain that leads me into museums and my love of still life paintings. Or I could ask myself, what do flowers remind me of? And that would take me into my love of gardens and gardening. So you start by using an object to generate a memory. You write a little bit of what that memory is: I might describe what it feels like to be on my knees, planting dahlias, wondering if I need fertilizer. But then you don't stay with that memory; instead, you ask: what does that in turn remind me of? The word *knees* might remind me of the time my partner needed knee surgery, and I'd be off jotting down memories of his recovery. In other words, in a memory chain, you use one memory to elicit another . . . in a chain. You do this focused freewriting for about fifteen or twenty minutes, but what is so surprising is that when you start you have no idea where you're going to end up. And every one of the little constellations of memory that emerge could be the kernel for a piece of writing. Moffett wanted writers to start with lots of material, not with a blank page, material you can go back to, that you can shape. And how do you shape it? You bring it to a group. So Moffett also modeled that with us. We wrote our memory chains and then we shared them. We laughed out loud so often! Some people produced memory chains on a single theme; others jumped all over. I remember once this really clever guy wrote about all the shoes in the room. Someone else wrote about Italian food. The memories come from whatever is elicited by the object, and if you choose a different object, you'll go in a different direction. And then after sharing these in groups, you select one of the memories and you do more freewriting on that.

SHERIDAN: That's just so terrific. I feel embarrassed that I never knew about this because I never read Moffett's methods text. I've read almost all of his other books, but I thought, "Not that one—that's not for college teachers, though I remember that its title refers to K–13. I'm afraid my snobbishness blocked me from discovering writing activities that could have enriched my teaching and workshops over the past fifty years!

SONDRA: To this day, Jim's memory chain and freewriting exercises are among the most reliable, generative, and fun activities I use in writing classes, helping to create the kind of community and relationships that Jim would say need to be part of a writing classroom.

SHERIDAN: That's another way Jim was ahead of his time—in recognizing that play and a playful attitude need to be part of the experience of composing, partly to free your attention and also to invite creativity. So, all of your writing project teachers knew about this memory chain exercise, because you did it every single summer?

SONDRA: Yes. That is a staple of my practice that comes from Jim. And then, that summer he also had us writing dialogues and monologues—all of the different genres he valued. And we did this fast, so it was a lot like freewriting: non-stop, pell-mell, conducted in a "don't worry about it" attitude. At one point, I recall writing some dialogue and Jim suddenly said, "Introduce a third voice." And, of course, doing that shifts the direction you are going in.

SHERIDAN: This is the movement to drama.

SONDRA: Exactly, and his notion of drama—that classrooms should be filled with drama—and also songs and limericks and haikus. Jim broadened the base that was otherwise available for most teachers and teacher educators. And it lent our writing project institutes an extra richness in the way we explored a wide range of genres. I have relied on Jim's work ever since as a practitioner—as a classroom teacher and teacher educator for forty-five years.

SHERIDAN: What a wonderful story. I just love it. I feel sort of brokenhearted that I missed working with Jim in the same way.

SONDRA: I'm surprised. You never did any of that with him?

SHERIDAN: Well, maybe he never had enough time with us. When he visited our writing project, I always invited him to do whatever he wanted to do or simply tell us about what he was writing at the time. And he usually did that, presenting some new and provocative ideas, typically accompanied by a new chart reflecting his latest theory. Sometimes he would play with some ideas he was still formulating and talk about more general issues in writing, like the importance of writing from plenitude and the ladder of abstraction. And he once did a meditation with us. But he never had a whole day to lead our writing project. I'm so sorry now that I never thought of it. We would typically have him for a morning presentation for two or two-and-a-half hours. I think we saw him too much as a guru and not enough as a master teacher. Ach! We could have read the guru, but we missed our opportunity to learn from our experience with the master teacher. My fault!

SONDRA: Well, speaking of the meditative part, it seemed to me that in *Teaching the Universe of Discourse* and elsewhere in other theoretical pieces, Jim explored Western consciousness until he got to its limits. You know, rational, logical, cognitive stages. There is a way that Western thinking about intellectual development focuses entirely on mental states and cognitive development, and Moffett was perhaps the first in our field to develop a model for intellectual growth and development relevant to the language arts that took into account the connection between the mind and the body. And now we are beginning to see more of that kind of understanding in the field of writing studies.

SHERIDAN: I agree. And I think Louise was also discovering something similar fairly late in her career, around the same time that Moffett did.

SONDRA: That's interesting. I didn't know that.

SHERIDAN: She wrote an essay in about 1981 called "On the Aesthetic as the Basic Model for the Reading Process," in which she comes to the edge of denying the equality of efferent and aesthetic, essentially saying that all reading, if it's to be meaningful to the reader, has to be experienced aesthetically, because if you don't get it in the body, as it were, you're not getting it at all.

SONDRA: Right. I can see that logic. I thought Moffett had the sense that Western thinking in the end was sort of closed at the top or didn't get beyond consciousness, and what I'm remembering now is how he loved the concept written about by Julian Jaynes of the bicameral mind [1976], and its implications for education. I think what drew Moffett to Eastern thinking was its much more subtle and fluid understanding of the mind in its relation to the body and the idea that there are different levels and states of consciousness. I think Prana was drawn toward Yoga and Eastern mystical thought because standard academic Western conceptions of mind didn't satisfy him. Eastern thinking around transcendence and spirituality really spoke to some core part of him.

SHERIDAN: I'm sure that's right. And I assume that throughout your long and close connection with him he was especially drawn to all the work you were doing with felt sense, and he must have seen your work as closely linked and important to his own deepest interests and seen your research as having much in common with his own ongoing studies. But was Moffett drawn to Gendlin too? It was the philosopher and psychologist Eugene Gendlin, wasn't it, whose writing introduced you to the concept of felt sense.

SONDRA: Yes, it was Gendlin who coined that term. You know, I knew Moffett best in 1979. I had already worked with Gendlin's notions, publishing "Understanding Composing" in *CCC* in 1980, but while I'm sure we shared an appreciation of the body–mind connection, I was also shy about all of that as well.

SHERIDAN: Shy? I remember you did a powerful workshop on felt sense for my writing project in about 1982.

SONDRA: I remember that—in the beautiful location, overlooking the ocean, right? And yes, I did introduce the guided process I developed. But I was always a bit nervous about that, worrying that folks might feel uncomfortable—even though the process is so safe and generative. In any event, I don't recall major conversations with Prana about it. Our ideas are certainly not dissimilar in approach and theory, and we share an appreciation of the connectedness between the mind and the body and going into the body to discover what isn't yet in words. Like Moffett, I was also interested in what's prior to words, what surrounds words, and the silence that is part of composing that we don't think about so much.

SHERIDAN: You know, as you say this, I actually am understanding some things about him better. He writes about the importance of meditation and about how writing comes from that. And I have to confess that I was always a little puzzled by that idea, wondering "how?" "How does it come?" And what you just said makes it less puzzling. Because meditation puts you in touch with things that are deeper. It puts you in touch with what you know from the body or from intuition, which is really what it means to experience a "felt sense"—something you know or feel but don't yet know in language.

SONDRA: Yes, yes, and then you can use that as a guide and ask, "Is this really what I want to say?" But there is also an important distinction between meditation and felt sense. Gendlin would say that the point of meditation is to get beyond your thoughts, to get beneath your thoughts, to sit, if you can ever get there, with no thought. And that the goal of using felt sense with writing is to generate thought, but from a really centered place. So Moffett and Gendlin are not writing about exactly the same thing and may have very different ends, but they're certainly connected.

SHERIDAN: With that distinction (that I would like to think about some more), Sondra, I think we must call an end to our meeting, which has already extended beyond the time limit I had promised. But it has also produced more discoveries and insights and useful information about Moffett and his teaching practices and our own experiences with him than I ever would have predicted. So I thank you for your generosity and your good memory, and your friendship, as well as for your important contributions to the field of writing studies and English education for the past half century, and I'll end this dialogical interview with the hope that we'll find future opportunities for similar conversations.

SONDRA: It's been a pleasure, Sheridan. Thank you for a very enjoyable afternoon thinking about the field of writing studies and the many ways in which Jim helped to shape it. He was a kind and caring person, and I am grateful to have had this opportunity to reminisce about him and about the exciting early days of the field.

Chapter Twenty-Two

Jim

Jan Moffett

In this poignant tribute to her late husband, Jan Moffett pays homage to his open-minded and paradoxical nature, his kind, loving support of her and their family, and the deep pain and anguish of his final days.

Jim was passionately and compassionately alive in his thinking that he stirred and awakened thinking in others. His words, spoken or written, were yeasty for me, empowering thoughts to move into new dimensions. Much power of love for everyone came through his mind and the light of it nourished me throughout our lives together. I believe Jim was capable of intuitive thinking as Rudolph Steiner defines it—a merging of feeling and will with the higher abstractive powers of mind so that thoughts include the full richness of experience while rising to the realm of universals.

At least that is my way of explaining Jim's extraordinary works. He had great humility in this intuitive thinking, as though he were passing it along from somewhere else. And, indeed, I believe he felt that in some sense he was, in spite of his long hours of concentrated work. I was awed by Jim's capacity for work.

As an *Interaction* coauthor put it, "Jim was the only man I ever knew who could work eighteen-hour days for four years." He worked so seriously at his writing and thinking, including thinking about thinking, and in such a highly disciplined way, it was as if he envisaged so many works to be accomplished that he could never complete them. His mind was intensely engrossed with what he felt needed doing, and it seemed a matter of such

Originally published in *California English*, (Winter, 1997), p. 9. Reprinted with permission.

importance that he never really concentrated on or fully enjoyed what he had accomplished.

This intensity concerned me greatly, for I felt I was helplessly standing by, watching him use up his essential force. I remember telling him of a vivid dream that I had early in our marriage. I dreamed I saw his head burning with fire. Desperately I tried to save him from what seemed to be imminent disaster, and I awoke in a panic, in mid-dream, not knowing how it ended. I think now that my dream came from at least partial misunderstanding. Recently I ran across a sentence from one of Jim's unpublished works, "Light is not to stare at, or even to see by, as I have been doing here, but to burn with."

Jim was a natural warrior. He labored, sacrificed and did battle through work for what he believed to be good, reasonable, necessary. He was a champion of the child—the learning, growing part of everyone, which could, perhaps, also be called the self. He espoused individualism because it was his intuition to do so, and because he knew the strength of the social fabric depended on the contribution of individuals. Jim worked hard for his own personal development, knew the power lay with him to do so, made his best continuing effort to learn, develop and contribute his increasing understanding through his works and days.

Jim built a remarkable solar office with some help from friends and family. He studied the subject of solar energy and learned how to install and use the equipment to capture it for lights, computer, printer and other office needs. He chose daily yoga study and practice as a way to develop physical flexibility and strength and to further the one-pointed power of mind through meditation practice. He used his travels as a consultant, his friends, his extensive reading, his life as husband and father, and, perhaps especially, his own writing to learn about himself and others in the world. In all this Jim taught me by example, at least as far as I could go in his direction. I believe this is how he taught others who knew him. I don't remember where, or even if, Jim ever wrote this, but he certainly believed that effective teachers always remain learners.

Jim gave me this wonderful ordinary life with home and children—a life of paramount importance for me and which our extraordinary life together so illuminated for me. When we first met on that October evening in 1950 (he was 21, I was 19), I recognized him in some way, felt destined to be with him in spite of my reluctance to consider marriage so early in my life. But, as Jim was a prophet in many instances, he was the cause of prophecy in others, and we married in the following September.

Jim was endearingly, wondrously funny and fun-loving. Images from our life together come to warm and encourage me; I see Jim brushing four-year-old Judy's long hair, distracting her with talk of the tangle-fairies who work while she sleeps, using a bit of jam, perhaps, to help with their intricate weavings. I listen, distracted, too. Jim is there at the barn with twelve-year-old Lisa and her new horse, Gypsy. Always the adventurer, Jim stands behind the horse to lift her right rear hoof for inspection. Gypsy, sensing another novice but a strong one, allows the lift but shakes off the inspection. Jim grins as he complains about her keeping the upper hoof. Words were his playthings as well as his work tools and he moved from puns to prophecies with ease and charm.

Jim concentrated on the self—his own and others'—recognizing that a sense of self is what all people on earth have in common. And he saw that the absolute uniqueness of each self is the way in which we are most alike. He was fond of the idea in Flannery O'Connor's story title "Everything That Rises Must Converge," and I believe he felt that if we were willing to make the great effort to lift ourselves in potential and output, we would feel the energy and benefit of convergence and, eventually, of unity. Jim also liked the sentence he found somewhere "Self Knowledge is bad news" because it was a humbling humorous reminder and a prompt to look actively for that bad news as the beginning step to outgrowing it. He had faith in the natural unity of mankind as well as in his own individuality. He saw them as unopposed.

Jim saw many things taken as opposites—the paradoxical nature life seems to hold for us—as part of circles that join to make up the wholeness of life. And he was unafraid of the apparent contradictions, so good a synthesizer was he. To mention a small example, I remember noticing, because of our many conversations, that over time words tend to move in meaning towards their opposites, sometimes evolving the whole way or even containing both meanings.

We talked a lot every day and I cherish that exchange for itself and for helping me develop in directions that, without him, I would have missed. No matter how busy Jim was, he was always a careful, tender listener for me. I never once felt he didn't have ample time for me. And I am in awe remembering, especially as I sort through his many unpublished works.

As an individual who is not especially verbal by nature, I moved seriously in that direction from my close association with Jim. And Jim began to be involved with the language of art and architecture, a more natural realm for me, and to pursue his quest for knowledge and understanding through ancient works and their special language that spoke a different way to him. Bringing the unspoken to word level was a special talent of his and I would love to know what he would have written about the ancient pictographs and petroglyphs that came to interest him so greatly.

I was reminded recently of our telepathic experiences over the years by hearing a tape recording of Jim's talk and discussion with AEPL members at Snow Mountain, Colorado, in 1995. I missed hearing the talk and only heard the recording after his death. Jim mentioned the developmental progression from passion to compassion to dispassion in connection with the spectrum of discourse—the heat and personal intensity of interior and dramatic monologue, diaries, letters bridging to the identifying compassion of varying kinds of narration and memoir; the transpersonal aspect of anonymous narration. This was a progression that was on my mind at the time as I painfully reached for dispassion and the balance of that, as I watched and tried to help Jim in his struggle with disease. I believe we never discussed that progression but it was on both our minds, for different, perhaps not unrelated, reasons.

Hamlet's words (II, 2) "noble in reason . . . infinite in faculties" had for me always been the perfect description of Jim. But a quality of a different order, of which I had only had glimpses before, was showing in his last two days. I saw Jim walking and talking before me in a luminous state, a warm and liquid purity, having dropped the cloak of personality, standing there as he really was. And he left me with the gift of personal knowledge that, much as we may distract each other with our passions and compassions of personality, we are all fundamentally that dispassionate, luminous purity.

In our youth Jim introduced me to the writings of many poets and I remember he liked Yeats' words for his own epitaph, "Cast a cold eye on life, on death. Horseman, pass by." In the intense emotion of my youth I couldn't see the wisdom in those words; now, in the intense grief of my age, I turn to their wisdom for survival. Perhaps Jim was born knowing; perhaps he learned detachment during childhood with an alcoholic father, but I see now that he understood well those not indifferent but purely dispassionate words.

Index

Note: A page number followed by "f" denotes a figure. A page number followed by "n" denotes a note.

Editors

Sheridan Blau is a professor of practice in the teaching of English and former director of the English education program at Teachers College, Columbia University. He is also emeritus professor of English and education at the University of California, Santa Barbara, where for thirty years he directed the South Coast Writing Project and Literature Institute for Teachers. He is a former president of the National Council of Teachers of English (1997–1998). In 2007 he was awarded the NCTE Distinguished Service Award for leadership in the profession of English, contributions to teaching, and exemplary writing. In 2012 he was named Rhetorician of the Year by the Young Rhetoricians Conference in recognition of his career-long contributions to the teaching of writing through his professional development work and his own research and publications. He has published extensively in the areas of seventeenth-century literature, the teaching of composition and literature, professional development for teachers, and the ethics and politics of literacy. His book *The Literature Workshop: Teaching Texts and Their Readers* (2003), was selected by the Conference on English Education as winner of the Richard A. Meade Award for outstanding research in English education.

Jonathan M. Marine is a writing teacher and doctoral candidate in the Writing and Rhetoric program at George Mason University, where his research focuses on writing engagement, graffiti rhetorics, and the pedagogy and theory of James Moffett. He is the reviews editor for *Kairos: A Journal of Rhetoric, Technology, and Pedagogy* as well as an associate editor for *Prompt: A Journal of Academic Writing Assignments* and the WAC Clearinghouse's *Perspectives on Writing* book series. He has published extensively on Moffett, including a master bibliography of Moffett's work (https://wac.colostate.edu/books/landmarks/moffett/bib/) and *Toward a Re-emergence of James Moffett's Mindful, Spiritual, and Student-Centered Pedagogy*. A two-time winner of NCTE's James Moffett Award, he was recently named the incoming editor of the *Journal for the Assembly of Expanded Perspectives on Learning*.

Paul M. Rogers is an associate professor of writing studies at the University of California, Santa Barbara, where he also received his doctorate in education. He is the former director of the Northern Virginia Writing Project, a cofounder and former chair of the International Society for the Advancement of Writing Research, and the coeditor of eight scholarly volumes of international research on writing, including *International Models of Changemaker Education* (2022). A recipient of the K. Patricia Cross Award for leadership in higher education and the Janet Emig Award for research in English education, Rogers's research focuses on longitudinal studies of writing development from early schooling through professional life, the history of English education, the role of feedback in learning to write, writing engagement, and the role of writing in fostering social progress. For more than twenty years he has taught a wide variety of undergraduate and graduate courses, including academic writing, qualitative research methods, professional and technical communication, and social entrepreneurship.

Kathleen (Buchan) Kelly has been an educator for more than twenty-five years in public and independent school settings. She has taught at the middle school, high school, college, and graduate school levels on the East and West Coasts. Along the way, she has earned two master's degrees and a doctorate. Kathleen is the author of several articles and has coedited another book on James Moffett, *Toward a Re-emergence of James Moffett's Mindful, Spiritual, and Student-Centered Pedagogy*. She currently teaches English at a small independent school in Southern California. The subject of her current book project is Sheridan Blau.

Contributors

Kim Donehower's research on rural literacy began in her maternal Appalachian hometown, which had seen three waves of literacy interventions by outsiders. Since then, she has continued to investigate issues of rural literacy in the US Great Plains. She is a professor of English at the University of North Dakota, where her work focuses on the impact of literacy practices on the sustainability of rural communities. With Charlotte Hogg and Eileen E. Schell, she coauthored *Rural Literacies* and coedited *Reclaiming the Rural: Essays on Literacy, Rhetoric, and Pedagogy*. With Sara Webb-Sunderhaus, she published the coedited volume *Rereading Appalachia: Literacy, Place, and Cultural Resistance*. Her essays and book chapters have appeared in the *Journal of Appalachian Studies*, *Women and Literacy: Local and Global Inquiries for a New Century*, *Rethinking Rural Literacies: Transnational Perspectives*, and *Literacy, Economy, and Power: Writing and Research after "Literacy in American Lives."*

Bill Green is emeritus professor of education in the Faculty of Arts and Education at Charles Sturt University, New South Wales, Australia. His research interests include English teaching, literacy education, and curriculum inquiry. Recent publications include *Engaging Curriculum: Bridging the Curriculum Theory and English Education Divide* (2018) and the coedited volume *Rethinking L1 Education in a Global Era: Understanding the (Post-)National L1 Subjects in New and Difficult Times* (2020). He is a life member of the Australian Association for the Teaching of English (AATE).

Denise Maltese has taught English since 1992 and currently teaches at Onteora Middle School in upstate New York. She has been a teacher consultant with the Hudson Valley Writing Project since 2001 and completed her yoga teacher training at Shakti Yoga in Woodstock in 2010. In 2007 she was the ELATE James Moffett Memorial Award winner. She would like to thank the editors of this volume for their encouragement, especially her mentor, Sheridan Blau, for creating the opportunity for this chapter to be written. Maltese is also indebted to Linda Lalita Winnick, Kate Naughter, Jackie Denu, and Jonathan Marine for helping her think through the ideas presented in this piece. She is grateful to be able to keep James Moffett's spirit alive through the work she does with her students every school year.

Ruth Nathan, formerly an elementary and middle school teacher, university instructor, and researcher, has recently retired as a visiting scholar at the University of California, Berkeley. Prior to her position at Berkeley, she served as a school-based language and literacy consultant. She received her doctorate in reading from Oakland University, eventually becoming the co-director of their Reading Research Laboratory with Keith Stanovich. Nathan's publications appear in such diverse journals as *Child Development, Reading Research Quarterly*, and *Language Arts*. She has also written several books on literacy, including the national bestseller *The Beginnings of Writing* (4th ed.). Along with Anne E. Cunningham and Katie Schmidt Raher, she is the coauthor of "Orthographic Processing in Models of Word Recognition," a chapter in the 2011 edition of the *Handbook of Reading Research*. Currently, Nathan regularly writes for *California English*, the journal of the California Association of Teachers of English (CATE).

The floor in **Shannon Potts's** middle school ELA classroom closet is covered in gold glitter. After fourteen years of teaching, she has accepted that many great ideas come with a mess. She often commits herself and her students to too many wild projects, but always with the same earnestness and enthusiasm. One of these whims became the children's book *Who Is Florence Price?* (2021). In recent years, she has also managed to find the time to complete a PhD (2024) at Teachers College, Columbia University in English education, with a dissertation that constitutes the most extensive and authoritative intellectual and professional biography of James Moffett, a study that is reflected in her groundbreaking historical chapter in this volume. Now, in the break between her PhD research and her attempt to turn her dissertation into a book, she can be found traveling, standing on docks waiting for crew boats, or walking her dog in Central Park—all while usually thinking about her teaching and the life of James Moffett.

Jessica Rivera-Mueller is an associate professor of English at Utah State University, where she directs the Department of English's concurrent enrollment program and teaches courses in English education and writing studies. Her teaching and scholarship focus on facilitating teacher learning for undergraduate students who are pursuing their teaching license, graduate students who are teaching in the college classroom, and practicing high school teachers who participate in the professional development programs she creates. Her work has appeared in *Teaching/Writing: The Journal of Writing Teacher Education, Prompt: A Journal of Academic Writing Assignments, Journal on Empowering Teaching Excellence, Utah English Journal*, and edited collections in the fields of writing studies and education. She is also the current president of the Utah Council of Teachers of English.

Wayne Sawyer is emeritus professor in the School of Education at Western Sydney University. Before joining WSU, he was a secondary school head of English. He is a past president of the New South Wales (NSW) English Teachers Association (ETA) and past chair of the NSW Board of Studies English Curriculum Committee. He is an honorary life member of both the NSW ETA and the Australian Association for the Teaching of English. Sawyer's doctoral research was on English curriculum history in NSW, and he currently researches in the areas of secondary English curriculum, curriculum history, literacy policy, literary knowledge, and pedagogy in low socioeconomic status schools. His most recent book includes the coauthored *Literary Knowing and the Making of English Teachers*.

Patrick Sitzer is a former English teacher and current doctoral candidate in English education at Teachers College, Columbia University. Starting his teaching career in a self-contained elementary classroom, Sitzer has taught at multiple grade levels and is interested in the ways teachers create communities of practice in their classrooms by fostering connections between students' lives and the texts they read and write. His research involves the power of stories that students and teachers bring with them to the classroom. Besides his work providing professional development for teachers, Sitzer has taught graduate students at Teachers College and Hunter College in New York City and presented his work at a variety of academic conferences. A member of NCTE since 2017, he is proud to join the conversation about the ongoing importance of James Moffett's work in the field of English education.

Karen Tellez-Trujillo is an assistant professor at California State Polytechnic University, Pomona in the Department of English and Modern Languages. Her educational background and research interests are in border, feminist, and cultural rhetorics. She is a graduate assistant advisor for rhetoric and composition and works with undergraduate students as a mentor for the Research through Inclusive Opportunities (RIO) program. Her work has appeared in the interdisciplinary journal *Writers: Craft and Context*, and she has a forthcoming chapter in the edited collection *Revising*

Moves. Trujillo is also the recipient of the 2022–2023 NCTE Early Career Educator of Color Leadership Award.

Ashlynn Wittchow taught English and creative writing in secondary schools in the Low Country of South Carolina for several years before entering the doctoral program and completing her PhD in English education at Teachers College, Columbia University. She is now an assistant professor of English in the Department of English at Louisiana State University in Baton Rouge. Inspired by several summers as a graduate student at the Bread Loaf School of English at Middlebury College, she wrote her dissertation, which she is now revising as a book, on the history of posthuman pedagogies and the environmental humanities at Bread Loaf, where she is an alumna of the Bread Loaf Teacher Network. She also serves as chair of the ELATE Commission on the History of English Education. Her historical research and her teacher research have yielded articles and chapters published and forthcoming in *English Education*, *English Journal*, and professional volumes in press with NCTE.

This book was typeset in Sabon LT Pro.
Typefaces used on the cover include Abadi MT Condensed Light, Gotham HTF, HTF Didot, and Norwester.
The book was printed on 50-lb. white, offset paper.

Praise for
The Healing Wisdom of the Forest

"A wise and engaging guide to the many insights offered by trees. Filled with practical advice and gentle invitations, our humanity and joy expand through attention to our leafy cousins."

—**David George Haskell,** biologist and Pulitzer-finalist author of *Sounds Wild and Broken, The Songs of Trees,* and *The Forest Unseen*

"*The Healing Wisdom of the Forest* by Anthony D. Fredericks is a beautifully reflective and practical guide that draws timeless lessons from the natural world to inspire our personal growth, resilience, and inner peace. Through engaging storytelling, actionable advice, and journaling prompts, the author invites readers to reconnect with nature's quiet wisdom and find strength, gratitude, and joy in everyday life. A nurturing and thoughtful read for anyone seeking to deepen their connection with nature and with themselves."

—**Holly Worton,** author of *If Trees Could Talk: Life Lessons From the Wisdom of the Woods*

"I came away from *The Healing Wisdom of the Forest* with a sense of peace—no small thing in today's world—and a newfound appreciation for the extraordinary lessons trees can continue to teach us. With poetic insight and ecological grace, Fredericks draws from the lives of trees to offer us a map for our own futures."

—**Daniel Lewis,** author of *Twelve Trees: The Deep Roots of Our Future*

"Optimistic and generous, *The Healing Wisdom of the Forest* offers tree-inspired lessons and reflections to reduce stress and increase happiness and well-being. This book is a story-rich manual that invites readers to engage their curiosity outdoors and discover for themselves what the local environment demonstrates about living a fulfilling life."

—**Heidi Beierle,** author of *Heidi Across America: One Woman's Journey on a Bicycle Through the Heartland*

"Just as trees achieve a balance of roots below ground while its branches reach for the sky, Anthony Fredericks has achieved a singular balance in his writing: part memoir, part information, and part inspiration. This is a gentle, intriguing read that will motivate you to observe, reflect, and embrace the balance, music, and magic embodied by trees. Read this book—and find a tree."

—**Suzanne I. Barchers,** writer

"With wit, charm, and wisdom, Anthony D. Fredericks weaves inspiring life lessons with evocative arboreal imagery into every page of this delightful volume. Like taking a leisurely walk along a verdant forest path with a beloved guide, let *The Hidden Wisdom of the Forest* take you deep into Nature to reveal your own nature, teaching how to live fully, gratefully, and with grace. Beautifully written, I was so enchanted, I could hardly put it down."

—**Cathy Katin-Grazzini,** sustainable chef and author of *Love the Foods That Love the Planet* and *Love the Foods That Love You Back*

"Anthony D. Fredericks reaches deep into your soul to remind you of your power, resilience, influence, and above all, humanity. This is not just a book—it's a quiet forest path that leads you back to yourself."

—**Crystal Robertson,** leadership coach and employee experience consultant

"*The Healing Wisdom of the Forest* is a gentle and enjoyable ramble through not only lovely forests and trees, but also through wise and gentle ways of handling life more enjoyably, and with a lot less stress. Just as the ancient trees withstand the varieties of life, this book will help you emulate their natural strategies and become, like them, adaptable, unflappable, and ultimately wiser for it. Recommended for all who wish to live more at peace with themselves and the world."

—**Michael Zajaczkowski,** author of *The Owner's Manual to Life: In Case You Missed That Day in School When They Handed It Out*

"A nurturing book, full of thought-provoking observations and insights."

—**Tristan Gooley,** author of *How to Read a Tree: Clues and Patterns from Bark to Leaves*

"I love this book! So wise! *The Healing Wisdom of the Forest* has a simple but profound message, told with poetic elegance. Most importantly, each chapter contains a wealth of practical and life-changing advice."

—**Rob Taylor,** author of *Professor McPhadden's Absolutely Essential Guide to Ghosts and Ghost Hunting*

"This book is beautiful! The writing is silky and cheerful. It will refresh your senses and restore calm. Dip in a toe or plunge fully in. It's a stunner!"

—**Diane Osgood,** author of *Your Shopping Superpower: Follow Your Values and Better Your World One Purchase at a Time*

"Fredericks masterfully gifts the reader with a work that is part magical, part self-help, and part scientific. Artfully written, the author shares personal stories, details of insight and inspiration acquired from trees, and concludes each chapter with straightforward strategies for self-improvement. Without reserve, Anthony D. Fredericks is 'Author Extraordinaire!'"

—**Dr. Susannah Richards,** author of *A Work of Heart: Connecting with Kids in a Chaotic World*